Our Three Selves

Our Three Selves

THE LIFE OF RADCLYFFE HALL

by

MICHAEL BAKER

QUILL
WILLIAM MORROW
New York

First published in 1985 by Hamish Hamilton Ltd, Great Britain

Library of Congress Cataloging-in-Publication Data

Baker, Michael, 1948–
Our three selves.
Bibliography: p.
Includes index.
1. Hall, Radclyffe—Biography.   2. Authors, English—
20th century—Biography.   3. Lesbians—Great Britain—
Biography.   I. Title.
PR6015.A33Z56   1986   823'.912   [B]   86-12714
ISBN 0-688-06673-9 (pbk.)

Printed in the United States of America

First Quill Edition

2 3 4 5 6 7 8 9 10

For Cathy

Contents

Illustrations   ix

Acknowledgements   xi

Preface   xiii

PROLOGUE   I

PART 1: MARGUERITE 1880–1907   5

PART 2: LADYE 1907–1915   31

PART 3: UNA 1915–22   59

PART 4: JOHN – [1] The Novelist 1922–1928   147

              [2] The Martyr 1928–1934   199

PART 5: SOULINE 1934–1939   293

PART 6: A SINGLE SOUL 1939–1943   327

POSTSCRIPT   353

Notes and Sources   358

Published Works of Radclyffe Hall   375

Index   376

Illustrations

Between pages 114 and 115

The infant John with great-grandmother Elijah Jones, Granny Sarah Diehl, and mother Marie Diehl Visetti. (*Photography Collection, Harry Ransom Humanities Research Center, University of Texas at Austin, Texas*)

The portrait of John as a child as it looked after she had it altered to make her appear more boyish. (*Nicola Rossi-Lemeni*)

John as a débutante. (*H. R. C., University of Texas*)

John with Jane Randolph, her two sons Thomas and Decan, and Marie Visetti. (*H. R. C., University of Texas*)

Mabel Batten (Ladye) in full vocal flight, as painted by John Singer Sargent in 1897. (*Glasgow Art Gallery*)

Ladye at about the time that John met her. (*Cara Lancaster*)

The White Cottage, Malvern Wells. (*Cara Lancaster*)

John and Ladye on the verandah of the White Cottage, with Cocky (parrot), Claude (terrier) and Rufus (collie). (*Cara Lancaster*)

Una Troubridge in 1915.

Mrs Osborne Leonard, the celebrated medium

Ladye's tomb in Highgate Cemetery. (© *copyright John Gay in co-operation with the Friends of Highgate Cemetery*)

Cara Harris, Ladye's daughter. (*Photograph by Baron Gayne de Meyer*)

Admiral Sir Ernest Troubridge, K.C.M.G. (*Felix Hope-Nicholson*)

Una's daughter, Andrea. (*Felix Hope-Nicholson*)

Toupie Lowther and members of her all-women ambulance unit. (*Imperial War Museum*)

Una and John at Crufts, 1923. (*B.B.C. Hulton Picture Library*)

Romaine Brooks. (*Meryle Secrest*)

Colette with Winnaretta Singer. (*Mrs James Lees-Milne*)

Between pages 242 and 243

John's literary agent, Audrey Heath (Robin). (*Patience Ross*)

John as seen by *T. P.'s Weekly*, 1926. (*By permission of The British Library*)

John by 'Pax' in *The Popular Pictorial*, 1927. (*By permission of The British Library*)

Havelock Ellis. (*B.B.C. Hulton Picture Library*)

'St Stephen', cartoon lampooning *The Well of Loneliness*. (*Brush and ink drawing by Beresford Egan, 1905–1984*)

John in her Chinese silk smoking jacket. (*National Portrait Gallery*)

John photographed by Howard Coster to mark the publication of *The Master of the House*, 1932. (*National Portrait Gallery*)

John and Una at a First Night, 1933. (*B.B.C. Hulton Picture Library*)

Edy Craig with 'the Boys', Chris and Tony. (*Photograph taken by the late Anthony Marshall. Reproduced by permission of the Westminster City Libraries*)

Mickie Jacob with John and Una, Sirmione 1934. (*Audrey Atcheson*)

Mickie and John. (*Audrey Atcheson*)

A photograph of herself that John sent to Souline. (*H.R.C., Univesity of Texas*)

Private View (1937), by Gladys Hynes. (*Michael Parkin Gallery*)

John's study at The Forecastle, Rye. (*H.R.C., University of Texas*)

John with Fido, one of her last dogs. (*H.R.C., University of Texas*)

John in her 50s. (*H.R.C., University of Texas*)

Acknowledgements

This book would have been impossible without the help and co-operation of certain people. I owe special thanks to Rache Lovat Dickson, Radclyffe Hall's literary executor; to Michael Thomas of A. M. Heath & Co; to Cara Lancaster, who gave me full access to Mabel Batten's private diaries and letters; to Nicola Rossi-Lemeni, who put Una Troubridge's Day Books at my disposal – and showed me great hospitality; and to Eleanor O'Keefe of the Society for Psychical Research. A number of libraries and librarians proved invaluable in my researches, notably Ellen Dunlap of the Humanities Research Centre at the University of Texas.

Many others have contributed in various ways. I should particularly like to mention Audrey Atcheson, Sybille Bedford, Maria-Victoria Berardinelli, Dr H. J. R. Bussey, David Chesanow, Beresford Egan, Mme V. Eldin, Ursula Fanthorpe, Barbara Fearon, Victoria Glendinning, Jane Hanslip, Alison Hennegan, Felix Hope-Nicholson, Michael Holroyd, Evelyn Irons, Rosemary Manning, J. Fraser Nicol, Nigel Nicolson, Stanley Olson, Dickie Payne, Michael Rubinstein, Sonya Reuhl, Patience Ross, Joan Slater, Ted Troubridge, and Bill Waterfield.

Finally, I wish to thank my agent, Gill Coleridge, and my editors in London (Penelope Hoare) and New York (Harvey Ginsberg) for their unfailing tact, patience and support.

Preface

It is now ten years since the publication of the first and only full-length biography of Radclyffe Hall, Lovat Dickson's *Radclyffe Hall At The Well Of Loneliness: A Sapphic Chronicle*. In that time interest in the novelist and her work has shown a marked increase on both sides of the Atlantic and several of her books have been reissued. In addition, new sources on her life have come to light, notably diaries belonging to her first great love Mabel Batten, some material written by 'John' herself about her childhood, and scores of journals kept by Una Troubridge relating to the 1930s when the two of them lived in Rye and Radclyffe Hall was engaged in a passionate but tortuous affair with a third woman. This fresh evidence makes it possible to present a far more comprehensive account of the writer's life than in the past.

One problem encountered by any biographer of Radclyffe Hall is the scarcity of source material written by herself. She never kept a diary and, until she became famous, does not appear to have been over-addicted to letter-writing. This means that her early life in particular remains too often shadowy and indistinct. Much of what we know thereafter — with the exception of the well-documented furore surrounding *The Well of Loneliness* — is derived from the private diaries and letters of her lovers, principally of Una, sources whose objectivity must inevitably be questionable. It is only in the last eight years or so of the novelist's life, when she was embarked on a prolific correspondence with her third great love Evguenia Souline, that we get the chance to examine her own view of events on a more or less routine basis. Her story is thus predominantly one told by others. This unevenness in the pattern of the evidence must be taken into account in appraising her life as a whole.

I have not attempted a work of literary criticism. This is very much a 'life' and, besides, Claudia Stillman Franks' recent study, *Beyond The Well Of Loneliness*, has more than adequately examined Radclyffe Hall's fiction. At the same time, the prose and poetry provide rich biographical sources and I have tried, by characterising and quoting from them, to show how they mirrored the author's prevailing concerns and preoccupations. Radclyffe Hall's reputation as a writer rests, uneasily, on *The Well Of Loneliness*, her fifth novel. In fact, critically speaking, she enjoyed far more success with her fourth book *Adam's Breed* and, to my mind, wrote a first novel (*The Unlit Lamp*) and a couple of short stories that bear comparison with some of her better contemporaries. She was no experimentalist, preferring the traditional narrative form, but there are times reading her work when one feels she could have been a deeper, more angular, altogether more original writer than she allowed herself to be.

I have tried to resist playing the amateur psychiatrist, not always, I fear, successfully. The conflicts and divisions in Radclyffe Hall's temperament often made her deeply unhappy, creating the stimulus behind her work. She came to believe, rightly or wrongly, that she was born a homosexual and sought to back up her claim with a good deal of pseudo-scientific theory. It is impossible not to attempt to answer some of the questions which her own assertions beg. However, I hope I have avoided the worst excesses of modern psychiatric jargon and placed my speculations in the context of her own times rather than what passes for fashionable thinking today.

Radclyffe Hall was an extremely complex personality, more so than her 'notoriety' has usually allowed for. She was not always likeable, sometimes absurd, often her own worst enemy. But she had great style, undeniable courage, and a touching capacity for compassion, her own vulnerability making her keenly aware of it in others. Life with 'John', Una Troubridge once wrote, was never dull. I would like to think this book proves her right.

Stockwell, 1985

Prologue

On the morning of February 7, 1917, three women sat round a table in a darkened room in Maida Vale, London. The only light came from a fire burning in the grate and a small red lamp. The woman in the centre, her dark hair gathered in coiled plaits over her ears, sat with a rug over her knees and her eyes closed. This was the celebrated medium Mrs Osborne Leonard.

On one side of her sat a slim, extremely handsome woman who looked far more youthful than her thirty-seven years. A pale oval face with thin lips, high cheekbones and a prominent aquiline nose was framed by striking ash-blonde hair tied severely in a long plait round the crown of her head. She held herself erect with an air of authority and wore a high stiff collar, a gentleman's stock, and a plain grey jacket with wide lapels and a fob-chain in the button-hole. From her neck hung a square eye-glass on a velvet ribbon. Her name was Marguerite Radclyffe Hall, but she always preferred to be known by her friends simply as 'John'.

The third woman in the room was John's lover, Mrs Una Troubridge. Not quite thirty, she had pale blue eyes and wore her blonde hair in the style of an Eton crop but swept sharply back from the forehead. Although five feet seven inches in height, her petite features and frail physique made her seem smaller. She too sported a tailor-made gentleman's jacket and high collar, but the severity of her appearance was softened by a bow floppant in place of a cravat.

According to the notes that John took of this sitting, for about an hour and a half nothing out of the ordinary happened. Then, quite suddenly, the familiar piping voice adopted by the medium in her trance-state fell silent. It was a long pause, broken by a heavy coughing or choking sound in Mrs Leonard's throat. There followed a steady exhalation of breath, remarkably prolonged, which Una later likened to an uncapped air-cushion being slowly squeezed empty.[1] Peering intently at the medium's face, Una noticed large tears escaping from beneath her closed eyelids. The next moment Mrs Leonard's body shuddered and she grasped convulsively at Una's hand, slumping heavily against her shoulder as if losing all consciousness.

Una signalled excitedly to John to help her support the medium. As they took hold of her, Mrs Leonard twitched slightly. 'Is that you, Ladye?' asked Una. In reply, the medium spoke in a quiet but audible voice, mellow in tone and quite unlike her own. 'Yes,' she said. She then hugged Una tearfully as if claiming a long-lost friend. 'Not unnatural perhaps,' commented Una afterwards, 'taking into consideration the many long and intimate sessions which I have attended at Mrs Leonard's ... and the fact that today was the first time when – given the control to be genuine – I have spoken directly to MVB since her passing over.'[2] MVB stood for Mabel Veronica Batten, or 'Ladye' as she was always called by John and Una. Ladye had been John's lover before Una and she had died unexpectedly nearly nine months previously.

Still in a trance, Mrs Leonard now turned from Una to John and hung on her sleeve. In the same low voice, she asked anxiously after John's health. John assured her she was well. She in turn wondered why Ladye was distressed. A smile creased the medium's face and she explained she was not upset, her tears were caused by her joy and excitement at 'coming through'.

Ladye's 'control' of Mrs Leonard lasted some ten minutes. The medium had never met Mabel Batten in her lifetime, and Una, speaking for John as well as herself, summed up her feelings later:

> Although distinct traces of Mrs Leonard appeared in the voice, there were certain phrases in which to my thinking the voice resembled that of MVB, shades of intonation and phrasing which it is difficult to define, but which nevertheless to me were rather convincing ... Having seen at other mediums several instances of what purported to be MVB controls, I can only say that that of Mrs Leonard was by far the most convincing that I have yet seen. And I can perhaps best express my condition of mind by stating that towards the end of the control, my arm being around Mrs Leonard's waist, I became quite suddenly conscious of a feeling of astonishment that MVB's waist should be so very much slimmer than it had been during her earth life.[3]

This considered, dispassionate judgement betrays little of the deep emotions aroused in John and Una by their dramatic experience. For John's affair with Una had started while she was still living with Ladye and had caused much pain and bitterness. When Ladye died, John's grief was fuelled by guilt and remorse. In a desperate bid to make amends, she sought to 'contact' Ladye through Mrs Leonard's reputed powers of mediumship.

Suppressing her own feelings, Una devotedly aided and abetted John's spiritualist mission. The sitting of February, 1917, was the first occasion that the two women together witnessed Ladye's 'appearance'. It marked the beginning of an extraordinary triangular relationship. Throughout the stormy years that lay ahead, whatever the scandals and humiliations, whatever the friendships sealed and broken, whatever the claims of fame and ill-health, John and Una would always find time to sneak quietly off to that darkened room where they could 'commune' with Ladye. In the early days the séances might be as often as two or three times a week. Later, as John's professional career flourished, the visits became less frequent, sometimes months apart. But they never ceased altogether until John's health broke down in her last years – and even then Ladye's name would often be invoked.

Ladye, alive, had proved a source of friction and guilt between John and Una. Dead, she was transformed for both into a combination of idol, confidante, and ultimate arbiter. Every home that the two women would share in the twenty-eight years they lived together became in part a shrine to the goddess, containing pictures, photographs, trinkets and other innumerable mementos of Ladye. Important anniversaries in Ladye's life were solemnly celebrated long after her death. She acquired an indispensable place in the couple's Catholic devotions: masses were ordered for her, flowers laid at her tomb, votive candles in their hundreds burnt to her memory.

Initially, John was the driving force behind this obsessive act of worship. Yet Una too came to believe implicitly in the ritual, invoking the exclusiveness of their holy trinity. Indeed, as other commitments began to claim John's attention, Una increasingly became the one who, with her flair for practicalities, shouldered the responsibility for tending the flame. In the mid-1930s, when John embarked upon an affair with another woman, subjecting her relationship with Una to its severest test, it was to Ladye that Una turned for guidance and consolation.

During John's lifetime only their closest friends were entrusted with the secret of the enduring connection with Ladye. After the novelist's death, however, when Una came to write her own account of their life together, she decided the world should know the truth. She was concerned about inaccurate public speculation over a dedication which had first appeared on the fly-leaf of John's novel, *Adam's Breed*, and in all her published work thereafter. This dedication read: '*To Our Three Selves*'. Una explained:

> The Three Selves referred to in the dedication were Ladye, who had encouraged [John's] first efforts in prose and of whose continued interest she was firmly convinced; myself, whose glad and humble service to her talent she chose thus to acknowledge and honour and ... Radclyffe Hall, since, generous as she was in her tribute to Ladye's influence and to my service, she could not deny that the books were her own creation.[4]

Couched carefully in terms of literary achievement alone, Una's explanation gave no hint of the profound emotional undercurrents which had originally united the three women.

There is a curious incident early on in *The Well of Loneliness* where one of the servants at Morton Hall, a young woman called Collins, develops a painful 'housemaid's knee'. The seven-year-old heroine Stephen, who has conceived a crush on Collins, acquires the idea that, if she too can hurt her knee, she can relieve her beloved of her suffering. 'I'd like to be awfully hurt for you, Collins,' the child says, 'the way Jesus was hurt for sinners.' And so she secretly sets about scrubbing her nursery floor, punishing her knees until holes appear in her stockings. The nanny finally discovers her odd behaviour and puts a stop to it. Later, in her prayers, Stephen reproaches God: 'He loves neither me nor Collins – He wants all the pain for Himself; He won't share it!'[5]

Radclyffe Hall too wanted to share the pain, to take others' suffering upon herself, and in a sense her whole life represented a search for some kind of martyrdom. The notion was reinforced by her strong religious convictions, but its roots lay deep within her early emotional development. If, as has been said, the past is a foreign country where they do things differently,[6] childhood is its capital city. The capital John hailed from was not a happy place and she never forgot it.

Part One

MARGUERITE

1880–1907

Chapter One

The house in the Christchurch district of Bournemouth was called 'Sunny Lawn' – an absurdly inapposite name in view of the misery and strife that would take place under its roof. John was born here on August 12, 1880. She was the second child, having been preceded by Florence Maude barely a year before. However, within a few weeks of John's birth, Flo died of mysterious convulsions.

By her own account,[1] John entered the world prematurely: the midwife had gone to the chemist and had to rush back, arriving in time to cut the umbilical cord – an act of impetuosity on the part of the baby which John would later interpret as the first sign of her 'masculine' temperament. She was christened Marguerite, the choice of her mother Mary, an American who evidently considered that a French name bestowed breeding for she preferred to be addressed herself as Marie.

John was an unwanted baby. At the time of her birth her father was absent, apparently philandering in new pastures, while Mary had made every effort to terminate the pregnancy. When Flo died, Mary ascribed the cause to syphilis inherited from her husband. Just weeks after John's arrival, her father deserted the marital home for good. Looking back on this unhappy beginning, John wrote later:

> Somehow it all seems rather dreadful; a night of physical passion and then me, created solely of bodily desire, of an animal impulse and nothing more, for I cannot believe that those parents of mine can ever have known the love of the spirit.[2]

The Halls originally came from Lancashire, and John felt that she owed her stubborn fighting qualities to her north-country blood.[3] Her great-great-grandfather, the Reverend Samuel Hall of Manchester, served as a tutor to Thomas De Quincy, author of *Confessions of an English Opium-Eater*. John regarded Sam Hall as an indomitable pioneer of higher education for the people, but De Quincy remembered him only as an uninspiring preacher and a stern, almost sadistic taskmaster.[4] In 1776 Sam married Elizabeth Russell, bringing the distinctive 'Radcliffe' into the family name, for she was the daughter of the vicar of Easingwold in Yorkshire, the Reverend Radcliffe Russell.

The Radcliffes were connected with the Earls of Derwentwater. The second Earl, Edward Radcliffe, had married Lady Mary Tudor, an illegitimate child of Charles II, and two of their sons had given their lives for the Jacobite cause: both had lost their heads on Tower Hill, one during the 1715 Rebellion, the other during the '45. John was proud of this colourful pedigree and in later years read widely in the history of the period and proclaimed herself a staunch supporter of the Stuarts. The turbulent Radcliffes had stood for a romantic lost cause, sacrificing their lives for their notion of honour and justice, and this powerfully appealed to John who, all her life, would be quick to side with the underdog.

Sam Hall's son John, the eldest of eleven children, was the first to add the Radcliffe name to his own, no doubt for reasons of social pretension. He became successively a surgeon, a magistrate and an alderman, and moved the family to Congleton in Cheshire – where Hall relatives still existed in Marguerite's lifetime. A fair, handsome man of clear-cut features he bore, according to Una (who had seen a portrait of him), a striking resemblance to his great-granddaughter in a bad temper.[5]

John Radcliffe Hall's son Charles made the family's fortune. Like his father, he went into medicine. After contracting tuberculosis, he settled in Torquay, where he helped to establish a new sanatorium for consumptives in 1851. The treatment of TB was then in its infancy, and Charles's energetic promotion of natural cures was destined over the next decade to make him extremely rich and to turn Torquay into a fashionable spa.

Charles called his grand town house 'Derwent' and lived in great style. Not that he was ever reckless or extravagant. His intricate and precise Will suggests a sharp, careful business mind: relatives who owed him money, for example, had the sums deducted from their legacies. He assiduously cultivated his social and professional standing. By his death in 1879 he had acquired a knighthood, served as president (in 1860) of the British Medical Association, and provided the family with armorial bearings as well as a pedigree which, by a precarious route, traced his descent from William Shakespeare. It was Charles who took to spelling Radcliffe with a 'y', quietly yoking it to Hall with an elevating hyphen. 'Such an unnecessary thing to do,' commented John,[6] who later banished the hyphen when she became a novelist.

Names obviously mattered to the good doctor from Torquay for he christened his only son – Marguerite's father – Radclyffe Radclyffe-Hall, an unwieldy mouthful even by Victorian standards. Before long the boy's friends had dubbed him simply 'Rat'. Rat's mother was a widow, Esther Westhead, who already had three children from her first marriage, a son and two daughters. The younger girl became a special favourite of Dr Radclyffe-Hall and her death shortly after his marriage to Esther dealt him a blow from which he never fully recovered. John considered her grandfather a sensitive man of strong emotions underneath his wordly exterior. Certainly he never let those around him forget his grief for his little step-daughter, for he plunged the household into an atmosphere of gloom for the remainder of his days. Under such circumstances Rat developed an early sense of rejection. As he grew up, relations with his father deteriorated and he began to show a marked reaction against the vigour and ambition that had driven Charles to the pinnacle of social success.

Rat went to Eton and from there to St John's College, Oxford, where he matriculated in 1869. No record survives of his having taken a degree. Like much else in his life, his courses were probably abandoned when he lost interest. Charles intended that his son should become a barrister, but Rat protested laconically that he found dinners in chambers indigestible. Furnished with a generous family allowance, the young man had no incentive to work for a living.

There was a flamboyant side to Rat. At Oxford he sported the fashionable long side-burns known as 'Dundreary whiskers' and developed a talent for conjuring. He adored expensive clothes and jewellery, especially diamonds, which he wore in his shirt-front, in his cuffs, and pinned to his cravat. He was not a tall man but his fair hair and blue eyes gave him a certain presence and he must have cut an elegant, dandyfied figure in all his finery.

Perhaps these extrovert tastes prompted Rat to take his first, and only, job – as an actor. He adopted the stage name Hubert Vane and joined a provincial touring company. In the 1870s acting was still frowned on as a career for a gentleman and the outraged Dr Radclyffe-Hall cut off his son's allowance. Whether Rat had any talent for the stage is not recorded, but his appearance as Charles Surface in a Torquay production of *The School for Scandal* did nothing to heal the family rift, indeed it looks suspiciously like a deliberate snub. However, either because he began to feel the pinch or grew bored, he soon abandoned the theatre. His father's Will, drawn up in 1872, confirms Rat as the chief heir to the family fortune, so perhaps there followed some measure of reconciliation with Charles.

Rat was not without interests, though most were the natural

pursuits of a monied Victorian gentleman with time on his hands. He loved dogs and hunting, and he kept a succession of yachts in which, with a valet in attendance, he sailed about the English and French coasts. He had inherited his father's weak chest and in winter he would set off for warmer shores. According to John, he once sailed round the world – an achievement which, if genuine, one suspects was less planned than the fortuitous result of chronic restlessness. He loved music and later took up painting. In both spheres, however, he seems, characteristically, to have dabbled rather than persevered. Even John, normally so eager to believe the best of her father, considered his land- and sea-scapes 'appalling'. He played the mandolin well and composed many songs, but he lacked the application to turn these skills into something lasting or rewarding.

John thought that women were her father's chief undoing. It is known that a scandal linking him with a fisherman's daughter in Torquay once drove Dr Radclyffe-Hall to bar him from Derwent House. In his Will, Rat left this woman an annuity and, significantly, made provision for another woman and her child in London. Whether the child was his is not indicated.

In 1878, the year before his father's death, Rat married a pretty young American widow, Mary Jane Sager. She was the daughter of Edwin Diehl, a Philadelphia businessman of Dutch extraction who had died during her childhood. Her aunt Jane had married James Reade, a Cheshire cousin of the Radclyffe-Halls. Reade brought his wife to England to meet his family and Mary accompanied them. At Southport in Lancashire she was introduced to Rat. The wedding took place in the town and was conducted by the Reverend Walter Begley, a classical scholar who had tutored Rat for Oxford and was to become one of his few lifelong friends. John always believed that Begley loved Rat as a son and that Rat saw in him something of the father he felt he had never had.

The marriage got off to an uncertain start. At the wedding breakfast Rat proposed the toast: 'We've all heard of the glorious stars and stripes. Well, I have married one of the stars. May I never deserve the stripes!' The strait-laced, class-conscious Halls were not amused. Americans were thought to be vulgar. A Hall cousin enquired of Mary with waspish innocence: 'Tell me, what language do you speak on the other side of the Atlantic ocean?' 'Choctaw and Cherokee!' shot back the bride with a defiant glare.[7]

With the Hall relatives keeping their distance, Rat and Mary went to live in London, taking rooms in Piccadilly. Shortly afterwards they visited her family in Philadelphia. The trip was not a success. Rat appears to have behaved off-handedly, provoking the Quaker reserve of his American in-laws by dressing in a green velvet coat, loud check trousers and flottant bow, and letting his hair grow down to his shoulders. 'So poor Mary has married a painter,' ventured the neighbours. 'No,' replied Mary's mother, 'poor Mary has married a side-walk artist!'[8]

On returning to England, the young couple settled in Bournemouth at Sunny Lawn. Rat always preferred the country to London, and Bournemouth at this date possessed the spacious grandeur and balmy sea air which suited his gentlemanly tastes and poor health. He especially loved the nearby New Forest, making many sketches of it and roaming its length and breadth on horseback. John too would grow to love the Forest and many years later that same 'enchanted gateway' served as the sanctuary and final resting-place of her tortured hero in *Adam's Breed*.

Within weeks of their marriage, her parents, according to John, were quarrelling. Marie (as we shall now call her) proved a shrewish wife. Spoiled as a child by a doting widowed mother, she soon manifested innumerable petty vanities, a propensity for wilful extravagance, and an ungovernable temper. These traits were to grow more extreme over the years and at times, reading her own shrill letters or John's accounts of her hysterical tirades, one is forced to the conclusion that she was mentally unstable. John characterized her as 'violent and brainless, a fool but a terribly cruel fool, a terribly crafty and cruel fool, for whom life had early become a mirror in which she saw only her own reflection.'[9] In marrying Rat, she had probably made a fairly precise calculation of his worth – which, after the death of both his parents, amounted to well over £100,000, in those days a very considerable sum indeed. That Marie's share of this fortune was to decline abruptly as a result of their separation, and at the very moment she was left with a baby she did not want, no doubt contributed to her lifelong resentment of her daughter. John believed, more charitably, that her mother had married for love and that her unreasoning hatred of Rat reflected a genuine bitterness and disillusion.

For his part Rat, restless and unfulfilled, was hardly suited to the routine demands of conventional married life. His temper, which John would inherit, could be no less uncontrollable than his wife's. He succumbed to sudden moods and morbid thoughts – a man of 'vast discontents', as John put it, never happy with the present, always for moving on, but with no sense of where to go. When the black mood took hold of him, he would saddle his horse and ride for hours at a time, galloping wildly across country in all weathers until the depression lifted.

In 1882 Marie petitioned for divorce on the grounds of cruelty, claiming her husband had abused and assaulted her. In his defence, Rat claimed he had been provoked by his wife's outbursts and had only tried to restrain her. The court sided with Marie, awarding her custody of the infant Marguerite and a settlement of £2,000.[10] Rat was furious and refused to pay. Instead he settled £200 on his daughter and, curiously (unless he was the father), a further £200 on the child of Marie's housemaid. However, Marie's lawyers discovered that Dr Radclyffe-Hall's Will permitted his son to leave his personal estate to one child only, his heir – Charles's way, no doubt, of preventing the dispersal of the fortune he had so assiduously built up. After further wrangling, Rat eventually laid aside £10,000 in a trust fund to be administered by his London solicitors Hastie & Co on behalf of Marguerite's care and education. Marie never received her court settlement and many years later the £2,000 became a bone of contention when she claimed John owed her the money.

After her father's departure from Sunny Lawn, John saw him on less than a dozen occasions during the rest of his life. All practical arrangements for her welfare were handled by Mr Hastie who, when the child was old enough to speak for herself, would call once a quarter and question her about her progress. Hastie impressed upon her the special position she held as an heiress and she developed an early sense of the responsibility that such wealth bestowed upon her.

Rat, meanwhile, beat a retreat to his yacht and continued his idle, aimless existence in a succession of foreign ports and first-class hotels. He kept a flat overlooking Hyde Park but rarely stayed there. John could recall one visit from him when she was still quite small. He arrived out of the blue, a romantic figure on horseback, tall (to her eyes) and bearded. He called her 'Daisy' and promised to buy her a cream-coloured pony for her birthday. In the event, much to John's dismay, she received only a doll. Rat's excuse was that ponies could be bad-tempered and dangerous. With characteristic charity to her father, John put the episode down to her mother's interference.

When she was eighteen John went with her grandmother, Sarah Diehl, to see Rat at the Paddington Hotel in London. It was October and he was preparing to take the train to Dover and there board his yacht for a winter trip to Cannes. While Granny Diehl waited below, John went up to her father's rooms. The once elegant dandy, now sporting a bushy moustache, presented a sick, emaciated shadow of his former self. Racked with bladder trouble and the shattering cough of advanced pulmonary tuberculosis, he had difficulty breathing. John expressed her concern but he insisted casually it was only asthma and what he needed was a few weeks in the sun. He seemed to realize, for the first time, what a beautiful daughter he had. He treated her with affection and showed an interest in her welfare. He wanted her to send him a photograph of herself. Musing on his misspent life, he advised John never to become a jack-of-all-trades like him but to stick to one thing. He promised to alter his Will to make her the sole heir to all his property (some of which was destined for John's Cheshire cousins). For once this appears to have been a genuine resolution on Rat's part for, before leaving London, he contacted Begley (now his trustee) and gave him notice of the proposal.

He did not live long enough to carry it through. John probably guessed she would never see her father again. She was touched by the terrible change in his appearance, by the depression and despair he breathed. Afterwards, Granny Diehl stopped off in the Bayswater Road to visit her bank. Sitting alone in the waiting cab, John broke down and wept silently.

Rat never reached Cannes. Too ill to sail from Dover, he sent his yacht ahead while he crossed the Channel by ferry and started his journey south overland through France. By the time he reached Paris his condition had worsened sharply and the party returned to England, putting up at the Lees Hotel in Folkestone. He drifted into a coma and died there ten days later. He was only fifty-two.

Chapter Two

In old age Marie wrote petulantly of John: 'She had not an ounce of my blood in her – she was Radclyffe through and through morally and mentally.'[1] From her earliest years John endured this spirit of maternal rejection. Her mother never had another child and so Marguerite remained the sole object of her violent resentments – which sometimes took the form of physical beatings. As John's face began to acquire the aquiline features so marked in the Halls, Marie took to commenting contemptuously on her appearance. 'Your hands are just like Radclyffe's!' was a favourite put-down.

Deprived of her mother's love, John sought it elsewhere. As a small child, the natural objects of her affection were the servants whose responsibilities centred on the nursery. There was a nanny, much loved, known as 'M'Nana' – later sacked for protesting at the bruises left on the child's body by Marie's beatings. Then came a governess Miss Knott, always called 'Nottie'.

Animals too figured largely. Her first pet, a pug named Joey, was followed by a succession of dogs and caged birds of various breeds and sizes. To the unloved child these creatures represented more than simply objects of passing sentiment. They were defenceless friends whose lives were irrevocably linked to her own in ties of loyalty and ownership. Throughout John's life animals aroused in her a strong, at times mawkish, protective instinct. She could never tolerate the slightest harm or cruelty towards them and repeated incidents in her adult life – taking in strays, releasing caged birds, reproaching other pet owners – show her going to inordinate lengths to relieve their suffering, real or imagined. As she grew up, people too came to be regarded in the same light, for defencelessness in whatever form would always attract her ready sympathies.

John's most lasting attachment as a child went to her grandmother, Sarah Diehl. Marie, after her divorce, had stayed for a time with her family in Philadelphia. When she returned to England she persuaded Sarah to come back with her, to act as both her chaperone and as a 'baby-sitter' for young Marguerite: Marie had no intention of letting her child become a tie. Granny Diehl had been married at seventeen and widowed by twenty-three. At the time of John's birth she was still in her forties. John remembered her as a short, stout woman with innocent blue eyes. As photographs of her attest, she bore more than a passing resemblance to Stephen's beloved governess Miss Puddleton in *The Well of Loneliness* – who is described as looking like 'a miniature box . . . neatly spliced at the corners'.[2]

This 'miniature box' gave John most of whatever tenderness and affection she received as a child. Sarah called the girl 'Suggie Plum', which John shortened to 'Tuggie'. Sarah would read to her for hours, mostly Dickens and Shakespeare. On one memorable occasion they both went to see Henry Irving act with the lovely 'misty-voiced' Ellen Terry. Sarah was religious but in an undogmatic, 'protestant' way. 'To her,' recalled John, 'I owe an early religious training of the kind that could only envisage God as love.'[3] Granny Diehl tolerantly believed that all Christian creeds led to heaven. She was neither educated nor particularly bright – 'weak and foolish' were John's words – but John could forgive her everything for her warm-heartedness.

Sarah became devoted to her grandchild, protecting her as best she could from Marie's violent storms. As John grew taller, and proved better able to fend for herself, the roles reversed. Marie bullied and intimidated her mother and John now did the defending and comforting. Like the pets, Granny Diehl too acquired a claim on John's self-consciously protective role. Even as a young girl John, in her solemn, grown-up way, would help her grandmother to cross the busy London streets, taking her arm and saying: 'Hold on to me, granny, I'll take you over. Don't be afraid . . . '[4]

Before long Marie married for a third time. She had soon left Bournemouth for the more desirable social world of London – she had always hated the stifling provincialism of the south coast. She had started taking singing lessons. Her teacher was a robust Italian called Alberto Visetti. Visetti, in his early forties, was on his way to becoming a music master of some eminence. He had started his career at the Milan Conservatoire but settled in London in 1870, eventually adopting English nationality. When Marie met him, he was a professor of singing at the Royal College of Music and principal conductor of the reputable Bath Philharmonic Society. Several of his star pupils at the Royal College went on to become famous singers. They remembered him as an enthusiastic and generous teacher provided, it seems, the voice under tuition showed sufficient promise to repay his time and attention. He would tell pupils with any prospects that they had 'gold in ze throat', the implication being that he alone could capitalize it for them.[5]

Marie's movements at the time of Visetti's courtship are hazy. It appears that in the summer of 1889 she decamped from London and went, with her mother and John, to reside in Bruges in Belgium. There Visetti followed her. If the trip started as a family holiday, it was a very prolonged one, for by February of the following year Marie still lingered in Belgium. In her *Life* of John, Una suggests that this curious peregrination reflected a calculated move on Marie's part to bring a hesitating suitor to the boil.[6] On the other hand, both parties may have preferred to conduct their wooing at a safe distance from the hot-house atmosphere of upper-class Kensington. Whatever the reason, Visetti proposed and was accepted in Belgium – and probably wed Marie there as well, since no record exists of their marriage in any British registers.

And so, at the age of nine, John acquired a step-father. Even though Rat was still alive, the right man could in time possibly have won John's trust and affection. Visetti was not that man. As a maestro he could mean little to the child. As a father-figure he proved unprepossessing, and certainly no match for the romantic horseman who had once dismounted at her door. He seems to have been vain, petty, excitable, quarrelsome, and he did not scruple, with Marie's help, to use John's trust fund in the pursuit of his own lavish social pretensions. In reality, Visetti was probably not as black as John later painted him – just a busy music professor too wrapped up in his own concerns to give much thought to an unhappy, unloved child. But his neglect hurt, and she never liked him.

The Visetti home was a large house, Number 14, in an imposing terrace in Addison Road, Earls Court, in those days a district with some claims to gentility. The family lived in comfortable circumstances, with a proper complement of servants and a two-horse carriage. Visetti had a studio in the house where he gave music lessons. Some of his Royal College pupils lodged with the family as paying guests, an arrangement which provoked jealous eruptions from Marie when Albert's attentions strayed too conspicuously towards his prettier students. If he resembled Rat in little else, Visetti shared his roving eye. Whereas John came to view her father's infidelities with a certain detached amusement, as pardonable male foibles not without their rakish glamour, in Visetti she found them merely disgusting.

Almost nothing is known of John's schooling. It was probably fairly rudimentary: she never, for example, learned to spell properly. She herself seldom mentioned her education and in her fiction school as an institution, a dominant influence in so many childhoods, scarcely figures at all. As a young child she was taught at home by governesses – like her Victorian heroines in *The Unlit Lamp* and *The Well of Loneliness*. Then again her mother's restless travels in the 1880s between England, America, and the Continent precluded a regular schooling. On the other hand, Una tells us that in her teens John did attend a number of day-schools, notably a fashionable establishment in Kensington run by a Miss Coles.[7]

However, the overwhelming impression remains that John was a solitary and self-absorbed child. Photographs show a thin, bony girl, awkward, shy and sensitive. She already suffered from asthma, now recognized as a classic psychosomatic condition. As a small child she had had double pneumonia followed by scarlet fever. In her late teens she contracted a severe bronchial complaint which kept her seriously ill in bed for weeks. Other bouts of ill-health recurred throughout her childhood, so she must have spent long periods alone in her sick-bed.

She had no real family either. Not only no brothers and sisters, but no relatives. Granny Diehl apart, her mother's family were all in America, and Marie refused to see any of Rat's English relations. John remembered other children asking her 'Haven't you got any relations?' and she never knew what to reply.[8] Even the family she did know was bewildering. Her real father was English but absent, her step-father was Italian but had become an Englishman – and her mother was American.

John fell back on her own resources and an imaginative world of her own making. She showed an early aptitude for music. The famous conductor Arthur Nikisch stayed with the Visettis and was so impressed by John's piano playing that he urged her to come and study composition as his pupil in Germany. John played entirely by ear, being unable to read a note of music. Nothing came of this proposal, however, apparently through lack of parental interest.

She had a precocious talent for improvization as well. At three, she started inventing her own verses and rhymes, and never lost the habit thereafter. Later, when she could write and play the piano, she composed verses to her own tunes, singing out the lines repeatedly until she had them right. The poems were then put down on paper and the musical settings forgotten. As an adult poet, she would employ the same technique. Since she never learned to transcribe music, almost all her published songs would be put to settings by others. Given that Albert Visetti was a professional music teacher, it says much for his lack of interest in John that she never received a proper musical education to back up her talent.

With no one to criticize or encourage her efforts (Granny Diehl was too admiring to be constructive), John's childhood poetry showed little development and appears unremarkable. Her subject matter was taken from simple natural phenomena and the sentimental joys they inspired. Titles such as 'Poor Robin', 'On A Vase of Flowers', 'Joey' (about her pug-dog), 'Moonbeams' and 'To A Tree', speak for themselves. In her teens, though nature remained her favourite theme, she also wrote about music, patriotism ('My Native Land'), and the passing of time (one of these last, celebrating the arrival of the New Year, contained the lines: 'Oh, innocent year, your life's begun, / Who knows the sin 'ere you are done?' – a surprising thought perhaps in a girl of fourteen). Childish though it is, John's versifying suggests her early preoccupation with the musical quality of words and therefore prefigures the later elegance and lyricism of her prose style as a mature novelist.

In 1894 some of John's poems were put together in a little home-made volume and presented to Visetti's colleague, the composer Sir Arthur Sullivan. The young author signed herself 'Marguerite Toddles', Sir Arthur's nickname for her.[9] The verses impressed Sullivan and he urged Marie to watch her daughter's education carefully. 'She has ink in her blood!' he remarked. Marie's reply is not recorded, but she never bothered to act on the advice.

The alienation and rejection John experienced as a child left an indelible mark – as her fiction later bears witness. In all her major works we are treated to the spectacle of children growing up without fathers, without proper maternal love, and with warring or disharmonious parents. Servants – nurses, maids, governesses – and other amiable outsiders provide an alternative source of trust and affection.

When she does write about happy families, it is often in idealized terms far removed from any daily reality. A proper marriage is viewed as something spiritual, not to say sacred. The good mother is described in reverential tones as placid, gentle, Madonna-like in her serenity and perfection – the very opposite, in fact, of Marie Visetti. John recalled that her childhood home 'had neither dignity nor repose, and, moreover, was deplorably lacking in beauty'.[10] She believed that houses, like all places, could and should possess spiritual values.

In later life John professed to be what she called a 'congenital invert', that is, a born lesbian. Such women, according to certain contemporary sexologists, exhibited masculine characteristics of physique as well as manner. When Una Troubridge came to write her account of

John's life, she drew a picture of a tomboyish girl who prefers drums to dolls, loves ponies and hunting, and hates the fluffy confections which as a young débutante she is compelled to wear. Una admits that 'such tastes are common to many girl children'. But then she adds: '. . . and might seem to have had little if any significance had the future not confirmed the fact of her sexual inversion.'[11] She goes on to discuss an early photograph of John as a baby.

> Its fists are clenched and its expression fierce; there is a quite definite resemblance to the Radclyffe Hall of later years when she had made up her mind about anything and meant to see it through . . . No one would doubt for a moment that this was a male child, and indeed, as I write this, a memory crops up that she was told at one time that throughout her infancy strangers always mistook her for a boy. She was still very young when she shed the baptismal name of Margaerite (sic), selected by her mother, and became known to her friends as Peter . . . a name that later was replaced so universally by John that for years many people knew her by no other.'[12]

Una's version must be treated with some caution. She accepted implicitly John's view of herself as a 'congenital invert' and, writing shortly after her lover's death, was anxious to promote Radclyffe Hall's reputation as the pioneering author of *The Well of Loneliness*. Significantly, John's own unfinished memoir entitled 'Forbears and Infancy' makes no mention of anything unusual about herself beyond the misery she suffered as a lonely, unloved child. Her earliest photographs show an apparently normal little girl with strong features. In adolescence she became thin and gawky, then blossomed into a very pretty young woman, slim-waisted and narrow-shouldered, neat and dignified rather than elegant, and carrying herself, as she always would, with an upright bearing. Leonard Woolf's mother sent her eldest daughter Bella to Miss Coles's school in Kensington at the same time as John. She recalled Miss Radclyffe-Hall visiting their house and looking very much 'a regular society girl'.[13]

It is also known that she was not always called Peter as a child. There was the early 'Tuggie', her father had called her 'Daisy', and to Arthur Sullivan she became 'Toddles'. None is a particularly masculine appellation. Perhaps John herself hated such nicknames, but they hardly suggest, as Una would have it, that other people 'always mistook her for a boy'.

Nor, it seems, was her hair a preoccupation as a child. She wore it long, allowing it to grow to waist-length, and as a young woman she tied it on top of her head in a chignon or plait. She did not cut it short, in fact, until she was well over forty.

When John was five years old, Granny Diehl commissioned a

portrait of her in oils from the fashionable society painter, Mrs Katinka Amyat. The picture has survived. It depicts a blue-eyed child in a white muslin dress with frilly ruffle and puffed sleeves. In her hands she clutches a small bouquet of ox-eye daisies. The painting is utterly conventional in its studied arcadian prettiness. As it stands today, it shows John's fair hair cut short above the ears and at the back, giving her face a boyish look that sits somewhat at odds with the girlish costume. In fact, as painted, the portrait presented John as she then appeared, with a thick mass of curls falling to her shoulders, making the child look as wholesomely feminine as her grandmother doubtless intended. This did not suit John's later theories about herself, however, so she had the curls painted out.[14]

If John was a rather less unorthodox child than she later liked to imagine, by her late teens she knew, like her fictional heroines, that she was 'different' from other girls of her own age. She was drawn neither to men nor marriage. Marie's hatred of Rat and the noisy skirmishing between husband and wife that punctuated life at Addison Road provided a poor advertisement for the married state. Men as a breed had little to recommend them. In her fiction they are almost invariably portrayed as weak, untrustworthy, insensitive and complacent. What was a husband, after all, speculates the beautiful Padrona in *Adam's Breed*, but 'a thing it was always essential to possess and pet into comparative good temper'?[15]

One man only was the exception: her father. For all his faults, John wanted to believe he was good. Her mother's rejection of her, the way in which she constantly denigrated her resemblance to Rat, only pushed the girl towards identifying with her father ever more strongly. Marie's loathing of him, so violent and unreasoning, suggested he was more sinned against than sinning. Rat's early death, after the poignant Paddington Hotel meeting and before John got to know him more intimately, preserved forever untarnished the fantasy of the romantic exile and benefactor whose patrimony would provide her escape from an oppressive home.

One question would nag her: if Rat had really loved her, why had he deserted her almost as soon as she was born and rarely seen her thereafter? Her explanation was characteristically charitable to the man and hard on herself. Had she been a disappointment to him? she wondered. Years later she confided to a friend her conviction that Rat had desired a son, that she had dashed his hopes at her birth.[16]

The real Rat, the deserting father and the unfaithful husband, would be replaced in her mind by a more romantic figure. Once she acquired her independence, John would gradually assume the squirely tastes and style she imagined had been her father's, even down to the flashing diamonds he wore. She rode to hounds, took up the mandolin, exhibited his moods and restlessness, and later, as Radclyffe Hall, even adopted his name as her own. By the time she came to write *The Well of Loneliness*, the feckless playboy had become a paragon of masculine virtue. 'What is honour, my daughter?' Sir Philip Gordon asks Stephen. 'You are honour,' the girl replies. [17]

At eighteen, however, John still lived at home, the victim of her mother's whims and rages. Even now Marie was capable of flying at the girl with her fists. Frequent conflicts over clothes arose as John resisted the showy, ultra-feminine style imposed by her mother, preferring instead plain high-necked blouses and simple tweed skirts. On one occasion, according to Una, Marie tore a plumed hat off John's head in exasperation, pulling her hair with it. [18] Her suspicion by this time that Marguerite was not 'normal' added to the tensions.

But John knew that before long she would be free. Under her grandfather's Will, at the age of twenty-one she would inherit the large personal estate he had built up. The bulk of this was made up of investments and was held in trust. Knowing his son only too well, Charles had stipulated that Rat could live off the income but must not touch the capital. Since Rat died leaving almost £52,000 of his own money – and he was by no means a parsimonious man – this income must have been considerable. As her father's only heir, John would receive the whole of her grandfather's estate, capital and income together, making her a rich and independent woman. But, because Rat failed to change his Will as he told John he intended at their last meeting, his fortune went not to her but to her Cheshire cousins. The final irony, therefore, is that for all her devotion to Rat, John technically owed her wealth and all its advantages not to him but to her grandfather.

She did not take this inheritance lightly. She saw it as a solemn responsibility and all her life she would be supporting relatives or others in need. A photograph of John as a young woman shows her, pale and grave, at the centre of a family group. No men are present, only women and children – her smiling American aunts and cousins, two young boys in sailor suits and, on the sidelines, her mother looking stern and huffy. Perhaps it is a birthday snapshot, for all attention clearly focuses on John. One is struck by her air of quiet dignity. Like a royal prince flanked by his retainers, she seems confident of her position as heir-apparent, yet conscious as well that it bore with it almost feudal allegiances and duties towards those about her. One cannot doubt that in this gathering John is the 'man' of the family.

Chapter Three

In Radclyffe Hall's first novel *The Unlit Lamp*, a minor character called Harriet Nelson makes a brief appearance. Harriet is a student of singing at the Royal College of Music. She is clever, plump, pretty and domineering. She is worshipped by a timid fellow-student, Rosie Wilmot, who slavishly obeys her every beck and call. Harriet wilfully plays with Rosie's affections, sure in the knowledge that, however sorely she provokes the girl, Rosie will never dream of spurning her. But just as Rosie is spellbound by Harriet, Harriet is in thrall to her own voice, a brilliant soprano, 'pure, sexless ... the voice of an undreamt-of choirboy or an angel'.[1] Nothing and no one must stand in the way of its practice and perfection, its well-being dominates all other considerations. Harriet's larynx is a veritable tyrant.

The pathetic picture of Rosie Wilmot and Harriet Nelson was loosely based on John's own relationship with Agnes Nicholls. Agnes was three years older than John. She had won a singing scholarship to the Royal College of Music in 1894. The *Musical Times* quickly singled her out at the College concerts as a singer of future greatness: she sang with an 'expression' and 'abandon' rare in young performers.[2] She won the College's coveted Dove Prize in 1898, and in 1900, her final year, she was awarded the Gold Medal for 'the most generally deserving pupil'. Years later Una heard her at Covent Garden and pronounced her voice 'unique' and 'unforgettable'.[3]

In her last years as a student Agnes boarded with the Visettis at Addison Road. She often practised in Alberto's studio and John was familiar with that 'unforgettable' voice before she met its owner. Physically, Agnes was of a type that invariably attracted John in her youth: somewhat heavy in the chin, broad-faced with a sensual mouth, statuesque in figure with a tendency to plumpness. Theirs was not a sexual relationship. John saw their friendship in idealized terms, emotional and spiritual rather than physical. Never having known normal maternal affection, she sought a companion at once older and more self-assured than herself – and there was no doubt that Agnes was supremely self-confident. John had the idea that romantic love entailed an act of service and self-sacrifice on behalf of the beloved. In

practice, this meant subordinat ing her life to the endless demands of
Agnes's voice and the ambitious future career that it promised.

Such a prospect did not deter John. Her own ambitions were as yet
unformed. She continued to write poetry in a sporadic fashion, but the
knowledge that when she left home she would not need to work for a
living did not induce her to seek a direction for her talents. Una tells us
that for a short time she attended King's College, London. No record
of this exists, though the Ladies' Department of King's was then in its
infancy and John possibly served as a part-time student there or simply
enrolled in its evening classes. She certainly never took a degree. Since
her father died in 1898, she may have changed her mind at this date
about university – rather as Joan Ogden in *The Unlit Lamp* gives up the
idea of going to medical school when Colonel Ogden dies.

After leaving the Royal College, Agnes embarked on her career. She
was immediately in demand on the concert circuit. A singer in the
grand manner, she made a name for herself performing in the most
popular oratorios of the day. By 1901 she had made her debut at
Covent Garden and was shortly appearing as 'Madame Agnes
Nicholls' on programmes – the first step on the ladder to divinity for
every prima donna.[4] By this stage, however, her involvement with
John was over. John, as Una reminds us, was not naturally a 'satellite'
personality.[5] For a time, eager to show her adoration, John threw all
her energies into supporting Agnes in her career:

> Whatever engagements in opera, concert or oratorio took the young
> singer, there also went John, listening, encouraging, sympathising and
> adoring. Holding cloaks, mufflers, bouquets, gargles and inhalers; in
> hotels, lodgings, trains and dressing-rooms, her existence entirely regula-
> ted by the imperious demands of that wonderful voice.[6]

Such self-effacement in the name of love might have been tolerable
had it been reciprocated with equal devotion. It was not. As Agnes's
professional commitments grew, and her reliance on Visetti's step-
daughter lessened, John was all too often taken for granted. At the
same time, both sides knew they were not emotionally in tune. Agnes
progressively pushed to arm's length an intensity of adoration which,
whether she understood its true nature or not, was becoming too disturbing for comfort. For her part, John perceived that Agnes did not
share her indifference to men. Within a couple of years of their parting,
the singer was to marry the composer-conductor Hamilton Harty.

After John's death in 1943, Agnes (by now Lady) Harty rang Una
and 'waxed eloquent on her brutal treatment' of John in those early
days.[7] John's comment on that painful time had already appeared,
more obliquely but no less pointedly, in *The Unlit Lamp*:

Years afterwards when . . . Harriet Nelson had become famous . . . Joan, seeing an announcement of the performance in the papers, would have a sudden vision of that little crowded sitting room, with Harriet hunched fatly in the wicker armchair, the rotund inhaler clasped to her bosom.[8]

In August 1901 John came of age and inherited her grandfather's fortune. Relations with her mother had already reached breaking-point. Going over her financial affairs with the solicitors, John learned that the Visettis had managed, against Hastie's advice, to overspend her maintenance allowance by the enormous sum of £12,000. When she asked Marie for an explanation, her mother flew into a rage. John moved out. She found a house on the corner of Kensington Church Street and Campden Hill Terrace, and took a lease on it. Granny Diehl went with her, to become a blend of companion, confidante, chaperone and housekeeper. Under her grandfather's Will, John inherited the Hall family portraits. These, together with several photographs of Rat, were installed in the new house in pride of place, daily reminders to John of her 'real' roots.

John's early twenties are frustratingly sketchy. For many writers, confident at an early age of their future destiny, these years are the most eloquently chronicled. John, by contrast, was shy, diffident, and intensely private. She kept no diary and wrote few letters. In spite of her poetic inspirations, she had no urge to be a professional writer. Apart from Visetti, whom she despised, her background had thrown up few positive cultural influences. The two dominant figures of her childhood, her mother and grandmother, were supremely conventional women, whereas Rat's influence proved too nebulous to be translated into an artistic ambition. Above all, her wealth and her class dictated she should not work but marry and settle down. She knew in her heart that this was not a choice open to her.

Having established herself in Campden Hill Terrace, John became restless and felt the urge to travel. It was a pattern which would assert itself throughout her life whenever she began to put down roots. She decided to visit her Diehl relatives in America, making two separate trips across the Atlantic.

On her first visit she stayed for a year, mostly in Washington. There she met Jane Randolph, a widowed cousin with two unruly small boys and a daughter. Jane came from the Jones branch of the Diehl family and was some ten years John's senior. She had a plain face, with small eyes and buck teeth, but she captivated John with her long auburn hair, exquisite hands and feet (a feature John always noticed), and

infectious smile. A strong, vivacious personality, Jane attracted many
admirers of both sexes. Una surmised from what John had told her
that Jane was 'a hard-going, reckless, and somewhat fickle but
loyal-hearted seductress'.[9]

The two women embarked on a tour of the southern states together,
leaving Jane's boisterous children with her mother in Washington.
They travelled in an old jalopy with one sparking plug, John doing the
driving while Jane sat beside her clutching a fierce bull-terrier called
Charlie in one hand and a revolver – 'handy for obstreperous negroes,'
as Una put it – in the other. John remembered this trip in later years
with great nostalgia. For the first time in her life she was free from
oppressive family pressures and could let her hair down. She started to
smoke, cigars as well as cigarettes, inaugurating a lifelong habit. Like
her father, she never took to alcohol in a big way, but on this extended
spree there were apparently a number of hard-drinking escapades in
which John followed the lead of her energetic cousin.[10]

At the end of a year John became homesick for England, as she
always did when abroad for long, and she soon returned to London.
She persuaded Jane to come with her. She assumed all Jane's financial
responsibilities and the family stayed at Campden Hill Terrace. At
some stage John and the Randolphs returned to America, where Jane
remarried, this time to a wealthy Texan from Houston called Harry
Caruth. Once again, John's protection was no longer needed and their
close friendship petered out. The two women remained on amicable
terms, corresponding for many years. John would always retain a soft
spot for Jane, even though, as a subsequent meeting in England several
years later proved, they had long ceased to have anything in common.

During her second visit to America John met another cousin,
Dorothy Diehl, the only daughter of her mother's brother William.
Dorothy was younger than John, still in her late teens, and one can
guess that this change in the pattern of John's affections gave full rein
to her ever alert protective instincts. The American girl conformed to
the physical type John preferred.

> She was plump and very pretty in a blue-eyed, golden-haired, pink and
> white style suggestive of the Dutch maiden of the musical comedies of our
> youth. She certainly had a charming mouth with deeply indented up-
> turned corners and an infectious smile, and when I met her long afterwards
> I thought her very amusing; but her wit had a cutting edge to it and her
> nature a crudity that was revealed in the coarsest hands I ever remember
> seeing on any woman.[11]

Una's own 'cutting edge' is apparent in this description, for relations with Dolly subsequently turned very sour indeed, but at the time

John obviously found her young cousin delightful. Dolly too came to England with John and settled under the protective roof at Campden Hill. There followed some travels together in Europe, principally in Italy. Una tactfully inclined to the view that John's interest, though affectionate, was primarily a family one, with John acting as her young cousin's self-appointed chaperone in a foreign country. Judging by later events, however, the bond between John and Dolly went deeper than mere friendship.

Dolly eventually followed the path taken by Agnes Nicholls and Jane Randolph: she married. Sometime around 1907, while still living with John and her grandmother (they had now moved to Albert Gate, Kensington), she fell 'violently in love' (the words are Una's) with an impecunious young composer called Robert Coningsby Clarke. Clarke was in his late twenties. He began as an articled pupil to Sir Frank Bridge at Westminster Abbey, then studied law at Trinity College, Oxford, where he was the chapel organist. He became a prolific composer of popular songs. His connection with John went beyond Dolly, for he was to set much of her poetry to music in the coming years and helped to make her reputation as a lyricist. In 1907, however, his fortunes had yet to flourish and John bestowed an allowance on the young couple, to assist 'what she was assured was true love to run more smoothly', commented Una.[12] Dolly married her composer at St Paul's, Knightsbridge, in 1909, John acting as one of the witnesses.

We know so little about John's early love life that it is difficult to come to any but the most tentative conclusions about its influence on her development. Whether her involvement with Agnes, Jane and Dolly was the limit of her youthful experience or merely marked the high points among a number of attachments is impossible to tell. She was certainly of a passionate nature and had a roving eye, but in her early twenties she was still shy and lacking in confidence. Moreover, her strong sense of loyalty and protectiveness makes it unlikely that she transferred her affections lightly. It is perhaps significant that each of these three women came from her own family circle, Jane and Dolly being cousins and Agnes a guest of the Visettis. In other words, friendship with them could arise naturally and without undue effort. By the same token, the chances of finding under such circumstances a love match that wholly satisfied her needs were bound to be slim.

One factor united Agnes, Jane and Dolly: each of them left John for a man. This was an option shut off to John if we are to believe her claim in later life (and we have no reason not to) that she was never in the slightest attracted to men. It must have powerfully reinforced her feelings of isolation and further promoted her growing conviction that *her* homosexuality was 'congenital'. Radclyffe Hall's heroines often become involved with women who are either already married or who end up so (even if, in some cases, they have to be pushed). However contrived this appears, it matched John's own experience. Ladye and Una, her most fulfilling lovers, would both be married women with children. This pattern had another effect. It induced in John the notion, unconscious or not, that she competed with men for women, thus underlining her natural tendency to reject her femininity and cultivate a mannish image. By the time she met Ladye and Una, this image was already well developed, and she would take some pride in the fact that she was supplanting both women's husbands in their favours.

It was during these years that John took a lease on a house, 'Highfield', in the village of Malvern Wells in Worcestershire. It was a large gabled mansion of Gothic grandeur. The stables were the chief attraction for John, for she had developed a passion for riding and hunting. Malvern's location enabled her to hunt with three different packs and during the season she would stay there for weeks on end. At one time she had as many as five horses stabled at Highfield, including a fierce, unruly jumper called Xenophon (which even John's grooms would not ride) and her favourite hunter, Joseph. Occasionally one of these horses would be transported up to London and John would ride in the Row in Hyde Park. Joseph would be the model for Stephen's beloved Raftery in *The Well of Loneliness*. Una tells us that once, when the horse tore its legs badly on barbed wire, John refused to follow the vet's recommendation to have it put down. Under her devoted nursing, the animal recovered and survived into old age.[13]

John continued to write, pouring out her feelings on paper in poetic verses. She still worked from the piano as she had done as a child. The first two lines usually came in a flash spontaneously, suggested by some tune which her fingers would idly discover as they toyed with the keys. She could never be sure how this opening would be used or followed up, but gradually the succeeding lines would emerge as her tinklings inspired new cadences and rhythms and rhymes.

In the summer of 1906 the Oxford Street publishers John and Edward Bumpus Ltd brought out her first volume of poems. She paid for the publication out of her own pocket and entitled it *'Twixt Earth and Stars*. A slim book, dedicated self-consciously to 'My Inspiration', it contained some eighty short poems. The majority were love lyrics, some apparently addressed to specific individuals but discreetly

Marguerite 1880–1907

entitled 'To -----'. None of the compositions suggested that homosexual love was the theme, and certainly the composers who later put
some of these verses to music would hardly have done so had that been
obvious. Many of the poems have the feel of ballads and John
probably wrote them with at least half an eye to the thriving popular
song market of her day. These songs provide the most successful
poems in the volume, being light, economical, and without pretension. 'On the Lagoon' is a typical example:

> A gondola, the still lagoon;
> A summer's night, an August moon,
> The splash of oars, a distant song,
> A little sigh, and – was it wrong?
> A kiss, both passionate and long.

The sentiments in *'Twixt Earth and Stars* are never very profound
and frequently repeat themselves in different forms. The triumphs and
joys of love are there, but the overwhelming impression is of love
turning sour, of regret, of yearning unfulfilled. The technique does
not always match the emotion, but accumulatively the bleakness of
the poet's outlook seems genuinely personal – as summed up in the
lines: 'A joy that passes, a pain that stays, / Such is life.'

'Twixt Earth and Stars brought John's name before the public for the
first time as a serious writer.[14] The response was encouraging enough
not to put her off. The *Queen* magazine praised her 'felicitous' gift of
expression and feel for rhythm.[15] The *Lady* considered she had 'real
talent'[16] and the *Publisher and Bookseller* judged her work 'of considerable merit'.[17] Within two years several of the poems in the collection
would be set to music (by Hubert Bath, Robert Coningsby Clarke and
Eathorpe Martin) and republished as popular songs.

It was the first indication John had received that she had some talent
deserving of the world's respect. However, for the moment her
wealth shielded her from the full implications of this knowledge. She
would continue to dabble with poetry, but in 1906 it still took a very
definite second place to the pleasures of hunting, travelling, and
amusing herself. In fact, despite Rat's advice to her at their last
meeting, John seemed set to become, like him, one of life's dilettantes.

Part Two

LADYE

1907–1915

Chapter Four

At the German spa of Homburg the morning ritual of drinking the spring waters began at 6 am. There followed a pre-breakfast dip in the saline baths. King Edward VII as Prince of Wales had made the resort fashionable and it now attracted some four thousand English visitors every season. The waters reputedly helped chronic rheumatism and were recommended to people who had lived in India or other tropical climes. This is what brought Mabel Batten to Homburg in 1907. However, she resolutely avoided the early morning rituals, preferring to lie in till midday. Her conduct raised a few eyebrows, but then Mabel was a woman who had always gone her own way.

It is unclear why John too was in Homburg that summer. Una tells us simply that she had gone there 'for some frivolous purpose'.[1] Likewise, the circumstances of her first meeting with Mabel Batten are shrouded in mystery. However, we do know the precise date they met – August 22 – for this anniversary would be cherished by both women ever after.

On the face of it, they had little in common. Mabel was fifty to John's twenty-seven. She was married with a grown-up daughter and grandchildren. Family ties gave her many connections in aristocratic society. In her youth she had been a noted beauty and rumour had it that she had enjoyed an affair with Edward VII before he became king. Certainly, he was godfather to her eldest grandchild and she owned a signed photograph of him.

But there were depths to Mabel which did not conform to the traditional image of the Edwardian grande dame. She radiated an unusual warmth and sensuality, while her wit and intelligence suggested a worldliness uncommon among women of her station. The drooping, languid eyelids, with their air of detached amusement, the delicate line of the mouth, and the slight tilt of the head, proclaimed a sexuality that lay outside conventional definitions, being neither coquettish nor sultry. She was at once bohemian and bourgeois. She believed strongly in reincarnation, later explaining the remarkable empathy that sprang up between her and John as evidence they had known each other in a former life.

Mabel's great-grandfather had been a Genoese Italian. There were also French and Irish strains in her ancestry. She was born, however, in Barrackpore in India, the daughter of an officer in the British Indian Army who ended his career as Judge Advocate General of Northern India. She enjoyed a musical education, being sent as a young girl to Dresden and Bruges to study harmony and composition. Later she spent several years in Florence and read widely in French and Italian.

In 1875, having returned to India, she married George Batten, then Commissioner of Inland Customs for the Central Provinces but shortly to become private secretary to the British Viceroy, Robert, Earl of Lytton. Mabel was eighteen and George a widower of forty-three – in John's time she would refer to her husband as 'my old George'. The couple settled in Simla and within a year of the marriage a daughter, Cara, arrived.

The British community was isolated and close-knit. The young Mrs Batten was accounted one of its prettiest women and she soon attracted numerous male admirers, among them Robert Lytton himself. In 1879 the poet and traveller Wilfrid Scawen Blunt arrived in Simla. A forceful, romantic figure, Blunt quickly made an impression and befriended Lytton. Blunt and Mabel were immediately drawn to each other but they took care, under the Viceroy's jealous eye, to maintain a platonic friendship only. The following year, however, Mabel pursued the poet to England where she stayed at his country house, Crabbet Park. She had promised Lytton before leaving India that she would not have an affair with Blunt. At Crabbet such promises meant nothing. Blunt recalled later: 'I found her door ajar at twelve o'clock and stayed with her till daylight.'[2]

Blunt believed he was the first man to satisfy what he called Mabel's 'nameless cravings'. He found her an intriguing blend: 'gay, fond of pleasure, quite depraved, but tinged too with romance.'[3] He observed in her an unquenchable restlessness of spirit, a quality summed up in lines from 'Butterflies', one of several poems he addressed to Mabel: 'Thy skies of blue, thy broken happiness, / The hopes thou chasest never to attain.'[4]

In 1882 George Batten retired and the family moved to England, settling at 3, Ralston Street, off Tedworth Square in Chelsea. Mabel set about seriously training as a singer. Her voice was a mezzo-soprano and possessed a warm, mellow timbre which contemporaries ascribed to her 'foreign descent'. She became noted, under George's coaching, for her clear enunciation as well. By the 1890s Mabel Batten was recognized as one of the leading amateur lieder singers of her day. Music, in fact, became her whole world. She played the piano and the Spanish guitar. She composed her own songs. She befriended Reynaldo Hahn and Gabriel Fauré and later sponsored the young Mischa Elman and the up-and-coming Percy Grainger.

Such a rich combination of beauty and talent made Mabel a favourite subject of painters and photographers. Koopman painted her, so did Sir Edward Poynter. Perhaps the best known portrait is the oil by John Singer Sargent, for whom she posed in 1895 when in her late thirties. The picture shows her in full vocal flight lit by lamplight – she actually sang to Sargent as he worked, a friend accompanying her on the piano. It is not altogether flattering to its subject, revealing a heavy throat and the beginnings of a double chin. One commentator suggested that it looked more like a lady yawning.[5] Mabel herself was not entirely happy with the portrait. She arrived at the studio one day to find that Sargent had cut away portions of her arms by reducing the width of the canvas. She was not amused.

Mabel's friends knew her as 'Ladye', an ironic nickname intended to point up the contrast between herself and her sister Emmie, whose aristocratic pretensions were well known. But 'Ladye' also spelled out an essential truth about Mabel: she was accustomed to receiving homage. At fifty she had begun to lose her hour-glass figure but her presence in a room still commanded attention. Una, who was a distant cousin, recalled:

> If she was no longer slim, she was no more than graciously ample and she had great dignity and length of line. She had that characteristically Irish colouring of a pale complexion, dark blue eyes and dark hair and not only her beautifully produced singing voice, but also her speaking voice, were quite enchanting.[6]

According to Una, John fell 'head and heart and soul in love' with Ladye at first sight.[7] A close relationship developed only slowly, however. Ladye had family ties and was a busy woman of some position (though her hey-day as a singer had passed). Moreover, 'she had no intention,' as Una put it, 'of sharing her life to any extent with what she regarded as a half-educated young cub who ignored all the important aspects of a civilised existence and preferred hunting to literature, music or the arts.'[8]

John felt overawed by such self-assurance and sophistication. However, she presented Ladye with a signed copy of '*Twixt Earth and*

Stars. Ladye had read the reviews and wondered whether the collection might offer any poems which could be turned into songs. She introduced John to several popular composers (among them Robert Coningsby Clarke). John invited her to tea at Albert Gate and took Visetti round to see her at Ralston Street. According to Una, Ladye told John bluntly that she expected her friends to make their mark. Eager to impress, John applied herself to her poetry.

In the summer of 1908 John and Ladye took a holiday together in Belgium. John appears to have been the moving spirit behind the trip, for Ladye always maintained that she went along for lack of anything better to do. The plan was to visit Bruges, where both women had spent part of their childhoods. However, all we know of this holiday is that in Ostend they had to move hotels owing to a double booking and spent most of their days in the local casino indulging Ladye's passion for roulette.

What is clear is that the two women who left England as friends came back as lovers. From this time onwards they would rarely be out of each other's company. The date they crossed the Channel to Ostend was August 12, John's birthday. Ever afterwards this anniversary became a double celebration.

The change wrought in John was evident from her second volume of poems, *A Sheaf of Verses*, published by Bumpus in the autumn of 1908. She dedicated the collection to 'Sad Days and Glad Days'. In spirit the poetry reflected the latter: 'Believe me, the world is a place full of joy, / And happiness stretches afar.' The technique and the emotion revealed a growing maturity. The love poems suggested greater confidence. John's homosexuality received an oblique mention with an 'Ode to Sappho' and, more strikingly, in 'The Scar' where she alluded to her abnormality as a thing of symbolic beauty, a cause of pride not shame, 'a path to gained respect'.

Ladye was responsible for John's new optimism. One poem in the collection, entitled 'Reincarnation', spoke directly of the poet's peculiar 'thrill' at first meeting her: 'Some compelling force of will, / Sprung from sympathies complete.'

On Christmas Eve 1908 John was thrown by Xenophon while hunting near Malvern and suffered concussion. The doctors believed she would have broken her neck and died instantly had the ground not been so soft. This near-miss deeply impressed John and later she and Ladye consulted a guru of the Raja Yoga movement as to what would have happened to her had she died so unexpectedly. It was an early indication of their mutual pre-occupation with the non-material world. John's poetry already showed an instinct for the mystical and she would always retain a respect for the irrational, intuitive processes. It stemmed in her from what Una later called 'that generous, highly spiritual element that in the end burnt up any lesser thing and pervaded and possessed her entirely'.[9]

John's hunting accident left her with a bruised spine and severe headaches. The doctors recommended prolonged rest and sea air. In April 1909, therefore, she set off with Ladye on a cruise to Tenerife, the first of many extended holiday trips they would take together. It also marked the first step in a more or less conscious programme of re-education that Ladye intended for John. Ladye admired Spanish culture and she proposed that John should learn to appreciate it too. In addition, she began reading aloud to her lover from 'improving' books, mostly French and English novels, remarking on their style and technique as she went along.

Tenerife enchanted them. For John the sights and sounds proved new and exotic. Even the ubiquitous beggars, wooing them with haunting love songs in strange minor keys, had a peculiar charm. The two of them went for long walks, picknicked, drove in open carriages, and rode on mule-back. Certain spots on the island became their favourites and they returned to them time and again, such as a wood where arum lilies grew. The place they loved the best was the old town of Orotava, sitting on the slopes of the Teide volcano. When years later John came to write *The Well of Loneliness*, it was in Orotava that her heroine Stephen and her lover Mary enjoyed their most carefree and blissful period together.

In Tenerife John and Ladye could let drop the guard which they had to keep up in England. In the coming years they would travel widely together and 'dear abroad' became a favourite catch-phrase of theirs. It signified much more than simply the thrill and glamour of foreign places; it meant being able to enjoy each other's company in a way that was impossible in England.

There was no question of Ladye leaving her husband. Such a course would have been unthinkable. George made little difference in any case. Now in his seventies, he spent most of his days at his club and viewed Ladye's attachment to John with a benevolent, paternal eye. Whether he suspected the true nature of their relationship is uncertain, but he did not mind taking separate holidays and regarded John with genuine affection. He was especially touched when on one occasion she helped him out after he had lost money on a bad speculation.

By this date John was lunching or dining at Ralston Street almost every day, for she and Granny Diehl had moved from Albert Gate to a flat just round the corner from the Battens in Shelley Court, Tite Street. A favourite rendezvous was the Bath Club, where Ladye indulged her love of swimming, the one form of exercise she enjoyed. Here the two women would sit for hours taking tea and chatting to mutual friends such as Dolly and Bobby Clarke, whom they had introduced to each other. Since their marriage the Clarkes were living at 1 Swan Walk, Chelsea, a stone's throw from Tite Street. In return for the annuity that John bestowed on them, Bobby Clarke had turned several of her poems into songs. Chappell & Co. published *A First Sheaf Of Little Songs* in 1908, following it up in 1909 with *A Second Sheaf Of Little Songs*. The latter included an unpublished poem of John's entitled 'Take Me With You When You Fly', which became an audience favourite at ballad concerts.

Apart from the 'Bobbies', as Ladye nicknamed the Clarkes, John also grew friendly with Ladye's daughter Cara. Cara was some five years her senior. She was married to a banker called Austin Harris and had two children, Peter aged twelve and Pamela, known as 'Honey', aged ten. The Harrises lived in Thurloe Square, South Kensington, and kept a country house, Aspenden Hall, at Buntingford in Essex. At weekends John often accompanied Ladye down to Aspenden and she became especially fond of Austin and Honey, joining them for long afternoon rides or country walks while Ladye and Cara stayed at home.

Ladye's relations with her daughter were not always easy. Cara felt that her mother had pushed her into a marriage she did not want and on the eve of the wedding there were stormy scenes at Ralston Street. Thereafter, however, Ladye came to regard the Harrises' friends, many of them business colleagues of Austin's, as somewhat too 'common' for her taste. Cara was a moody, quirky woman and one suspects that, though she accepted John, she also harboured a certain jealousy towards her intimacy with Ladye. Later, this situation provided rich ground for misunderstandings between John and Cara.

In February 1910 John and Ladye paid a second visit to Tenerife. As always during the English winter, Ladye had succumbed to coughs and colds and hankered for 'dear abroad'. She started a diary at about this time and it rarely fails to record every little ailment that afflicted her or John. This hypochondria suggests that Ladye had too much time on her hands, but it also reflected her pervasive restlessness, the 'nameless cravings' that Wilfrid Blunt had noted in her.

On the voyage out to Tenerife their ship encountered a terrific storm. It lasted four days and many passengers thought the vessel would founder. 'If we had not been in such grim danger,' Ladye wrote to Cara afterwards, 'the situation would really have been funny. Wild-eyed Germans in pyjamas struggling along and stewards actually hanging on for dear life to the handrails & not attempting to help one! ... Johnnie said she wanted "most awfully to live" & I quite agreed with her.'[10]

On the worst night of the gale John made Ladye get up and dress, ignoring her insistence that she be allowed to drown in her nightgown. Returning to her own cabin, however, John climbed into bed and fell fast asleep clutching a rosary. At the time Ladye scolded John for the inconsistency of her behaviour, but the story later became a favourite with them as proof of John's coolness in an emergency. Another, from the same holiday, told of how John rescued them from the clutches of a drunken coachman by taking the reins from him and steering their carriage safely home to Santa Cruz.

They were back in England by the end of April. On May 6 Ladye's diary read: 'King Edward VII (God rest his soul) died at midnight.' The following day Ladye dressed in mourning and remained so for over a month. Her rumoured affair with Edward had taken place many years previously, but she had retained a special affection for the king and always took a close interest in his activities. It made her a staunch monarchist and patriot, an outlook which exercised an important influence on John, who would always hold politically conservative views.

The king's death was the first of several in 1910 that would affect Ladye and John personally. In the autumn George Batten became seriously ill. In October he was operated on for an undisclosed ailment and his condition worsened. John, meanwhile, was coping with an unexpected crisis of her own, for Granny Diehl suddenly fell gravely ill as well. She died peacefully on October 18. John attended the funeral with her mother on the 22nd and the following day knelt beside Ladye and Cara in Westminster Cathedral praying for George who was failing fast. He died at Ralston Street on the evening of October 24, his head in Ladye's hands.

Within the space of a few days two of the most important people in the lives of John and Ladye had gone for good. Genuinely grieved as they were, both women understood only too well that this double blow at once removed the chief obstacle to a more permanent union between themselves. Ladye was now a widow, comfortably off in her own right, for George had left her the house in Ralston Street and some £8,000. For John likewise it meant the end of her last real family tie: she was now living on her own.

After a decent interval of mourning, they took another trip abroad, this time to the French and Italian rivieras. They spent most of the holiday looking at villas. However, none of the houses measured up to their fastidious tastes and they detested the English ex-patriates whom they encountered – 'thoroughly common & 2nd class,' Ladye informed Cara.[11] In April 1911 they abandoned house-hunting and crossed to Corsica for three weeks, thankful to have escaped 'the well-worn and boring old maids which filled Alassio & Bordighera'.[12]

In mid-May John bought the lease on a large unfurnished apartment at 59, Cadogan Square, conveniently near Harrods and the elegant stores of Sloane Street. In her excitement, she purchased Ladye a house-gift in the shape of a small Yorkshire terrier which they christened Claude – 'he is loving, un-smelly, very quiet, only barks if anyone knocks loudly at my door,' Ladye proudly told Cara.[13] A few days later Otero, a French bulldog, was added to the growing menagerie of pets – which now included John's old sable collie Rufus and a noisy parakeet called Lorim. To John the idea of a home was inconceivable without animals. Ladye liked them well enough but she was not inclined to put herself out. She would pet and spoil them, but she was too lazy to bother herself seriously with such chores as grooming and exercise. These tasks invariably fell to John.

Cadogan Square did not become vacant until October. In the meantime John set about selling Highfield House in Malvern. On April 28 her old horse Joseph, too infirm to go on, was shot in her presence. The event marked the close of a chapter in John's life. Since meeting Ladye she had devoted less and less time to riding and hunting. Ladye had formerly ridden in her India days, but horses made her nervous and she often urged John to give them up, especially after her accident on Xenophon in 1908. John proved reluctant to abandon one of her greatest pleasures, but the new life she had found with Ladye left little room for such pursuits. As Una put it in her memoir, 'brawn was giving way to brain' in John as Ladye introduced her to new intellectual influences.[14]

John did not give up riding entirely by selling Highfield. Though she no longer owned horses, she would still hire them from time to time, both in London and in the country. Nor did she intend to leave

Malvern. The plan was to find a smaller house in the district and accordingly the two lovers spent the summer of 1911 scouring local properties and consulting builders. The weather turned oppressively hot and the pace of their search bordered on the leisurely. Most days Ladye lay in till midday. She urged John to do the same, to 'take it out of your bed', as she put it, but John was accustomed to country habits and rose early (she enjoyed gardening and could sometimes be found digging and watering at 5 am). Ladye, by contrast, spent long hours pottering about her bedroom, reading, nibbling biscuits, and preparing her toilet. On one occasion she killed nineteen wasps before noon and 'invented' a net contraption to hang across the windows for keeping insects out. Both achievements were recorded in the diary in a tone suggesting that a good day's work had been accomplished.

On August 30 they visited a house a mile down the road from Highfield. It was called The White Cottage and they took an instant liking to it. The low gabled villa had originally been two separate but attached premises, an inn and an ancient cider house. The front windows gave an uninterrupted view of the Severn Valley and distant Bredon Hill. The village school stood opposite, St Wulfstan's Catholic church to the right, and beyond that, in Little Malvern, the ruins of the twelfth century Benedictine Priory. John's offer for the cottage was accepted and they hired a local builder to start extensive renovations on the interior.

In London in September the two women made final preparations to move into 59, Cadogan Square. Ladye let Ralston Street, marking the occasion by posing for photographs taken by a fashionable society portraitist: they show her, in a white china crêpe tea gown trimmed with fur, clutching Otero to her bosom. She also redrafted her Will to make provision for John. A new parlour-maid, Bryant, arrived, as did antique Italian pillars for Ladye's sumptuous bed fittings. The couple finally occupied the flat on October 2.

1911 ended on a note of cheerful optimism. On November 1 Ladye came out of mourning for George and friends dropped by to inspect their new home. A round of parties proclaimed the start of the festive season. Ladye introduced John to Liza Lehmann, a composer who would set several of her poems to music, and they met Sir Edward Elgar, a fellow resident of Malvern. At Christmas they attended two sumptuous fancy dress balls, one of which took place at the opera house in Covent Garden. Ladye went to one as a Lady of Baghdad, to the other as a Lady of Seville. John appeared at both as her Persian slave boy, her hawkish features and high cheekbones lending a convincingly 'foreign' air to the part. 'John looked ripping,' thrilled the diary on the day they both tried on their costumes for the first time.[15]

At the end of 1910 John had had another anthology of poetry published. Entitled *Poems of the Past and Present*, the volume was dedicated to 'Mrs George Batten' and represented John's tribute to Ladye. One poem, 'The Garden', expressed the unprecedented joy John had experienced since becoming Ladye's lover: 'I knew a region desolate / Unfruitful and without name, / Where all my loving was regret, / Before you came.' New literary influences were reflected in a homage to Elizabeth Barrett Browning, before whose 'simple, kind profundity' John felt humble and inadequate. The Brownings would always remain among John's favourite poets.

Here and there a note of anxiety intruded into the new collection, a feeling that such love and happiness could not last and when it ended would quickly be forgotten. In 'Non Omnes Moriar' she imagined them both dead: Ladye would be remembered, but all John could hope for was that someone someday might say 'She had yet one more lover in her day, / A poet fellow; I forget his name!' The tone was ironic but the unease genuine. John's nature contained a deeply fatalistic streak that inclined her to see the sorrow behind every joy.

Chapter Five

Having made her home with Ladye, John took another dramatic step. On January 3, 1912, the two women attended a performance of Max Reinhardt's *The Miracle* at Olympia. The play was a mime which told the story of a nun lured from her vows by the wiles of a 'spielman' or trickster, then brought to repentance by the miraculous intervention of a statue of the Madonna. The play's religious sentimentality greatly appealed to contemporary audiences. 'We both loved it,' Ladye recorded in the diary.

The Miracle triggered a deep response in John. For some time she had inwardly been debating the question of her religious beliefs. In *A Sheaf Of Verses* she had written a poem which began: 'Ah! Faith, I'd barter all I own to know / But one brief moment of your magic charm.' She wished desperately to believe in the existence of a scheme, an order that gave meaning to the apparent misery and chaos of existence. More than this, she hankered for a routine and a ritual, a sense in fact of belonging, something notably absent from her childhood.

Sooner or later she might have discovered Catholicism for herself but, as in so much else, Ladye served to hasten the process. Ladye was herself a Catholic convert, though neither very orthodox nor doctrinaire. Her tolerant curiosity in spiritual matters impressed John in a way that Granny Diehl's undogmatic brand of Anglicanism had done earlier.

Instead of trying to convert John, Ladye sensibly chose to let her make up her own mind by a gentle introduction to the forms and rituals of her faith. She took John to services at fashionable Brompton Oratory or the Jesuit chapel at Farm Street. Their travels abroad led them to Catholic countries, where the Church could be seen as part of a whole way of life, a cultural climate at one with the sunny, exotic Mediterranean character. John's imagination was fired by the mysteries of Catholicism.

A further consideration swayed her. Embracing Catholicism intensified her union with Ladye, for it gave hope of an after-life together in which their love could endure eternally.

The day after attending *The Miracle*, Ladye took John to Brompton Oratory to see Father Sebastien Bowden. Now in his seventies, Father Bowden was reputed to have been the priest whom Oscar Wilde sought out to receive him into the Church after his release from Reading Gaol (in fact, it appears that he refused to take Wilde in). Bowden agreed to put John under instruction and a month later, on February 5, solemnized her conversion at the Oratory. She followed Ladye's example and took St Anthony, the patron of lost things, as her name-saint and Antonia as her baptismal name. The next morning she attended her first mass.

The alterations to the White Cottage, meanwhile, were taking longer than they had expected. They did not move into the new house until August 4. For the first few days they happily shifted furniture around and hung curtains. Ladye began reading aloud to John from Marjorie Bowen's *God and the King*, an historical romance about William of Orange – and John's introduction to one of her favourite novelists. John planned a 'smoking room' for herself and they purchased a fine antique bureau for it.

Friends and relatives descended on them: Ladye's brother Arthur Hatch, the Visettis ('we are both longing for Wednesday when they depart – they are both *so* untidy,' Ladye told Cara)[1], and then the 'Bobbies'. In the diary Ladye's familiar recital of ailments began again, too. She complained of shingles and heart pains (which she called 'heart-attacks'), then took to her bed with acute lumbago and a nurse in attendance. The servants also proved troublesome. Mrs Sheridan the cook received her notice for appearing 'rather the worse for wear' and Ladye dismissed her personal maid Redding. 'Slaves', as Ladye called them, never quite lived up to their exacting standards.

John's conversion to Catholicism decided them to take their winter holiday in Rome. The object was not simply to show John the home of her faith but, if possible, to procure an audience with the Pope. They left London by train on November 17, accompanied by Ladye's new maid Sibelle, John's maid Linz, and in a cage a grey parrot called Cocky. They stopped off for a night in Pisa – Ladye longed to put the Leaning Tower straight, 'it *is so* aggravating!' she told Cara[2] – and arrived in the Eternal City on the 20th, booking into the fashionable Hotel de Russie. Their first day was spent sight-seeing, chiefly around

St Peter's where the cobbled square gave Ladye 'an attack of "Roman feet"'. Next morning the diary noted: 'Roman feet so painful had to send for Roman pedicure!' Ladye took an inordinate pride in her feet, which were slim and petite, and the slightest blemish on them caused her untold distress.

In keeping with the religious purpose of the trip, they were drawn less to the Rome of Antiquity than to the city of the Early Fathers. They visited all the great churches, prayed, lit candles, ordered masses and attended Benedictions. They bought religious medallions for the children at Malvern school. John found silver clasps for her prayer book in the Via Sistina and Ladye presented her with a gold pendant set in pearls which bore the inscription '*Antonia. Roma, Dec. 1912*'.

Their audience with the Pope was meanwhile being arranged. The great day arrived on December 10. Una takes up the story:

> The saintly peasant-Pope abhorred ceremony and his humility deprecated homage. John has told me of how the Cardinal [Gasquet] warned them to omit the customary three genuflexions and of how, when in her shyness and reverence she forgot and fell on her knees, the Cardinal clutched her by the scruff of the neck and hauled her to her feet, hissing 'Get up! What did I tell you!' In any case it was Ladye who was the success of that audience. Her Italian was quite tolerable, while John's had not yet come into existence. Ladye was self-possessed and said and did the right thing, putting the Pope (who was himself a desperately shy man) at his ease, while John hovered in the background tongue-tied. The result was that when the Cardinal presented two photographs for signature, Ladye's bore a lengthy inscription: 'Alla diletta figlia Veronica ... ' while John's received only an unadorned autograph.[3]

They arrived back in England to find that Chapman and Hall had published John's fourth book of poetry, *Songs Of Three Counties And Other Poems*. The new collection celebrated John's love of nature. Half the poems dealt with the countryside around Malvern that she knew so well (the three counties being Worcestershire, Herefordshire and Gloucestershire). As the title suggested, many of the offerings were songs and several had already been set to music by Bobby Clarke and Liza Lehmann.

In tone, *Songs of Three Counties* drew closely on the rural poetry of A. E. Housman. Housman's outlook and temperament matched John's. His verses were simple and economical and exuded that mixture of melancholy and nostalgia that John too felt so strongly. Ludlow represented Housman's land of lost content; Malvern represented John's, though it evoked wistfulness rather than exuberance. Watching the Ledbury train wind its way through the Wye valley, John felt like a child again for whom 'fairy tales come true'. She had known Malvern only as an adult, but for that very reason it could be vested with all her nostalgia for the untrammelled childhood she wished had been hers. Her vision as a writer would always be rooted in a deep English romanticism, in an anti–modernist attachment to the land. She harked back to a pre-industrial era where, as she saw it, modern complexities (by which she really meant the dislocation and disillusion of her own life) gave way to simpler certainties.

The most popular poem in the anthology would be 'The Blind Ploughman', which Bobby Clarke turned into a successful song. It told how the ploughman's loss of sight had actually intensified his love for the beauties of nature because it enabled him to see with his *soul*. The idea was central to John's outlook. She regarded her homosexuality as a handicap which had often made her unhappy. As a practising Catholic, she now believed that such suffering must all be part of God's scheme too. It existed for a purpose, to grant her deeper understanding, to make her better not worse.

Songs of Three Counties marked the peak of John's reputation as a poet. Though critics never quite accorded her the status of a serious poet, partly because of her connection with song-writing, the reviews for the new collection praised her skilled, economical technique. The *Daily Telegraph* considered her one of the few lyricists whose work was as enjoyable to read as to hear.[4] The *Lady* magazine, more fulsomely, likened her 'deft workmanship' to the 'chiselled setting of a precious stone'.[5]

In her memoir Una speaks of John's early years with Ladye as 'amongst the happiest of her life, for they were shared with a most delightful, sympathetic and versatile companion'.[6] Since John had never known the emotional support of a mother, Ladye admirably met her need for an intimate who fulfilled the dual role of guardian angel and loving counsellor. At times they seemed more like teacher and pupil or parent and child than lovers.

But Ladye was not always the dominant partner. Where she proved so 'versatile' was in combining sophistication with a strong streak of childishness, thus enabling John to indulge her protective instincts and more masterful inclinations. In public Ladye projected a stately, undemonstrative exterior. In unfamiliar or uncongenial company she had a habit of withdrawing into herself in such a way that people sometimes thought she was trying to be superior. She invariably wore heavy stays, even in hot weather, and consequently tended to sit somewhat stiffly in chairs and give the appearance of gliding rather than walking. She made a point of doing everything at an unhurried pace and resolutely refused to rush even if late for a train.

In private, however, this regal façade was replaced by a girlish gaiety. She loved being petted and spoiled. She showed herself lazy, hopelessly impractical, accident-prone (she was always straining her wrists or ankles) and a prey to ailments. She thus projected a helplessness, studied or not, which aroused John's urge to play the 'man' – and undoubtedly attracted her sexually. As their love affair lapsed into a more regular domestic routine, to John fell the tasks of fetching and carrying, of attending to the animals, of arranging their travel plans, of supervising Ladye's investments – everything, in fact, expected of a dutiful husband.

Ladye revelled in private jokes and secret pet names. It was Ladye who first changed Marguerite to John, probably after great-grandfather John Hall, who so resembled John in looks and whose portrait Ladye adored. When all their friends became accustomed to John or Johnnie, Ladye privately began calling her Jonathan, in reference to the Biblical friends Saul and Jonathan who were 'lovely and pleasant in their lives, and in their death they were not divided'.[7]

But even inanimate objects acquired names and personalities. Ladye called her two hot-water bottles (she never slept without them, even in summer) 'Jones' and 'Charlie'. A favourite pendant was always known as 'The Pink Plump of Pekin'. She owned a parasol with an ivory handle in the form of a monkey's head: this was 'Bimi', after Kipling's fictional monkey. She also introduced John to a private baby-language. Thus 'poon' and 'sporkish' were words applied to people whom they considered, respectively, decent or tiresome. 'Sneevish', suggesting a cross between 'peevish' and 'snivelling', referred to pettiness in others. 'Pogging' meant making eyes at people: 'poggers' were very infra dig.

Ladye liked her creature comforts. She once remarked, not wholly in jest, that the very best was only just good enough for her. Her tastes were extravagant, exotic, and highly particular. She spent days being fitted for new clothes for special occasions, such as Ascot (which she never missed) or a 'Court' at Buckingham Palace (she attended one in 1912 accompanied by John and Cara). At the flat in Cadogan Square she insisted on fresh flowers daily and an orange motif on all the furnishings, arranged to her own design, as a reminder of Spain. She collected Chinese jade and prepared her own scent (a mixture of verbena and white lilac). She loved food and when abroad devoured lobster and crab in the more bohemian sort of restaurant with an abandon that appalled John, who automatically suspected foreign standards of hygiene. She kept a small box in her bedroom (John nicknamed it 'The Larder') full of sweets, nuts and biscuits.

By contrast, John's tastes were somewhat austere and spartan. She still wore stays and light feminine shoes at this date, but the rest of her clothes were plain and severe – tailor-made jackets in black or grey, stiff collars, and long heavy skirts. She hated the contemporary fashion for light, flowing dresses modelled after the ancient Grecian style. Whereas Ladye loved long, elegant ear-rings, John preferred simple diamond studs after her father's example. Ladye gave her a string of pearls, but she hid them by wearing them under her blouse.

Ladye did not try to discourage John's masculine image. She drew the line at John cutting her hair short – John once suggested it and she reacted with horror – but for the rest she rather liked John's husbandly style. 'I find Jonathan delightful to be with,' she once wrote to Cara. 'Of course, her temper is hotter than Tabasco and she is very impulsive – but what does that matter? She is true grit all through & a real poon in her outlook on life – and is so kind and darling to me. I admire & respect her downright honesty and she is awfully clever too.'[8] Two of John's traits were less appealing to Ladye: her swearing and her smoking. Ladye tried her best to persuade John to give up both habits, but for once her advice fell on deaf ears.

Through Ladye, John made her first real acquaintance with other homosexual women. Not that London boasted a clearly defined lesbian coterie, but Ladye's wide network of social connections had brought her into discreet contact with like-minded women. One of these was Winnaretta Singer, the widow of Prince Edmond de Polignac and a wealthy patron of the arts (she was the daughter of Isaac Merrit Singer, the American sewing-machine tycoon). She had a house in the King's Road, Chelsea, and Ladye first mentions her in the diary at about the time she and John were moving into 59 Cadogan Square. The three women developed a mutual interest in ancient Greek culture, notably the works of Sappho.

John also met at this time the composer and suffragette, Ethel Smythe, whose former lovers included Winnaretta herself and Emmeline Pankhurst. It seems that, for a period at least, Ethel's influence turned John and Ladye into supporters of the Votes-For-Women campaign – though, sadly, there is no record of how active they were. The movement did attract lesbians and some elements in it were stridently hostile to men, but it is more likely that John and Ladye felt a sympathy for women's rights in general. Una tells us that both admired George Sand as a woman before her time, both advocated Divorce Law reform (unusual for Catholics), and both took a philanthropic interest in prostitution as it affected women. This last proved a popular cause with contemporary feminists and Ladye's diary reveals that in the summer of 1912 she and John attended a special Sunday performance of Shaw's play *Mrs Warren's Profession* in the company of numerous suffragettes.[9]

Yet John's feminism was at best ambiguous, her sympathies complicated by her curiously divided nature. She saw herself increasingly as a man trapped in a woman's body. Accordingly, she tended to identify primarily with men, an outlook reinforced by her resentment of her mother and by a desire for acceptance in 'normal' society. She invariably chose men as her doctors and lawyers – two breeds to whom she would have frequent recourse throughout her life – though she could be scathing about their competence. When in later years she came to make public pronouncements on the subject of women, her views proved unhesitatingly traditionalist and patriarchal: a few women would always excel, she asserted, but most remained happier as wives and mothers.

Something of this dichotomy in John's attitude is apparent in a remarkable letter she wrote (anonymously) to the *Pall Mall Gazette* on March 4, 1912. It appeared in the next day's edition of the paper. On February 29 the miners had embarked on an all-out strike that rapidly threatened to close down industry. At the same time the suffragette campaign was reaching a peak with widespread acts of civil disobedience. A suffragette demonstration planned for March 4 in Parliament Square was banned by the police, so hundreds of women went on the rampage through London smashing windows. Many big stores in Knightsbridge and Kensington had their panes broken and ninety-six arrests were made. *The Times* inveighed against 'turbulence and hysteria'. John instantly put pen to paper:

> Sir – Have the Suffragettes no spark of patriotism left, that they can spread revolt and hamper the Government in this moment of grave national danger? According to Mrs Pankhurst, they are resorting to the methods of the miners! Since when have English ladies regulated their conduct by that of the working classes? But, indeed, up to the present, the miners have set an example of orderly behaviour which the Suffragettes might do well to follow!
>
> I was formerly a sympathiser with the cause of female suffrage, as also were many women who, like myself, are unrepresented, although taxpayers. Women who are capable of setting a revolutionary example at such a time as this could only bring disgrace and destruction on any Constitution in which they played an active part.
>
> Yours, etc.
> A FORMER SUFFRAGIST[10]

The letter speaks for itself. John could be deeply moved by social injustice, but she instinctively sided with the Establishment and held to the hierarchical view of society to which her class subscribed. The novelist Frank Danby (author of *Pigs in Clover*) once privately proposed a scheme whereby employers and servants could be brought together in a sort of revival of the feudal system. Danby argued that domestic peace would never prevail until servants felt they were able to come to their masters or mistresses for advice in the knowledge that the real interests of both sides were as one. John proved sufficiently intrigued by the idea to take it seriously, much to Ladye's amusement. Shortly afterwards *Punch* got wind of the scheme and lampooned it in a cartoon in which a butler earnestly regales his mistress with his personal problems. Danby quickly dropped the subject, as did John. But the incident aptly reflected her unsophisticated, reactionary political instincts – not to say a humourless streak in her too.

On June 30, 1913, John dined with Bobby and Dolly at Swan Walk. Also present was Phoebe Hoare, the wife of Oliver Hoare, a banking colleague of Austin Harris. According to Ladye's diary, John had lunched with the Hoares in mid-May. This is the first time they are mentioned. If John had been in touch with Phoebe in the interim, Ladye did not report it. From June 30, however, the diary is preoccupied with John's burgeoning interest in Phoebe. Dolly played the go-between in this strange affair and Swan Walk became the trysting-place. The fact that Ladye recorded so many of John's visits to Phoebe suggests that she knew at an early stage what was going on. She always insisted on frankness in relationships, so perhaps John made no attempt to conceal her intentions. In her memoir of John, Una would describe this episode as 'a trivial, passing lapse' which Ladye dismissed with 'a tolerant smile'.[11] This was not how it appeared at the time.

The day after seeing Phoebe at Dolly's, John took her to the theatre. The day following they again saw each other at Swan Walk. A break of some three weeks intervened (according to the diary at any rate) until their next meeting on July 16. A recurrence of Ladye's 'heart-attacks' signalled her distress. For the next two weeks John was meeting Phoebe almost every other day. She could not ignore Ladye's misery, however. On July 19 Ladye helped her revise a new poem. That evening Winnaretta Singer dined at Cadogan Square and read to them from a book about Sappho. These literary reminders of lesbian love gave John 'remords de conscience', as Ladye put it, and she could not sleep that night. But it did not stop her seeing Phoebe again.

On July 28 John and Ladye went down to the White Cottage for the summer. In early August Ladye's great friend Adela Maddison, a composer and former pupil of Fauré's, came to stay. Adela lived in France and must have been somewhat eccentric to judge by a rhyme coined by Ladye: 'Adela Maddison, Mad as a Hattison'. After a week of music-making, singing songs to Ladye's guitar under the walnut tree in the garden, the guest left on August 12, John's thirty-second birthday. The diary mentions no present from Ladye – an unusual omission – cataloguing instead a fresh list of ailments.

On August 20 Austin Harris, who had arrived without Cara for a short spell at the cottage, took photographs of John and Ladye on the verandah. In spite of the heat, both women wore their smartest outfits (Ladye sported her solar topee from India), perhaps because the occasion was intended to commemorate the imminent fifth anniversary, on the 22nd, of their first meeting. They both smiled sweetly for the camera, but John felt out of sorts: 'J. upset me by being furiously angry with Otero,' noted the diary. On the 22nd itself, however, Ladye presented John with a diamond safety-pin and John proved 'very loving'.

Three days later, in an unprecedented move, John left Ladye in Malvern and joined Phoebe and Dolly for a week's holiday in Southbourne, near Poole in Dorset. The visit had obviously been planned in advance and with Ladye's knowledge. No record survives of what transpired in Southbourne, but Ladye had no illusions that John was conducting a full-blown affair with Phoebe. She felt depressed and breathless while John was away, and on her return they talked and argued 'far into the night'.[12]

It rained throughout September and John felt cooped up and 'weather-bound' in Malvern. Otero sickened and had to be destroyed, leaving Ladye terribly upset. John was not in consoling mood. She remained 'fighty', as the diary put it, and most days went off riding on her own. Ladye retreated to bed with 'shingles', then announced she would go and stay with Cara, who had written to say she was expecting a baby in May. In retaliation, John went off to Brighton for four days, ostensibly to see Dolly.

Back in London in the autumn John resumed seeing Phoebe, leaving the flat first thing in the morning and only returning late at night. The strain began to tell, however. Ladye's heart gave further trouble and she was plagued with insomnia. John looked thin and ill. She understood only too well the emotional blackmail behind Ladye's persistent hypochondria and yet she felt guilt-stricken at the intolerable situation she had created. They quarrelled frequently, disagreeing for the first time ever about their annual spring holiday (Ladye wanted to go to Spain, John insisted on San Remo).

At Christmas they joined the Harrises at Aspenden. On Boxing

Day the whole family attended the local meet at Brent Pelham, John, Austin and Honey riding with the hunt. Ladye's last diary entry for 1912 (when they were in Rome) had read: '1912 was a very happy year.' Her tune had changed now. 'Felt very pleased that this *horrid* year was finished!' she wrote on December 31, 1913.

1914 saw a marginal improvement. In the second week of February, John and Ladye set off on their continental holiday, having finally agreed on Tamaris, near Toulon in the south of France. They were accompanied by two new personal maids, (Julia) Meyer and (Gertrude) Garry. 'A lovely place,' proclaimed the diary when they arrived, but it rained for a month.

Florence, however, cheered them up. Ladye knew Florence from her youth, but it was John's first visit to the city associated with her beloved Robert and Elizabeth Browning. 'It leaves Rome far behind,' she wrote to Cara. 'It has remained in the middle ages (sic), one feels a strange and yet familiar aura of the 15 & 16 centuries, the moment one sets foot in its streets ... As I *know* that I lived in the 15th century myself it appeals to me strongly.'[13]

Back in England in May John was soon visiting Phoebe again. Ladye had other worries on her mind, for on May 8 Cara's baby Karen was born at No. 10, Catherine Street, where the Harrises had moved the previous year. John was conspicuous by her absence. She had once expressed a wish to be the godfather if the baby was a boy,[14] but on the day she was taking tea with Phoebe and treating her to a theatre in the evening. In July, however, it seems that Oliver Hoare became suspicious of his wife's involvement with John and thereafter many of the lovers' meetings took place in his presence. But they managed to escape for a day together at Southbourne on July 17 (with Dolly acting as 'chaperone') and in succeeding days to slip off to restaurants and theatres on their own (seeing Chaliapin perform at the last night of the Russian Opera on the 25th).

On July 28 Ladye wrote in the diary: 'War threatening with Germany.' It was the first indication she had given of the worsening international situation provoked by the assassination of the Archduke Franz Ferdinand in Sarajevo at the end of June. On August 1 she reported that Germany had declared war on France and invaded Luxembourg: 'City news very depressing,' she added, voicing the concern felt by her class for their investments.

That weekend she and John joined the Harrises at a large house, Horsey Hall, they were renting in Norfolk. Ladye wrote beforehand to Cara about sleeping arrangements at the Hall. Ladye stated that she did not mind sharing a two-bedded room with John (both at the White Cottage and Cadogan Square they had separate bedrooms) so long as they had a dressing-room where John could change in privacy. 'We have never all these years shared one room *without* a dressing room . . . Perhaps you'll find you can put [John] up in a small bedroom not next mine? She says she'd far rather do that if you haven't got a dressing room for her.'[15] It is possible that these instructions reflected the continuing friction between Ladye and John, but John was certainly a stickler for what one might call 'husband's rights' in the home, chief of these being her own study and dressing-room. It seems extraordinary, nevertheless, that she should have insisted on them in somebody else's house.

While they were at Horsey they heard the news that Germany had declared war on Russia. 'Everyone – especially Johnny – depressed – Heard that the Banks were refusing to pay out gold,' Ladye reported.[16] The inevitable happened on August 3. While everyone at the Hall was bathing in the swimming pool, Germany invaded Belgium. The next day England was at war. John and Ladye arrived back in London on August 6 to find the streets 'full of Territorials leading droves of horses' and Harrods empty of sugar – 'owing to the enormous orders selfish people gave ten days ago,' Ladye com-plained.[17] The following day both women, along with many other people, drew out gold from their bank, fearing the worst in the coming conflict.

Yet the outbreak of war did not stop them from escaping to Malvern on August 9 for their usual summer sojourn at the White Cottage. The previous day John had taken tea with Phoebe. They did not know it, but this would be the last time they would see each other for several years, for the war was about to separate them as it separated many others. In September, when it became clear that the conflict would not be short-lived, John and Ladye decided to stay in Malvern and let the flat in Cadogan Square. By this date Phoebe had left London with her husband in any case. The affair had run its course.

What prompted this amorous adventure that caused John so much heart-ache? We have only Ladye's side of the story, and a scanty version at that. The likeliest answer is that John had simply begun to tire of Ladye – of her self-indulgence, of her hypochondria, of her dependence on her – and sought fresh sexual conquest with a younger woman. From Ladye's diary we get a suggestion, in early 1913, that her laziness had begun to irritate John. 'John told me she expected me to housekeep in future and she seemed awfully angry about nothing which upset me.'[18] Then again, in *Songs of Three Counties*, a mood of regret, even desperation, had crept into some of the poems, reflecting a new unease on John's part. In one of them, 'Willow Wand', the poet yearns for the perfect lover, 'the ladye of my heart' (note the allusive archaic spelling of 'lady'), with whom she will dwell for ever: 'We will quarrel never – never, / Oh! never – never!' This was a far cry from the joyful love lyrics of *Poems of the Past and Present*.

John was too aware of the enormous debt, emotional as well as intellectual, that she owed Ladye to commit an infidelity without incurring the severest reproaches from her conscience. She felt frustrated and oppressed by their relationship, but she could never have completely broken the ties of loyalty that bound her to Ladye. At the same time, had not the war taken Phoebe from her, it is equally possible that their affair would have lingered on without any real resolution. Such a tortuous emotional tangle was to recur in John's life.

The tranquil Malvern neighbourhood made a natural centre for war wounded. The Red Cross set up three hospitals in the area and the Order of St John two. Women flocked to join the two local Voluntary Aid Detachments (VADs). Three battalions of soldiers were also stationed in the district, many of them camped on the golf links in Malvern Wells.

In September 1914 fresh newcomers arrived: Belgian refugees. They were given an emotional welcome and dispersed among the population. Malvern's first allocation consisted of thirty Ursuline nuns and a party of mothers and children, who were shortly joined by their menfolk. The Belgians proved a troublesome lot. Fights broke out between the Flemish speakers and the French Walloons, and by the war's end popular sympathy for them had greatly waned in the locality.[19]

In the days following the declaration of hostilities, John and Ladye busily attended Red Cross lectures and learned first-aid. They offered to put two rooms in the White Cottage at the disposal of wounded soldiers – and, unlike many others, were prepared to take German casualties if necessary. They helped ferry wounded Tommies between hospitals in their motor car and transported library books to and from the casualty wards.

Had John been a man, she would have enlisted without hesitation. Her natural instinct was to take an active role in the war effort. Had she been on her own, she might have enrolled in one of the all-women ambulance units which later patrolled the French and Belgian fronts. As it was, she felt she could not leave Ladye – an added source of frustration for her.

She therefore did the next best thing to joining up: she encouraged others to do so. John wrote her own recruitment leaflets and she and Ladye drove round the district distributing them to outlying farms. Ladye reported to Cara: 'I infused a wholesome dread of invasion by Germans into some of the lazy cocksure yokels who would keep on repeating – One Englishman can beat a dozen Germans, etc etc! ... We've had shamefully few recruits in answer to the "Kitchener" call in this part of the country – tho' they all flock to see the Worcester Cricket Match!'[20]

At a private meeting in nearby Castlemorton, John made an impromptu speech urging the audience (all women) to persuade their menfolk to enlist – 'It simply poured out with no effort & I was quite taken aback at her eloquence!' Ladye told Cara.[21] They put up large recruitment posters on the walls of the White Cottage. When some-body defaced these, John wrote an indignant letter to the local press denouncing the perpetrators for insulting not only King and Country but their own manhood. 'What manner of men have we in these parts?' she fumed. 'Their women should be ashamed of them!' Perhaps not surprisingly, the local paper assumed its irate correspondent was a man and printed her name as 'Mr M. Radcliffe Hall'.[22] Pacifists received short shrift. A schoolmaster who expressed himself opposed to his son enlisting was damned as 'odious' in the diary. The war did not improve John's humourlessness.

Neither woman had near relatives at the front, so their experience of the conflict remained essentially vicarious. Ladye worried whether Adela Maddison would get safely out of France (she did in mid-August). They ordered masses to be said at St Wulfstan's for the soldier brother of John's maid, Garry. Bobby Clarke attracted their concern when he joined the Volunteers in September. Dolly wrote to say they were penniless and would have to let Swan Walk while she undertook war work. John assured her that she would continue her annuity and the Clarkes' two dogs, Toto and Clayton, were des-patched to the White Cottage for the duration (Ladye called them the 'animal refugees').

On September 19 John and Ladye had a farewell lunch in London with Bobby in his 'new khaki'. They stayed with Cara at Catherine Street and packed up the flat at Cadogan Square in preparation for the arrival of tenants. With its searchlights and darkened streets, the city looked 'sad and unusual', Ladye noted.[23] They returned to Malvern on September 22 in the 22-horse power limousine they had hired since 1912, driven by their usual chauffeur, Serpell. At Burford crossroads the car was struck broadside on by another vehicle and careered into a low wall. The injuries to John, Garry and the chauffeur were slight (Serpell wept hysterically until John ordered him to get a hold of himself), but Ladye sustained cuts to the head, broken ribs and, more seriously, damage to her lower spine.

John quickly took charge and had Ladye carried into a nearby house owned by a Mrs Pigott, where she was attended to by a Dr Cheatle. John then faced the driver of the other vehicle, Mrs Lakin, and roundly accused her of trying to kill them: 'I advise you never to drive a motor car again, because you neither sounded your horn nor put on your brakes!' Mrs Lakin protested she was travelling 'dead slow' but she admitted that Serpell had had right of way.[24] In the subsequent court proceedings between the insurance companies, it became clear that Mrs Lakin had put her foot on the accelerator in mistake for the brake. John and Ladye felt she had lied in the witness-box and, after winning the case, Ladye informed Cara, in a tone of vindication, that Mrs Lakin's own counsel had confided to them that 'she was a terribly unpleasant client'.[25]

Ladye remained at Mrs Pigott's for eleven days, too ill to be moved. This at least was the opinion of Dr Cheatle who suspected a fracture to the base of her spine. However, Frank Romer, the Harrises' doctor, announced it safe to take the patient to Malvern. In the light of subsequent events, John was to question Romer's diagnosis and came to believe that Ladye had been moved too quickly, thus hastening the onset of her final illness.

The Burford crash turned Ladye into a virtual invalid. John took over the housekeeping and sat for hours rubbing Ladye's neck or playing soothing tunes to her on the mandolin. One suspects that Ladye quietly relished such undivided attention, but it tested John's patience to the limit. When in December Ladye received a pessimistic report from her stockbroker and agonized over her dividends, John exploded angrily, railing at her preoccupation with trivialities in a time of war. But her anger was directed as much at herself. She realized acutely the cosiness of her existence in Malvern while others were actively serving their country. Yet how could she leave Ladye now? It is hard to resist the conclusion that much of this angst was self-dramatization on John's part, for even in Malvern she could have occupied herself more usefully than she did.

John had not neglected her writing. After the success of *Songs of Three Counties*, she planned to experiment with blank verse and to give her next collection of poetry a unified theme. She had been corresponding with Professor Quiller-Couch of Cambridge, who complimented her on some of her unrhymed verses. 'With me [he] thinks that there is a great future for this style in English lyrical poetry,' she wrote importantly to the writer Douglas Sladen.[26] Sladen replied magnanimously that she was following in the footsteps of Shelley and Matthew Arnold.[27]

Chapman and Hall published the new anthology in the spring of 1915 under the title *The Forgotten Island*. John's idea was that the poems represented someone's recollection of a previous incarnation on a mythical island like Lesbos and, taken as a whole, they told the story of a love affair which runs from the heights of passion to the dull yearning for new pastures. Though the way in which John had planned the collection suggests she was engaged in a literary exercise, it is tempting to discern references to her frustration with Ladye and the thwarted affair with Phoebe. A recurring image, for example, is of a ship taking the tide and sailing purposefully towards new shores. The poet longs to go with it.

The Forgotten Island proved to be John's last published volume of poetry. Though some reviews were admiring, she was disappointed that it did not attract more widespread notice. The war was largely to blame. The poems were out of step with the patriotic spirit that prevailed in 1915.

John's poetry represented her passport to prose. Without either a formal literary education or the drive of economic pressure, she nevertheless felt compelled to write. Poetry was not her forte – her talents would lie with narrative description and psychological detail – but it came naturally out of her childhood precocity as a lyricist and musician. The fact that she was well past thirty before realizing her false start suggests how little she regarded herself as a professional. Douglas Sladen observed of her in 1915: 'To see her, even to speak with her, one would think that she thought more of her hunting-box and her horses than of abstractions like poetry ... There is no one I know who writes more from inspiration.'[28] This was true. As a novelist John would develop a relentless working routine, but as a poet she wrote largely as the mood took her.

John later claimed that Ladye was the all-important influence upon her development as a writer.[29] True, Ladye encouraged her efforts and widened her literary horizons, providing useful social connections along the way. Yet Ladye's temperament was altogether too easy-going to supply the kind of stimulus John needed and some of John's frustration with her in their later years may have stemmed from a subconscious awareness that Ladye's presence actually held back her creative growth.

John had already tried her hand at some short stories. These are mentioned by name in Ladye's diary from the summer of 1914 onwards. None of the stories was ever published and they were destroyed by Una after John's death. But in May 1915 Ladye had hit on the idea of sending a batch of John's best short stories to an acquaintance of hers, the publisher William Heinemann, who had a reputation for spotting new talent.

Heinemann met them for lunch on June 1 and praised John's stories extravagantly. But, far from offering to publish her, Heinemann proposed she should abandon short stories and write him a novel instead. John was appalled at the prospect. Una recalled John telling her in later years:

> She protested that she had not the faintest idea even of how to set about writing a novel, had never thought of undertaking a work of any length and felt quite certain that she would never be able to do it, would, as she put it, 'never stay the course'. 'Oh yes, you will', replied Mr. Heinemann. 'You don't know it yourself yet, but I know it. You can and you will and you will bring it to me.'[30]

Una's account is inaccurate on one point. Despite her protests to Heinemann, John had already toyed with the idea of a novel. In her diary entry for March 26, 1915, Ladye noted that John worked almost all day on a book she called *Michael West*. From a later source, John's notes to Mrs Leonard's spiritualist séances, there is mention of a novel which John began while living with Ladye but never finished. The early part of this book dealt with an unhappy childhood. If *Michael West* was this book, then we may reasonably conclude that John tried to write an autobiographical novel at about this time. The attempt apparently failed and she abandoned it.

Heinemann's offer to John reflected a shrewd appraisal of her real talents, but she was not yet ready to accept the challenge.

Part Three

UNA

1915–1922

Chapter Six

On Sunday, August 1, 1915, John and Ladye attended a tea party in Cambridge Square hosted by Ladye's sister, Emmie, now a widow for the second time after the recent death of her husband Lord Clarendon. Emmie had also invited, among others, her cousin Mrs Una Troubridge. Una never much cared for Emmie – 'very countessy' was her verdict – but she admired Ladye and as a young woman had dined on a number of occasions at Ralston Street with her mother. She had met John only once before, in June 1912, at a gathering in Cheyne Walk. Afterwards Ladye had offered her a lift home. The meeting had left no impression and Una did not keep in touch. On this occasion, however, her reaction proved very different. Writing of the event thirty years later, she could still recall in perfect detail John's impact upon her:

> She was then thirty-four years of age and very good indeed to look upon. At that time, short hair in a woman was almost unknown and she had not yet cut hers. Ladye would have been horrified at the mere suggestion! It was silver-blonde, and she ruthlessly disposed of its great length and abundance (it reached nearly to her knees and its growth defied frequent pruning) by wearing it in tight plaits closely twisted round her small and admirably shaped head. Her complexion was clear and pale, her eyebrows and very long lashes nearly as golden as her hair and her eyes a clear grey blue, beautifully set and with a curiously fierce, noble expression that reminded me of certain caged eagles at the Zoological Gardens! Her mouth was sensitive and not small. It could look very determined; indeed in those days it sometimes looked hard, but was liable to break into the most infectious, engaging and rather raffish smile that would spread to her eyes and banish the caged eagle. Her face and the line of the jaw were an unusually pure oval ... it was not the countenance of a young woman but of a very handsome young man. Like her father she was only of medium height but so well proportioned that she looked taller than she was and the very simple tailor-made clothes which she wore, even in those days, fostered the illusion. Her hands, and here again, they were not feminine hands, were quite beautiful and so were her feet. Altogether her appearance was calculated to arouse interest. It immediately aroused mine and for reasons much less obvious that interest was returned. Our friendship, which was to last through life and after it, dated from that meeting.[1]

Una was not her real name. She was christened Margot Elena Gertrude Taylor. But in a family much given to pet-names, 'Una' had somehow attached itself to her and stuck. Her upbringing was very different from John's. Indeed, in some ways it was the sort of childhood that John would have chosen for herself.

Una's father Harry was a tall man (six feet two in his socks) and for as long as she could remember his hair was completely white. He was the son of Sir Henry Taylor, a senior civil servant at the Colonial Office but better known as the author of several popular historical melodramas on the Victorian stage (a piece called *Philip Van Artefelde* made his name). As a young man Harry studied music and harboured ambitions to become a concert pianist. Sir Henry, however, like many artistic fathers, looked to a less precarious career for his son and procured him a commission in the army. Though Harry rose to the rank of captain, military life did not suit him. So, shortly after marrying Una's mother, Minna, a beautiful Irish woman of genteel but penniless origins, he moved (by dint of Sir Henry's string-pulling) to a post as Queen's Messenger in the Consular Service. The job demanded a passing knowledge of the more important European languages and little else, but the pay was poor and Harry spent long stretches abroad delivering diplomatic despatches to places as far afield as Moscow and Istanbul.

Una was born on March 8, 1887, almost five years after her elder sister Viola. Despite constant financial pressures, they were a happy, close-knit family. The two girls grew up in a cultured and cosmopolitan atmosphere. From the age of seven, Una had a Belgian governess and soon acquired fluency in French. In the early years the family resided in Rottingdean, near Brighton, and the Taylors could count among their friends several famous artists and writers who had bought houses there, notably Sir Edward Burne-Jones, Sir Edward Poynter, and Rudyard Kipling (whose daughter Josephine was Una's playmate). At an early age Una displayed a natural talent for drawing. Harry Taylor arranged for her to have art lessons at the Victoria and Albert Museum, where she attended classes (she was then aged seven) in sun-bonnet and frilly drawers. She quickly showed an exceptional aptitude and acquired a reputation as a child prodigy.

With a dramatist grandfather in the family, theatre-going was encouraged. By the time Una was eleven, the Taylors had moved to London (to Montpelier Square) and she began attending plays regularly, a pleasure she never lost. Sir Henry knew the actor-manager

Sir Herbert Beerbohm Tree and Una became a privileged visitor behind the scenes at Her Majesty's Theatre (she estimated she saw Tree act Malvolio twenty-six times). All her earliest heroes were actors and romantic historical characters. The two came together in Sarah Bernhardt's role as Napoleon Bonaparte, Una's 'number one historical god'. For months after the performance Una avidly sought out photographs of Bernhardt, sketched her, and tried to imitate her, 'to pose,' she recalled, 'with a languid hand upon the hip, and to long, how utterly in vain, for dark, mysterious narrow eyes, a high-bridged nose, a questing, haunted expression and an interesting past.'[2]

She was a bright, extrovert child and 'acting a part' became almost second nature to her. She possessed a strong streak of exhibitionism. She later admitted she enjoyed being ill as a child because it meant the whole household rallied round her: 'these interludes I distinctly recollect as rather bright spots in the monotonous weave of daily existence.'[3] In their play-room the two sisters had a trapeze on which they devised impromptu 'performances' for indulgent parents and friends. In later life Una marvelled at the patience of the adults who bore with her interminable showing-off. She was a child, she confessed, with 'a prodigious memory, supreme self-confidence and a total absence of all sense of humour'.[4]

Clothes and dressing up always appealed to her, particularly boyish or androgynous styles. She could recall her 'utter bliss' as a child of eight when, on a holiday near Boulogne with Lord William Cecil and his four sons, she was allowed to wear one of the boys' suits and become the 'fifth brother'.[5] At the age of sixteen she shocked her parents by appearing one day in the most outré fashion: 'My abundant hair was collected into a stiff pompadour, my neck confined in the highest of stiff collars attached to a flannel shirt with cuffs and cuff-links. I sported a very narrow ribbon bow-tie pushed well up to the top of the collar, a severe coat and skirt, and specially made patent leather oxford shoes with low heels.' There followed a Stuart phase (lace collars and cuffs and large flat hats with ostrich plumes), an interlude in the eighteenth century, and a French Revolutionary get-up: 'A gold lorgnette completed the outfit, and an occasional interpolation of the adverb "vastly" gave realism to the illusion that I had been born 150 years earlier, of varying and uncertain sex but naturally of high degree, and had with other fortunate ones of my rank managed to escape the guillotine.'[6]

Una was able to satisfy her theatrical tastes in clothes because by sixteen she had achieved a certain economic independence through her artistic talents. At the remarkably early age of thirteen she had won a scholarship to the Royal College of Art, where she started modelling in clay, a medium in which she soon showed such ability that, while still a student, she rented a small studio of her own and began exhibiting her figurines. Before long she began to receive commissions. The prima ballerina Adeline Genée posed for her in 1907 and the finished statuette was exhibited at the Royal Academy the same year.

In her teens Una flirted with Buddhism and Shintoism. Then, at the age of twenty, she visited Florence and stayed for many months with some Italian cousins, the Tealdis. Living in Italy gave her her first introduction to Catholicism and she sensed that those around her frowned on her lack of faith: 'it needs strength of mind to live comfortably among people who honestly believe that you will be damned,' she later remarked.[7] Whether this pressure was really irresistible or whether she sought to shock her Anglican relatives, with characteristic impulsiveness Una converted to Catholicism before leaving Italy.

Una's trip to Italy in 1907 was prompted by Harry Taylor's death. The family had no inkling that Harry had tuberculosis until he suffered a violent haemorrhage one August night in 1906. Edward VII (Harry was now a King's Messenger) sent him to a private sanatorium in Midhurst. From there, apparently recovered, he went to convalesce in the milder climate of Pau in the foothills of the Pyrenees. However, his condition suddenly worsened and he died at Pau, attended by the family, on March 5, 1907 – three days before Una's twentieth birthday. He was only fifty-two, the same age as Rat when *he* died.

Her father's death not only left the Taylors in straitened circumstances (they had had to accept 'loans' from friends to pay their expenses at Pau) but removed one of Una's closest friends and allies. She was devoted to Harry and he adored her. Harry was a gentle, unassuming man with a propensity for private family humour of the Victorian nonsense variety. He gave pet-names to cherished household objects, calling his foot-bath 'Moab' and his hot-water bottle 'Sammy'. He also nicknamed his acquaintance after the animals in a book of comic verse by E. T. Reed entitled *Tails With A Twist* (the children dubbed him 'The Rabbit' after one of these characters). As a small child Una addressed her father as 'Petit', which became 'Petchiot', in ironic allusion to his tallness, but as an adolescent she always knew him as 'Harry' and regarded him more as a brother than a parent. He was a companionable man but not very clubable. He rarely accompanied his wife Minna socially, preferring to be on his own, with a close friend or two, or just with his family. 'He avoided society with a passive determination,' was how Una put it later.[8]

Shortly after her father's death Una married. Ernest Troubridge came of a long line of distinguished military men. The family motto was 'Ne Cede Arduis' – 'Yield To No Obstacle'. Ernest was educated at Wellington, a school with a long services tradition, and entered the navy in 1875 at the age of thirteen. By 1901, when Una was still only fourteen, he was a captain and a widower with three small children.[9] He was big, bluff and handsome – Una was told he was 'the handsomest man in the Navy' – with a reputation for vigour and bravery.

In March 1907 Troubridge was appointed Flag-Captain (that is, chief of staff) to Sir Charles Drury, Commander-in-Chief of the Mediterranean. He was due to leave for his station on Malta towards the end of the month. For some time he had been paying court to Una but Harry Taylor's illness removed her to France. There seemed no prospect that Troubridge would see Una again before he left England. Then, on March 5, Harry died and a few days later the family returned to London unexpectedly. Troubridge did not waste his chance. On March 18 he proposed to Una and was accepted. In later years Una would often wonder how different her life might have been had she not returned home before the captain's departure.

Why did she decide to marry this much older man (he was forty-five)? Almost certainly because he could take the place of Harry, whose death left her distraught and bereft. Troubridge was a family friend, safe, solid, avuncular. Harry had approved of him, calling him 'your Captain'. He even had Harry's snow-white hair (aboard ship his men called him 'The Silver King'). There was, moreover, little to keep Una at home. Despite a flair for practicalities, she could be impulsive. Marriage into the navy held out a dash of glamour, the prospect of foreign travel, above all escape to pastures new. 'Having chosen for my husband a man old enough to be my father,' she later recalled, 'I set to work to look his age.' She began wearing sweeping black velvets and purple face-cloths. 'I know now and understand the intense amusement it aroused in those who beheld it.'[10]

In the summer of 1908, now engaged to Troubridge, Una made another prolonged visit to Italy, this time with her sister Viola. They stayed in Levanto, with Una's friend May Massola, an English woman married to Baron Cencio Massola. Una gloried in her freedom, spending whole days in the sun 'without hat or gloves and love it'. She swam twice a day, plunging 'just like a man' through the crashing breakers and relishing all the big seas. There was dancing every night 'with scores of young sailor men over from Spezia but I don't ever dance & the young men failed to interest me wch was sad as I might otherwise have had a better time.'[11] Young men rarely appealed to Una.

As Troubridge was still stationed on Malta, he and Una were married in Venice, at the British Consulate, on October 10 (her 'rank or profession' was given as 'sculptor' on the marriage certificate). Within weeks Troubridge was transferred to England as Commodore of the Naval Barracks at Chatham. The posting hardly appealed to an officer of his calibre, but he accepted with good grace and expected Una to conduct herself with a dignity appropriate to the leading naval wife on the station. She dutifully did so, surprising both herself and her friends by submerging her normally spirited personality in her husband's – further evidence of her chameleon-like ability to adapt herself to those around her.

In the autumn of 1909 Troubridge took up new duties at the Admiralty. London would be their home for the next three years. Una gradually picked up the threads of her former life, reaffirming old friendships, visiting theatres and exhibitions, returning to her painting and sculpture. She started daily singing lessons. This reassertion of her independence was not to Troubridge's liking. He had assumed her wifely role was permanent. The steady progress of his career – he was now private secretary to the First Sea Lord – and the birth of a daughter, Andrea, in November 1910 reinforced these assumptions.

Shortly after the birth of Andrea – whom they nicknamed 'The Cub' or 'Cubbie' in the Taylor tradition – Una started to suffer from recurring nausea and depression. Visits to doctors and specialists brought no lasting remedy. Then, towards the end of 1912, her GP recommended a specialist in nervous disorders, Dr Hugh Crighton-Miller. Psycho-analysis was just beginning to become fashionable and Crighton-Miller (who later founded the Tavistock Clinic) was in the process of building up a lucrative practice in Harley Street. Una made an appointment to see him in the New Year.

By this date Troubridge's career was on the move again. After a year as Winston Churchill's Chief of War Staff at the Admiralty, he was promoted to rear-admiral in command of the Mediterranean Cruiser Squadron. It meant that Una would be returning to Malta. The prospect did not appeal. On January 10 she paid her visit to Crighton-Miller, accompanied by her sister Viola. The specialist thought he could cure her but only if she stayed in England for treatment under his supervision. Troubridge reluctantly consented. On January 14 Crighton-Miller hypnotized Una for the first time. She had begun to keep a diary and she reported that she felt 'much better and more cheerful'. On the 18th Troubridge left London alone to take up his new duties.

Una wrote her husband a letter almost every day and he wrote back.

He showed himself loving and sympathetic, but he was not the sort of man to wonder deeply about the possible psychological causes of his wife's ill-health. He was all for her consulting this 'nerve chap' so long as it brought her swiftly back to his side ready to take up her social duties again. If Una, for her part, considered there was anything seriously wrong with her marriage, she did not express it at any conscious level. When in February she received two letters from Troubridge in one day, she declared herself '*so so* happy'.

Crighton-Miller quickly realized that Una was intelligent, spirited and highly suggestible. He began to teach her how to hypnotize herself as a means of relaxation, and she voraciously read the books on psychology and hypnotic techniques which he recommended. As always, Una gave herself wholly to her new preoccupation. On February 3, after several practice attempts at self-induction, she was able to record in her diary: 'suggested to myself that I should become completely unconscious and found myself fighting it just like chloroform. Still very lightheaded [sic] tho I have woken up.'

In March Troubridge became restless at his wife's prolonged absence. The pressure on Una manifested itself in a renewed bout of headaches and nerves. She eventually agreed to join him on a temporary basis. On the eve of departure, however, her resolution failed her. 'Tried to leave England tonight,' she wrote in the diary on March 18, 'no go – saw Miller.' After two months of treatment Crighton-Miller had become the new mentor and father-figure in her life. He calmed her, and Una finally set off for the Mediterranean on March 22, leaving Andrea and the nanny in the hands of her in-laws.

Troubridge's superior in Malta, the new 'C-in-C Mediterranean', was the dapper Sir Archibald Berkeley Milne (popularly known as 'Arky Barky'). Because Milne was a bachelor, Una ranked as the First Lady in the British naval community on the island. It meant a host of official duties. While 'Zip', as she affectionately called Troubridge, went off to play tennis or polo, Una was expected to call upon other wives. She had to host a relentless round of entertaining and make herself available at numerous functions. The company did not excite her. A typical entry in the diary – 'We dined Blunts – Oh Lord!' – reflected her boredom at these gatherings. Her seediness returned and she took to staying in bed in the mornings as a form of protest.

The couple returned to England on leave in early July. Una immediately visited Crighton-Miller, with whom she had corresponded regularly while away. He was now treating Viola as well. Viola's marriage to a journalist, Maurice Woods, had run into trouble and she suffered depression. Woods was an intellectual type and the specialist confided to Una that Viola's problems stemmed from a basic incompatibility with her husband. 'I wonder if two sisters so much alike in many ways as you two,' he wrote, 'ever married men so astonishingly different as your respective husbands.'[13]

He proved less candid about Una's own marital difficulties, which were clearly primarily of a sexual nature. By her own account, Una had experienced 'crushes' on other girls as a child,[14] but by the time she came to articulate such memories (in 1927) she was a self-confessed lesbian who had been living 'à deux' for over ten years. In 1913 she was still the wife of a distinguished rear-admiral and the mother of an adored child. If she doubted her heterosexuality at this stage, she did not mention it and all the signs are that she intended to persevere with her marriage. Crighton-Miller made out that he was treating her for 'nerves' and continued with her relaxation therapy. In the summer and autumn of 1913 she visited the specialist, at no small expense, on fifty-seven occasions. She became so proficient at certain hypnotic techniques that she was soon hypnotizing Viola and Troubridge's secretary.

That August she and Zip spent a week with the Cub at Hunstanton in Norfolk, where the Troubridges owned a house called 'The Castle'. Una resumed her sculpting and set to work on a major new project, a marble bust of the famous Russian dancer Vaslav Nijinsky, which attracted considerable notice when it appeared in a London gallery in the late summer of 1913. But Una's career as a sculptor had to take second place to the renewed demands of her marriage. Zip returned to Malta in September. Una followed him at the end of October after completing her second course of treatment with Dr Crighton-Miller. The wearying round of official engagements began again. She took up Italian lessons (her diary for 1914 is written almost entirely in Italian) and tried her hand at French translation work. The diary recorded many a 'bad day'. As soon as she could, she escaped to the Italian mainland, visiting first Florence and the Tealdis, then the Massolas in Levanto.

On August 2, while she was still in Italy, Una noted that Germany had declared war on France and Russia. She returned to Malta, Cub in tow, only to discover that her husband had put to sea. For several weeks she had no further news, then learned that Troubridge had been re-called to London. The couple were finally reunited in Naples on September 14. As they took Cubbie round the local aquarium, Zip explained to Una for the first time his version of the events which had so suddenly thrown him into disgrace.

Britain's entry into the war had been imminent for some time before the official declaration of hostilities on August 4, and Churchill, as a bellicose First Sea Lord, was anxious for early naval triumphs. He saw his chance in the presence in the Mediterranean of two German heavy cruisers, the *Goeben* and the *Breslau*. On August 2 Churchill ordered that the two battleships be shadowed. As commander of the Second Squadron, Troubridge was the officer to whom this task was entrusted. Unfortunately, unknown to the British, Turkey (who was expected to remain neutral) had opened secret negotiations with the Austrians and agreed to allow the *Goeben* and the *Breslau* a safe haven in the Dardanelles.

By the time Troubridge learned that the two German battleships were steaming east, only his four armoured cruisers had the speed to catch them. They set off after the Germans on the night of August 6, intending to intercept them before first light – the *Goeben* had 11-inch guns to the 9.2 inch guns of the British cruisers, making a daylight attack a risky business. At 4 am Troubridge's flotilla had still not closed with the enemy ships. Rather than risk a daylight encounter, Troubridge ordered his ships back to their station in the Adriatic.[14]

It was a fateful decision. The escape of the German battleships into the Dardanelles meant that Russia's only access to the Mediterranean front through the Black Sea was now effectively sealed off. In the heat of the moment, however, what assumed even greater importance than these strategic considerations was the blow this failure dealt to the pride of the British navy and to the expectations of its political chief, Churchill. While Una waited anxiously on Malta in mid-August, Troubridge was being subjected to a volley of criticism from his masters in London. At the Admiralty opinion ran so strongly against his conduct that he felt he had no alternative but to apply for a court-martial to clear his name. It was to face a charge of negligence in his pursuit of the *Goeben* – 'being an enemy then flying', as the official wording put it – that he now returned to London with Una at his side.

The court-martial, held in camera, opened in Weymouth on November 5. The strain had told on Una and she spent the duration of the case in bed in London at the Charing Cross Hotel, visited by her mother, by Crighton-Miller and by friends. The hearing lasted four days. Troubridge insisted that his action was based on his understanding that he was not to risk his own forces needlessly. The logic and sincerity of his defence was irrefutable and at 8 pm on November 9 the court fully and honourably acquitted him of the charges. Throughout the proceedings he conducted himself with intelligence and integrity. Whereas his superior in Malta, Berkeley Milne, did little to try to exonerate him, seeking instead to save his own reputation in the affair,

Zip scrupulously went out of his way to avoid implicating Milne, taking upon himself full responsibility for his actions.

If not actually by his side during his ordeal, Una remained loyal to her husband. The case aroused considerable publicity and her photograph appeared in society papers such as the *Tatler* (May Massola wrote to say it was not nearly so good as the one Una had given them – which can hardly have been consoling).[15] Una explained the affair to her friends as a case of backstairs intrigue against an officer whose rise had been meteoric. Privately, she felt that Zip was not over-popular with his colleagues. He could be domineering, said what he thought (even to superiors), and tended to be scathing about less able officers. As a result, few of his naval colleagues rallied round in his hour of need.

Despite his acquittal, Troubridge never again held a sea command. The Admiralty neither forgot nor forgave. Instead, he was put in charge of a naval battery being sent to Belgrade to keep open the Danube for the Allies. For an officer of his promise it was a humiliating come-down.

Virtual exile to Serbia dismayed Una too. She accompanied Zip to Belgrade in early 1915, then returned to raise funds and volunteers for a hospital there for British servicemen. She took a house in Bryanston Street, near Marble Arch, and began the thankless task of writing begging letters to the Admiralty and her husband's former colleagues. Money gradually came in and soon a party of nursing auxiliaries had been formed. They were due to leave for Belgrade in September, Una accompanying them. The prospect depressed her terribly.

It was in this mood of despairing uncertainty that Una came face to face with John that August afternoon at Emmie Clarendon's.

Chapter Seven

Despite the supreme importance with which their first proper meeting was later vested – Una would fashion it into a destined encounter of Wagnerian proportions – the affair between John and Una began casually enough. Certainly on John's side, Una presented the prospect of an amorous diversion. John was in no mood to repeat the agonized entanglement with a married woman that had been her experience with Phoebe. 'How do I know if I shall care for you in six months' time?' Una recalled her saying with studied coolness in those early days.[1] The fact that Una's husband served abroad made matters more convenient, as did the knowledge that she would be leaving England in September. John saw the chance here for a short, sharp involvement that could be abruptly and painlessly broken when the time came for Una to depart. It suggests that John had decided to stay with Ladye while intending, like many husbands she knew, to 'play the field' at the same time.

However, none of this reckoned with John's natural tendency to commit herself to people who gave themselves to her. It also took no account of Una's remarkable blend of charm and persistence. Nor her impulsiveness. She knew quite well the sort of woman John was, for her cousin Mabel's 'ménage à deux' was common knowledge in the Taylor family. But this only attracted Una the more. She had always been drawn by the androgyne figure, by the ambiguity of gender. Now here was a handsome woman whose boyish manner and appearance was no stage effect like Bernhardt's Napoleon but an everyday reality. Depressed by her marriage and suspecting, consciously or not, that men did not satisfy her needs, Una threw caution to the winds with the same abandon she had displayed in marrying Troubridge. She admitted later:

> I thought little and felt a great deal. I was swept along on a spate of feeling, of learning the endless aspects of this strange personality, and all I knew or cared about was that I could not, once having come to know [John], imagine life without her. I had, at twenty-eight, as much consideration for Ladye or anyone else as a child of six.[2]

Before her death Una destroyed her diaries for 1915 and 1916, covering the period when her affair with John began. The reason can only be guessed at, namely that they contained disclosures about a delicate situation in which Ladye was to be the ultimate and tragic loser. For the day-to-day unfolding of this episode in John's life, we must therefore turn to Ladye's diaries – cautious in the knowledge that they are likely to give a one-sided view of events.

For a fortnight after Emmie's tea party, Una is not mentioned. Then on August 15 she appeared for tea at Cadogan Square and stayed over for dinner. She began 'dropping in'. On the 18th Ladye and John were invited by Una to Bryanston Street, meeting Andrea for the first time (Ladye thought the child 'a darling'). Una took the opportunity to present John with some of her earliest sketches for the bust of Nijinsky. On the 22nd Una met Dolly Clarke at Cadogan Square. Two days later John spent the evening on her own at Bryanston Street, reading Una a new story she had just finished called 'The Woman in the Crêpe Bonnet'. This marked an ominous development. Until now, no one but Ladye had been permitted to appreciate John's work in this way – and she wrote in the margin of the diary: 'After this date Una "set in".'[3]

The mutual visits, and mutual admiration of each other's work, set the pattern of the friendship. It turned out that John had bought Una's statuette of Adeline Genée long before they knew each other, which struck them as a happy omen, as also the fact that their fathers had died at the same age. Like Ladye, Una was intelligent, widely read, cosmopolitan in her outlook. Moreover, she was a professional artist of proven reputation. And she possessed a crucial advantage over Ladye: she had youth and a certain modernity (though she was not, artistically, avant-garde – an important distinction for John). She presented, in fact, a natural intellectual successor to Ladye at a point when John's development had begun to outstrip the older woman's capacities.

September came round and the hospital unit left for Belgrade without Una. She moved to a flat with a studio in Hay Hill, Mayfair, and began work on an etching of John's head. She 'dropped in' for meals at Cadogan Square and started to accompany John to early mass (which Ladye rarely attended). Una, like Ladye, had a girlish side to her which she quickly realized John found appealing. Before long, John was calling her by the pet name of 'Squig' or 'Squiggie'.

Towards the end of September, John and Ladye took their usual autumn holiday. Owing to the war, 'dear abroad' was out of the question and they chose to visit Watergate Bay, near St Columb Minor in Cornwall. Una and the Cub joined them a few days later, apparently by arrangement. For the first time the two younger women were able to see each other all day every day. In the mornings they would set off on long walks across the cliffs to St Mawgan or Bedruthan, leaving the child in the hands of the nanny and Ladye resting in the hotel. In the course of these walks their intimacy grew. Una recalled:

> There I saw [John] for the first time in rough country clothes, heavy short-skirted tweeds unusual in those days, collars and ties and, I remember, a queer little green Heath hat with a pot-shaped crown . . . and day by day I fell more completely under the spell of her enthralling personality. She was so intensely alive, she could be so kind and tender, and she was also so wilful, so humorous and, in those days, so intolerant! Her temper was so violent, so quickly spent, and her penitence, if she thought she had given pain, so extreme . . . She was so intuitive, so intelligent and yet so naive and simple. She was still a mass of sharp corners, prejudices and preconceptions that she was sure nothing was ever going to modify! She was at that time not only devout but, to my mind, bigoted in the extreme, and young as I was, and also devout, I rebelled at her militant theories. I remember saying to her: 'I believe you would be prepared to torture heretics . . . in another age you would have been a Torquemada . . . ' and to this extent I was right: I had met for the first time in my life a born fanatic. Not, however, as I then suggested, one who would persecute others, but one who, if the need arose, would go to the pillory or the stake for her convictions . . . [4]

Ladye adopted a maternal air towards the two younger women, seeing them off on their walks with a cheerful 'Bless you both,' or wandering a little way to meet them on their return. She loved stormy seas and the three would sit for hours on the cliffs at Bedruthan watching the tide rushing in. Then there were drives in jingles and paddling in the surf (it was too cold to bathe), and sometimes Una and Ladye, the two cousins, would leave John in the hotel and walk out on their own.

But Ladye was merely a side-show to the main event and she knew it. Behind the cheery exterior, she felt anxious and depressed. One night, after they had all gone up to their rooms, she accosted John and they had a long discussion, recalling similar occasions during the Phoebe affair. On another, more distressingly, she experienced terrible nightmares which woke her at dawn shouting and in a sweat.

On October 11 they heard the news that Belgrade had fallen to the Austro-Hungarians. The following day they headed back to London to enable Una to keep in closer touch with events. It appeared that Troubridge had managed to escape from Belgrade and Una reported that the hospital unit was being disbanded and sent home. Ladye entered this information in her diary with a heavy exclamation mark: there was now evidently no prospect of the interloper letting them alone. Since their return from Cornwall Una had proved a persistent presence. On October 13 a Zeppelin raid left many dead and wounded in the Strand and the following night she slept on the divan at Cadogan Square, fearing to be on her own.

John had discovered that Una shared her love for pets (as a child Una had owned a tame owl called Merlin which flew round the house hooting and soiling the furniture) and she bought a bulldog bitch for her from breeders in Maidenhead. They christened the dog Juno and began taking it for long walks in Hyde Park. Ladye felt left out. She described her mood as 'sad & rotten' and wrote plaintively: '*Wish* I felt stronger & more able to work!'[5]

Una meanwhile was in the habit of depositing her five-year-old daughter at More House, Tite Street, the home of her friend Jaqueline Hope's family (Jaqueline's mother, Mrs Laura Hope, was Troubridge's elder sister). Una would have been an unorthodox parent whatever her circumstances. Her own somewhat bohemian upbringing inclined her to treat Andrea with a casualness that to outsiders looked like indifference or neglect. She did not believe in mollycoddling children, favouring spartan methods (in Malta she used to hang Andrea out of the window in a muslin bag to dry after a bath) and holding strict views about good manners. The Troubridges regarded her as a poor mother because they believed she had victimized her three step-children, deliberately dressing them in down-at-heel clothes. Indeed, relations between Una and the children had deteriorated to the point where, in 1912, the youngest, Mary, then eighteen, refused to live with her any more (Troubridge entrusted the girl to the Hopes).

Andrea's clothes hardly suggest she was favoured above the other children, for Una dressed her in a strange assortment of garments, such as straight narrow tunics ending mid-thigh or knickerbockers without a skirt. In her own way, Una was genuinely fond of the Cub. She admired her for being tall and slim, disliking the Troubridge tendency towards plumpness, and if the child ever fell ill, she rushed to her side.

At the end of October 1915, in response to soaring costs brought about by the war, John decided to sell both the flat in Cadogan Square and the White Cottage. She and Ladye moved into a suite in the

Vernon Court Hotel, just round the corner from Cara in Catherine Street.

On November 29 Una and John travelled down to Malvern to take an inventory of the White Cottage. There, in the afternoon, they made love together for the first time. John was the first woman with whom Una had ever had sexual relations – and she would be the last. Twenty-three years after the event Una still cherished the memory:

> I can shut my eyes now & recall the luncheon she had prepared for me – & trying to eat while I summoned my resolution to leave immediately – & all that followed, & in the evening our walking along the valley road to where the lights ended and the hedges began – & so back to the White Cottage with a bond forged between us that has endured for over 23 years.[6]

In December Una had to vacate her flat in Hay Hill. She found another apartment with a studio at 13, Royal Hospital Road, Chelsea, almost next door to Swan Walk. A routine now became established whereby she would lunch and dine with John and Ladye at the hotel. John would saunter round to Swan Walk for breakfast. Sometimes John stayed the night at the studio, reappearing before Ladye in an irritable, nervous mood – always a sign of guilt with John.

Under the circumstances, Christmas 1915 proved less than festive for John and Ladye. On Christmas Day itself they exchanged the ritual presents (a fob watch for John, a pink fur-lined dressing-gown for Ladye) and dined *en famille* with the Harrises at Catherine Street. Afterwards they returned to the hotel deep in gloom. Ladye confided to the diary: 'Felt depressed & very sad. John upset – she talked with me till past 2 a.m.' Una was back the next day, and John again stayed the night at Royal Hospital Road on the 28th. On New Year's Eve the three women dined quietly at the hotel. At ten o'clock Cara and her son Peter put in an appearance in fancy dress costumes on their way to a party. They were accompanied by a French baroness in a Pierrot's get-up. It briefly enlivened an otherwise cheerless evening. At quarter to eleven Una went back to her studio flat. Ladye's last diary entry of 1915 read: 'John & I saw the new year in & both felt depressed.'

In late January 1916 Una came to live at the Vernon Court Hotel (though she continued to work at the studio during the day). John could have discouraged the move but did not. Ladye felt sick at heart. 'Thought seriously of going to live by myself,' she wrote in the diary.[7]

Una's pretext for moving to the hotel was her fear of the growing number of Zeppelin raids over London. The timing, however, suggests a more personal motivation. She had just received a wire from Troubridge to say he would be arriving back in England on February 3. After all that had happened between her and John, the prospect of resuming marital relations with Zip appalled her. Accordingly, when tonsillitis conveniently struck her down on January 30, she threw herself on John's protection. It was the kind of appeal, as Una well knew, that John could never resist. When Troubridge finally arrived in London on the express from Rome, he was dismayed to find his wife, not on the platform to greet him, but in bed in a hotel being nursed by a strange woman.

For the rear-admiral it provided a bleak climax to months of drama and hardship at the Balkan battle front. After the fall of Belgrade, he and his men had retreated across the Albanian mountains under terrible conditions of privation – as John and Ladye heard from him over the dinner table at the hotel while Una languished in bed above them. King George V commended him for his part in the Serbian campaign and he would shortly be promoted again, this time to vice-admiral. 'He did splendid work,' Ladye informed her grandson Peter, 'and has helped to make history!'[8]

But the war hero was also a husband and his stirring exploits could only briefly banish from all their minds the more pressing domestic crisis which his return had now provoked. With brutal candour, John suggested to Ladye that they settle abroad, taking Una and the Cub with them. Even had Ladye agreed, such a course was hardly practicable in wartime. Moreover, John was just about to buy a new flat for Ladye and herself, at 22, Cadogan Court, near Sloane Square. John signed the lease on February 18. Two days later she accepted an offer for the White Cottage.

By this date Una was up and about again, but Zip, camped disconsolately at his club, had sensed that he was unwelcome and began to lose patience. On February 22 Ladye reported: 'unexpected upheaval by Troubridge' ('upheaval' was a Ladyeism for a row or violent outburst). John, too, felt the strain – and took it out on Ladye, haranguing her for an hour and a half one evening. 'Atmosphere sad beyond words,' the diary concluded forlornly.[9]

Troubridge finally insisted on finding a home for his family. Una dutifully rushed round Chelsea looking at flats and houses. A small house came up for let in Beaufort Gardens and they took it, moving in on May 6. But relations between husband and wife were tense. 'J. very worried re Troubridges,' Ladye noted[10] – a curious display on John's part in view of her own responsibility in the matter.

John and Ladye meanwhile made final preparations to move into Cadogan Court. The White Cottage had new owners and in mid-

April John made a last visit to Malvern to supervise the hand-over. The transfer made her nostalgic and she wrote a 'darling' letter to Ladye describing the passing of 'our White Cottage'.

The event temporarily brought them closer. At fifty-nine Ladye was in fragile health. Her legs were swollen and discoloured with varicose veins and she suffered constant pains in her neck. Her blood pressure could be dangerously high. She hated air raids and fretted if John remained away from her side for any length of time, especially after dark. The prospect of Ladye becoming an elderly invalid had not escaped John. Such a burden did not bear contemplating for a woman of thirty-five, but John knew it was a responsibility she could not bring herself to shirk. 'Let her begin to feel,' Una observed of John many years later, 'that anything or anyone is dependent on her and immediately they stake an eternal claim in her universe.'[11] The tension between this constraint of John's personality and her desire to break free lay, once again, at the root of her depression and frustration.

At the end of April Ladye became aware of black specks floating across her vision. She described them graphically as looking like 'chenille caterpillars'. The oculist diagnosed a small blood clot in her left eye. She attended mass with John on May 7 and could hardly read her prayer book. Afterwards, walking back to the Vernon Court, she suffered a bout of breathlessness and heart palpitations. But she laughed at herself, remarking: 'I know that I shan't make old bones!' In hindsight, John believed that Ladye had had a sudden presentiment of what lay ahead.

On the whole, though, Ladye felt more cheerful during these early summer days of 1916. The move to Cadogan Court proceeded smoothly – one evening she and John lit the stove in the new flat and gaily pretended they were already living there – and John was seeing less of Una now that Troubridge had put his foot down. Ladye had witnessed a similar phase in John's affair with Phoebe after Oliver Hoare's intervention. She had hopes that John's infatuation with Una would peter out in the same way. After attending a Red Cross concert with John (at which Agnes Nicholls and Clara Butt sang Elgar's 'Dream of Gerontius'), Ladye noted: 'I felt tired but extremely happy.'[12]

Juno, the French bulldog that John had given to Una the previous October, proved a sickly creature and they returned her. John insisted they find a replacement. Accordingly, on May 14 they revisited the kennels at Taplow, near Maidenhead. Ladye stayed in London and spent the day with Cara. The weather turned cold and raw and Ladye complained of feeling 'rather shingly'.

Having purchased another bulldog, John and Una stayed the night at Skindles Hotel in Maidenhead. The following morning they returned to Taplow, where John bought a second bulldog pup for herself. The weather cleared, becoming warm and sunny, and the two women felt reluctant to go back to London. They debated spending another night at Skindles but John opposed leaving Ladye on her own longer than planned. All the same, by the time their train steamed into London, it was dark and almost dinner time.

That afternoon Ladye had sung one of her own compositions, the patriotic 'Mother England', at a private tea party. She rarely performed these days, but the song was proving popular at wartime concerts and her recital received enthusiastic applause. She returned to the hotel in buoyant mood, hoping to regale John with her success. To her dismay, John was not back from Maidenhead. As it grew dark, Ladye anxiously telephoned Una's studio and the house in Beaufort Gardens. After several attempts she got through to Una, who had just arrived home from the station. Una reassured her that John was on her way to the hotel. Ladye laughed when Una told her that John had bought a puppy too, remarking ruefully ' "Not *another* dog!" '[13]

When John arrived at the Vernon Court, she and Ladye sat down to a quarrelsome dinner. Ladye reproached her for gallivanting with Una while *she* fretted alone at the hotel. John lost her temper. Afterwards, as they went up to their rooms, Ladye suddenly felt unwell. She complained of being cold and experiencing a numbness in her legs. It was the onset of a stroke. John rang Una and asked her for her doctor's number. Una complied and hurried round to the hotel. By the time she arrived, Ladye had sunk into unconsciousness.

Ladye lingered for another ten days. A bed was made up in the sitting-room overlooking the gardens of Buckingham Palace and she lay there with a bandage wrapped tightly round her forehead. Paralysis had set in down one side of her body, affecting her speech. Several times she tried to say something to John but the words would not come. Gradually she lapsed into a coma, surfacing only once to grasp John's hand and raise it feebly to her lips. She died on May 25.

John's grief was intense, all the more so because she blamed herself for what had happened. Her late return from Maidenhead and the row at dinner over Una had been responsible, she felt, for triggering Ladye's cerebral haemorrhage. Further, she saw her conduct as symptomatic of a more general selfishness in which her affair with Una had led her to neglect Ladye at a time when her health was evidently in decline. This remorse had grown to monstrous proportions during the long days and nights that John had watched over Ladye's unconscious form. She had desperately waited for some opportunity to speak to Ladye, to reaffirm her undying devotion and to receive in return some sign or word of forgiveness. Her anxiety had become so conspicuous that the doctor even suggested he administer an injection which could induce consciousness in Ladye. John had declined, fearing that Ladye would feel pain.[14] But her craving for absolution remained unrelieved.

Ladye's Will designated Cara as her executrix, but John was made responsible for her funeral arrangements and the disposal of many of her personal effects. Indeed, John's favoured status was implicit throughout the document. Ladye referred to her as 'my friend' and bequeathed her not only all her books, but all her furniture from the White Cottage, all her photos, and many of her most cherished personal possessions, including the portrait by Sargent. The Will expressed Ladye's hope that John would never forget her and that they would meet again beyond the grave.

When Ladye had first drafted the Will, in February 1915, she had intended to give Cara a greater role than she now had. John had strongly opposed this, however, on account of Cara's behaviour after the Burford car accident. Cara had never once showed up during the ten days that her mother had lain at Mrs Pigott's, and only later agreed to visit her in Malvern after John had written her a pleading letter. When she finally arrived, Cara accused John of exaggerating the urgency of the matter. John never forgave Cara for this apparent callousness and argued fiercely that she did not deserve to be left in charge of arrangements after Ladye's death.[15] Ladye had conceded and amended the wording of her Will accordingly.

John's concern was entirely genuine, being characteristic of her over-protective attitude. However, by delegating effective responsibility to John, the Will stored up future trouble between her and Cara – something Ladye recognized, for she expressly enjoined them to act in concert after her death in carrying out her wishes.

Cara resented John's arrangements for the funeral and burial. A requiem mass took place at Westminster Cathedral on May 30, with the embalmed body of Ladye lying before the altar in an open coffin. John allowed no music, only Gregorian plain-song. Afterwards, the coffin was laid to rest in a catacomb vault that John had purchased in Highgate Cemetery. The imposing chamber contained four stone shelves, two of them intended for John and Cara when their time came to join Ladye (the fourth shelf was for balance). Over the stone entrance with its iron grille ran a carved inscription *Mabel Veronica Batten*. Cara was further upset when John had barbed wire erected around the tomb to keep out trespassers.

John tried her best to appease Cara, in accordance with the spirit of Ladye's wishes. She presented her with some of Ladye's choicest pieces of jewellery and furniture, including a valuable diamond and emerald tiara that she (John) had bought Ladye for her 'Court' with King George V in 1912. She also allowed her to take Ladye's music scores. These belonged to John under the Will, but late one night Cara forced her way into the flat at Cadogan Court, roused John from her bed, and volubly claimed the scores were hers. The incident gave an early warning of Cara's increasingly aggressive behaviour towards John.

A fortnight after Ladye's death, John moved out of the hotel and into Cadogan Court. The flat became a shrine to the departed loved one. Ladye's bedroom was left undisturbed, exactly as it had been on the day she died (though she had never actually slept there). John placed fresh flowers – Ladye's favourites, delphiniums and lupins – beside all her framed photographs. She wrote to Rome requesting that masses be said for Ladye at the Vatican. She approached Father Worswick at St Wulfstan's in Malvern Wells and asked that a wall tablet be erected in the church to Ladye's memory. To her dismay, Worswick turned her down – ostensibly because he disliked wall tablets. We may guess the real reason, for the relationship between the curious occupants of the White Cottage had been the subject of persistent rumour in the village. In the coming months, John would have frequent cause to lament, as she saw it, the speed with which others forgot Ladye.

Before long John moved out of Cadogan Court, its reminders of her life with Ladye too poignant to bear. She went to stay instead with Dolly Clarke. The choice was significant, for Dolly too had been touched by tragedy. In 1915 she had learnt of Bobby's death in action. She was expecting her first child at the time. The baby was born in February 1916 and Dolly went to stay with friends in Purton, Wiltshire. It was here that John now joined her.

From Purton John wrote a series of letters to Cara, expressing her terrible remorse at Ladye's death and, implicitly, working out her guilt. 'My love for Ladye,' she explained,

> was always the greatest emotion of my life while she was here, but now it has exceeded all bounds. I love her differently and with a sort of spiritual force, that makes me wonder at myself sometimes . . . I gave to her the best

8 years of my life – and although other people took my surface interest twice during that time, they never touched my soul, or penetrated into my mind . . . I think the only two intimate friends I had for a short space, namely Phoebe and Una, always felt that they got only my left over energy and thoughts. They used to say so in moments of annoyance . . . I am longing to go and join her . . . If only one were a man and could go to the front, one would pass over so honourably, and so well and so soon . . . From now on no interest shall ever blur her memory for me. There shall not be even a shadow to come between us . . . I never told her an untruth except once in all these years, and I never kept anything from her. Now that she has passed over I find it difficult to care about money and comforts & the pleasures of this life. These things were only dear to me because of her, and her need of them.'[16]

Undoubtedly, Ladye *had* been the love of John's life – precisely because she had represented so much more than simply a lover. She had been the only woman to fill that all-important emotional gap left by John's mother while also providing the perfect intellectual companion for her. At the same time, it seems clear that she was the first partner to satisfy John sexually, giving her a fresh confidence by overcoming her inhibitions about her homosexuality. In short, Ladye's influence enabled John to grow up – and, ironically, in so doing, encouraged her to go her own way.

When John returned to London in the late summer, she accepted Dolly's offer to become a paying guest at Swan Walk and let off part of 22, Cadogan Court (from time to time she would sleep on a divan in the study, the only room in the flat without overpowering associations with Ladye). Una too invited John to stay, at the studio in Royal Hospital Road, but she declined. In her remorse, she now deliberately held Una at arm's length. Her 'desire for expiation was such,' Una later admitted, 'that I think there was a time when, had she only considered herself, she would have put me out of her life and offered me up as a sacrifice to loyalty.'[17] That this ultimately did not happen, Una put down to John's unselfish, protective attitude towards her: 'she realised that she had become the be-all and end-all of my life.'[18] This was only half the truth. John also needed Una, not only as a shoulder to cry on, as a confidante who had known both her and Ladye intimately, but also as an audience to her self-flagellation, one that could be alternately wooed and castigated yet would never tire of the performance. With her singular capacity for submerging herself in a role expected of her, Una provided the perfect handmaiden to John's self-regarding martyr.

In hindsight, the eventual coming together of John and Una as a couple after Ladye's death seems a foregone conclusion. So long as

Ladye lived, it could have never happened, for John's strong sense of loyalty would not have tolerated it. With her death, however, the obstacle was removed. Yet this underestimates the penitential intensity of John's determination to punish herself. She was, as Una had noted, a born fanatic. Ladye's whimsical outlook had kept John's humourless tendency towards self-dramatization within reasonable bounds. Her death removed such a restraining influence, for Una had none of Ladye's placidity and could be every bit as 'hysterical' as John.

In the immediate aftermath of Ladye's death, therefore, all the signs were that John's affair with Una would founder. The two women continued to meet frequently, but as often as not the atmosphere was heavy with mutual recriminations and smouldering silences. Thus the paradox of this legendary partnership-to-be, spanning some twenty-eight years (of which, Una calculated, they spent only four nights under separate roofs), was that it began (on John's part at any rate) as a casual fling rather than a coup de foudre, and revived after Ladye's going in the form of a slow, painful drifting together that contained many false starts and was dictated as much by expediency as by mutual affection.

Chapter Eight

On August 23, 1914, took place the first battle between British and German forces in the First World War. While John and Ladye were attending ambulance lectures in Malvern, two divisions of the British Expeditionary Force beat off six German divisions at Mons in southern Belgium. By later standards the casualties (some 1,600) were not high, but they seemed so at the time. Ladye, whose diary reported all the major engagements of the war until her death (she kept a running total of the number of days the conflict had lasted), noted: 'Great British losses at Mons.'

Mons acquired legendary importance. It was widely reported that during the battle British soldiers observed angelic hosts in the skies. Some regarded this as merely a German trick, an illusion created by projecting magic-lantern slides at the clouds (for what purpose was not explained). It seems more likely that mass suggestion was at work, occasioned by the intense patriotic emotions which the war had released. It was in this feverish climate that the 'religion' of spiritualism took hold of the popular imagination and grew into a fashionable cult of remarkable proportions. As the casualty lists lengthened – 50,000 British losses at Loos (September–October 1915); 420,000 on the Somme (July–November 1916) – people who had lost loved ones clamoured to be put in touch with them 'on the other side'. This gave wide prominence and heightened credence to a variety of phenomena – clairvoyance, telepathy, trance mediumship, ouija and planchette boards, table-tilting – associated with the supranormal, as well as to the hoaxes and frauds which inevitably accompanied them.

One man did more than any other to lend respectability to this war-time movement: Sir Oliver Lodge. Lodge was a distinguished physicist and pioneer of wireless telegraphy. A Fellow of the Royal Society and Principal of Birmingham University, he had been knighted in 1902. He and his wife Mary had a large family of six sons and six daughters. When war broke out in 1914, only their youngest son Raymond remained eligible for military service. He was a sweet-natured youth of great promise to whom the Lodges were deeply attached and, when he met his death at the front in September 1915, their grief was profound.

As a member (and former president) of the Society for Psychical Research, Sir Oliver had undertaken many investigations into spiritualist phenomena. Through friends who had also lost a son, he was introduced to a well-known medium, Mrs Osborne Leonard. Mrs Leonard quickly gave every sign that she was in communication with Raymond and over a series of lengthy sittings built up an elaborate picture of the young man's life in the 'beyond' (where cigars and whisky sodas could apparently be obtained). The Lodges were undoubtedly comforted in their distress by this information and in 1916, driven by a desire to help others similarly bereaved, Sir Oliver published his account of the sittings under the title *Raymond, or Life after Death*. The book's enormous success suggests that Lodge had tapped a deep reservoir of spiritual need in the war generation. Between 1916 and 1919 *Raymond* went through twelve impressions.

John was a natural convert to spiritualism. She and Ladye had always believed in the existence of supra-normal forces. As we have seen, they put down their own remarkable empathy to the fact that they had known each other in a former incarnation. They were receptive to instances of telepathy and coincidence. They had visited clairvoyants together and for a time shown an interest in theosophical ideas. They had always said that their love would survive death. John – and the mystical streak in her poetry underlined this – was much attracted by the ineffable, by a vision of life that emphasized the unity and timelessness of all creation.

But her immediate reasons for considering spiritualism were more emotive. She was driven by a deep-rooted guilt. She desperately wanted to know if Ladye blamed her. What had Ladye tried but failed to say to her during those last anguished days as she lay paralysed? Neither prayer nor confession had supplied John with the solace she craved.

She first thought of visiting a medium after Una's mother, Minna, claimed that Ladye had tried to communicate with her at a séance held by a Mrs Scales. Though this seemed somewhat unlikely given that Ladye had never really liked Minna, John was in a mood to clutch at any straw. She visited Mrs Scales half a dozen times. At first she was impressed, but gradually it became clear that the medium not only cheated but was mentally unbalanced. Una suggested that they approach Sir Oliver Lodge and ask him to test Mrs Scales. The great man agreed and eventually confirmed their suspicions. At the end of

July, Dolly decided to visit the celebrated Mrs Leonard in the hope of making 'contact' with Bobby. She suggested, however, that John should first test the medium for her.

At thirty-four Mrs Gladys Leonard was two years younger than John. As a child she had reported seeing visions. She had hoped for a career on the musical stage, but diphtheria ruined her singing voice and she eked out a living as an actress in repertory (a theatrical training which must have helped her later in the impersonation of her 'communicators'). Marriage to a fellow-actor, Osborne Leonard, somewhat eased her financial worries and she began to develop her talents in the spiritualist line. She first discovered her 'gift' while experimenting with table-tilting. She had passed into a trance and was told afterwards that a young girl called Feda had spoken through her. Feda became Mrs Leonard's principal 'control'. The girl purported to be a thirteen-year-old Indian whom an ancestor of Mrs Leonard's had married and who had died in childbirth in 1800. Feda spoke in a high-pitched voice and, like a child, sometimes got her grammar wrong and mistook the meaning of words. She always referred to herself in the third person ('Feda says . . .', 'Feda sees . . .') and her manner towards Mrs Leonard was a strange mixture of flippant tolerance and jocular contempt. In the spring of 1914 Feda warned Mrs Leonard that the world was about to be overtaken by a terrible catastrophe and many people would need her help. When the war came, Mrs Leonard accordingly took rooms in London and began to hire out her services at both public and private sittings. Sir Oliver Lodge was the first scientific researcher to investigate her skills in depth and, through *Raymond*, made her famous.

John's first visit to Mrs Leonard's rooms at 41, Clifton Avenue, Maida Vale, took place on August 16, 1916. She went on her own and was careful to preserve her anonymity.

> Arrived at Mrs Leonard's flat, I was shown into the room where her séances are held by Mr Leonard her husband. Mrs Leonard joined me in a few moments, and I can confidently assert that we had never met before. As I was testing this medium for someone else [Dolly], as well as being most anxious myself to obtain evidential results, I addressed practically no conversation of any kind beyond saying good morning to Mrs Leonard, prior to the sitting. She informed me that she had received my letter reminding her of the appointment. She then darkened the room with curtains, lit a small red lamp, and proceeded to suggest that I should take notes, handing me at the same time a piece of paper and a pencil, which I had forgotten to bring.[1]

Mrs Leonard closed her eyes and for a few seconds there was silence. From the measured pace of her breathing it became apparent that the medium had sunk into a trance. She then began speaking in the high, childish voice characteristic of Feda.

Feda: There is a soldier standing near you – he is showing the letters RJ. He has an aquiline nose and is rather dark. He wants you to help his family, who are in doubt as to whether he has passed over. He is tall and slight. I think he had an accident to his head.

John: I do not know him. Is there no one else?

Feda: Yes, there's a lady of about 60 years old, perhaps.

John: Please describe her, she interests me more.

Feda: The soldier knows you, Feda had to describe him, he insisted on it. He may know you on the Astral Plane. You often go out to the other side at night. Now he has put his hand on your arm.

John: Please leave him as I do not know him, I am afraid I cannot help, though I would do anything I could. Will you describe the lady of about 60?

Feda: The lady is of medium height, has rather a good figure but is inclined to be too fat, Feda thinks. She has a straight nose, a well shaped face, but the face is inclined to lose its outline a little. The eyebrows are slightly arched. Her hair is not done fashionably.

John: Is it worn in the neck?

Feda: No, it's done on the crown of the head. She has passed over quite recently. She had not been well for some time prior to passing, she was sometimes conscious of this, but put it behind her. Feda don't mean to say that she worried over it much or that she suffered much, she didn't. Feda thinks she didn't know how ill she really was. She went about doing things just as usual. She gives Feda the impression of internal weakness. You were much with her in her earth life. You gave her vitality, you kept her up with your vitality.

John: That is so, I think.

Feda: She is worried about you and says, 'You always had, and seem now to have, so much responsibility that I sometimes want to come back.' She is wearing a dark dress and a brooch with a twisted pattern in the middle . . .

John asked whether the purporting lady communicator had a name but Feda could not supply it. Feda then suggested to John that Mrs Leonard might do better to try a table-sitting, at which point the control announced her departure and Mrs Leonard woke from her trance. John told the medium of Feda's suggestion and Mrs Leonard agreed to it. At a table-sitting messages came through movements of the table according to a recognized code, the medium supervising the proceedings in a conscious state. Mrs Leonard began by declaring:

If there is anybody there who wishes to speak, will they please try to understand the rules which are:- The table to move three times for yes – once for no – and twice for doubtful. The alphabet to be called by me, the table to keep moving meanwhile, but to stop when the desired letter is called. Do you understand?

In reply, the table jolted three times, denoting 'yes'. Under such a system deciphering the message could be slow and laborious, especially since there was no clear indication where a word ended and another began. Taking down the letters as the table 'spelt' them out was obviously crucial.

Mrs Leonard:	Kindly give your name, you see we must have a proof.
Table:	Mabel Veronica Batten.
John:	Correct.
Table:	I have been trying to write, I have been with you so much, especially at night. Been so anxious about you. Am lonely, so miss you.
John:	Whom do you live with?
Table:	George. Do you remember a place we went to called Watergate?
John:	Yes, has it no other name?
Table:	Yes. Bay.
John:	Correct. Watergate Bay, that is a fine proof you have given.
Table:	That's why I wanted to talk this way.
John:	Have you any more to say, my dear?
Table:	Heaps. You were so good to me I didn't like it just at first here.
John:	Can you give the name you always called me by?
Table:	Yes. John.
Mrs Leonard:	No, no, you must be wrong, John is a man's name.
John:	It is correct.
Table:	I want you badly. I did try to take you once.

This ended the table-sitting – and the session, which had lasted over an hour and a half. John thanked Mrs Leonard and made a further appointment with her. The medium suggested that next time John should come with a friend who could take notes for her: it would make it easier to concentrate on her questions while also ensuring a full record was kept of the proceedings.

John was no blind believer in spirits. Her acquaintance with a scientist as eminent as Sir Oliver Lodge and her assiduous background reading in the subject had taught her to be alert to the risks of fraud among mediums. Nevertheless she could not help being impressed by Mrs Leonard at this first sitting. She wrote to Cara:

I am prepared to take my oath that I was not cheating, that the table *stopped itself*, as far as I am consirned [sic], and that in my opinion the medium did not stop it, as she cannot have known the names Veronica Batten – George – John – & Watergate Bay. The table *felt alive*.[2]

This is not the place to discuss at length the plausibility of Mrs Leonard's skills. Part of the medium's talent lay in a combination of adroit 'fishing' and a shrewd assessment of her sitter's personality and motives. John's inexperience helped, too, on this occasion. Mrs Leonard's opening gambit – the soldier with the 'aquiline nose' (i.e. related to John) – was a standard one, given that most of her clients were seeking relatives or loved ones lost in battle. It is noticeable, too, that the description of the 'lady of 60' is only *appropriate* to Ladye, not *distinctive* of her. John thought the point about the hair particularly good since Ladye invariably wore hers up, but such a style was not improbable in a woman whose tastes would have been moulded in the late-Victorian years. On the nature of Ladye's illness, Feda proved vague in her diagnosis, hinting at an 'internal weakness' – which would be difficult to fault.

Mrs Leonard had remarkable powers of telepathy and some of her most striking answers were arrived at in this way. John was aware of this, but pointed out (in her notes to the sitting) that when the table had mentioned Watergate Bay, she herself had been thinking of Orotava in Tenerife, the scene of some of her happiest times with Ladye. Where Mrs Leonard showed herself to be singularly sensitive was in divining, while in the trance, that it was something to do with Ladye's condition before she died that was worrying John. Used to meeting many sitters from different walks of life, the medium was a good judge of character. John's grave and nervous disposition suggested a natural worrier. '"You always had, and seem now to have, so much responsibility that I sometimes want to come back",' Feda reported Ladye saying to John. They were words of comfort which might be applied to many a grieving sitter, but one can see how, in her own circumstances, John felt they constituted a special message to her from Ladye. As always, the sitter's desire to believe was the medium's strongest ally.

At her second sitting with Mrs Leonard on August 25, John was accompanied by Dolly as her note-taker. However, the results of the table-sitting (there was no trance this time) were almost wholly unintelligible. John made no further appointments with Mrs Leonard, returning instead to Mrs Scales (who at this stage had not yet manifested signs of what John called her 'neurotic mania'). When the Lodges finally assured her that Mrs Scales was as suspect as she had thought, John was visibly upset. She felt her love for Ladye had been somehow exploited and dishonoured. The Lodges were touched and suggested they make a special appointment for John and Una with Mrs Leonard. At the time John did not connect this Mrs Leonard with the one she had already visited twice (an indication perhaps of her over-wrought state) and gratefully accepted the Lodges' offer. Una had not been to Mrs Leonard's before nor had John told her of her own visits since Dolly had sworn her to secrecy.

Dolly reacted angrily to thus being supplanted and much of the trouble they would encounter from her in the future dated from this assumption by Una of her place at John's side in the spiritualist 'quest' for Ladye.

Not that relations between John and Una had improved. Una was making herself ill with worry, claiming that a painful heart condition she once suffered as a child had returned. Life at Beaufort Gardens with Zip and the Cub had done nothing to revive her faith in her marriage, yet John wallowed in grief and continued to rebuff her as a lover. The pressure eased somewhat in September when Troubridge left to take up new duties in Greece. Una and little Andrea, now almost six, moved back to the studio in Royal Hospital Road. Since this was just round the corner from Swan Walk, Una once again began 'dropping in' on John.

Shortly after Troubridge's departure, Una persuaded John to come away with her. Accompanied by John's ageing collie, Rufus, they stayed for a week in a hotel at Llanberis in Wales. The autumn landscape was breathtakingly wild and beautiful. They went for long, bracing walks, climbed to the top of Snowdon, and tramped round Carnarvon Castle, each trying to cheer the other with a hearty show of jocularity. But it did not rekindle the romantic spirit of their affair prior to Ladye's death. John studiedly resisted any show of physical affection between them and they returned to London as hopelessly miserable as they had left.

Despite her despair, Una knew in her heart there could be no going back. She was not the woman she had once been. Characteristically, even her appearance had changed since meeting John. Whereas previously she had worn her hair long, parted in the middle and coiled in saucer-like plaits over her ears, she had now ruthlessly cut it and adopted a page-boy crop. The style was still unconventional at the time (it had been pioneered before the war by girls at the Slade School of Art) and denoted an emancipated woman. Una added her own embellishment by sweeping her hair back from her forehead, making her look more boyish. She altered her clothes at the same time. The low-cut, full-bodied dresses and tent-like tea gowns she had once thought appropriate to an admiral's wife were exchanged for plain tailor-made suits and simple blouses in a soft imitation of John's severe style.

John's and Una's joint sitting with Mrs Leonard, on October 2, proved the most fruitful yet. John introduced her companion as 'Una' but, beyond that, both were careful to say nothing which might disclose their identities. The medium went into a trance and Feda began giving further details of Ladye's appearance. Both sitters were struck by the accuracy of Feda's reference to Ladye's habit of looking sideways without moving her head, a very distinctive gesture of hers.

John then asked if Ladye had suffered much when she died. Feda replied:

> She says not as much as one would think – something had come up to her head and before she passed over, worked up to the brain and formed a small clot on some part of the brain that stopped her feeling – it doesn't seem to worry her . . .

This tallied correctly with a cerebral haemorrhage. John enquired if Ladye had still recognized her while semi-conscious.

Feda: She says it's hard to explain, but Yes – she did know you but was not sure if you were part of the dream or real – she says 'I could *feel* you – you seemed to be mentally impressing me with all your might with . . . (sotto voce: Old lady? Old Lady? Oh! Lady?) She says you said 'Oh! Ladye! Oh! Ladye! It's all alright.' And (she says) 'now and again holding me physically as if wanting to hold me up.'

John: Did she ever doubt my devotion?

Feda: She says 'No, I never, never doubted it, never, never, I give you my word.'

John: Does she know that I am devoting my life to her as though she were here?

Feda: She says 'Yes, but don't deplete yourself too much – don't overdo things. I know you better than I've ever done before.'

John: Does she love me more than anyone else?

Feda: She says 'Silly question, more than anyone – there is more in our love than there has ever been between two women before.' At least it seems so to her.

John and Una had recently discussed the possibility of going to Italy to do war work. John hinted at this in the sitting, to which Feda replied that Ladye seemed anxious about it. John reassured her that Una would look after her. Did she permit Una to do that?

Feda: She says Yes, she is very glad if she will, that is if you will let her, she says she has got a very difficult task.

John: Doesn't she know I want to join her?

Feda: She says Yes, but the end of her life had come, the sands had run out. You must not come yet, nor neglect anything that will keep you on the earth plane.

John pursued the point. Would she then live to be very old? Ladye did not think so. She might even see her in three or four years' time – though Feda added that such things were difficult to predict. Ladye returned to the exclusiveness of their love for each other: it had more depth than other people's, it was like a married couple's, they belonged only to each other.

John: Will she be glad when I go over?
Feda; Yes.
John: Una says she hopes she won't have to live very long now that you have gone and I'm going.
Feda: She is afraid she has to disappoint Una. Una must not come yet. Una must not think that all has gone yet.

The trance ended with Ladye signing off, according to Feda, with her characteristic, 'Bless you both.' It was an impressive finale to an impressive sitting.

Once again, on closer examination, this séance seems weightier in advice – and the sort of advice which John wanted to hear – than in the number of accurate 'hits' it scored. Moreover, it is hard to resist the conclusion that much of the consolation sought by John represented equally a rebuff to Una. In her line of questioning John was naturally keen to establish that Ladye's love for her remained unbroken, but the lengths to which she pursued this theme, the pointed emphasis that she made on the exclusiveness of her relationship with Ladye, conveys an impression of studied insensitivity towards Una's feelings in the matter. This was Una's first joint sitting with John and John may, perhaps unconsciously, have put on a performance calculated to snub her.

At the end of the October 2 sitting, John arranged for a series of regular séances with Mrs Leonard, averaging about two a week at a guinea a time.

John was anxious to put the record straight on the question of Ladye's stroke and the quarrel she feared had provoked it. The matter arose at a sitting on October 9.

John: Something happened before she went over between us that made her unhappy. I want her to tell me that it won't interfere with our meeting and being together.

Feda: She says 'I say most emphatically nothing could or shall prevent our meeting or my coming to you as long as God permits. I will come to you, and you help me by wishing it. I love to come.'

John: Has she forgiven me?

Feda: She says: 'I've both forgotten and forgiven. You were not responsible, I know now what lay at the bottom of it, if you had known it would hurt me it would have been different.' Do you know, she says: 'I'd forgotten about it.'

John: Tell her I didn't know she was ill, her passing was the shock of my life.

Feda: She says: 'You needn't tell me that. I see right into you – I understand you better than I ever did, you know I loved you when I was here, I understand you and know you never hurt me intentionally; of course you didn't know I was ill, I didn't know it myself till too late, perhaps it was coming on for some time. I couldn't expect you to know what I didn't know myself.'

John: Tell her we had every doctor and fought for her life. Is she happy?

Feda: She knows that. Yes, she is perfectly happy. She says nothing could have been done for her, unless something had been done to her whole system, not only part of it, two or three years ago, and that would only have kept it at bay. She says after all she was spared suffering and a long illness.

At one point during the sitting Una looked up from her note-taking and asked John plaintively how *she* was going to be able to join her and Ladye after death if, as Feda reported Ladye saying, the door was to be shut behind them. John tried to deflect the question but Ladye, through Feda, interrupted to reassure Una. John would come over first, she stated, and naturally they would want to be alone together for a few weeks. However, when Una died, she would get the same treatment, staying exclusively with Ladye for a time. Ladye, it appeared, was already showing a judicious sense of tact towards the competing claims upon her.

Una became the questioner for the first time at a sitting on October 13. She lost no time in soliciting Ladye's help in her own cause.

Una: Tell my Lady she's got to help me to take care of Twonnie [Feda's name for Johnnie].

Feda;   She says yes, she wants that, she puts her in your charge.

Una: Tell her I am honoured and will do my best.

Feda: She says she's afraid you hardly appreciate the magnitude of your task, it will be perfectly awful sometimes, terrible.

Una: Tell her I'll stick to it all right.

It struck Una that this notion of John being hard to handle was one Ladye had often confided to her in a half-jocular way when she was alive.

At another sitting in October Una asked if Ladye was glad that she (Una) was so fond of John. Ladye said yes, that they were both 'good children'. She then asked Una, through Feda: 'Will J mind your being so very fond of Twonnie?' By 'J' it transpired she meant 'T', that is, Troubridge. Una replied that she was as nice as she could be to her husband, but she could not help her true feelings towards John. Ladye agreed that John should come first but that Una must be careful not to display her affections too openly in front of Troubridge, something she might be inclined to do.[3] This was a shrewd observation of Una's character.

At several further sittings Feda relayed from Ladye some remarkably detailed descriptions of the White Cottage. So accurate was Feda's version that John began to suspect that, after all, Mrs Leonard might know more about her than she claimed. She therefore hired private detectives to check whether anyone had made enquiries about Ladye at the Registry of Deaths or in the Malvern district. John herself went down to Malvern Wells and interviewed the new owner of the White Cottage as well as their former servants, while Una checked that no one had been talking to the staff at the Vernon Court Hotel. All these enquiries drew a blank. It seemed Mrs Leonard was above reproach.

Gradually, as the sittings multiplied, their character changed. John's original motive – to seek Ladye's forgiveness – had been swiftly answered. She continued to impress upon Ladye that she missed her, and the element of putting Una down persisted in the early months, though Ladye began to show some impatience with John, urging her to make an effort to be jollier – 'when you and Una have a joke and laugh together about something, it lifts her up so much more than you can believe,' Feda commented.[4] The sittings became a kind of therapy for John, Mrs Leonard acting more like a psychiatrist than a medium, wooing John back to a normal life, sowing harmony between her and Una, giving practical, common-sense advice.

The séances began to acquire an additional interest, as evidence of spirit survival after death. Neither John or Una had lost close relatives in the war (Bobby Clarke was the only casualty of any consequence either knew), but their rising excitement at the accuracy of Feda's evidence grew into a conviction that research in this field provided the true war work they should be doing. By now they were sending their notes of the sittings to Sir Oliver Lodge and he praised their intelligent, cautious approach. He urged them to become members of the Society for Psychical Research, on whose executive council he had a seat. John and Una applied and the Society accepted them at a council meeting held on October 25 at its offices in Hanover Square.

Lodge's backing was important because the Society for Psychical Research regarded itself as an august and exclusive body. It had been founded in 1882, largely under the impetus of a small group of Cambridge academics. The aim was to investigate a number of contemporary phenomena – mesmerism, clairvoyance, telepathy, mediumship, hauntings and such like – which appeared to challenge the prevailing advance of scientific materialism. Some of the Society's early members undoubtedly hoped that, by finding proof of these phenomena, it would be possible to show that science did not contradict religious experience but confirmed it. However, all these researchers were wholly committed to conducting their enquiries in an impartial, scientific spirit (the founding committee firmly rejected including the word 'occult' in the Society's title).

In its first thirty years of existence the SPR attracted some of the ablest contemporaries to its work. The philosopher Arthur Balfour (later to be Prime Minister) immersed himself in its activities, as did his brilliant sister Eleanor, who married Henry Sidgwick and became the second principal of Newnham College, Cambridge. Oliver Lodge joined in 1884. Two other distinguished physicists, Sir William Crookes and Professor Balfour Stewart, were also members. When John and Una joined in 1916 the president was the classical scholar Professor Gilbert Murray and the Society had over a thousand members.

As members of the SPR, John and Una felt their visits to Mrs Leonard took on a new importance. After every sitting, they would retire to the studio at Royal Hospital Road and Una would type up the notes which John dictated to her. Copies would be forwarded to Sir Oliver and the Society. Soon they were visiting other mediums besides Mrs Leonard in order to test their claims. Much time and effort were devoted to verifying abstruse points made in sittings. Before the end of the year the pressure of this work was such that they were obliged to hire a secretary. Phenomena outside séances began to draw their attention too. Both imagined they heard rapping noises on furniture or felt strange currents of air pass over them. Ladye was often saying at Mrs Leonard's that she visited them at night in their flats. Was this evidence then of her presence? Ladye suggested that it was – though the dates and circumstances of these occurrences rarely tallied with her predictions of them.

In January 1917 John and Una were invited to stay at Mariemont, the Lodges' home in Birmingham. If either of them had any doubts about the value of their work with Mrs Leonard, Sir Oliver was the man to reassure them. As a respected scientist, his belief in spiritualism could not easily be dismissed as mere crankiness. He had a hearty contempt for his critics, of which there were many after the publication of *Raymond*. To religious objectors, he opposed the traditional claims of science, asserting that he was simply responding to the evidence. To fellow-scientists who ridiculed his whisky-and-cigars vision of paradise, he replied that the intellectual establishment was always much slower to accept newly discovered scientific phenomena than ordinary folk. History would seem to suggest that the reverse was truer, but Sir Oliver was a man with a mission and such people are inclined to interpret the facts to fit their case.

His brand of fervour was not always in step with mainstream opinion in the SPR. One can see, however, that Sir Oliver had just the right credentials to appeal to beginners in the field like John and Una – both too intelligent to swallow everything they were told but intense enough to make a crusade out of those aspects they did believe. Moreoever, both women were chronic hero-worshippers. John in particular was flattered by the attention paid to her by so eminent an intellectual. Lodge even looked the part. His balding domed head, the piercing but kindly eyes, and the bushy beard and moustache, lent him the appropriate gravitas of a Victorian sage.

The visit to Mariemont was recorded in Una's diary with suitable reverence. Having deposited the Cub at the Hopes' in Tite Street, they reached their destination at five in the evening. 'Such dear delightful people I have never met,' Una wrote, 'and one could not long be shy.'[5] Sir Oliver had asked Una to translate *Raymond* into French and she worked at this task in the mornings. After dinner each day there would be a sitting, sometimes at the ouija board or it might be table-tilting, or they simply linked hands on the table top.

On their last night John suffered a nose-bleed and had to retire to bed, leaving Sir Oliver and Una talking psychic matters until the small hours. Una was enthralled. 'So *very* interesting and a great & adorable man.' John expressed her satisfaction that the great man had appreciated 'her Squig' so highly.[6] The two of them had acquired favourite pupil status and before the visit was over Sir Oliver added honour to compliment by asking them to relieve him of some of his correspondence (from persons applying to see mediums he recommended). They accepted the task gratefully.

They took their leave of the Lodges on January 12. On both sides there was a self-conscious dramatization of the moment of departure, as if disciples were being sent on their mission by the master.

When [Sir Oliver] said goodbye to John he said 'This isn't the last we see of you' & to me he kissed the fingers of his hand and then put them to my forehead – a benediction I shall *never* forget![7]

The postscript proved rather more down-to-earth. They planned to spend a couple of days in Malvern before returning to London and at Birmingham station they were 'claimed' by a scruffy and pathetic wire-haired terrier which turned out to belong to one of the porters. Una promptly bought the animal off its owner for four shillings, christened it Billy, and gave it to John as a gift. That night they put up at the Imperial Hotel in Great Malvern and gave the dog a thorough scrubbing in Jeyes fluid.

Revisiting Malvern brought back all John's memories of Ladye and the following day saw her sunk in another deep depression: 'Poor J cried nearly all afternoon,' Una wrote in the diary, adding 'so did I.' Both women were still a bundle of nerves and hypochondria. Doctors were consulted and second opinions taken. One diagnosis of Una's chest pains put them down to indigestion. It was a circumspect way of saying she was simply unhappy.

For John still led her a tortuous dance. Some days she could be sweetness itself. On others her black mood descended and she would reduce Una to tears with harsh outbursts and cold rejections. When John fell ill, she would allow Una to stay overnight at Swan Walk – not in her bed but on the divan. Una proved pathetically grateful for such crumbs of comfort. But, when the whim took her, John could withdraw her favour with unexpected ruthlessness. 'Much upset at my walking home!' read one plaintive entry in the diary after Una had read aloud to John at Swan Walk until the early hours.[8]

John used sexual abstinence as a means of punishing both Una and herself. The gesture was characteristic of a fastidious, humourless streak in her nature. Its unhealthiness revealed itself all too clearly in her constant ailments and bewildering moods – as also in the relentless, obsessive sittings with Mrs Leonard. She had begun addressing Ladye directly through Feda, calling her 'darling' and expressing a desire to have a proper conversation with her. She sometimes excluded Una from the sessions and sat alone with the medium.

On January 19, at one such solo séance, it seemed that her wish was granted for Ladye dislodged Feda and took 'control' of Mrs Leonard for the first time. 'What you trying to do?' Feda suddenly exclaimed in her childlike manner. She apparently directed this at Ladye not John, for the medium's body began to tremble and she stretched out her left hand, groping the air. In a barely audible whisper, she murmured: 'Where are you, darling?' John leaned across and took hold of Mrs Leonard's hand. 'Is that you, Ladye?' she asked. The medium replied: 'Yes,' and turned and embraced John with a low sob. When John could find the words, she said: 'Call me by my name.' She had asked this of Ladye on previous occasions, but the nearest Feda had achieved was 'Donnie' or 'Twonnie'. Now the medium answered, still in a whisper: 'I can't think! Oh, why can't I say your name? I'm so stupid, I can't say it!' John told her not to worry and soothed her with endearments. Mrs Leonard continued to cling to her, feeling her face with her hands and stroking her sleeve, as an anxious blind person might do.

After about a minute the medium became calm and released John. Feda's voice, in her normal tone, announced that Ladye had gone. When Mrs Leonard awoke from the trance, John told her: 'You were controlled this morning by someone with whom I often communicate.' The medium expressed surprise and replied she had been unaware of it.[9]

Communicating with Ladye served to reinforce John's religious beliefs. The Catholic Church, on the other hand, condemned spiritualism and that worried her. She had confessed to a score of different priests her involvement with mediums and been roundly reprimanded for her pains. She sought Ladye's advice. Ladye was reassuring. It was not the Church which condemned her, she remarked, but its 'exponents' – implying that if John looked long enough she would find a confessor who approved. She talked vaguely about a Spanish Carmelite priest 'at a church that is across the river, across the Thames'. John begged her to reveal his name, but the vital information tantalizingly eluded Feda. John was advised to think the matter through herself.[10]

In February John discussed her problem with Father Norbert Wyllie, of the church in Cheyne Walk that she and Ladye used to attend (Church of Our Holy Redeemer). He would not sanction her activities but nor would he condemn her, preferring to leave the matter to her own conscience. For the moment this satisfied John. Una had no such qualms. 'Tell [Ladye] I never confess it,' she told Feda, 'I don't think it's wrong, and I say nothing about it.'[11] It neatly illustrated a basic difference in the two women's temperaments – John cautious and conservative, Una impulsive and unconventional.

In February Una was obliged to move. She found a new flat at 42, St Leonard's Terrace. 'I am very much depressed at new start in another squalid little lonely abode,' she confided to her diary, 'but one must just do one's best & go on – I am very very tired.'[12]

In March, John went down with German measles. Fearing for her baby, Dolly summarily asked her to leave Swan Walk – a tactless gesture which pained John but expressed Dolly's continuing resentment at her exclusion from Mrs Leonard's sittings. Una immediately persuaded John to be nursed at St Leonard's Terrace – and despatched the Cub to the ever tolerant Hopes for the duration. Una relished the cosy domesticity. She started John on Ovaltine and made her take a complete rest from her psychical reading.

On March 28 John proved well enough to attend their regular sitting with Mrs Leonard. Afterwards she took Una to lunch at a favourite haunt, the Prince's Grill Room in Regent's Street – since Ladye's death they had avoided places like the Bath Club or the Berkeley Grill which were especially associated with her. John seemed in mellow mood and sought to allay Una's fears. She assured her that Ladye would not desert them or advise anything that would not turn out happily. 'I have often felt so,' Una commented, 'but glad to hear J say so too.'[13]

Her relations with Dolly still prickly, John moved permanently from Swan Walk and took up residence again at Cadogan Court. Una had meanwhile decided to buy a small house at 6, Cheltenham Terrace, a short walk from John's flat in Draycott Avenue.

On May 28 Una learned, to her consternation, that her husband would be arriving in London the next day. She had not seen him for nine months. She had written to him, not very regularly, and letters came back which she dutifully read out to the Cub. From his own family as well as Una herself, Troubridge knew of his wife's deepening involvements with both John and SPR. He worried in particular about the impact on the Cub.

The enormous amount of time that Una was now spending with John on spiritualist matters meant that Andrea led an unsettled existence. The Cub could find herself farmed out at a moment's notice to the Hopes or any other amenable child-minder – which sometimes meant the servants or the chauffeur even. On one occasion a policeman discovered the little girl wandering by herself about the streets in the middle of the night.[14] John had no real feeling for children (though, curiously, her fiction shows an acute grasp of child psychology). She accepted Andrea as an unavoidable part of Una's life rather than felt any special affection for her.

Having fetched out Troubridge's 'civvies' from Taylor's Depository (where most of their possessions were in storage), Una met the admiral off the train on the evening of May 29. If Zip had hopes that Una's presence betokened a less bleak homecoming than last time, he was to be quickly disillusioned. She had booked him a room at the Charing Cross Hotel.

This time there was no question of even a formal resumption of marital relations between Una and Troubridge. Throughout his leave of three months, the admiral stayed in a hotel while Una slept at John's (as often as not on the divan in her study) or at Cheltenham Terrace. For a brief period, while John went outside London to conduct a psychical investigation for Sir Oliver Lodge, Zip moved into her flat at Cadogan Court – and doubtless discovered, if he did not know already, the true nature of John's past relationship with Ladye.

If he felt upset at the way matters stood, the admiral manfully held his feelings in check: this time there were no 'upheavals' from him. Una, on the other hand, found the strain intolerable, succumbing to renewed heart pains and nervous exhaustion. Zip took her to see a Harley Street specialist, who confirmed she was suffering from anxiety: 'no remedy,' Una wrote, 'except being perfectly happy & other still more impossible circumstances – so I back to 6 Cheltenham Terrace where John awaiting me. Bless her – the best friend ever woman had.'[15]

On August 1 – the second anniversary of her meeting with John at Emmie Clarendon's, Una noted – Troubridge saw off his wife and child (plus nanny and two dogs) on the bus to Southbourne. The plan was to give Andrea a summer holiday by the seaside while Zip attended to duties that required him at the Admiralty. As arranged, John met Una on her arrival, having travelled down separately to Southbourne from another spiritualist investigation outside London.

While apart, the two women had corresponded daily, sometimes twice a day. Despite John's moods, proximity was becoming a habit, a drug they both needed, the company of each other preferable to anyone else's. Yet Una despaired. What on earth could she do about her marriage? So long as she remained Troubridge's wife, how could there be any real happiness with John? Sometimes depression overwhelmed her. At Southbourne she felt so ill and tired that she wondered how she could go on living. On August 12, she reported, 'John scolded me & chaffed me & I cried!' She went early to bed, feeling miserable – at which point 'John very dear to me & put me in her bed & gave me milk & biscuits.'

A few days later they both sat up late discussing 'all sorts of sad possibilities in the next state of existence till we hardly knew which was the most unhappy of the two'.[16] Both women liked to dramatize a crisis, winding each other to fever pitch, it seemed, in order to heighten the ecstacy of emotional release afforded by the inevitable reconciliation that followed. One suspects that this ritual served as a substitute for, or possibly a prelude to, sexual relations between them, being the only way John's guilt over Ladye would allow her to be intimate with Una.

The pressure on them eased as Troubridge's leave drew to an end. Una wired him on August 15 to persuade him to join them at Southbourne. The gesture was largely for form's sake. She must have known that the prospect of holidaying with both her and John could hardly appeal to him, and he found an excuse to decline the invitation. He did not see his wife and child again before his departure. On August 26 Una noted without comment: 'True left at 1 pm for Greece.' With the coast now clear, the two women broke their holiday and returned to London the same evening.

Chapter Nine

If Ladye was providing consolation for John and Una on the spiritual level, in the physical world she was fast becoming a source of contention. The trouble originated with Cara. Since her mother's death, she had behaved towards John with a volatile mixture of ill-disguised resentment and brittle chumminess. At first she had taken little interest in John's 'communications' with Ladye. Gradually, however, as she learned of the remarkable results being obtained at Mrs Leonard's, she began to show signs of wanting to take part in the séances herself. John and Una opposed this, believing the presence of an outsider would undermine the delicate ambience they had so carefully built up with the medium. Ladye appeared to agree, intimating that her daughter would be a difficult sitter who would muddle and misinterpret the 'evidence' (not least because Cara had a chronic hearing disability which obliged her to carry an ear trumpet).[1]

Matters reached a head in August 1917 when a 'disagreeable' letter arrived from Cara accusing John of influencing her mother's spirit against her. She again asked why she should be barred from Mrs Leonard's. Una suspected that Dolly was behind the letter. 'Unspeakable of Dolly to want to queer John's pitch or mine,' she wrote, 'we have neither of us so very much that she need envy.'[2] Ten days later a letter arrived from Dolly herself, reiterating Cara's case. John was furious. She wrote the same day, reminding Dolly that her meddling was poor gratitude for the support that she (John) had always given to her and Bobby. This appeared to do the trick, for a second, more conciliatory letter arrived by return of post from Dolly, 'scared at last,' Una noted triumphantly, 'into leaving John in peace.'[3]

Cara, however, could not let the matter rest. On September 14 John and Una paid a visit to Pittleworth, the Harris's country house in Surrey. Cara, in argumentative mood, made it plain that she objected to John's continuing interest in Ladye through mediums. She also demanded that John return her mother's personal diaries (which, along with all her books, Ladye had left to John in her Will). These attacks 'made John quite ill with nerve strain', Una reported. Two days later Cara turned abusive. In a swipe at Una's credibility as a psychic researcher, she remarked that of course all Crighton-Miller's patients were known to be lunatics. John, losing her temper, warned Cara to 'cultivate an amiable disposition' or else. 'This acted like magic,' Una observed, and they heard no more on the subject before leaving Pittleworth.[4] The row had one positive result for Una. John now promised her that *she* would be buried in the vault at Highgate should she die before Cara. 'So I am happier,' Una wrote.[5]

But John knew that Cara's disgruntlement continued to rankle. To show goodwill, therefore, she arranged a sitting with Mrs Leonard for her. This took place on September 25, with Una acting as her recorder. The séance was muddled and vague. Feda appeared to have difficulty getting through. Some man kept trying to communicate, then someone called George, whom they thought might be Cara's father. But the evidence was too slim to draw any coherent conclusions. Cara acted nervously throughout, which may not have helped. Her mood was not improved. On October 3 Ladye warned John and Una, through Feda, that Cara was now convinced that they were trying to block her path. John said she thought Dolly could not be trusted either. Ladye agreed. Dolly was selfish, she observed, and her indebtedness to John rankled. It was all getting bewildering and Una commented wearily to Feda: ' "Sometimes one feels rather overwhelmed and as if there were inimical people all round." '[6]

Una could take some comfort from the fact that her affair with John was now proceeding more smoothly. She was beginning to regain ground lost through Ladye's death. In October John told her that she intended to leave her all her clothes and 'little personal things' in her Will. 'It is good of her as means *so* much to me,' Una commented.[7] On the night of October 19, while they were sleeping in separate rooms at Cadogan Court, the air raid sirens went off. John insisted Una get dressed and they take refuge in the lobby of the building on the ground floor. But Una could not find her clothes. They rushed into John's study, then opted 'to go to bed *together* in her room & await alarms [i.e. the All Clear] which came the moment our heads touched the pillow – finally we spent the rest of the night sleeping soundly in *my* room – John transferred at 3 oc'. Decorum – that is, the arrival of the servants in the early morning – demanded they sleep apart in separate rooms, but the unmistakeable tone of excitement in Una's description of the incident suggests that she regarded the opportunity to be in John's bed as a rare privilege to be cherished.

But Una had to be careful not to presume too much. Two days after their little escapade, she carelessly made a slighting reference to a photograph of Ladye, the one in a travelling case which customarily sat by John's bedside and accompanied her whenever she went away.

John took offence and they quarrelled bitterly. 'We both said very hurtful things,' Una wrote, 'but made it up before bedtime – tho' I remained miserable & wild with myself that *any* provocation should make me unkind to John.'[8]

Back in the summer Isobel Newton, the Secretary of the SPR, had asked John and Una to prepare a research paper based on the results of their sittings with Mrs Leonard with a view to presenting it to a meeting of the membership. This was an honour for such new members and the two women set about their task with all the earnestness of bright pupils whose praises have been sung by the headmaster in front of the whole school. Many days of their holiday in Southbourne were spent typing up their notes and writing a first draft. In early October the paper was ready. After reading it, Mrs Salter, the editor of the Society's journal (*The Proceedings of the Society for Psychical Research*) was so impressed that she suggested it run over two meetings instead of the usual one.

Both women felt exhausted after finishing the paper and, at their next sitting with Mrs Leonard, Ladye suggested they take a holiday.[9] On October 22, therefore, they went to stay for three weeks at the Cottage Hotel in Lynton, Devon. Much to John's delight, she found horses could be had for hire. Una had never ridden before, but she gamely bought breeches and puttees and placed herself under John's expert tuition. She surprised herself by taking to it quite quickly. 'John said I had a lovely seat wch pleased me much – no one can know what a joy it is to me to find I *can* ride with her.'[10]

As always, Una took it for granted that John knew best, whereas Ladye had tried to discourage John's sporting enthusiasms. Una was content to play the child-woman 'Squiggie' to John's 'leading man' when the occasion demanded. As the supplicant in their affair, Una acted towards John with a certain calculation, projecting the girlish ingenue when she felt this would win John round. But her 'versatility' was the equal of Ladye's, if not more so, for when required she was just as adept at assuming the role of intellectual companion, common-sense confidante, elegant woman-about-town, or indispensable organizer. In any one of these roles she might have quickly lost John's attention, for John had a restless, mercurial side to her nature. It was Una's remarkable ability to quick-change from one guise to another that made her compelling as a lover and, ultimately, irresistible.

On their return to London from Lynton, Una rented a small house called 'Grimston' in Datchet. The idea was partly to secure a safe haven for the Cub away from blitz-ridden London. But it also facilitated the work with Mrs Leonard, who was now permanently installed in a cottage in the locality. Though John still occasionally slept at Cadogan Court, Grimston now became her base – and in effect represented the couple's first home together.

On November 25 Una underwent an operation for a gynaecological complaint. During her early married life she had had a misconception which damaged a Fallopian tube and gave her occasional trouble. The operation left her in considerable pain and she frequently burst into tears. What hurt more, though, was John's apparent lack of sympathy, for she talked repeatedly of meeting Ladye 'in the next state'. Una wondered miserably if there would ever be an end to her loneliness, 'here or beyond'. She was further dismayed when John placed little significance upon the fact, which Una had carefully noted, that their menstrual cycles were now running in tandem – a precious symbol to Una of the bond between them. John insisted instead on regaling her with a dream she had had in which Ladye appeared in petticoat and pink blouse, looking as young as when they had first met. Was this, one wonders, a real dream or was John playing upon Una's anxieties in the brutal manner she sometimes adopted as a way of signalling her resistance to (and guilt at) their living together?

In February 1918 Una tried another tack when she started to record instances of telepathy occurring between her and John. To her delight, she found that their minds were highly attuned to each other's. The exercise was meant to have a 'scientific' basis, as a contribution to their spiritualist researches, but it soon became little more than a game, each devising thoughts or utterances as unlikely as possible in order to test their telepathic powers to the utmost. This still produced, or so they believed, a remarkably high number of accurate 'hits'. 'I invented Squig words to a Congo tune & sang them while John thought same,' Una reported triumphantly on February 13.

Both women were highly suggestible. At a sitting on January 2, Ladye asked if John had recently seen a small light. John confirmed that several days previously she had observed a flash of blue light. She also recalled seeing a yellow light in the shape of an egg hovering against the bedroom curtain. Ladye stated that these phenomena indicated she was watching over them. Inevitably, Una too now began to observe lights, notably a blue luminous haze hanging over the foot of John's bed at Grimston (where they slept in a twin-bedded room).

These hallucinatory experiences probably owed a good deal to the continuing state of tension between them. Over the Christmas period another black mood had descended on John, who raged at the slightest inconvenience. Life at Grimston did not help. The heating boiler kept going out, good food was proving hard to get (on Christmas Day they lunched on hare and an ordinary dessert), the dogs were sickly and badly house-trained, and the Cub's toys encroached on every room. John blamed Una for her inability to run a proper home and compared their circumstances unfavourably with the ordered comforts of life with Ladye. 'I am in despair,' cried Una miserably.[11] Then the cook walked out and Una tried unsuccessfully to fill the gap: 'we agreed the stew had been a failure & I wept in John's arms.'[12]

Ill-health stalked them both. Many of their ailments were psychosomatic. When the doctor examined Una, he usually found little organically wrong with her. On March 8, her thirty-first birthday, she had her colon X-rayed. It proved 'quite decent' and, to celebrate, she went and ordered herself a blue serge suit.

Their joint research paper, meanwhile, had gained them further success at the Society. Entitled simply 'On a series of sittings with Mrs Osborne Leonard', it dealt only with the period between August 1916 and August 1917. The central focus was upon Ladye (identified merely as 'M.V.B.') and the accuracy of her revelations about her past life with John. The last section described more contemporary 'evidence' which, though unknown to the sitters, had turned out on enquiry to be true. The paper was long and detailed (over two hundred pages when subsequently printed) and needed the two meetings over which it was spread.

In tone and presentation the piece was sober, lucid and rigorously 'scientific', admitting as evidence only that knowledge which Mrs Leonard could not possibly have learned either from her sitters or anyone else. The question of telepathy was not discussed. Deprived of the emotional context in which the séances had begun and proceeded, its findings sound at times both banal and distinctly humorous. For example, as evidence of trying to overcome her well-known fear of horses, Ladye revealed she was trying to ride in the spirit world. She also stated that she had her own private swimming-pool, remarking pointedly that, unlike on earth, on the 'other side' people did not 'come and look over your wall' when you bathed.[13]

There was no disagreement as to who should read the paper: Una naturally proposed John and John did not demur. The first instalment of the lecture took place on January 31, 1918, the second on March 22, John carefully rehearsing her delivery in front of Una before each occasion. The January meeting was held privately for members at the

Society's premises in Hanover Square. The March meeting, chaired by Sir Oliver in the Steinway Hall, was thrown open to non-member ticket-holders, enabling friends and relatives to attend – among them Minna Taylor, Marie Visetti, Cara and Dolly.

At the end of the private reading John was dismayed by the stupidity of some questions from the floor, but after the second, enthusiastic applause greeted her. Miss Newton assured John that everyone regarded the paper as 'flawless'. Una thought John had read 'beautifully' – and was flattered when Gerald Balfour, an eminent Council member, told her she was 'the finest recorder he had ever known'.[14]

On June 3 they returned to the Cottage Hotel, Lynton, for a repeat of the previous summer's successful holiday there. The train was crowded, but John's tips to the guard and Una's determined ('more force than dignity', as she put it) rearrangement of another passenger's luggage on the rack secured them seats in a first-class apartment. Travelling in comfort was a cardinal rule for both of them.

On June 11 their holiday mood was rudely shattered when a letter arrived containing a bombshell: Cara wrote informing them that she had made an official complaint to the SPR about their research paper. One of the Society's 'shining lights', she stated, had thought it best if she be allowed to examine the lecture before it went to print in the *Proceedings*.

The 'shining light' was none other than Mrs Salter, with whom Cara had had a formal interview on June 7. Cara claimed that John's paper was inaccurate. She and her mother, she declared, had been 'like sisters', and John and Una had deliberately prevented her from sitting with Mrs Leonard. Cara went on to accuse the two women of being too 'emotional and excitable' to be reliable investigators. Much of her criticism was directed against Una. Cara pointed out that Ladye had disliked Una and had quarrelled with John about her just prior to her stroke. Una was in any case unbalanced, she asserted, because she had been treated by Dr Crighton-Miller.[15]

Not knowing the full details of this meeting until they returned from Lynton, John's first response to Cara's letter was one of defiance. The very same day Una penned a long and aggrieved letter to Mrs Sidgwick, the Honorary Secretary of the Society and one of its most influential members. She protested strongly that their report should require Mrs Harris's endorsement.[16] Mrs Sidgwick was a mathematician, by profession and by temperament. She privately viewed the affair as a storm in a tea-cup. She was in favour of humouring Cara without conceding that she had any rights in the matter.[17] In her reply to Una's letter, therefore, she counselled permitting Cara to see the paper, but only under Mrs Salter's auspices. At most, she believed, a slight alteration of wording here and there would satisfy Cara's objections.[18]

This advice, eminently soothing and reasonable, had its desired effect. John and Una agreed to hand over their paper to Mrs Salter. In her reply to Mrs Sidgwick, Una apologized if the Society had been put to any inconvenience. She regretted that Cara had not come direct to them with her complaints from the first – 'instead of telling me that [John's] interest in Psychical Research & the Bible were making her too boring to invite to the house!'[19]

John, much more so than Una, was deeply sensitive to any charge of bad faith in front of her eminent colleagues. She was proud, with all the self-consciousness of a largely self-educated person, to have been admitted to the company of these intellectual giants, and the idea that they might think she had somehow offended against their high standards appalled her. Accordingly, she wrote to Sir Oliver Lodge, the fatherly mentor whom she respected above all others.

> To have to admit such things about the daughter of the most wonderful friend a woman ever had is painful beyond all words. To you it is not so difficult as it would be to write this to most people, because one always feels that you will understand. Then again we never forget that you were our first master in Psychical Research, and we feel that you have a right to know all that concerns us in this branch of our lives.

Point by point the letter refuted Cara's principal charges. It ended:

> Mrs Salter now has the matter in hand, and we believe intends to inform Mrs Harris that she must either put her accusations in black and white, and affix her signature thereunto, or else withdraw them, also in black and white, in toto. If she does the former, the matter will be dealt with by our solicitor, as it will constitute a very grave slander, but we both pray that she will not compel us to such steps. I can never forget who she is, and Una feels as I do. On several occasions relations of Mrs Harris's have told us that we had no right to encourage her to take an interest in Psychical Research, as they considered her unbalanced to the extent of being mentally deranged; this has lately weighed with us. I think her lack of balance and excitability are perhaps the kindest and truest explanation of what she has done.[20]

This sounds damning in its magnanimity, but John intended to be charitable. She was always ready to forgive if not forget.

A few days later a message came back to John through the Society assuring them of Sir Oliver's full support. In the event Cara never pressed her charges (though she never made a written retraction either). John's paper did not go to press until October, much to her exasperation, and finally appeared in the *Proceedings* in December 1919. All the signs are that the issue remained a sensitive one at the Society (in July 1919 Mrs Sidgwick instructed that the initials MVB in the paper be changed to AVB to protect Ladye's identity and avoid any possible offence to Cara).

Cara and John were permanently estranged by the episode, as were Dolly and John. John shed few tears for Cara. Only her devotion to Ladye's memory had kept the relationship alive. Dolly was another matter. John's ties to her were deep-rooted. They were cousins and John had brought her to England from America. John had begun as her lover, remained a close friend, and always been her protector. Bobby Clarke's career as a composer owed a good deal both to John's financial support and her talent as a lyricist. Dolly's ingratitude was hard to forgive under such circumstances and John finally cut off her allowance.

Dolly's conduct is puzzling. It seems that her jealousy of Una lay at the root of the matter, which suggests that she still possessed strong emotional feelings towards John. And yet there had been no ill-will between Dolly and Ladye, still less between Dolly and Phoebe. John admitted that she had only once lied to Ladye about an infidelity and one wonders if Dolly, at a time when John's relations with Ladye were under strain, had not found momentary consolation in renewed intimacy with John. It is equally conceivable that Dolly and Una were simply incompatible personalities. Dolly was conventional in the sense that she had neither occupation nor independent means. Una, by contrast, possessed recognized artistic talents and an intellect to match her beauty, as well as social self-assurance. She could be forthright and, where John was concerned, undoubtedly possessive. If, after Ladye's death, Dolly had somehow hoped to re-establish herself as foremost in John's affections, she must have quickly realized that in Una she confronted a formidable, and ultimately unbeatable, rival. Resentment was hard to conceal under such circumstances.

The row over John's research paper marked the first occasion on which her private life was exposed to public gaze. The episode made a deep impression on her, not so much because it threatened to expose her homosexuality but because it reinforced her view of human relations in general. If Helen Salter or Mrs Sidgwick ever wondered why John's friendship with Ladye and Una generated so much emotion, they did not say so. Their concern was exclusively to prevent the quarrel passing beyond the portals of Hanover Square.

John had won the argument against Cara but she saw, with characteristically clear-sighted fatalism, that the victory represented a kind of defeat. To Cara, still more to Dolly, she had extended the hand of friendship and protection only to have it spurned and to receive in return a slap in the face. Was this the fate of all good intentions, she wondered, to be misunderstood and to be used as a stick to beat their bearer? Only someone with an acute and fastidious sense of the ties of loyalty and trust could have agonized in this way. When John became a novelist, her work would revolve round the theme of rejection. Her favourite characters would be 'misfits' doomed to see their selflessness exploited and their virtue unrewarded. John's childhood laid the foundations for such a personal vision but her turbulent adult experience supplied the bricks and mortar.

Chapter Ten

A semblance of a life together began to emerge for John and Una. They tentatively embarked upon some joint entertaining at Grimston. Their first dinner guest was Una's friend Iris Tree, a daughter of the actor-manager Sir Herbert Beerbohm Tree. Iris was a large, strikingly blonde woman of some eccentricity (she would stand in the street and whistle for taxis through her fingers). 'We all laughed a great deal,' reported Una,[1] who wore a black evening gown with paste bandeau. John appeared in a blue and red tea-gown.

Bicycling became a fad after the doctors recommended they should take more exercise. John's birthday present to Una in March was a new Sparkwood model and even the Cub was equipped with a small cycle (John taught the child to ride it in one lesson, Una noted proudly). They now cycled to the shops in Windsor and even to Slough for early morning mass – though Una rang her bell so enthusiastically that John was obliged to discourage her.

They made friends with a couple in Datchet called Bill and Ida Temple. The Temples lived at 'Ormonde', a large house near Grimston, and had children of the Cub's age. Ida Temple held classes for local children at the house and Andrea was soon taking her lessons there. Inevitably, the Temples rapidly joined Una's list of child-minders.

The Temples also adored animals, owning a parrot and several dachshunds which Bill Temple trained for show. John's old collie, Rufus, had died in the New Year and she replaced him with a tiny Blenheim spaniel named Prudence. One of Una's three miniature terriers had also died in early 1918, and in June John presented her with a red dachshund bitch bought from Bill Temple. The dachshund was a show dog officially known as Champion Brandesburton Caprice, but Una rechristened it Thora and allowed it to sleep in her bed. Under Bill Temple's tutelage, Una started to learn how to train dogs for exhibition – and was rewarded in November when her terrier, Ben, won several prizes at the Canine Society Show. Bill Temple also advised them where to buy an African grey parrot when John thought they should obtain a replacement for Ladye's Cocky. In the end they opted for Harrods, always one of their favourite shops, purchasing a talkative bird called Karma which had formerly belonged to the music-hall comedian George Robey (the parrot said 'Good night' in a tipsy voice and made loud hiccupping noises).

No sooner had they started to put down roots than John became restless and wanted to move. Ostensibly, she now thought Grimston too small, but her real motivation was a desire to buy a country house of her own – a plan which she claimed Ladye had always harboured. It was Una who rented Grimston and John felt *she*, like most husbands, should be the property-holder of any home they shared. In the spring of 1918, they began inspecting houses in the Windsor area.

In May, however, their plans received a set-back when Troubridge wrote to Una saying he refused to move to Datchet and expected her to come back to him. This put Una on the spot, since it threatened both her relationship with John and their work with Mrs Leonard. The renewed pressure shattered Una's delicate nervous balance. In September, for the first time since 1914, she visited Dr Crighton-Miller and embarked on a new course of relaxation treatment. It proved only partially successful, for her chronic digestive troubles returned. A particularly sharp attack of colitis forced her to bed before supper on October 10: 'John sat with me & Karma & he talked & we read the Iliad,' the diary recorded.

Exactly a month later the Kaiser abdicated. The following day the Armistice was signed. The news was received in England with wild rejoicing. All work came to a halt and crowds surged through the streets of London commandeering omnibuses and throwing impromptu parties on their upper decks. John and Una heard the signal for the Cease Fire as they wandered across Sloane Square. They joined the cheering crowds which greeted the King and Queen on the balcony of Buckingham Palace, then went in search of a place for lunch. All the restaurants were packed, so they bought buns and munched them at the SPR's offices in Hanover Square. 'We then to Flat [Cadogan Court], to Crighton M who had gone on a bust – to Mace [their dentist], who hadn't, to station & Datchet & bed.'[2]

The war had been curiously remote from their lives and its end signalled not hope but renewed uncertainty. On December 4 they vacated Grimston and moved into temporary accommodation in another Datchet house, 'Swanmead'. Ten days later Troubridge wired from Salonika requesting that his great-coat be sent over to

Paris. The telegram threw Una into fresh anxiety and she rushed round to see Crighton-Miller. His calming influence helped her to come to a decision. She would not go back to her husband and on December 21 she wrote to Zip telling him so.

On January 2, 1919, the lovers inspected a strange house called 'Chip Chase', to the north of London at Hadley Wood. Mock battlements adorned its front – 'an unfortunate peculiarity', in Una's opinion – and from the outside it looked 'rather like the sort of castle that you would buy in Harrods' toy department'.[3] Yet it stood in beautiful wooded countryside and, as the prospectus boasted, Marble Arch lay only twelve miles away. The interior contained every modern convenience and comfort, and the very reasonable price included carpets, curtains and fixtures, 'the selection of which,' Una recalled, 'the owner, wisely mistrusting his own judgement, had entrusted to Burnetts of Covent Garden.'[4]

Last but not least, in nearby Oakleigh Park there was for sale a cottage which would suit Mrs Leonard. John made an offer on both properties – a measure of the extent to which their 'work' now dominated their existence. Una gaily descended on Maples, the department store, choosing 'my curtains' and purchasing a leopard-skin rug and a bear-skin rug. The only disappointment was a letter from the nanny on January 9 announcing she would not be continuing in their service. The 'upheavals' of life at Grimston had evidently taken their toll, for their maid Ivy had already given her notice in December. Finding and keeping servants would pose as much of a problem for John and Una as for John and Ladye.

On January 18 Una heard that Troubridge had been promoted to full admiral with seniority. His war record was distinguished and despite the *Goeben* incident, the Admiralty had to acknowledge it. The promotion made Troubridge even less inclined to accept the break-up of his marriage, for fear of provoking a public scandal. He wrote to Una from Paris stating that he would not let her leave him. She took to her bed at Cadogan Court, her temperature rising to 102°.

The admiral arrived back in England at the beginning of February. On the 3rd he turned up unexpectedly at Swanmead. John was working there alone while Una spent the day in London. When Una returned, she refused to see Zip except in John's presence. It proved an unpleasant meeting for both sides. Troubridge quickly realized that his wife was adamant about leaving him. Hurt and bewildered, he insisted on a proper legal separation. John put Una in touch with her father's solicitors, Hastie and Co.

A deed of separation was the only course open to Catholic couples wishing to part. It primarily took the form of a financial settlement, with arrangements for any children or property involved. Solicitors dealt with the matter out of court, which had the advantage of avoiding any unwelcome publicity. On February 6 John and Una saw Hastie to approve the terms. Before consenting, Una again consulted Crighton-Miller. As well as maintenance, the deed gave Una sole custody of the Cub. A story later circulated that John was named as co-respondent in the document. This was untrue. Unlike divorce, separation did not apportion blame for the break-down but simply acknowledged a fait accompli.

On February 8 Hastie's clerk telephoned to ask if Una would pay half the stamp duty required for the deed. Troubridge evidently intended not to pay a penny more than he had to, which Una thought showed a lack of magnanimity. However, she agreed and the clerk rang back ten minutes later to say that the admiral had signed. Una rushed round to Minna to announce the news, then to her sister Viola.

John and Una sat up late discussing the day's momentous change in their lives. 'A great peace & relief upon me,' Una noted. She finally signed the deed herself on February 10. 'Deo Gratias!' exclaimed the diary. Una had a serious talk with the Cub, putting her in the picture. Then she and John took Ladye's aspidistra to Wills and Segar to find out why it kept wilting. However dramatic the events in their lives, ordinary routine always quickly re-established itself.

The move to Chip Chase proceeded smoothly – too smoothly for John's liking, for she felt that it augured some disaster at the eleventh hour. Ladye assured her that nothing would go wrong because it was 'imperative' that the 'work' should go ahead undisturbed – implying that she was keeping a watchful eye on events from the 'other side'.[5]

Chip Chase was John and Una's first real home, for John finally relinquished Cadogan Court and Cheltenham Terrace was let to the Crighton-Millers. The two lovers were as excited as newly-weds, making numerous shopping expeditions to hunt for furniture. John's preference was for antique oak, which Una quickly grew to love too. They purchased old settles, a refectory table, and several ornate chests. John took over Ladye's resplendent four-poster bed from Cadogan Court. Una wanted something similar and they toyed with buying a beautiful Elizabethan specimen but in the end thought it too expensive. Some of their more unusual purchases John gave to Una as gifts: a chandelier for her bedroom, a wooden hutch for a pet rabbit, and an item described in the diary as a 'po-stand'.

Oak was not unsuited to Chip Chase's somewhat baronial air. John and Una particularly liked the large, high entrance hall with its minstrel's gallery and sweeping staircase. They decided to make this the dining-room – though they soon discovered they needed a screen to conceal diners from visitors at the front door. The two other most important rooms downstairs were an office for their secretary and a large study for John which opened out onto the garden. The drawing-room at Chip Chase seemed superfluous to them (an indication of how little they entertained), but once they had moved in, they came up with a typically idiosyncratic solution to the problem of this wasted space. They had linoleum laid on the floor and wooden partitions erected to turn the room into a makeshift kennels for the growing number of show dogs they were acquiring.

Upstairs the rooms were reconstructed to suit their personal requirements. An archway was built into the wall between Una's bedroom and the next room, which became their dressing-room and led by a connecting door into John's bedroom beyond. Both women were bad sleepers and their lifelong preference was for separate beds if not separate rooms. 'Nothing has ever altered my views,' wrote Una years later, 'that comfortable repose can rarely be achieved with one's head "pillowed upon another's breast" or with someone else's head riding upon one's bosom.'[6] However, they did like to be within easy reach of each other.

In March Hastie's informed Una that they had received a letter from Troubridge in which he threatened to go back on the separation agreement and regain custody of Andrea. The fate of the Cub had been preying on Zip's mind. The day that he had signed the deed of separation, he had also instructed his lawyers to redraw his Will. This declared that, in the event of Una predeceasing him, his sisters Laura Hope (Jaqueline's mother) and Violet Gurney would be appointed Andrea's guardians during the periods when he was absent on foreign service. He further stipulated that 'my said daughter shall under no circumstances be left under the guardianship or care of Marguerite Radcliffe (sic) Hall.'

John felt the letter was a bluff on Troubridge's part. So did Crighton-Miller. To make doubly sure, they consulted the eminent lawyer Sir George Lewis. He advised that Troubridge would not dare risk the public scandal that would ensue from his breaking a legal agreement. Reassured, John and Una went off to say confession at the

The infant John with (left to right) great-grandmother Elijah Jones, Granny Sarah Diehl, and mother Marie Diehl Visetti

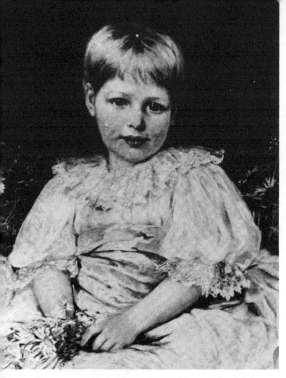

The portrait of John as a child as it looked after she had it altered to make her appear more boyish

John as a débutante

John with Jane Randolph and her two sons Thomas and Decan in sailor suits. Marie Visetti stands on the left in a flowered hat

Ladye at about the time that
John met her

Mabel Batten (Ladye) in full vocal
flight, as painted by John Singer
Sargent in 1897

The White Cottage,
Malvern Wells

Una Troubridge in 1915

John and Ladye on the verandah of the
White Cottage, with Cocky (parrot),
Claude (terrier) and Rufus (collie)

Mrs Osborne Leonard, the
celebrated medium

Ladye's tomb in Highgate Cemetery,
where John would also be buried.

Cara Harris, Ladye's daughter

Admiral Sir Ernest Troubridge,
K.C.M.G.

Una's daughter, Andrea

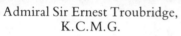

Toupie Lowther (second left, middle row) and members of her all-women ambulance
unit

Una and John at Crufts, 1923

Romaine Brooks

Colette (right) with Winnaretta Singer

Carmelite Priory in Kensington Church Street. Lewis was right. Troubridge took the matter no further. But it was not the last they would hear from him.

On April 12 they planned to leave the Cub with the Temples. At the last minute, the Temples were unable to take Andrea. A 'foolish & childish row' erupted between the lovers, John protesting that the child was always spoiling their arrangements and coming between them. This was unfair, of course, but the episode decided Una to send her daughter away to a boarding school, the Convent of the Holy Child at Mayfield in Sussex.

The Cub was proving to be a lively, intelligent child who had come out top among the children taught by Ida Temple at Ormonde. They noticed that she showed a precocious interest in ethical and religious matters: she had once remarked that 'we only had bodies so that other people should be able to see us!'[7] John was sufficiently struck by this aspect of the girl's development to suggest to Una that, if she turned out to be brainy, Andrea should be sent to university to receive a scientific education in order to become a good psychic researcher.

Almost every entry in Una's diary since she and John had started living together at Grimston began with the words: 'Breakfasted in our room.' 'Our room' meant the bedroom at Grimston, while at Chip Chase it designated their dressing-room. The practice had originated because either one or both of them were so frequently ailing that they preferred to dress and face the day only after they had eaten breakfast. This became a lifelong habit: breakfast was the time to open their post, read the papers (they took the *Daily Mail* and the *Daily Telegraph*), and discuss the day's arrangements. It was a sacrosanct hour when the intrusions of servants or callers (or even Andrea) were greeted with stern disapproval. Only the beloved dogs could claim their attention with impunity.

The establishment at Chip Chase was a grand one. As well as the Cub's nanny and a new personal maid, Rosina, the staff comprised four house servants and two gardeners. Miss Maclean arrived daily to type up any psychical work in progress. Then there was the usual menagerie of animals: Ben, Prudence and Thora were shortly joined by snub-nosed Brabançonnes, the first being Fitz-John Minnehaha, alias Tinkie, whom they liked so much that others of her breed soon followed – necessitating the drawing-room kennels. In Una's dressing-room two doves, Pelléas and Mélisande, billed and cooed and on the porch Karma chattered away, attracting the attention of the local urchins who, to John's annoyance, played in the vicinity of the house. In the sloping garden a donkey called Hilary stood tethered alongside hutches for the rabbit Lady Dionissia and a pet hedgehog named Warwick (after the King-Maker, who was buried in the locality).

Ladye's presence remained as conspicuous as ever. They had several new photographs of her framed and placed round the house. The Sargent portrait was hung in pride of place in the baronial hall. It was not long before they were wondering whether Ladye presided over Chip Chase in other manifestations. The first night Una heard a sound like a 'twang' coming from the landing outside her door. At a sitting with Mrs Leonard five days earlier, Ladye had forecast that she would make such a noise.

Back in March, when Una's nerves were still recovering from the drama over her separation from Zip, Crighton-Miller had suggested that she take a rest cure. Una agreed to the plan but treatment was postponed until after the move to Chip Chase. When the time finally came, Una was happily settling down in her first home with John and the idea of six weeks in a nursing home had lost its appeal. However, on June 2 she was admitted to Bowden House, the clinic which Crighton-Miller ran in Harrow-on-the-Hill. The Cub was despatched to Viola (who had just filed a petition for divorce against Maurice Woods) and Peggy Austin, an old friend of John's, came to stay at Chip Chase to keep her company.

John took over the writing of the diary in Una's absence. Una's diary was not a secret record. Like almost everything in her life, John had complete access to it. One wonders, in fact, to what extent the anguished tone of so many entries in the early, tortured stages of their affair was designed for John's benefit. The same might be said about the numerous flattering references to John.

The first night that Una was away at Bowden House, she and John tried communicating with each other telepathically – something they had planned in advance. The diary does not say if the results were successful, so they probably were not. On June 3, John noted: 'Minna rang up to say Una is now "A Lady". She meant that T[roubridge] had had K added to his threadbare CMG.' Una had no qualms about adopting the title of 'Lady Troubridge'. Such a handle still wielded a good deal of influence in those days, and in the future she never scrupled to use it ruthlessly if she thought it could help. The Troubridges were less impressed by Una's self-aggrandisement.

Only now, in Una's enforced absence, did John show how much she missed her. After a moonlight walk with Peggy in Hadley Woods one night, John noted: 'very lovely & longed for Squig to see it.'[8] When Peggy left, John felt lonelier than ever. She realized how much she had come to rely on Una. If Ladye had been cast in a motherly role, Una played the more wifely part. In fact, as the tribulations at Grimston had illustrated, Una was often no more domesticated than John (she admitted herself she found servants hard to handle)[9] and her real talents would blossom later as John's amanuensis. But her capacity for detail and a certain self-assured pragmatism, more worldly than John's, made her advice and support as a partner invaluable. Thus while she was away, John felt more at a loss than ever when the hot water supply at Chip Chase turned temperamental and one of the Brabançonnes developed mange and all the furniture had to be disinfected.

The lovers were soon reunited. Una hated the 'damned dull routine' of the clinic and suspected that some of the patients in the nursing home were 'loonies'. Crighton-Miller suggested a new course of treatment, but on June 20 Una informed him that she intended leaving the clinic the next day. The psychoanalyst was not amused. 'Very angry I think', recorded John, 'so was I but I concealed it – which he didn't.'

John can hardly have been too displeased. The episode demonstrated, as others had done in the past, the unshakeable primacy of her place in Una's affections. Even so admired and longstanding a confidant as Crighton-Miller could not hope to match John's influence when it came to the point. Alert to the position of rivalry in which she stood with men, John could take a special satisfaction in the eminent doctor's fall from grace so soon after Troubridge's.

In July Sir Oliver Lodge stayed at Chip Chase for a night. He was another man who had fallen from his pedestal in their eyes. While all their researches had tended to make them more cautious about mediumistic phenomena, Sir Oliver believed with ever increasing forthrightness that the evidence for survival was incontrovertible. 'He seems weak & odd in his head I think', Una wrote, '& rabid against all scientific criticism of spiritism – alas – we very distressed.'[10] The Society, however, continued to hold them in high regard. In the autumn Mrs Sidgwick proposed that one of them be co-opted onto the Council – 'We to decide which', wrote Una, adding: 'I persuaded John to accept – I should have been miserable otherwise attending meetings from which she was excluded.'[11]

For the most part the honeymoon period in their first home together was working well. But weeks of tranquillity and content could be punctuated by days of sudden, unexpected squalls. John's fits of depression were often the cause. Deep-seated frustrations welled up inside her, making her tetchy and unreasonable or so miserable that she would cry inconsolably and refuse to eat. Una tried her best to be patient and sympathetic at such times but as often as not John goaded her into angry exchanges and tearful recriminations. In the coolness that came after, the two women would solemnly discuss parting for ever, convinced they were hopelessly incompatible. But reconciliation invariably followed.

At one level these quarrels constituted a self-conscious ritual, as if their relationship required the spur of periodic emotional crises in order to thrive. On John's side, there was a more disturbing aspect to it. Like the religious hysteric, she sought pain to achieve ecstasy. She seemed to need to hurt and humiliate, not only Una but herself, before, in the heat of apology and forgiveness, she could love.

On September 19 Andrea started her first term at Mayfield and John and Una drove down with the child to see her settled in. Returning to Chip Chase the following day, they found the place had been burgled and all the dogs drugged. Ironically, they had recently been scouring pet shops for a guard dog. The thieves were caught within twenty-four hours and later sentenced to several years in gaol. Touched by the plight of one of the men's family, John gave his wife £5. A few days later they bought a Great Dane pup to guard the house. It became John's dog and she named it Olaf.

On December 1 John announced that she had obtained permission for Una to be buried with her and Ladye in the vault at Highgate. Una was in seventh heaven: 'I feel I can never be *really* unhappy again & thank God's mercy.' The following day, while a gale raged about the house, Una read aloud to John from Clemence Dane's recently published *A Regiment of Women*. Privately, they were beginning to display a conscious interest in the subject of lesbianism. As if to proclaim her allegiance to her regiment of women, Una bought herself a tortoise-shell monocle and, unlike John (who normally wore her eye-glass for reading only), began publicly to sport it in her eye. The gesture was typical of her theatrical inclinations – and, ironically, it made her appear even more severe than John.

Christmas 1919 proved the happiest the two women had known together. They attended a fancy-dress party as a Red Indian chief and his squaw, with the Cub wrapped in a tricolour to represent 'France' and the dog Tinkie decked out as Cupid. On New Year's Eve they flung wide the windows at Chip Chase and listened to the sound of the bells. 'John was sad & silent – & I think hated it', noted Una, 'still, I'm glad I saw it in with her & prayed that all good may come to her.' John often found it difficult to join in with other people's gaiety. A sense of detachment, of the hollowness of it all, overwhelmed her on such occasions.

Chapter Eleven

1919 marked an important year for John as a writer. After a long break of several years, she returned to prose. Not a short story this time, but a novel, her first attempt at this form since abandoning the abortive *Michael West*.

She actually started work on the book on Boxing Day. She kept at it in a continuous burst of inspiration for five days, Una reading aloud and commenting on each section as it was completed. The idea for the novel had in fact been brewing in John's mind for some time. Una first became aware of it during their third summer holiday in Lynton.

> We were staying, as on former occasions, at the Lynton Cottage Hotel and one evening, while we were at dinner, sitting at the end of the long room, we watched a couple of fellow guests making their way to the table: a small, wizened old lady and an elderly woman who was quite obviously her maiden daughter. The latter was carrying a shawl and a footwarmer and clutched a bottle of medicine. She fussed for several minutes round the old lady, putting the footwarmer under her feet, the shawl round her shoulders and inquiring if she felt warm enough and not too warm before she herself attempted to sit down. And John said to me in an undertone: 'Isn't it ghastly to see these unmarried daughters who are just unpaid servants and the old people sucking the very life out of them like octopi!' And then as suddenly: 'I shall write it. I shall write Heinemann's book for him and I shall call it *Octopi*.'[1]

The book would take well over two years to complete and would pass through many transformations. John was a writer who worked from inspiration. This was true of her song-writing and poetry and it remained true of her as a novelist. Regular daily hours at her desk, with so many words a day, did not suit her temperament. But she began to try to work like this. One practical result of the years of psychical research was that, for the first time in her life, she had grown accustomed to applying herself, to putting in long hours of writing up notes and dictating them to the typist. She tried to impose the same discipline upon herself as a novelist. As often as not the result proved disheartening. 'I have seen her', recalled Una, almost unaffected by incredibly long spells of continuous writing and I have also seen her grey with exhaustion when, determined to dispose of some situation, to complete some section or chapter, she has wrestled vainly, hour after hour, against an inspirational blackout.

Knowing the devastating effects on her health and nerves of such fruitless battling I have many times implored her to desist, to wait until the spirit really moved her, and occasionally I would prevail, but much more often I would be told I was a fool for my pains ... though later, when mournfully but firmly destroying the results of her persistence she would generously admit that I had been right![2]

Despite such admissions, John continued to wrestle with the blank page. The 'ordeal' of writing strangely appealed to her ascetic, obsessional temperament. In later years, as an established novelist, she began working into the night, sometimes all night – a practice which inevitably took a toll of her health. The image of the lonely writer closeted for hours in her study, burning the midnight oil, was one that John found heroic. Increasingly she came to regard the agony and exhaustion of marathon sessions at her desk as inseparable from a writer's achievement. This developed into what can only be described as a positive lust for suffering – which affected her writing for the worse.

According to Una, John's method of working never varied:

She never herself used a typewriter, in fact she never learned to type and the mere thought of dictating her inspiration to a typist filled her with horror. She always said that the written word was to her an essential preliminary and she wrote her work with pen or pencil, very illegibly, generally mis-spelt and often without punctuation. Sometimes she wrote in manuscript books but, especially in later years, often on loose sheets of sermon paper or indeed on paper of any kind, and to this day I will find scraps covered with sentences and sometimes discover 'try outs' on a bit of blotting paper or an old cardboard box.[3]

She was seriously ashamed of her spelling, which suggests her sensitivity to her lack of education, but never learned to correct her mistakes. Una was obliged to check all her letters for spelling and John insisted on rewriting them if any errors were found.

Once the first draft of a section was completed, John would have Una read it back to her. 'I would read and read again as often as she desired and as I read she would dictate alterations and corrections and these I would put down and incorporate in the next reading.' After this stage, the draft would be dictated to the typist, who was required to remain silent and motionless every time John paused – for words and phrases continued to be 'polished' even as she read them out. The typed script would then go back to Una for a further reading and,

almost invariably, further correction and amendment, before being
submitted to the typist for a second time.

This painstaking process might be repeated several times and take
many weeks. It required enormous tact and sympathy from Una, for
John was alert to any fall in her usual high standard of prose and her
confidence easily deserted her.

> After a day or night spent like Jacob, wrestling with the angel of her own
> uninspired obstinacy, she would hand me the resulting manuscript with an
> excellent simulation of self-confidence and command me to read aloud.
> This I would solemnly proceed to do with the best imitation I could of
> approval and appreciation. But in spite of my efforts there would be a
> growing flatness in my voice that infuriatingly confirmed her own infall-
> ible judgement; and having been asked whether I was tired and told that I
> was reading abominably and sometimes informed that my ineptitude was
> ruining the beauty of what I read, the manuscript would be snatched from
> my hands and torn to shreds or thrown into the fire. Physically and
> mentally exhausted, black depression would overwhelm her. She had seen
> the last of her inspiration, she would never write again . . . What she had
> written was as dead as Queen Anne, it would shame a child of seven . . .
> why had she ever imagined she could write? Nothing like this had ever
> happened to her before . . . and so and so on until, in spite of chronic
> insomnia, sleep would come, and days perhaps of stagnation and
> recuperation.[4]

Writer's 'block' and John's inexperience with the novel form were not
the only reasons that *Octopi* proved slow to materialize. Hardly had
1920 begun before ominous storm clouds gathered on the horizon.
The source of the trouble lay, as so often before, with Troubridge.
Shortly after receiving his KCMG, the admiral had been appointed
president of the Inter-Allied Danube Commission, an international
board set up under the terms of the peace agreement to ensure the
victors' control of this important water-way. The Commission's
headquarters lay in Paris, with a general secretariat in Budapest, so for
the rest of 1919 Troubridge's duties took him abroad again. He
returned to England on leave in December.

In January he called at his club, the Travellers', where he
encountered St George Lane Fox-Pitt. Fox-Pitt was a member of the
SPR Council, having first joined the Society in 1883. He and Troubridge had met on previous occasions and discussed the subject of
psychical research in the light of Una's involvement in the Society.
This had been before the admiral's separation and at that time he had
adopted a rather amused attitude to spiritualism. His view was very

different now. Fox-Pitt had obtained him a copy of John and Una's lecture on their sittings with Mrs Leonard. The admiral was angered by what he read. He called the paper 'immoral' and declared that his wife's interest in such matters had adversely affected her mind and caused the break-up of their marriage. He made it plain that Miss Radclyffe Hall had somehow exploited the Society's authority to gain a pernicious influence over Una for her own purposes. He left little doubt in Fox-Pitt's mind as to what those purposes were and expressed his outrage that the Society should countenance such goings-on.

Fox-Pitt came away from this meeting deeply disturbed. Even before hearing Troubridge's outburst, he had had his own reservations about John's paper. Though he had been a member of the Society almost from the beginning (and was one of the longest serving Council members), he also professed Buddhist beliefs and was violently opposed to the Society's current preoccupation with spirit survival after death. He took exception even to the term 'spirit', claiming that the very notion of a spirit world was a pernicious delusion responsible for much of humanity's greed and selfishness.[5]

In December formal notice had been given of the intention to co-opt John onto the Society's Council, the election to take place on January 28. Troubridge's allegations confirmed Fox-Pitt's view that she was not a fit person to receive such an honour. On January 14 he therefore went to the Society's offices and confronted the Secretary, Isobel Newton. He called John 'a grossly immoral woman' and repeated what Troubridge had told him at the Travellers' Club. The following day Fox-Pitt returned to Hanover Square and took the matter up with Mrs Salter. He again called John 'thoroughly immoral', explaining that she had once lived with Mrs Batten, whom he characterized as 'a most objectionable person'. He expressed his determination to oppose John's election to the Council, if necessary by forcing the issue into the open.

The first John and Una heard of this incident was when Mr J. G. Piddington, the Society's Treasurer, telephoned Chip Chase on January 17. He advised them to get in touch with the SPR solicitor, Mr Scott. 'Long interview with Mr Scott anent* Pitt Fox (sic),' the diary recorded the same day. There followed forty-eight hours of hectic activity. Una went through all her recent letters from Troubridge and typed up extracts from them at John's dictation. They saw their solicitor, Sir George Lewis, on several occasions. On the 22nd he

*'(mainly Scot.) prep., in a line with: against: towards: in regard to, concerning, about.' Chambers Twentieth Century Dictionary 1982. A usage much favoured by R.H., it often appears in her fiction.

showed them copies of statements which he had taken from Miss Newton and Mrs Salter. John and Una went round to the Society the same day and obtained further clarification of the matter from the two women themselves, Mrs Salter coming back to Chip Chase for dinner.

John felt shocked not simply for herself but on behalf of Ladye. The implication that Ladye was a notorious and perverted woman was not a charge that John could ignore, especially since Ladye could not answer for herself. Loyalty alone dictated that she act against Fox-Pitt. However, she wished to avoid legal action if possible and Sir George Lewis wrote to Fox-Pitt demanding that he withdrew his slander and apologise. Fox-Pitt was unrepentant. He expressed his amazement at their insolence and, adopting a position that would remain his defence throughout the affair, pointed out that in calling John 'immoral' he referred not to her personal morals but to her research paper.

This was an extraordinary line to take. Although it conformed to Fox-Pitt's longstanding views on psychical research, it was hardly what he had meant when he spoke to Miss Newton and Mrs Salter. Having threatened legal action, John now had no alternative but to sue Fox-Pitt for slander. The prospect was alarming, as much for Una as for John. In his allegations to Mrs Salter, Fox-Pitt had assured her that Troubridge would be quite prepared to back up his charges against John and Ladye in public. Even if this assurance was hollow, which seemed likely, the admiral would have to be sub-poenaed by John to give evidence. Una had no illusions that this invited a public post-mortem on her marriage. 'Where should I be in this terrible trouble without [John's] devotion and friendship,' she wrote plaintively.[6]

The case did not come up until the autumn. In the meantime, dogs were becoming a growing preoccupation. In February Olaf the Great Dane, still only a year old, had to be shot by the vet when it developed an epileptic condition. John was heartbroken. 'I can suddenly remember John's face as we sat waiting for the sound of that shot,' Una wrote many years later.[7] In April Una's dachshund Thora developed incurable follicular mange and had to be put down too. Both women wept miserably.[8]

But owning dogs had its compensations too. Breeding and exhibiting was now an integral part of their life. They attended together all the main dog shows in and around London, kitting themselves out in fedoras, capes, boots and riding breeches. They specialized in Braban-çonnes, or griffons as they are usually called, and they brought to their new-found hobby all the zeal and thoroughness which had characterized their psychical work. They quickly excelled, bringing home trophies from almost every contest they entered. Griffons are delicate, neurotic small dogs providing many difficulties for the breeder. When the drawing-room kennel at Chip Chase was full, the mess and the noise (not to speak of the stench) frequently got on their nerves – John's in particular – provoking further 'upheavals' between them. On one occasion Tinkie disgraced herself by having an attack of diarrhoea in Sir George Lewis's office.

John and Una presented a formidable, somewhat intimidating couple in the arcane world of professional exhibiting. They did not hesitate to criticize other dog owners whose standards of love and care fell short of their own. They were against anthropomorphism. 'One must bear in mind,' declared Una, 'that the dog has as good a right to be purely canine as the human being has to be purely human.' The central question was 'whether the dog has as good a cause for satisfaction in his owner as that owner has cause for gratification in ownership'.[9] To John and Una, the owners were more often found wanting.

On March 29 they lunched at the Savoy with 'Toupie' Lowther. Toupie was about thirty and had first been introduced to John by Ladye in their Cadogan Square days. Ladye was very fond of her and used to call her 'Toupée'. Her real name was Barbara and she was the eldest daughter of the sixth Earl of Lonsdale. A bulky, tall woman of extremely masculine appearance, she had a considerable reputation as a fencer and tennis player. A story about her, probably apochryphal, told how she was once arrested at the Franco-Italian frontier for masquerading as a man. On the return journey she wore skirts but was again arrested – for masquerading as a woman. Her athletic prowess followed in the family's sporting tradition, for her aunt had been a well-known horsewoman and crack shot while her uncle, the fifth Earl, had excelled as a long-distance walker and boxer (he gave his name to the Lonsdale belt). In 1914 Toupie married Lieutenant-Colonel James Innes. Not long afterwards he sued her for divorce.

The war saw Toupie come into her own. In 1917 she and Miss 'Desmond' Hackett formed an ambulance unit which, despite initial opposition from the authorities, eventually operated alongside the French army on the Compiègne battle front. The unit consisted of twenty cars and some twenty-five drivers, all women, most of them British but also seven Americans and one Frenchwoman. They took part in the big retreat of June 1918 and the subsequent advance of August, ferrying thousands of casualties from the battlefield to dressing stations. The unit was mentioned in despatches and five of its drivers, Toupie among them, won Croix de Guerre.[10]

Toupie's war experiences marked the high point of her life. Interviewed later by *The Times*, she said: ' "It was a wonderful time. We were often 350 yards from the German lines awaiting the wounded, under camouflage. Out of it all we carry the most profound respect and admiration for the 'poilu', the most courteous and gallant gentleman imaginable." ' When the unit finally disbanded, the French commander had told her: ' "If there is another war, mon lieutenant, I shall send for you.' "[11] Toupie lived for that day but it would not come again.

Following the Savoy lunch, John and Una began to see Toupie regularly – their friendships always went in intense bursts. John admired Toupie as a woman who had proved herself the equal of any man, not only in sports but on the battlefield. But for Ladye, John's war might have been like Toupie's. She deeply envied the younger woman's service in action, with all the opportunities for honour and courage which it had afforded. Only on getting to know Toupie better did she realise that this model of gallantry was in fact deeply insecure, afflicted by financial and emotional worries that made her tiresomely clinging and chronically self-absorbed.

In the spring and summer of 1920, however, John and Una thought her 'a dear'. They were amused by the imitation flowers she wore in her buttonhole and impressed that she was one of the first women in England to have ridden a motorbike. Una started work on a bust of Toupie in uniform intended for the Imperial War Museum. Toupie came for weekends at Chip Chase accompanied by her dog (called 'The Priest') and would appear at dinner attired like a Chinese mandarin in black satin trousers. Lunches with Toupie at the Savoy or the Hyde Park Grill became a regular fixture, followed by tea at her flat in Egerton Mansions at the top of the Brompton Road.

In August all three women went to Brighton for the summer break. John and Una put up at the Prince's Hotel while Toupie stayed at her mother's house in Hove. Toupie's current girlfriend, Nellie Rowe, who had been much in evidence in previous months, joined John and Una at the hotel. However, the situation proved awkward, for Toupie was trying to wind down the affair. She liked to boast slyly of her 'conquests', but the truth was that her love-life was a mess. In Brighton she became so intent on keeping Nellie at arm's length that John and Una hardly ever saw the two women together. Matters reached a head when Nellie retired to bed early one evening, at which point John and Una crept out of the hotel to join Toupie at some night spot: 'we all talked & howled till 1.30 am!'[12] Nellie finally got the message and left Brighton the next day.

Motor cars were one of Toupie's passions. While in Brighton she took John and Una round various garage showrooms, with the result that John ended up buying a black Singer Saloon as a present for Una (who thought it looked like a 'little bug beetle'). Before taking delivery of the vehicle, John drove it on a test run accompanied by the garageman – and managed to back it into a fence. For the next two weeks the three women did little else but drive and tinker with their cars, for Toupie had bought herself an Overland tourer. Picnics provided the favourite excuse for taking out the cars onto the Sussex downs, where Toupie explained the finer points of the combustion engine and gave John and Una driving lessons. They soon found Toupie could be difficult. She was sensitive to imagined slights and there would be days when they had to calm her out of a 'puerile rage' or avoid her black mood. On one occasion they sneaked off without her to a dog show in Guildford – where they bought a successor to Thora, a red dachshund called Thorgils of Tredholt, whom they came to know as plain Thor.

In the autumn the Singer started giving trouble. The gear-box played up and they had to ring Toupie for advice ('We howled with mingled despair & amusement,' Una noted).[13] They now affectionately called Toupie 'Brother' and referred to her as 'him'. Despite Brother's expertise, the car continued to break down and they finally sold it in early October for £400. Psychical research no longer claimed all their attention. They were socializing more and having a determinedly good time. 'We spent nearly all day preparing for the unheard of event of dining out decolletées!' gushed the diary[14]. They attended the much talked about production of *The Beggar's Opera* by Nigel Playfair at the Lyric Theatre, Hammersmith, and 'adored' it. Brother stayed the weekend of October 23 along with her cousin Claude Lowther ('Claudie'), a dandyish figure in his late forties who owned Hurstmonceux Castle and was an old friend of Ladye's. The weather turned wet and they all remained indoors playing games, mainly trials of strength to humour Toupie. When the rain held off, Brother had them help her wash and polish her car. The two Lowthers were again at Chip Chase the following weekend. This time table-turning kept them amused: 'no results – but much laughter.'[15] Toupie stayed a night a week later. It was her third consecutive weekend with them and the novelty of her presence was beginning to wear a bit thin. 'Toupie had the usual scare over her car & we tested it *all* the morning!'[16]

The hectic merry-making of October had something of the air of a last fling, for in November their thoughts were overshadowed by the approaching slander action against Fox-Pitt. On Sir Oliver Lodge's advice, John had reluctantly requested that her co-option onto the SPR Council be postponed until after the case. As consultations with Sir George Lewis and John's counsel Sir Ellis Hume Williams proceeded, they studiedly avoided any contact with Troubridge. On one occasion when they dropped the Cub off at Cheltenham Terrace for a weekend with her father, the admiral himself appeared and tried to speak with them, but they turned their backs on him and hurried away.

The strain on them began to tell. On November 1 they both purchased, for luck, statuettes of John's patron saint St Anthony and several St Christopher medals. Una's nerves again plagued her and she frequently felt nauseous and tearful. Three days before the case opened they went to have their hair done at the salon in the Great Central Hotel and caused a scene when Thor was refused entry.

Finally, at midday on November 18, the proceedings got under way. Sir Ellis Hume Williams began by outlining the background to the case. He explained how John and Una had become friends, how they had joined the SPR, and how they had come to write their paper. He naturally gave no hint of the homosexual nature of the two women's relationship. Turning to Fox-Pitt's slanderous statements to Miss Newton and Mrs Salter, Sir Ellis declared they could only be taken to refer to his client's sexual immorality, namely that she was 'addicted to unnatural vice', and as such constituted 'as horrible an accusation as could be made against any woman in this country'.[17]

John was the first witness. She was soberly dressed in a long dark jacket and skirt with a pale stock and high stiff collar. She was cross-examined by Fox-Pitt, who had elected to conduct his own defence. Fox-Pitt contended that the statements attributed to him were incorrect, that they were uttered under privileged circumstances, and that they referred solely to John's abilities as a psychical researcher. He therefore sought to undermine her credibility as a scientific investigator.

Have you had any training in science? – Not as you understand it, only in psychology.
Do you know anything of physiology? – I have read something.
Do you know anything of physiology in relation to psychology? – I know it in connexion with the Society for Psychical Research.

The defendant [i.e. Fox-Pitt]:- This paper of yours is scientific rubbish, quite unworthy of the society, and its publication is extremely harmful. It has produced a condition of mind which I consider immoral.[18]

At which point the Lord Chief Justice intervened to remark that the charge against Fox-Pitt went rather further than the issue of whether the paper harmed the public interest. In fact, the Lord Chief Justice showed a marked inclination to intervene, largely with amused or sceptical comments which, to the delight of the public gallery, drew attention to the more ludicrous aspects of spiritualism. As Fox-Pitt tended to phrase his questions in the arcane terminology of psychical research and with all the blithe unawareness of an absent-minded professor lecturing to the converted, he became something of a butt for such comments, to the detriment of his case. But the experience proved hardly less pleasant for John, for Fox-Pitt singled out those references in her paper which, taken out of context, sounded particularly absurd.

His Lordship:- How does a spirit bathe? I see later on that the lady has a private bathing pool in the spirit world. (Laughter) You must bear in mind that hearsay evidence is not admissible.[19]

John was not amused.

The day's proceedings were adjourned at 5 pm. That night John and Una lay awake into the small hours discussing the case (they often left open the door which connected their bedrooms). Una was due in the witness box the following day and in the morning she bought herself a veil to go with the mauve silk hat and heavy brown cloak she was wearing.

Asked by Sir Ellis whether their paper intended to show that they had actually communicated with the dead, Una made it clear that it expressed no such opinion. It merely recorded what had been said at the séances and remarked upon the apparent coincidences thrown up. This was the careful answer of a good scientific investigator. Fox-Pitt pursued the point when he came to cross-examine. He insisted that the paper offered evidence of a spirit world. Una replied that it was only evidential in the sense that the descriptions of Ladye were characteristic of her when she was alive. But Fox-Pitt pressed his attack home by pointing out that Ladye's appearance purported to have changed in the beyond, implying that a whole after-life existed. This was pushing Una onto dangerous ground, but relief came in the form of a further interruption from his Lordship who sought to know whether Feda was the medium or someone else. Una explained, somewhat cryptically, that when Feda spoke of the medium's body, she spoke as of another person, to which the judge retorted: 'I don't say that I understand, but I see what the witness means.'[20]

Thereafter Fox-Pitt spoilt his case by a descent into incomprehensible jargon, prompting the judge to disallow any further detailed questioning about psychic research. He insisted that the court concern itself with the accepted meaning of the term 'immoral'. Here Fox-Pitt stood on shakier ground, especially after Miss Newton and Mrs Salter both testified that they had no doubt that the charges he made to them about John related to her relationship with Ladye and not to her lecture. Mrs Salter made the point that when Fox-Pitt had called John 'a thoroughly immoral woman', he had shown some embarrassment. Fox-Pitt continued, against interruptions from his Lordship, to assert his own definition of 'immoral' (and resorted to a dictionary), but under cross-examination did admit that Troubridge had told him Mrs Batten's name was linked with that of several *men*! He claimed, finally, that Miss Newton and Mrs Salter were part of a conspiracy against him within the Society because of his opposition to 'spiritism'. He labelled this conspiracy a 'junta' and, to the amusement of the court, described it as 'a breathing together' which produced lies about him.

Despite this extraordinary performance from Fox-Pitt, the verdict proved close. The jury believed that the statements attributed to the defendant were correct, but they accepted his claim that they were not intended to apply to John's personal character. This was tantamount to a decision against John. However, her junior counsel, Mr St John Field, argued that the question of intent was immaterial. The Lord Chief Justice agreed and instructed the jury accordingly. They finally returned at 7.30 pm with a verdict in John's favour and an award of £500 in damages. 'Home to a much relieved & happy evening,' wrote Una.[21]

The victory, of course, was a fairly hollow one and John and Una knew it. Though they could be thankful that no detailed probing had taken place into either John's past relations with Ladye or the break-up of Una's marriage (in the end Troubridge had not been called as a witness), the case left no one deceived as to what Fox-Pitt had really meant when he called John 'grossly immoral'. Moreover, the Society and its works had come through the proceedings with dignity badly mauled.

This was the end of Fox-Pitt's association with the SPR. In December he resigned both from the Council and as a member. The usual expression of regret in such circumstances was not recorded on this occasion. Instead, a vote of confidence was proposed in Miss Newton and Mrs Salter and carried unanimously.[22] Fox-Pitt had a history of entering in where others feared to tread – and usually on insufficient evidence. He had bankrupted himself in a series of lawsuits defending his claim to have invented the electric light. During his Buddhist phase, he joined the Theosophical Society but soon found himself at the centre of acrimonious wranglings which led to a fine for assault against a fellow-member. He had once been married to the daughter of the Marquess of Queensberry, the one who clashed with Oscar Wilde. The marriage was annulled, allegedly on the grounds of Fox-Pitt's impotence. This humiliation may have turned him against women in general and fuelled his defiance of the small group of formidable females who now dominated the SPR's affairs.[23]

The slander action had a postscript. True to form, Fox-Pitt decided to fight on and gave notice to appeal on the grounds that insufficient attention had been paid to his defence of privilege. The appeal came to court in March 1921. Fox-Pitt was represented, according to Una, by 'a common young man who used many dishonest shifts'.[24] However, he won his point and a new trial was ordered, but Sir George Lewis advised John not to go on.

The Fox-Pitt case confronted John in stark terms with the dilemma of the homosexual woman: however much she chose to be herself in private, society's attitude forced her to adopt a deceitful standard to defend her integrity in public. Indeed, one of the ironies of the trial was the spectacle of Fox-Pitt desperately trying to avoid the obvious implication of his words under pressure from an opposing counsel who had raised the bogey of 'unnatural vice'. Since John regarded her sexual orientation as neither a vice nor unnatural, winning on such terms deeply troubled her conscience.

She was not yet ready to speak what she felt, but she was already displaying her defiance of convention in other ways. Throughout 1920 her appearance and habits underwent a conspicuous change. Her clothes became increasingly masculine. To the plain tailored jackets, ties and skirts (she did not adopt trousers until the 1930s, like most women) were added men's socks with garters, heavy, thick-soled shoes with a broad toecap, and (in winter) spats. In August she was fitted for a brocade smoking jacket. To go with this she bought two pipes at Dunhill's and Una gave her a tobacco jar for Christmas. Pipe-smoking was a purely private indulgence but she soon gave it up when it made her tongue and lips sore and returned to the strong, unfiltered cigarettes she habitually smoked.

In November she asked Ladye if she could cut her hair. This time reluctant permission came from the 'other side.'[25] She did not take the momentous step, however, until after the court case, perhaps to avoid undue comment. On December 17 Una's diary noted: 'after tea I cut off John's hair & we washed it.' The next day it was properly trimmed and waved at the hairdresser's. In place of the luxuriant plaits, she now sported a uniform short-back-and-sides. The severity was relieved by striking kiss curls which grew down the side of the face and projected forward to her cheekbones in an exotic imitation of sideburns. Her slim, neat figure and her flair for the theatrical touch always ensured her style remained wholly original. She and Una loved clothes such as capes and tricorn hats which recalled a more romantic era and they had taken to buying garments at Nathan's, the theatrical costumiers. After having her hair cut, John wondered whether to order the sort of coat which a Spanish grandee would have worn in the seventeenth century. In the end she decided it might look too much like fancy dress.

Chapter Twelve

In December John had put Chip Chase on the market. They were bored with its dull suburban neighbourhood and frustrated by the twelve-mile drive into the heart of London – 'a dreary penance of tramlines and traffic', as Una described it.[1] The house was anyway too big for them and, after the expense of the Fox-Pitt case, the upkeep of so many servants seemed a wasteful extravagance. John finally accepted £5,000 for the house and they rented a furnished flat at No 7, Trevor Square, opposite Harrods and a short walk from Toupie's.

In January the Cub fell into disgrace for an undisclosed 'naughtiness' which had led to her temporary suspension from school. The poor child was lectured sternly by John and Una over a forty-eight hour period before being forgiven. In fact, Una could be proud of her daughter's record. At the end of the summer term of 1921 Andrea came home with two prizes, a good conduct medal and first-class exam honours. At ten the child possessed all the natural talent and cheerful resilience that Una had shown at a similar age. They were qualities she needed, for the impression remains that she did not always get the encouragement and attention she deserved. Una rarely visited her at school and her parents' separation subjected the child to pressures which the diary hints at only too clearly. When in the summer of 1921 Una announced a long autumn trip to Europe with John, the Cub was visibly upset and returned to school at the end of August in floods of tears. 'Poor lamb' commented Una, and John sent her a photograph album, but once the child went out of sight she was largely out of mind too.

Despite Fox-Pitt's resignation, the ripples caused by the affair were still being felt at the SPR. Some members considered that, though John had been vindicated, the court case had damaged the Society's good name sufficiently to warrant keeping her off the Council. As a result, her name was left off the agenda of the annual general meeting due for January 31. On learning this, Una immediately telephoned Isobel Newton and threatened her with their resignations. John's name was restored and Mrs Sidgwick duly proposed her co-option – which finally took place at a Council meeting on February 7.

New friends helped John and Una to take their minds off these pressures. In November 1920 Toupie had introduced them to Gabrielle Enthoven. Like Toupie, Gabrielle had also known Ladye well. Her husband, Major Charles Enthoven, had died the same year as George Batten, and Gabrielle had turned her hand to amateur acting and playwrighting. In 1916 John, Ladye and Una had attended her play *Ellen Young* at the Savoy, but she was best known for an adaptation of d'Annunzio's poetic drama, *The Honeysuckle*, which first appeared in 1915. During the war she took charge of the War Refugee Committee and, from 1916, worked with the Red Cross to supervise the welfare of British prisoners-of-war in Germany, Turkey and Russia. In recognition of these services she was awarded the OBE. Now in her fifties, she was a big, broad-faced woman, almost Slavic in features, with the air of someone used to having her commands obeyed.

Through Toupie and Gabrielle, John and Una encountered a circle of women who were united by their homosexuality and their shared wartime experiences. As often as not we know no more than their nicknames – such as the tempestuous couple Poppy and Honey, who became regular dinner guests at Trevor Place, who loved dancing till the small hours, and who frequently caused scenes with their violent quarrels. Others, like Enid Elliot and Eileen Plunkett, had been drivers serving in Toupie's ambulance unit.

In the company of these friends John and Una began to socialize in a way that had been inconceivable a year before. After the war years of austerity, London was now abandoning itself to a hectic gaiety. Jazz, of the twanging banjo and relentless rhythm variety, was all the rage and with it came a bewildering series of jerky dance fashions with names like the 'Jog Trot', the 'Vampire', the 'Elfreda' and the 'Camel Walk'. The Licensing Act of 1921 partially lifted the wartime restrictions on drinking hours and restaurants began introducing dance-floors. Those who wanted to escape the limitations on drinking and dancing could now go to private night-clubs, which were invariably expensive, however squalid, but always packed and popular. In the summer of 1921 John and Una were often to be found at the Orange Tree Club, where they would dine and dance the night away with Toupie, Poppy, and the others. The sight of women dancing together was not unusual, a hangover from the war kept alive by the continuing scarcity of eligible men.

In May John and Una befriended two established female novelists who, in their different ways, were to influence John's career as a writer. The first of these was Violet Hunt. John had first met Violet during the war, and sought her advice at about the time she was writing her short story, 'The Woman in the Crêpe Bonnet'. By this date Violet was a successful novelist with a dozen titles to her name, including the acclaimed volume of short stories *Tales of the Uneasy*. She had drifted into writing through journalism. She later became a reader for Ford Madox Hueffer's *English Review* and claimed to have 'discovered' D. H. Lawrence. She went to live with Hueffer, whose wife refused to divorce him, and was involved in an unpleasant libel case when the wife sued a magazine for referring to Violet as Mrs Hueffer. Shortly after this Hueffer (who now called himself Ford) fell in love with someone else and by the end of the war their liaison had stumbled towards estrangement. Ford was obviously a difficult man to live with – Richard Aldington said that he 'drew no hard and fast distinctions between writing a novel and living one'[2] – but Violet remained a staunch admirer of his work (his novel *Ladies Whose Bright Eyes* was dedicated to her). She was essentially an Edwardian grande dame of letters, still very good-looking (she was fifty-five in 1921), amusing, distracted and loquacious, with a certain reputation for innocent tactlessness. She held distinguished literary parties at her home Holly Lodge on Campden Hill, where a bust of Ezra Pound by Gaudier Brzeska stood on a pedestal in the garden. Like many other women writers of the period, she had been a suffragette, standing with her fellow-novelist, May Sinclair, in Kensington High Street making collections for the cause.

Violet is first mentioned in the diary on March 16, when John and Una met her while exercising the dogs in Hyde Park, in the early morning – to avoid the 'dirty folk', as Una put it. They invited her to dinner and she stayed till after midnight confiding to them her 'troubles', namely the whole sad Madox Ford saga. She returned the invitation in June and presented them with several copies of Ford's novels, including *The Good Soldier* – which Ladye had read to John in 1915 and pronounced 'a really clever book'.[3]

The second novelist who came into their lives at this time was Ida Wylie. Born in Australia, she had spent most of her childhood in England and Europe, ending up (after Cheltenham Ladies College) at a finishing school in Karlsruhe. Her mother had died when she was very small and relations with her father became increasingly strained as she grew up, not least because of Ida's manifest homosexuality. She stayed for eight years in Germany after completing her education, an experience which she later turned into her first really successful novel *Towards Morning*, published in 1920. She was an active suffragette and did war work in France. In 1917 she went to America, where she was highly regarded as a short story writer. She put down roots there and returned to England only at intervals. Ida was a spirited, volatile woman, promiscuous in her affections (Una thought her pathologically unfaithful), with a love of motoring, riding, and – to John and Una's delight – English bull-terriers.

In June they dined with Ida and met her lover, Rachel Barrett. Ida drove them home afterwards in her Singer, nicknamed 'Fiametta'. The experience was not one they would forget for Ida, a notoriously reckless driver, scared them out of their wits – which prompted her to write:

> I have mentioned your caustic criticisms on my driving to other friends whom I fondly believed to be admirers & the ice having been broken it appears that everybody felt that they had said goodbye to this earth when they came on board. This has shocked me very much. Since then Fiametta and I go about with our tails between our legs. We sidle ... up to street corners & peer round honking hideously throughout, and then make a dash across with nervous squeaks of thankfulness.[4]

Despite the 'caustic criticisms', they were fond of Ida and she of them. 'I count meeting you both as one of the really nice things that have happened to me,' she told them.[5] She was someone with whom they could talk easily about writing and the current state of the market – which interested John as a fledgling novelist. Ida recommended them Sheila Kaye-Smith's *Joanna Godden*, which had just appeared, and A. S. M. Hutchinson's *If Winter Comes*, which she said she had wept copiously over. Her verdict on Sinclair Lewis's American bestseller *Main Street*, however, was: 'frightfully long & dull in parts'. About here own work Ida was always modest. 'It makes me blush every time I think of it,' she wrote to them, 'It's most painful – this really knowing what's what & not being able to live up to it.'[6]

At a party given by Toupie in June, John and Una met the American painter, Romaine Brooks. In the course of the following weeks they spent a lot of time in her company. A resolutely independent woman, both in means and outlook, Romaine was at forty-seven firmly established as a portraitist with a wholly original style. Her route to fame, however, had not been easy and she would always be a natural rebel against convention.

Like John, Romaine had seen little of her father after her parents' early divorce. She had also suffered miseries at the hands of a bullying mother who had time only for her mentally deranged son. Unlike John, though, Romaine had little respect for her father, who was an alcoholic. 'Belonging to one parent was a disagreeable experience,' she once wrote, 'I had no desire to belong to another.'[7] When her mother died, leaving Romaine a fortune, she gravitated to the artistic colony on Capri, where she met and married the homosexual poet John Ellingham Brooks. Intended as a marriage of platonic companionship, it became insupportable to Romaine when Brooks proved more conventional than he liked to appear by disapproving of her newly shortened hair and masculine shoes and trousers. They separated (Brooks extracting an annuity of £300 from her) and Romaine fled to London and Paris.

In 1910 Paris hosted her first solo exhibition. The Italian poet Gabriele d'Annunzio extravagantly admired her painting and the two of them formed a passionate, ambiguous friendship that lasted until his death. Romaine made him the subject of a number of memorable pictures. She also painted Jean Cocteau, the elegant Russian dancer Ida Rubinstein (who fell in love with her), and the remarkable American poet Natalie Clifford Barney. In 1915 Natalie became the central figure in Romaine's life, the two of them embarking on a love affair and a friendship that would span some fifty years. Both were wealthy American expatriates who had adopted France as their mother country. Their temperaments admirably complemented each other. Natalie was highly sophisticated, self-assured, witty, erudite. Romaine, by contrast, was moody, withdrawn, mistrustful, quirky, and singlemindedly dedicated to her painting. She saw herself as the embattled artist, noble in isolation and fiercely self-sufficient. 'One should be a slave to nothing except one's toothbrush,' was her motto.

Romaine fascinated John because she represented that awe-inspiring figure, the complete artist. She was someone whom John was not – a free spirit, apparently untrammelled by personal ties and obligations. While John envied such blitheness, she also found it difficult to tolerate in any but small doses since her somewhat humourless sense of conventionality was easily offended.

For the moment, however, Romaine added a touch of exoticism to John and Una's life, exciting them with talk of holidays abroad. The couple had been thinking of spending the summer in Italy and Romaine suggested they visit her in August on the island of Capri, where she kept a house called the Villa Cercola. The villa was ideal for dancing, for it possessed one of the few wooden floors on the island. Romaine owned a Decca portable gramophone and employed a Chinese manservant to play it, seductive Oriental melodies such as 'Ah Fim Loo' and 'Shanghai Lullaby' issuing from its cavernous speaker. Capri provided a unique haven for artists and homosexuals alike and Romaine was only one of a number of flamboyant women who helped to give the island its brilliant and exotic reputation. The tall, deep-voiced pianist Renata Borgatti gave fortnightly concerts at her studio on the Punta Tragara, playing 'with divine irresponsibility and some wrong notes, because she never practised enough.'[8] Renata had a tempestuous affair with another siren on the island, Mimi Franchetti, a noted society beauty who wore short pleated skirts and bow ties, sported a cane, and smoked cigarettes in a long jade holder. More extraordinary still was the Marchesa Casati, who arrived on Capri in the summer of 1920 with a gilded gazelle, a blue parrot, and a giant negro servant attired in blue plush tailcoat and breeches. Compton Mackenzie once arrived at her villa to find her lying on a bearskin rug completely naked.[9] Romaine described it all to John and Una in the same nostalgic tones that Faith Compton Mackenzie was to use when she recalled her own sojourn on Capri in the summer of 1919: it was a time 'for divertimento, for bathing at the Bagno Tiberio – lustrous brown bodies and red toe-nails – for moonlight academies under vine-roofed pergolas, for starlit duologues on magic terraces, with beauty veiled by the warm darkness and the mere touch of a slim hand an electric shock.'[10]

John and Una were sufficiently impressed to alter their holiday plans. But almost immediately complications arose. Toupie had become infatuated by Romaine and followed her everywhere. Romaine did not discourage her but it is clear she regarded Toupie as a mere diversion. Matters reached a head in July when Toupie learned that Romaine had invited John and Una to Capri but not her. In a fit of pique she cancelled a party which the couple had planned to hold in her flat three days later. John and Una were furious. When Toupie tried to phone them after a week they hung up on her three times – finally relenting by ringing her back after dinner. As Una put it: 'he came round at 9. & apologised.'[11]

The episode made John and Una more circumspect. When Romaine left London at the end of July, they promised her only that they would come to Capri if they could – almost certainly intending not to. They had no wish to offend Toupie, but they also wondered if Romaine might be more trouble than she was worth. Starlit duologues and the electric touch of a slim hand might, after all, not be such a good idea. Ladye expressed similar reservations at their next séance with Mrs Leonard – which, as always, confirmed their feelings.

They finally left for Italy on September 1 – after a frantic last-minute hunt by Una for a new pair of strong brogue walking shoes. It was John's first return to the Continent since her holiday with Ladye in Tamaris and Florence in the spring of 1914. As if to inaugurate the trip in the right spirit, they stopped off at Calais for a few days to order masses for Ladye and to allow John a refresher course at the gaming tables in the local casino. In Paris they ordered another mass for Ladye at Notre Dame and John bought Una a Joan of Arc medal. They reached Levanto by first-class wagon-lit on September 10. Una had a joyful reunion with May Massola, whom she had not seen for eight years – 'just the same perfectly darling creature'.[12]

Idle, relaxing days followed, mostly in the company of the Massolas and their friends. John and Una stayed at a hotel in a suite of rooms linked by a connecting door – 'we shall sleep in one & use the other for clothes & dressing', noted the diary.[13] They were serenaded at dawn one morning by a tenor voice beneath their window singing 'Io v'ol haciarti, gli occhi neri, gli occhi neri' – a comforting sign that the Italy each had known before the war remained the same. A less welcome Italian custom was the keeping of birds in cruelly small cages. When they could, John and Una purchased the birds and set them free. They decided to keep a canary and placed it in a large cage, calling it Gabriele after d'Annunzio.

In early October a letter arrived from Romaine. Were they coming to Capri or not, she wondered, because Toupie had written to say they had set off to Italy? 'I hope to hear that you are ever so much better & are being well *fed up*. Personally I think all that dieting a mistake. Am getting quite thin here by mere exercise.'[14] John and Una had definitely decided to make their way to Florence after Levanto. Una wrote back tactfully explaining their change of plans. Romaine was disappointed but, judging by the tone of her reply, had half-expected as much. She was more concerned to explain her behaviour towards Toupie, who had been sending her recriminatory letters all summer: 'She is disatisfied (sic) with present state of affairs instead of being astounded that I even remember that somewhat fragile commencement. The ways of sentiment never surprise me, but then *I* never take things for granted.'[15] John and Una were by no means the first to be shocked by the ruthlessness of Romaine's self-sufficiency.

They arrived in Florence on November 6 and checked into the Hotel Albion. They were glad to be back in the city which held such happy

pre-war memories for each of them. Glad too to be in a good hotel at
last and eating decent food – two major preoccupations of all their
travels – for Levanto had left a good deal to be desired on both scores.
Towards the end of their stay there, relations with the Massolas had
deteriorated. May had become peevish with them. In a stormy
incident in a shop she had sided with a 'beastly' man whom Una told
off for allowing his dog to snap at her. Old friends who had known
John and Una separately found it difficult to adjust to them as a
couple. In the Massolas' case, a latent disapproval of the relationship
compounded the problem, for they had known Troubridge well. But
the real stumbling block was the exclusivity of John and Una's
friendship. Rarely out of each other's company and totally loyal to
each other, they blocked any outsider getting close to either one of
them. Former confidantes on both sides tended to react with jealousy
or resentment.

Winter had descended on Florence and the first thing they did was
buy overcoats, warm hats and knitted knickers. There followed a visit
to John's favourite Florentine church, Or San Michele. They were not
great sightseers, preferring to return to places they knew and liked
from previous visits. Simply shopping or wandering round the streets
often gave them greater pleasure. They bought each other Christmas
presents: jewelled cuff-links for John from Settepassi on the Ponte
Vecchio, a large sapphire ring for Una – which she would never take
off. Una prided herself on a discovery she made in a junk shop in the
Via della Vigna Nuova, a third-century reproduction of a miniature
statuette of the Volto Santo of Lucca. It was cast in bronze with
enamelled eyes and they picked it up for a song. When it had been
cleaned, its shoes proved to be silver and its crown gold. Moments like
this helped to create that special love they felt for the city, which they
were soon calling 'our Florence'.

In 1921 political turmoil prevailed in Italy and the central government was too weak to control the rival bands of Fascists and Communists roaming the streets. The carrying of arms was forbidden, but
the law was frequently ignored and ugly scenes of public disorder
constantly threatened the fragile calm. For reasons of class and religion
John and Una instinctively sided with the Fascists. At home both
staunchly voted Conservative. As Catholics they were horrified by
the advance of atheistic Soviet-style Communism (two Communist
MPs were elected to the House of Commons in 1922) and in Florence
the presence of Communist slogans on walls everywhere confirmed
their worst fears.

Sounds of shooting from across the river awoke them early one
morning (with characteristic precision, Una noted the time was 6 am

and judged some fifty shots rang out), followed by the insistent ringing of a church bell. They were told it was a 'brawl' between marauding groups of Fascists and Communists. Mussolini arrived in the city on another occasion and they watched the crowds surging towards the Ponte alla Santa Trinita to hear him address a Fascist gathering. 'I was desperately anxious to sally forth to see and listen, but John was adamant: I was to stay indoors. It was my Irish blood yearning for a free fight. I should get injured and embarrass my Italian friends by becoming an International Incident.'[16]

One day they went round the orphanage of the Innocenti and were touched by the sight of so many unwanted children. Her protective feelings thoroughly aroused, 'John was sorely tempted to buy a baby', Una tells us.[17] But, as always, ill-treatment of animals provoked John's strongest feelings. They were appalled at the brutality they witnessed at a circus. Una burst into tears and John immediately sent off a cheque to the RSPCA. Like Ladye, Una was sometimes amused or even exasperated by John's inordinate concern for the welfare of animals, but gradually, as in so many other areas, she adopted John's outlook, acquiring the 'seeing eye' which never failed to 'remark the underfed or overloaded horse or ass, the chained or neglected dog, the untamed bird in the dirty, cruelly tiny cage'.[18]

They left Florence on January 7, 1922, travelling to Paris by sleeper. On the 9th Romaine turned up in an open motor at their hotel to take them to lunch at her flat in the Avenue Victor Hugo. The meeting had been arranged by letter while they were still in Florence. Romaine stressed that lunch would be completely informal: 'I strongly hate servants . . . Such a thing as a well-trained butler would send me mad.'[19] She had cut her hair into a short, straight style in imitation of the Japanese fashion and she expressed her dislike of the wave which Una had recently put in hers. Una agreed to wash it out, but back in England she had it re-waved in deference to John's wishes.

On January 10 John and Una met Natalie Barney for the first time when they dined, with Romaine, at her house at 20 Rue Jacob. Romaine had described Natalie to them as someone with 'an unusual mind of the best quality'.[20] This understated Natalie's true talents. She was a poet and essayist, witty, intellectual, with a skill for turning accepted notions on their head in the form of striking aphorisms. But what made her stand out was her supreme serenity and self-confidence, a rare combination of tough-mindedness and courtly charm which drew people to her like moths to a flame.

From an early age she had been determinedly independent, strongly resisting the conventional demands upon women to subordinate their lives to men. In this respect, her lesbianism was very much an

extension of deeply held feminist views, so that when Rémy de
Gourmand dubbed her 'The Amazon' he signified much more than
just her appearance in the well known bowler hat, bow tie and
waistcoat that she wore to ride in the Bois de Boulogne every
morning. Physically, she was an attractive woman, with magnetic
blue eyes, luxuriant honey-coloured hair (invariably slightly
unkempt), and a voice which had the warm timbre of a cello. She
pursued women with great panache and her love affairs were numerous but, like her friend Colette, she remained essentially a person who
thrived on friendship, which placed fewer limits on her independence
than sexual entanglements. 'To live alone, my own master, was
essential, in order to give more freely of myself,' she once wrote, and
it remained a guiding principle of her life.

Because John and Una were leaving Paris for London next day, a
Thursday, they missed their opportunity to attend one of Natalie's
famous Friday afternoon salon parties. Since the war these gatherings
had become one of the great centrepieces of Left Bank intellectual
life, drawing a mixed collection of writers, artists, bohemians, and
homosexuals of both sexes. No 20, Rue Jacob was a seventeenth-
century house buried in a courtyard, with an enchanting enclosed
garden containing a Doric 'Temple d'Amitié'. Visitors felt they were
stepping out of time as they crossed the cobbles to be greeted by
Natalie's housekeeper, Madame Berthe, and were led into the sumptuous salon, full of mirrors and furs and tapestries, to meet Natalie
herself, invariably dressed in a long robe of white ottoman silk.
Natalie's flair for the theatrical touch ensured that the proceedings
retained their reputation as very special occasions. Guests were
served by a butler whose bald pate was lacquered and had hair
painted on it, all in French curlicues. Handfuls of rose petals once
descended from a skylight in the roof. Somebody would be asked to
play the piano, to dance a mazurka, or recite a poem. As Gide
commented, Natalie was one of the few people one *ought* to see if one
had the time.

In May 1921 John had purchased the freehold of a house at No 10,
Sterling Street, off Montpelier Square. The property required extensive renovation and the builders had been at work since June. It was
still not quite ready when the couple returned from Europe in January
1922, so they transferred to another furnished flat in nearby North
Terrace – and discovered sewer rats the size of rabbits were sharing
the tenancy with them. The house agent refused to believe their

complaints on this score, so when one of the rats died in the kitchen, Una wrapped it in a shoe-box and posted it to him.[21]

They finally occupied Sterling Street in mid-March. All their furniture and possessions, including some 2,000 books, were once again moved out of storage and crammed into the new home. It was much smaller than Chip Chase, with no garden to speak of, and they were content with a reduced staff of three servants. They scoured local antique shops for yet more Elizabethan oak chests, tables, chairs and panels. Somewhere they unearthed what they believed was an authentic Tudor portrait of Henry VIII to add to their growing collection of 'old masters'. The previous August Una had succeeded in tracking down one of the three sketches that Sargent had made in preparation for his oil portrait of Ladye. She presented it to John on her forty-first birthday on August 8. This too was now hung with all the other pictures and photographs which so conspicuously testified to Ladye's memory.

Friendships kept up by letter during their Continental travels were resumed once more. Toupie initially proved rather cool. 'Lord knows why & He doesn't care!' exclaimed Una,[22] but Brother's resentment of what she construed as their collusion with Romaine to exclude her plainly still simmered. All John and Una's friendships went in cycles, and if Toupie had now fallen out of favour, Ida Wylie was positively in. She and Rachel Barrett were frequent visitors to Sterling Street and the invitations were returned with equal regularity. In the summer John bought an Arrol Johnston motor car, which they christened Wilfred (later it became The Toad) and entrusted to a chauffeur, Beale. May and June were blazing hot months and the two couples, each in a separate car (no doubt to John and Una's relief), drove in convoy down to the south coast or into the Kent countryside for weekend picnics. One excursion took them through Winchelsea, Rye and Hythe, affording John and Una their first glimpse of the 'wonderful' Romney Marsh which they would get to know so well in later years.

Through Ida, John began to meet other established writers for the first time. In March she encountered the novelist J. D. Beresford, who was a reader for Collins. Ida also introduced her to May Sinclair, a shy woman in her fifties who had been writing novels since 1896. Unmarried, May was a feminist and ex-suffragette, and had worked with a Field Ambulance Corps in Belgium during the war. Her latest novel *Mary Olivier*, published in 1919, was an attempt to explore the sub-conscious mind and had struck a new style in the 'stream-of-consciousness' genre. Rebecca West and Rosamond Lehmann would both later acknowledge their debt to May Sinclair.

With Violet Hunt, May was a founder member of the newly formed international writers' club called PEN (standing for Poets, Essayists, Editors and Novelists). The club elected John Galsworthy as its first president and by 1922 an impressive list of distinguished writers from many countries had joined. Women writers were well represented. John was elected in the spring of 1922, along with Storm Jameson and Mary Webb. She attended her first PEN dinner on May 2 and accompanied Ida to *her* inaugural function as a new member in June. Literary clubs were in vogue in the post-war years and John had soon joined both the Writers' Club and the Women Writers' Club as well. Talks and lectures were organized by these bodies, but their meetings were primarily social occasions designed to bring writers together to enhance their professional solidarity. The emphasis was on informality (PEN rules stipulated that no formal speeches should be given and that members should make themselves as comfortable 'as if they were in their own homes')[23] and members could invite guests, which prevented Una feeling excluded.

All this rubbing shoulders with the great spurred John to renewed efforts on her book. She had managed to do some writing in Florence, in fact had worked so intensively that Una had tried to persuade her to stop – the first of many arguments on the subject of her over-working. Until they moved into Sterling Street, too many distractions disturbed the tranquil routine she needed for working at her best. She was not the sort of writer who could snatch an odd hour here or there. But when not writing, she was often reading – or rather, Una was reading to her, just as Ladye had always done.

> I would read to her endlessly and many times I thanked God that my voice had once been trained [as a singer] and never seemed to fail me. I would read by day and often by night in an effort to exorcise her constitutional sleeplessness. When we went away together to an hotel the first things to be unpacked were at least a dozen books of every description. I would have borrowed or bought them on various recommendations and have glanced through them provisionally or have read them myself.[24]

Una would keep lists in her diary of books to be read, which she would get out from *The Times* Book Club in Wigmore Street or buy from the book departments of Harrods and the Army and Navy Stores. As often as not these books were the latest best-selling novels – their 1921 list included Ethel Dell's *The Obstacle Race*, W. B. Maxwell's *A Little More*, E. F. Benson's *Lovers and Friends*, and (as Ida had recommended) Sheila Kaye-Smith's *Joanna Godden* and A. S. M.

Hutchinson's *If Winter Comes*. But sprinkled among them was a more personal selection, a judicious balance of classics, old and new, high-brow and low-brow (such as Baroness Orczy's Scarlet Pimpernel books or Charles Reade's *The Cloister and the Hearth* – which reduced them both to tears) and subjects close to their hearts (the 1921 list included Elizabeth von Arnim's *Elizabeth and her German Garden*, Mary Dowdall's novel *Three Loving Ladies*, and Freud's *Leonardo da Vinci: A Psychosexual Study*).

All John's reading represented a conscious attempt to prepare and improve herself as a prose-writer. Her taste was resolutely middle-brow. There is no evidence that she either liked or read systematically among contemporary authors whose style was experimental. Joyce, Lawrence, Virginia Woolf were not to her liking. May Sinclair was a friend but, though John read some of her novels, they do not appear to have impressed her. Her predilection was for the traditional narrative form, for the mainstream psychological novel. She adored historical novels. They confirmed her romanticized view of the past, but her favourites also appealed to her for their spiritual, other-worldly qualities. In this lay the key to her enthusiasm for Ford Madox Ford's *Ladies Whose Bright Eyes* – which Una read to her for the fourth time in March 1922 – and for Marjorie Bowen's novels with their Dutch or Italian historical backgrounds (they had read her *Burning Glass* and *The Unfortunate* in 1918). Again and again John would return to these books – and in later years to others like George du Maurier's *Peter Ibbetson* and Margaret Irwin's *Still She Wished for Company* – because they fulfilled what Una called the 'something in her nature that was dissatisfied with material life; the something that would occasionally make her say that she was feeling happy because for the moment she had a sensation that the veil between this world and another was very tenuous indeed.'[25]

Part Four

JOHN
[1] THE NOVELIST

1922–1928

Chapter Thirteen

At the end of July 1922 John and Una left London for the spa of Bagnoles de l'Orne in Normandy, where they hoped a course of carbonic acid bath treatment would help cure the inflamed leg which had troubled John since her hunting accident. They stopped off first for a few days in Paris. They saw Romaine and Natalie again. The two couples drove in the Bois and attended a costumed ball. They inspected Romaine's latest pictures and admired once again the nude study of Ida Rubinstein painted in 1915 and called 'The Weeping Venus': Una thought it had 'waxed in beauty' since their earlier visit.

On their last day in Paris they lunched with Elizabeth de Gramont, Duchess of Clermont Tonnerre, at her villa in Passy overlooking the Seine. Lily, as all her friends called her, was a tall, imposing woman of impeccable aristocratic ancestry who 'resembled King Ludwig of Bavaria and Rimbaud'.[1] Despite her background, she had Communist leanings (of a very idealistic sort) and was sometimes dubbed the 'Red Duchess'. She had known Natalie since 1910 and was successively lover and friend, overlapping for a time Natalie's affair with Romaine in a discreet, highly civilized ménage à trois. She had an encyclopaedic mind, spoke fluent English, championed music by Rameau and Debussy, and loved anything new or creative with a passionate intensity which sat somewhat oddly with her grande dame manner and appearance. She carried a lorgnette, being very short-sighted, and expected on-the-minute punctuality from the guests who attended her lavish candle-lit lunches and dinners. Like all the leading members of the Barney circle, Lily was capable of the grandiose gesture and the bon mot. She once remarked of a twice-married woman who kept complaining of never meeting her Tristan: '"You don't meet Tristan, you invent him. Anyway, is she so sure she's Isolde?"'[2]

Bagnoles seemed very dull after the heady atmosphere of Paris. It was a sleepy resort where everyone, according to Una, seemed to hobble around with game legs. But the lovers were always happy to revert to each other's company after a bout of hectic socializing. The baths, which Una sampled too, induced a delicious drowsiness in the afternoons and they lolled peacefully about their rooms in the Hotel des Thermes, Una reading aloud from Edna Ferber's *The Girls* and then Sheila Kaye-Smith's *Sussex Gorse*. Seclusion also gave John the chance to work on *Octopi* again. The quiet routine was broken only when, towards the end of July, Gabrielle Enthoven joined them. After over three weeks on their own, they felt glad to see her. But the novelty soon wore off. After a week Una was pronouncing Gabrielle 'snappy and dull'.

On the 31st they returned to Paris, stopping over for a day before taking the train back to London. August 1 marked the seventh anniversary of their meeting and they read together the poems of Renée Vivien, the tragic lesbian poet who had been one of Natalie's early *grandes passions* and who had died in 1909 from a combination of starvation and alcoholism. Her doom-laden verses, recalling Baudelaire and Swinburne, portray the lesbian as a social outcast whose forbidden love reaps more torment than joy. Such a theme did not fail to impress John, whose own poetry had dwelled, in a milder, disguised form, upon the solitary affliction of homosexuals like herself.

August 18 is heavily ringed in Una's diaries from 1922 onwards. It marked the date of what they later referred to as their 'marriage' and was always celebrated thereafter as a major anniversary in their calendar (along with August 1, the date of their meeting, and November 29, the date they consummated their love). On the face of it, August 18, 1922, was an unremarkable day. They went shopping, had their hair waved, and dined quietly together in the evening. The 'marriage' was clearly not a formal ceremony of any kind. Two small clues possibly indicate what Una meant.

First, August 18 marked the start of Una's period. We know this because she was in the habit of drawing a crude face symbol in the margin of her diary to denote when she was 'cursed'. John's periods were indicated in the same manner, except that her face symbol appeared in profile, highlighting the aquiline nose, while Una's looked squarely to the front. As is now well documented, it is common for two women's menstrual cycles to synchronize if they live in close daily proximity. This had been the case with John and Una since at least 1917. Recently, however, John's periods had become irregular. As she had just turned forty-two, she could well have been entering the menopause. On August 18, when John should have begun her period in unison with Una, she did not. In fact, she would not menstruate again.

The second clue lies in a letter which they received on August 18 from their gynaecologist, Dr Alfred Sachs. Unfortunately, this letter has not survived. Nor has the letter they sent to Sachs on August 11, to which Sachs's letter must have been the reply. We can only speculate what this correspondence was about. Was the start of Una's period related to the arrival of the doctor's letter? Throughout 1920 and 1921 Una had been undergoing treatment from Sachs for undisclosed gynaecological troubles. Her periods had proved irregular during this time. More recently, however, she seemed to have improved and Sachs stopped his treatment.

Did the simultaneous arrival of Una's period and Sachs's letter denote the same thing, namely that she was better? If they did, it meant that Una could regard herself as 'functioning' as a woman again after prolonged uncertainty. The fact that this occurred on the very day that John's periods were perceived (in hindsight) to have halted for good contained a symbolic significance that would not have escaped the two lovers. As they saw it, John's loss of this pre-eminent badge of womanhood marked the completion of her advance towards 'manhood'. For the first time since living together their concept of themselves as a couple united unto – and beyond – death acquired a physiological validity on a par with any heterosexual partnership. They were now, they felt, 'man' and 'wife', and Sachs's letter solemnized the transformation.

The autumn of 1922 saw John working hard on *Octopi*. The book was making good progress now they were settled into Sterling Street. Accordingly, they cut their outside commitments to a minimum. Instead of going abroad at the end of August, they contented themselves with short weekend breaks at familiar places like Bournemouth, Brighton and Hastings. Toupie and Ida were markedly less in evidence. Sittings with Mrs Leonard were rationed to monthly intervals. To prevent her style being influenced by other writers in the same genre, John would let Una read her only what they called 'shockers' – horror stories and detective thrillers. Only the dogs and John's PEN dinners were permitted to distract her.

Since moving out of Chip Chase, they had got rid of some of the griffons and were now concentrating on dachshunds. Thor had won many prizes at shows and was soon joined by Erda (who died in November). Then, in October, they bought a liver and tan dachshund which they had seen in Holland Park. They followed the old woman home who owned it and requested to buy it. They named the new dog

'Charles' but it was registered at the Kennel Club as Fitzjohn Wotan. Despite his lack of pedigree, Wotan was to be their most successful exhibit ever. At his first show in November, the dachshund won six first prizes and never looked back thereafter. He 'swept the benches', as Una put it, in every class he entered, losing just once – and then only, they felt, because the judge in question was piqued he had not bought Wotan himself.[3]

John finished her first draft of *Octopi* at 8 pm on October 26. They read Minna the first four chapters a week later – her opinion is not recorded – and the 'polishing' process continued into November and December. On December 20 the book's title became *After Many Days*, a reference to the biblical text: 'Cast thy bread upon the waters for thou shalt find it after many days'. The final corrections to the book were completed to John's satisfaction on Christmas Eve – at five past ten in the evening, Una noted with her customary precision. They had recently attended a party at J. D. Beresford's house in Regent's Park, meeting H. G. Wells and Walter De la Mere. Beresford offered to read John's manuscript in his capacity as a reader for Collins, as well as any short stories she might wish to give him. Hardly was Christmas over, therefore, before John and Una were back at work going through John's stories. The manuscripts were handed to Beresford on January 6.

After Many Days tells the life-story of Joan Ogden, a bright, sensitive, middle-class girl growing up at the turn of the century in the dull provincial resort of Seabourne. The chief focus is upon Joan's adolescence and her relations with her family, in particular her mother, a snobbish and neurotic woman whose empty marriage to the boorish Colonel Ogden has induced in her an inordinate emotional dependence upon Joan. Into this stifling atmosphere comes a breath of fresh air in the person of Elizabeth Rodney, an attractive Cambridge graduate hired to tutor Joan and her younger sister Millie. Elizabeth represents all the exciting possibilities which lie beyond the narrow confines of Seabourne. She quickly perceives that Joan is exceptionally intelligent and she determines to help her break the conventional mould by preparing her for university and a career as a doctor.

However, Elizabeth's ambitions for Joan soon provoke the hostility of her parents. Colonel Ogden expects his daughter to marry and settle down like any dutiful young woman. But Joan makes it clear that she is not attracted by men and repeatedly turns down the proposals of a likeable medical student, Richard Benson, who seems the perfect partner for her. As for Mrs Ogden, she becomes increasingly jealous of Elizabeth's influence over Joan. Fearing that Joan will eventually abandon her, the mother takes every opportunity to play on her daughter's sympathies, feigning helplessness and ill-health. Joan is torn between conflicting loyalties. She develops a deep affection for Elizabeth and knows in her heart that, to fulfil her potential, she must escape from her roots. At the same time she cannot help feeling sorry for her mother whose tragic, stunted existence calls forth all her most compassionate and protective instincts.

For a time, in her late teens, Joan's friendship with Elizabeth wins the day and the two young women make plans to set up home together in a flat in London, where Joan can attend college while Elizabeth works. But the dream is destined to be thwarted by a series of disasters. First, Colonel Ogden dies, leaving the family in straitened circumstances. It is then discovered that he has wilfully squandered a legacy intended for Joan and Millie, on which Joan was relying to pay her way through college. The final blow is Millie's early death from consumption. Mrs Ogden is able to exploit each of these events in turn to tighten her emotional stranglehold on Joan until she finally agrees to stay at home. Devastated, the rejected Elizabeth retires from the scene to marry and live abroad, never seeing Joan again. The book ends many years later, long after Mrs Ogden's death, with Joan as a sad, wasted figure eking out a miserable existence as a live-in companion to an elderly relative.

John's first novel, like many others, was conspicuously autobiographical. Seabourne is reminiscent of Bournemouth, Southbourne, and all the other sea resorts John knew so well – and suggests that, though she liked visiting them, she was quite aware of their stiflingly parochial qualities for the permanent resident. Her descriptions of the Ogden household, of the girl Joan's boredom and loneliness, of her conflicts with her parents, of her tomboyishness and implicit homosexuality, all point to John writing herself and her own childhood into the book. Perhaps these parts were translated from the discarded *Michael West*. The novel also provides the clearest statement she was ever to make of her feminist views. The reader is left in no doubt that marriage is an awful experience for most women and a character called Lady Loo (she bicycles about in bloomers and a Norfolk jacket) who advocates that women should use their brains is given a sympathetic hearing. Richard Benson utters the same sentiments with more passion, eloquent in his opposition to women being 'shut out of things, bottled up, cramped', and it is plain that the author herself is speaking here.

Yet, this said, the book's feminism is strictly limited. The story's ending is deliberately contrived to satisfy John's chosen theme. Joan ultimately wastes the opportunity to fulfil herself because of her mother's vampyric intentions towards her. But John makes it very clear that Joan is also a willing victim in her own destruction. From the opening chapter the girl is cast as a person with a strong sense of duty and compassion, willing to take the blame, even at the age of twelve, for her sister's misdeeds. Half way into the novel we have few doubts as to how it will end, so helpless is Joan in the face of her own extreme urge to protect and defend.

The story is actually about three women – Joan, Mrs Ogden and Elizabeth – and the tortuous emotional strife that ensues when two of them vie for the affections of the third. Moreover, the nature of Mrs Ogden's relationship with Joan is a good deal more explicitly erotic than might be expected between mother and daughter. 'Then Joan's strong, young arms would comfort and soothe, and her firm lips grope until they found her mother's; and Mrs Ogden would feel mean and ashamed but guiltily happy, as if a lover held her.'[4] And later, when Joan is beginning to dread her mother's constant demands for affection: 'She pressed her cold cheek against Mrs Ogden's, rubbing it gently up and down, then suddenly she folded her in her arms, kissing her lips, seeking desperately to awaken her dulled emotions to the response that she knew was so painfully desired.'[5]

The erotic undertones to Joan's affection for Elizabeth, though never fully acknowledged by Joan, are equally unmistakable. In one scene, for example, Joan enters Elizabeth's room while she is asleep and watches her secretly with a mixture of fascination and guilt. For her part, Elizabeth grows so attached to her pupil that she is prepared to endure ten years in Seabourne (which she claims to hate) to be near the girl. At one point in the story, when Joan is studiously avoiding any discussion of her future with Elizabeth, Elizabeth exclaims desperately: '"Joan! If you loved me you couldn't make me unhappy about you as you do. Joan, don't you love me?"'[6]

Beneath the surface this is the story of John, Ladye and Una. The scene between the ageing mother and the slavish daughter which John had witnessed at the Lynton Cottage Hotel in 1919 struck her so forcibly not because she was interested in the plight of spinsters but because it touched a raw nerve within herself. Notice her choice of title: *Octopi*. Love was something which could trap its victims, crushing them in a tentacle-like embrace. John had felt trapped by Ladye's love and yet, like the dutiful daughter, she could not ignore the cry for help which it represented, however manipulative. What had happened to the pathetic spinster at Lynton and what happens to

Joan in the novel could, John discerned only too clearly, have befallen herself if Ladye had not died so unexpectedly.

After the Colonel's death, Millie's consumption is diagnosed and Joan has to move into her mother's room and share her bed. In describing Joan's agony at having to sleep night after night alongside the mother whose whole physical presence now repels her, the novel gives us a devastating picture of a love affair in which, on one side, the passion has died.

> Side by side, in a small double bed, lay the mother and daughter in dreadful proximity. Their bodies, tired and nervous after the day, were yet unable to avoid each other. Mrs Ogden's circulation being very bad she could never sleep with less than four blankets and two hot-water bottles. The hot, rubbery smell of these bottles and the misery of the small double bed, became for Joan a symbol of all that Leaside stood for. She took to lying at the extreme edge of the bed, more out than in, in order to escape from the touch of her mother's flannel nightgown. But this precaution did not always save her, for Mrs Ogden, who got a sense of comfort from another body beside her at night, would creep up close to her daughter.
>
> 'Hold my hand, darling; it's so cold.' And Joan would take the groping hand and warm it between her own until her mother dropped asleep; but even then she dared not leave go, lest Mrs Ogden should wake and begin to talk.[7]

That this, hot-water bottles and all, was a scene which John herself had experienced cannot be doubted.

After Many Days confirmed what John's spiritualist work had already indicated, namely the deeply traumatic effect upon her of her infidelity to Ladye. The book was an attempt to exorcise the memory, being part apologia for her conduct, part an essay in self-exploration. What comes through the fiction painfully clearly is the conflict felt by the author herself between duty and desire, restraint and passion, self-sacrifice and ambition. What also emerges is a terrible sense of regret, of wasted opportunity. John was only too well aware that, because she had stayed with Ladye, the war had passed her by. This feeling was reinforced by all the women she had met and befriended since who had performed honourable service for their country. It was with some bitterness that she reflected on the irony that while even 'little Una' had been in Serbia winning medals at the front line (both Serbia and the Admiralty had decorated her on her work on behalf of the hospital unit), she, the 'man of the house', had sat at home writing poetry. In all John's fiction artistic people are viewed with considerable ambivalence.

Yet, despite the yearnings and regrets, John's heroine is powerless to resist the impulses of her own nature. The novel suggests that people's lives are governed by an underlying determinism which only the strongest effort of will can combat. External events are less influential than Joan's own particular outlook and limitations, which are the root cause of her self-denial and hence the waste of her potential. Such a preoccupation was natural perhaps to someone with John's sexual proclivity and unhappy background, but also reflected the peculiar frustrations she experienced as a woman of pronounced masculine temperament and inclinations.

As a first novel *After Many Days* showed high promise. John's narrative skills and natural descriptive powers appeared to strong advantage. As a sensitive and sophisticated psychological portrayal of character, it would not be bettered by any other book she wrote. For the modern reader it is probably her most accessible and appealing novel. However, it presented difficulties for the contemporary publisher. John was an unknown author with no track record in fiction. The book was over-long and its grim vision depressing. It was not regarded as a commercial proposition.

J. D. Beresford hinted at these disadvantages when he returned John's manuscript on January 10. He told her he had read the novel with 'intense interest' but it was not the sort of book which Collins felt it could publish. He advised her to shorten it and made some helpful suggestions.

John decided to equip herself with a literary agent. Ida Wylie arranged an introduction to her own agent, Audrey Heath, a diminutive woman, shy but businesslike. Audrey had been a classical scholar at Cambridge before joining the Hughes Massey-Curtis Brown literary agency. When Massey and Brown separated, Audrey left the firm and set up on her own in 1919. By a stroke of good fortune, the Massey-Brown split procured her a ready-made list of reputable authors who sold well in America (Ida Wylie among them), for the large American agency Brandt and Brandt did not wish to be seen to favour either Massey or Brown. By 1923 A. M. Heath and Co was established at the top of a narrow winding staircase in cramped offices above the Burlington Arcade overlooking Piccadilly. The firm was keen to recruit more home-grown talent. Audrey read John's shortened version of *After Many Days* and expressed her approval. William Heinemann himself had died while John was still writing her novel, but Audrey decided that Heinemann's should be sent the manuscript first.

Audrey was no more sanguine about the book's chances of finding a publisher than Beresford had been. However, from someone came the suggestion that if John could write a short, light novel and get that accepted first, it might make it easier to sell *After Many Days*. Thus in mid-January, even before Audrey Heath had read the manuscript of her first book, John was embarked on a second, which she entitled *Chains* (her working titles were rarely very inspired). She was to write this new work in record time, going at it in furious bursts throughout the winter and spring of 1923. There began again the usual 'upheavals' between her and Una when the dogs' yapping disturbed her concentration. And back again came the familiar days of depression and frustration when she would tear up what she had written in a fit of temper – a habit which she gradually stopped when Una convinced her that some of her first drafts were superior to the second or third, obliging them patiently to reconstruct the torn fragments from the waste-paper basket. However, as early as the end of April she was able to deliver the first part of *Chains* (some sixty pages) to Audrey for her inspection.

In spite of *Chains*, John plunged into a hectic social life now that *After Many Days* was out of the way – a sign perhaps of the intense emotional involvement that the earlier book had entailed. New friends and new haunts commanded her attention. Most of these were associated with the smarter bohemian set in London who frequented that square mile between Soho and Bloomsbury called 'Fitzrovia'. In Percy Street, in the heart of Fitzrovia, lay the Eiffel Tower restaurant. The Eiffel Tower, like the Café Royal before it, was one of those places which summed up a whole artistic generation. Quite why it was so pre-eminent is unclear. The food was neither cheap nor outstanding, the décor consisted largely of potted ferns, and the proprietor was a fat, unprepossessing Austrian who spoke little English. It had become fashionable during the war amongst the more adventurous 'bright young things', notably 'arty' rich girls like Iris Tree, Lady Diana Manners and Nancy Cunard. By the twenties successful and up-and-coming artists, writers and actors were its patrons and it exuded that racy, glamorous atmosphere in which people like to see and be seen.

John had recently remet the actor Ernest Thesiger, an old friend of Ladye's whom she had nicknamed 'The Ace of Diamonds'. He introduced her and Una to the composer-conductor Eugene Goossens, 'a charmer' whom they came to know as 'Guy'. Guy and his wife Ida (nicknamed 'Boonie') frequented the Eiffel Tower and took John and Una for their first meal there in February. Afterwards they trooped off to the nearby Ham Bone Club. Guy also introduced them to another club, in Charlotte Street, called the Cave of Harmony, which was run by Harold Scott and the red-haired actress Elsa Lanchester. The club specialized in late-night cabaret and theatricals and, though without an alcohol licence, turned a blind eye to customers who brought their own bottles. Not that either John or Una were ever great drinkers, but the unique atmosphere of the Cave quickly made it a favourite haunt of theirs.

Through their Fitzrovian connections, John and Una began to circulate on the smarter, middle-brow fringes of mainstream London cultural life. They made the acquaintance of actresses such as Marie Tempest, Gwen Fargo and Gwen Farrar, and writers such as Edgar Jepson, Elizabeth Gilliat and Marjorie Bagot. The queen of the Body and Soul movement, the dancer Margaret Morriss, invited them to her parties, and Mrs Sidney Schiff, wife of the publisher and translator, introduced them to the Sitwells – who did not impress John and Una. Like many others, they regarded the Sitwell literary experiments as pretentious and pointless. The memorable first public performance of *Façade* which John and Una attended in June in the stuffy Aeolian Hall drew the damning comment in the diary: 'a *bad pain* afternoon of Miss Sitwell shouting down a megaphone'.[8]

Romaine reappeared in London at the end of April, thankful to have escaped from the 'horrible' Riviera and hoping to 'find you both glad to see me'.[9] They were, and spent almost every day in her company for the next week. Romaine was looking for a studio in London and Una, whose portrait Romaine wanted to paint, helped her. They eventually found one in the Cromwell Road.

When she felt in the mood, Romaine could be entertaining and the three of them spent long nights talking and laughing at her flat or dancing till the small hours at the Cave of Harmony. Her humour could change, however, with alarming speed and she took offence for the most irrational reasons (she once protested: 'How can I talk to her? She has such *ugly* arms!'). After one night at the Cave which ended at four-thirty in the morning, Una noted cryptically: 'Romaine très difficile & spoilt'.[10] Another day she was 'damnably rude' to them and they left her studio in a huff.

In June, at a dance given by the actress Gwen Farrar, they had been introduced to the American revue star Teddie Gerard. Teddie had made a name for herself in London as a sex-symbol of the arch and pouting kind then fashionable. She had pioneered the first backless evening gowns, an act of theatrical daring which drew gasps from her audiences and – from the gentlemen in the chorus-line – a spirited rendering of 'Glad To See You're Back, Dear Lady'. Behind the naughty stage image dwelled an even naughtier reality, for Teddie was a wild girl who took drugs, drank too much, and loved women hard and fast. 'I once saw her', recalled Beverley Nichols, 'so drunk at a matinée that she could not remember the chorus of "Limehouse Blues", which she must have sung at least a thousand times.'[11]

Teddie owned a house in the country, Orchard Cottage near Broadway in Gloucestershire, and she liked to fill it with friends at weekends. At the beginning of the year John had bought a new car, a six-cylinder Buick Philadelphia, and she and Una were soon driving frequently between London and Orchard Cottage in the late summer and autumn. There they met Teddie's current flame Etheline, a tragic Frenchwoman called Blue Leveaux (who treated them to sorrowful confidences about her affairs), and the famous author of *The Green Hat*, Michael Arlen, whom they drove back to London. Teddie also had a London flat in Sackville Street, and she and Etheline were apt to turn up on John's doorstep at the oddest hours of the day or night. These intrusions were not always welcome, especially if John had plans to work or Teddie proved the worse for wear. Teddie came round to Sterling Street one evening at 11.30 in the company of the American speedboat racer, Jo Carstairs. Both women had been drinking and stayed till 1.30 am – 'when we were glad to see the last of them', commented Una.[12]

Teddie seemed an unlikely companion for John and Una, who drank only in moderation, certainly never touched drugs, and were as monogamous as a happily married couple. The fact that Teddie was an American partly explained it, for (despite her mother) John always retained a soft spot for that side of her family. She discerned too, beneath the actress's racy façade, a charm and vulnerability which touched her. But another element explained Teddie's attraction for them. Like Romaine, she was a woman who responded to impulse, who did what she wanted without the restraining hand of duty or convention. On John, who inclined so much the other way, this quality exercised a particular fascination. That side of her own personality which yearned for escape and freedom and physical excitement could find expression through association with Teddie and reap a vicarious satisfaction.

Chapter Fourteen

At a tea party given by May Sinclair in September, John and Una first met Vere and Budge – that is, Vere Hutchinson and Dorothy Bur-roughes-Burroughes. Vere was the sister of the novelist A. S. M. Hutchinson and herself wrote novels and short stories (Cape published *Sea Wrack* in 1922 and was about to bring out *Great Waters*). Budge was an artist trained at the Slade and specializing in animal and figure illustrations. They were a slightly younger couple than John and Una, but the parallel partnership of writer and artist gave them much in common. They were soon meeting regularly. In October John took Vere as her guest to a PEN dinner and in November Una read them extracts from John's *Chains*: 'they howled with joy over it till past midnight.'[1]

Others were impressed by *Chains*, too. John delivered a completed draft of the novel to Audrey Heath on June 19, almost five months to the day after she had started it. Audrey liked it and sent the typescript – with a new title *The Forge* – to the London publishers Arrowsmith. They, too, expressed interest and in September, after John had made revisions to the text, offered her a contract which took an option on her next two novels. John's only stipulation was that her name on the cover should read 'M. Radclyffe Hall', which eliminated any obvious feminine connotations.

The prospect of Arrowsmith showing concrete interest in another two books encouraged John and Audrey to submit *After Many Days* to them. By this time the novel, now retitled *The Unlit Lamp* on Una's suggestion ('the unlit lamp and the ungirt loin' came from Browning's poem 'The Statue and the Bust'), had been turned down by Heinemann and several other British publishers. John began a third novel, *A Saturday Life*, another social comedy in the style of *The Forge*, intended to interest Arrowsmith. Suddenly, after spending years on one book, she now had three on her hands.

But in early January 1924 Arrowsmith also turned down *The Unlit Lamp* – and as a gesture offered to waive its option on John's third novel. Considering this very fair-minded, John insisted Arrowsmith have first refusal to *A Saturday Life*.[2] She always believed in honouring her word, whether under contract or not.

The Forge was finally published on January 25. John worried that publication would be held up at the eleventh hour, for three days before, just as Ramsay MacDonald was being sworn in as the first Labour prime minister, a railway strike began. However, the strike was settled by the intervention of the Trades Union Congress and John proudly received her six complimentary author's copies. On the day of publication itself John and Una did what they would always do when one of John's novels was published: they tramped round as many bookshops as they could, counting the number of copies in each and keeping a beady eye on the progress of sales. If a shop ran out of stock, they tended to alert the publisher in reproachful terms. John sent a copy of the novel to the Visettis, which suggests that, though she rarely saw them nowadays, she retained some hopes that they might be proud of her. Their reaction is not recorded. Una spent an afternoon writing postcards to friends and acquaintances informing them that the book was out and should be purchased before stocks disappeared. As it happened, this proved more than just a boast, for *The Forge* had entered its second printing by the beginning of March.

In *The Forge* John wrote a book to order. She achieved what was expected of her, namely an undemanding social comedy of contemporary life. The story revolves around Hilary and Susan, a wealthy young married couple who move to the country when the war ends, to a large Elizabethan mansion, Bambury Hall. We are told little of their backgrounds except that both once had artistic aspirations, Hilary to be a writer, Susan a painter. He has had some poetry published but dreams of being a novelist, she attended the Slade and broke off a promising painting career to marry Hilary. Though husband and wife are essentially compatible, they begin to grow restless and frustrated under the humdrum routine of their leisurely domestic existence. They move back to the city in the hope that this will cure their malaise. When it does not, and each feels as trapped and stifled as ever, their marriage starts to suffer.

The catalyst in this situation is a brilliant artist Venetia Ford, whom Susan meets at a masked ball in Paris. Venetia has a legendary reputation as a wild, erratic genius who left her husband and now lives on her own, free and untrammelled, dedicated only to her art. Under her influence, Susan determines to leave her husband and return to her career as an artist. Hilary, meanwhile, has come to similar conclusions about himself, having already started the great novel to which he thinks destiny beckons him. The couple therefore agree to part.

The experiment is a failure for both of them. Neither has the talent or the will to carry through their purpose, and Venetia bluntly tells Susan as much. Inevitably, Hilary returns and the couple are reconciled. In a long speech at the end of the book, Hilary points up the moral of the story, namely that we are all of us bound by 'chains' of some sort, even those who seem the freest, this being nature's way of preserving a sensible balance between man and his environment. This less than profound philosophy is Hilary's somewhat pompous way of saying that he and Susan are not cut out to be bohemians. The whole tone of the novel is heavily ironic and the reader is not intended to take this conclusion seriously.

Despite its comic approach, *The Forge* deals with a theme which also preoccupied John in *The Unlit Lamp*, namely the ties which bind people to each other. On the face of it, *The Forge* takes a different tack from the earlier book by demonstrating that such 'chains', far from being destructive, are life-renewing and the source of one's identity and security. And yet Hilary, voicing John's true sentiments, makes it clear that the heaviest chain one bears is love. It is deceptively light sometimes, giving the impression of freedom, but one cannot run far without being checked by its 'intolerable tug': 'The only way is to keep very close together, a slack chain doesn't hurt so much.'[3] Moreover, it is noticeable that Susan decides to go back to Hilary, not because she has had any fundamental change of heart about their former life-style, but because his hair has turned grey and she is suddenly overwhelmed by pity at his childlike helplessness. Joan's fate was sealed by similar emotions in *The Unlit Lamp*.

The second point of interest in *The Forge* is the heavily autobiographical character of its subject matter. Hilary and Susan represent John and Una and the story condenses their own life together between about 1918 and the present. John demonstrates that she knew her own character to a fault. Hilary is portrayed as a mercurial, often contradictory personality. Compared to Susan, who is much more placid and happy-go-lucky, he is a born worrier. He is also far less adaptable than his wife. Susan can derive pleasure and amusement from the most unpropitious circumstances, while Hilary is easily irritated and rages against modern progress, lamenting the loss of simple virtues everywhere. He supposes he might have made more of his talent for writing had he not inherited an income at the age of twenty-one. And, significantly, he had a bad war. His time at the front should have been 'epoch-making', but he was wounded after two months and invalided out for the duration without firing a shot in anger. The memory of this poor showing plagues him with sad regrets in his more melancholy moments.

Susan is implicitly commended for cheerfully putting up with all her husband's idiosyncracies. The novel is really John's tribute to Una (it is dedicated to her) and Susan is the chief focus of attention. The banal ending, which appears to recognize no middle ground between artistic freedom on the one hand and domestic security on the other, in fact expressed Una's true desire to subordinate her interests to John's. The fact that the story has Susan hankering after, and temporarily regaining, her independence as a painter suggests that John herself may not have been entirely at ease with the knowledge of what Una had given up for her sake – a situation uncomfortably similar to the sort of sacrifice John felt she herself had made on Ladye's behalf.

Much the most interesting minor character in the novel is Venetia Ford, who is a straight take-off of Romaine Brooks. Venetia symbolizes the uncompromising Artist. The novel displays a marked ambivalence towards her, just as in reality John was both impressed and disturbed by Romaine. Susan marvels at the way Venetia works at her easel, like a spirit possessed, totally absorbed by the task in hand. Yet the painter is an uneasy companion. She can be cruel, heartless, selfish, dissipated. Susan is never quite sure whether Venetia is secretly mocking her with her mysterious smile. Romaine Brooks had made an impact on John that compelled her to examine the very real differences between them. Whereas Romaine appeared to have been, in modern parlance, liberated by her lesbian orientation (to the extent that it could not be divorced from her whole feminist and artistic outlook), John's psychological make-up was such that she increasingly adopted a position in which her self-image and self-esteem were defined only in terms of her sexual abnormality.

Paradoxically, the same impulse drove John to identify with conventional values. Romaine felt no such need for social acceptance. John suspected, rightly, that Romaine regarded her attitude, and its outward emblem of mannish clothes and playing the 'husband' to Una, as ridiculous. She also suspected, again not without justification, that Romaine had eyes for Una. Hence their uneasy relations and the note of coolness towards Venetia discernible in the novel. But if great artists often behaved like cads, what was the use of conventional decency if it merely produced artistic mediocrity? In adopting a tone of affectionate irony towards Hilary and Susan, John suggests her awareness of the question – and of the lameness of her answer at the story's end.

On February 20 Una started a press cuttings book for John. '11 reviews [of *The Forge*] so far & all good', she reported. Ida Wylie, in the *Sunday Times*, thought the book a highly commendable first attempt at that most difficult form of fiction, comedy: scenes of 'genuine gaiety' went hand in hand with descriptions 'which insist on being read and remembered for their light-handed delicious rightness'.[4] The *Field* thought 'M. Radclyffe Hall' was a man. The *People* knew she was not but took the opportunity (alongside appropriate photographs) to regale its readers with John's preference for male dress, confiding that she had boasted she did not possess a single frock in her wardrobe.[5]

John's friends congratulated her. Violet Hunt wrote: 'You are a "clever cat" as we used to say at school – a "dog" in your case.'[6] Vere declared that she and Budge had adored the book: 'I think the wisdom lying beneath the lightness is quite remarkable. You have a delightful way of touching on the comic and making one not so much laugh as *think*.' She likened *The Forge* (as did the *Evening Standard* review) to Elizabeth von Arnim's *Elizabeth and her German Garden*. Vere also detected something of herself in the character of Hilary – 'my poignant sorrow for him is therefore really very funny!!'[7]

Romaine was not amused by the book. She had no illusions that Venetia was meant to be her and she thought the likeness trite and superficial. She would later tell Natalie Barney that John had watched her 'with the eye of a sparrow who sees no further than the window-pane'.[8] To John herself, however, she proved more circumspect, perhaps because she still hoped to paint Una's portrait. The book had amused her, she wrote. 'But I don't like laughing when I read, so do hurry on the sad & disagreeable volume [ie *The Unlit Lamp*]. Fatigue makes me long to hear of another's woe.'[9]

With *The Forge* safely in the bookstalls and, more importantly, doing reasonably well (in mid-March it reached the best-seller list of *John O'London's Weekly*), John could afford to relax. For several weeks she and Una indulged in a hectic round of late-night parties, theatre-going, and calling on friends. Teddie Gerard was back in town, rehearsing to take over Gertrude Lawrence's part in Noel Coward's revue *London Calling!* Teddie introduced them to Princess Violette Murat, one of those clever, titled lesbians who featured so prominently on the Paris salon circuit in the years before and after the First War. The Princess knew mutual friends from both the Polignac and Barney circles, which meant that John and Una were soon attending her lavish London parties (Una thought them 'dull'). Budge invited them to a private view of her work at the Leicester Galleries. Augustus John invited them to a 'thé dansant'.

One of Teddie's friends was the American star Tallulah Bankhead. Like Teddie, Tallulah had made her name as a stage vamp, but the sensuality she projected was smouldering rather than coy. In 1923 she had appeared in London for the first time in a play called *The Dancers*. Her part was small but it created a sensation. With her husky Southern drawl ('like hot honey and milk', wrote one critic), heavy-lidded eyes, and voluptuous red mouth, she was the embodiment of provocative sexuality. What made her unique, however, was her enormous following among young women, chiefly, it seems, of the typist and shop-assistant class. The press solemnly deplored the cult, without quite saying why, in articles with headlines such as 'The Hysterical Gallery Girl' – and thereby boosted the phenomenon still further.

Tallulah intrigued John. Here was another beautiful young American who had discarded all inhibitions, who drank heavily, took drugs, and was carefree about sex. Though she was not a lesbian, by her own admission she had had love affairs with women as well as men, having a penchant, it seems, for boyish females.[10] Perhaps she was, accordingly, drawn to John and Una. Certainly John, as a woman who saw herself competing with men for women's favours, would have regarded the Tallulah cult with interest. At all events, in the spring Tallulah suddenly became one of their closest friends. They ordered huge bouquets of flowers for her first night in a new play *This Marriage* at the Comedy in May. She was always inviting them to tea, where they met her amiable, heavy-drinking court jester, the amateur actor Sir Francis Laking. Dinners at the Eiffel Tower or the Moulin d'Or would be followed by dancing into the small hours at Brett's.

In March John had 'flu. After months of tension and excitement over her books, she was thoroughly run down. As soon as she was well enough to travel, Una took her to Weymouth and Bournemouth for a rest – though John insisted on doing some more work on *A Saturday Life*. She also wrote to the Society for Psychical Research handing in her resignation from the Council. She felt her writing was taking up too much time to do justice to her duties on the Council. Her recent illness convinced her, under Una's persistent prodding, that she must cut down her commitments. Her letter insisted, however, that she did not intend to give up psychical research and she would continue to sit for Mrs Leonard (whose powers, she maintained, were greater than they had ever been).[11] The Council accepted John's resignation with regret.[12] After an association of some eight stormy years, it proved a remarkably quiet and dignified exit.

In May John and Una moved house yet again. They had begun to find Sterling Street unbearably cramped. In its place John bought 37, Holland Street, an attractive Dutch-style town house off Kensington Church Street and conveniently close to the Carmelite church where they sometimes attended mass.

During May Una sat for her portrait by Romaine. Some seven sessions took place at the Cromwell Road studio, followed by two more in early June. Una wore a long dark severely cut jacket and pinstripe skirt over a white shirt with stiff wing collar and stock. Romaine was amused by this get-up and had Una pose standing up, her monocle set firmly in her eye and the two dachshunds, Thor and Wotan, placed on a table in front of her. In the finished picture the dogs look up adoringly at their mistress, directing the eye of the observer to the bold white splash of the shirt and the pale oval face above. Una looks curiously tall and angular, with an elongated arm sweeping down to an outsize hand in the foreground clutching one of the dogs by the collar – the whole effect like a reflection in a mildly distorting mirror. Her pursed mouth and knitted brows, framed by the helmet of close-cropped hair, lend her a somewhat exasperated expression. Whatever her original intentions, Romaine finished by creating a brilliant caricature of Una, one that caught both her eccentricity and that element of class arrogance which could make her seem so severe at times. Romaine wrote to Natalie that the portrait would perhaps cause future generations to smile.[13]

The sittings had not been easy for Una. In her casual way, Romaine had cast aspersions on *The Forge* which Una could not ignore out of loyalty to John, and some sharp words were exchanged – hence perhaps Una's look of irritation in the picture. When Romaine showed the portrait to John on June 9, John was politely unenthusiastic. Una told Romaine she was pleased, but to John and her friends she expressed surprise at the way she had been portrayed. 'Am I really like that?' she asked.[14] With the portrait still not finished, Romaine decided to leave London for the south. In a note to Una she hoped that a further sitting could be arranged when she returned. She ended brusquely: 'Don't bother bringing the dog (sic) to London, they must accept my colour scheme. Tant pis!'[15]

John and Una were also making plans to go away, to Bagnoles again for another rest cure. In the last week of May John finished the first draft of *A Saturday Life* and Una booked their reservations for June 12 on the boat-train to Paris. A few days before they were due to leave, Audrey Heath informed them that Newman Flower, the literary director of Cassell – the eleventh publisher to the approached – was highly impressed by *The Unlit Lamp*. She felt the prospects were good. No further word had come from Flower by the 12th, so John and Una made their departure as planned. However, arriving at the Hotel Normandy in Paris that night, they were greeted by two telegrams from Audrey saying Cassell had offered good terms for the novel. They immediately altered their plans and made arrangements to return to London. The rest of that evening they worked on the book, revising it in line with Flower's stipulation that it be reduced in length.

Over the weekend that followed they hurriedly made the rounds of their Paris friends, including Violette Murat, the actress Gwen Fargo, and Natalie Barney. By Sunday night they were back in London. On Monday they worked on *The Lamp* all day in collaboration with Audrey, reducing it to a final 108,000 words by Tuesday. On the Friday the contract with Cassell was signed. Audrey Heath was right. The terms *were* good. For the first time in her literary career John received an advance, of £50. Her royalties would be 15% on the first 3,000 copies (of a six-shilling hardback edition), 20% thereafter. In addition, Cassell retained an option on her next two novels, excluding *A Saturday Life* (to which Arrowsmith had already laid claim). Flower had built up a strong list of high-brow popular fiction at Cassell and John was joining distinguished company: H. G. Wells, Arnold Bennett, Robert Hitchens, Louis Bromfield, Olive Wadsley, Stefan Zweig, Sheila Kaye-Smith, Compton Mackenzie, Ernest Raymond.

On June 22 they again boarded the boat-train to return to Paris. They were in high spirits. Unlike John, who was an excellent sailor and loved grey British seas, Una detested the Channel crossing. She shut herself away in a private cabin and sipped dry martinis in an effort to forestall the effects of seasickness. Lunch on the Paris train, however, made it all worthwhile. In *The Forge* John had evoked the nostalgic feelings she always felt on entering those familiar French compartments, with their mud-coloured seats adorned by lace anti-macassars. The smell of good coffee, the passing of the waiter in his red and blue uniform, the babble of foreign accents, excited her with pleasurable expectations 'like a bugle call'. Lunch itself, fortified by an expensive wine, invariably culminated in their favourite indulgence, a towering bombe glacée followed by delicious hot coffee splashed into thick pale-blue cups.[16]

During the few days they stayed in Paris before proceeding to Bagnoles and the Hotel des Thermes, they were involved in a strange scene at Natalie Barney's. Natalie was her usual charming self and she made Una read *The Forge* out loud to her. At a certain juncture

Romaine put in an appearance and, seeing what they were doing, caused 'a hideous scene abusing The Forge, John & Natalie like a fishwife!'[17] It was a revealing moment, showing that beneath the casual exterior Romaine remained highly sensitive and insecure. Romaine's reaction impressed John. In the future she would be careful to disguise the real-life source of her fictional inspiration and always denied that her books were autobiographical. When, later in 1924, she sent Natalie a copy of *The Unlit Lamp*, she insisted it contained no portraits drawn from life. Natalie replied that as far as she was concerned, she had no quarrel with such portraits. With characteristic playfulness, she declared she would get Romaine to read the novel aloud to her, adding 'I think she may feel that you have treated an even more serious subject lightly – and that she was more worthy of the serious book!'[18] Natalie had long experience of Romaine's more irrational impulses.

John and Una remained at Bagnoles throughout July, quietly taking their daily baths and correcting batches of page proofs sent out to them from Cassell. On their return to London, John had her first taste of what it was to be a literary lion. At a party given by Vere and Budge, the guests included Leonard Rees (editor of the *Sunday Times*), Margaret Irwin, Michael Arlen, and the ubiquitous Violet Hunt. Word had got round about Newman Flower's high opinion of *The Unlit Lamp* and everyone made a great fuss of the new author. Elated by this unprecedented attention from her professional colleagues, John took Una on a spending spree, buying her a snow leopard coat at Welsman's and a cretonne coat for herself.

The Unlit Lamp was finally published at the end of September. For the first time the author's name on the cover read simply 'Radclyffe Hall'. One of the earliest reviews, in the *Sunday Times*, was by Alec Waugh, elder brother of the as yet unpublished Evelyn. Waugh expressed equivocal feelings about the novel. He found the subject interesting, but he deemed its treatment only 'adequate'. The best thing in the book in his opinion was the portrayal of Mrs Ogden, but he saw Joan's instinct for self-sacrifice as strange and disturbing. Interestingly, Waugh made the point that the novel was entirely feminine, men being merely incidental to the story.[19]

Una mentions Waugh's review in the diary without passing comment – a sure sign that they were disappointed by it. That same evening Francis Laking dined with them and got abominably drunk ('we had an awful time'), which did not improve their spirits. Two days later, however, they were thrilled by five further reviews, all 'magnificent'. Moreover, on checking at Harrods and *The Times* Book Club, they discovered that the book had sold out. There was more excitement when they learnt that the *Lamp* was being advertised in a giant display on the station clock at St Pancras. They wasted no time in going round to see it. Una persuaded John she should be photographed at this important juncture in her career, so she posed for the fashionable Lafayette studio.

John and Una dined with Vere and Budge on November 1 and sensed an 'atmosphere' between them. When they saw Vere a few days later, her behaviour was distinctly odd. On the 6th they had dinner with Gabrielle Enthoven, who was now in charge of the theatre collection at the Victoria and Albert Museum. On their return home, they were greeted by 'Budge's bomb' – a note from Budge informing them that Vere, who was only thirty-three, had contracted an unspecified virus which would eventually leave her paralysed. A further symptom of the condition was periodic bouts of insanity – which explained Vere's strange conduct. The situation was tragic. Vere's second novel *Great Waters* had been recently published by Cape to some fine reviews. The question arose as to how long she could now go on writing, and how Budge could support her on her meagre income if she had to give up work. John and Una spent the next day gloomily debating the matter with Audrey Heath. Nobody, least of all the doctors, seemed to know exactly what was wrong with Vere. For the moment she could still write (and would produce a new novel in 1925), but within a year she would be virtually a cripple.

In December 37, Holland Street was at last ready to receive them. John enjoyed supervising renovation work and had chosen much of the décor for their new home. Once again, their favourite oak style predominated. All the basins and mantelpieces had been taken out to be replaced by bathrooms and gas fires set in Old English red brick hearths. The rooms were large, with attractive casement windows and deep window-ledges where they would keep well-tended bulbs. The house was narrow, however, with few rooms on each floor. They decided to share the 'master bedroom' since the only other room on the same floor proved hardly big enough to hold a bed. To sleep on different floors was out of the question, so they installed twin beds in the main bedroom, each with linenfold oak panelling at head and foot, and made do without a dressing-room. They turned the small bedroom into a guest room, giving it over to Andrea when she was home for the school holidays. The drawing-room lay on the first floor, the walls painted a warm yellow – the only unusual feature in a beautifully appointed but otherwise conventional domestic interior. A staff of three, a cook and two maids, completed the establishment. John was a stickler for correct dress for the servants, insisting that her maids wore the traditional white aprons and brimless caps. Sloppiness or incompetence, as always, received short shrift. Within six weeks of moving in, the parlourmaid had been replaced, while the new chauffeur was promptly sacked for driving Una 'like hell' to the French cleaners one morning.[20]

Holland Street would be their home for the next four years – years which would mark the high-point of John's career as a novelist. She had, for the first time in her life, 'found herself' and was not plagued by that nagging malaise that in the past had expressed itself partly as a chronic sort of wanderlust. By the end of 1924 she was fast becoming known. Almost weekly, chiefly under the benevolent patronage of Leonard Rees, she was meeting new members of the British literary establishment: St John Adcock, the publisher John Murray, Netta Syrett, Rebecca West, Alec Waugh, E. V. Lucas, Edmund Gosse, all made her acquaintance at this time. At the PEN Club dinner in December many fellow-writers came forward to congratulate her on *The Unlit Lamp*.

This was also the period when John started becoming a regular 'first-nighter' at the theatre. She and Una sometimes attended as many as three or four different plays a week, matineés as well as evenings. Because they knew several successful actresses, this ritual was partly a service to friends. But the 'first night' in the Twenties was also a great social occasion, an opportunity to see and be seen. Though John was a shy, diffident person, she enjoyed the limelight of this particular arena. At a time when theatre-goers commonly dressed in evening clothes, John's appearance in high stiff collar, man's stock, and black military cloak, invariably caused a stir. The romantic actor in her thrived on this attention and, with her customary style, she rarely disappointed expectations.

Radclyffe Hall at a first night was an image of her which many people who saw her but never knew her would always remember – and smile in that slightly superior way. What they perceived, of course, was a woman trying to ape a man, overlooking the emotional need that gave life to her performance. Ironically, John never attempted to masquerade as a man – not by her own standards at any rate. Though she never carried a handbag and had special pockets sewn into her skirts, she drew the line at wearing trousers in public. To have done so would, in her book, have been to act out a deception. Therefore, from the waist down at least, she made no attempt to disguise her true sex. But it did not stop her *wanting* to be a man. Her own frustration and her awareness that other people regarded her with a certain amusement, merely confirmed her view that the sensitive individual lay at the mercy of overwhelming pressures in the ordinary world.

Chapter Fifteen

A Saturday Life was published on April 1, 1925 (with a jacket designed by Una). The book had sold nearly 700 advance copies. Arrowsmith planned to bring out a cheap second edition of *The Forge* in May to capitalize on John's growing reputation since *The Unlit Lamp*. As usual, on the day of publication John and Una rushed round the book stores checking on stocks. They found business 'thriving'. When the reviews came out, they were almost universally appreciative. Even those which had reservations (mainly about the story – plot was never John's strong point) praised her descriptive powers and her eye for character. The review which pleased them most was by Ida Wylie in *The Queen* magazine. John was, wrote Ida, a writer 'who sets out with no apparent intention at all of being funny but who surprises the chuckles out of you with the nonchalant air of a conjurer producing rabbits from the pockets of an astonished schoolboy'. The novel had a measured perfection, accomplishing exactly what it set out to do in exquisitely economic language, a quality Ida ascribed to John's early training as a poet: 'Laughter lurks in her description of a sofa. She can conjure up Italian memories in a line.' Ida expected John to write a big, important novel one day.[1]

Like *The Forge, A Saturday Life* was a comic novel with a serious underlying purpose. It represented a variation on the earlier book's examination of artistic experience and the conflict between egoism and social obligation that John felt so keenly lay at the heart of this experience. The heroine of the story, Sidonia, is a bright, vivacious girl who possesses an extraordinary array of artistic talents. She excels at dancing, drawing, poetry, piano-playing, sculpting and singing. What is remarkable about these aptitudes is that they arise spontaneously one after the other, wholly developed, at different stages of her childhood and adolescence. Once one talent has languished and been replaced by another, it is lost for good as if she had never possessed it. The explanation is that Sidonia is a reincarnation of former artistic lives, six of them. According to this theory, which is derived from Eastern mysticism and dubbed 'the legend of the Saturday Life', certain persons are destined to live seven times on earth. The seventh and last life repeats all the previous incarnations one after the other in rapid succession. In other words, the story has a large element of fantasy to it.

At the start of the novel Sidonia, as one would expect in such a precocious child, is wilful, headstrong and selfish. By the end she has mellowed and matured. She has given up all thought of the operatic career she was planning and has married a dull country gentleman called David, bearing him a child in the closing pages. Sidonia's story is, then, like Susan's in *The Forge*, a tale with a moral. In the process of 'finding herself', she is influenced by several important characters: an unmarried friend of her mother's called Frances, her art teacher Einar Jensen, and a close-knit Italian family, the Ferraris, with whom Sidonia stays in Florence while training to be a singer. Each of these mentors teaches the girl, in different ways, that there is a balance to be struck between artistic inspiration and ordinary life, that artistic integrity need not be compromised by a certain degree of social conformity.

A Saturday Life both looks back to John's earlier fiction and fore-shadows the work to come. The central relationship in the early part of the book, between Sidonia, Frances, and Sidonia's mother Lady Shore, has echoes of the threesome in *The Unlit Lamp*. Sidonia is jealous of Frances's friendship with her mother and, in a scene remarkably reminiscent of Elizabeth's pleas to Joan, begs her to try and love her more. Whereas in *The Forge* the artistic characters were not wholly sympathetic figures, in *A Saturday Life* the art professor Einar Jensen and the singing teacher Liza Ferrari are cast as exemplary models of compassion and humanity. This is not such a reversal as it looks for both are teachers rather than artists, in Jensen's case a failed artist even. Jensen is dwarf-like and has a crook back. Yet he is a brilliant teacher. He has a remarkable air of spirituality, being selfless and, in the literal sense of the word, pitiful. When Sidonia first meets him she thinks, significantly, that he looks like St Paul. The point John is making about Jensen is that he is saintly because he has known suffering. His grotesque physical shape and his sense of failure as an artist are sources of pain and humiliation which have had the effect of making him sensitive and caring.

Despite its stylistic resemblance to *The Forge, A Saturday Life* is essentially a 'spiritual' novel with strong religious undertones. Sidonia's quest for self-fulfilment takes her progressively down a path towards self-denial. In marrying David, she in effect consecrates herself to a life of service. While on one level this seems an appalling waste of a particularly dynamic individual, on another the novel suggests that Sidonia has attained a kind of spirituality.

John meant her moral to apply just as much to men as women. Because her fiction is principally about women and because she herself was homosexual, her novels have been eagerly scoured by modern commentators for her attitude to the 'woman question'. But this is to simplify her views. Her concern went beyond both women and homosexuals, whom she saw as just two kinds of 'victim' among many others. In *A Saturday Life* she can be seen reaching out for a more unified vision, one that embraced the material and spiritual elements of life, that affirmed the mystery and timelessness of all experience. The novel ultimately fails because such a theme cannot be satisfactorily accommodated in a story which, despite its supernatural elements, is so thoroughly grounded in a world of conventional realism.

Further evidence of John's preoccupation with the theme of spirituality comes from a short story which she started writing at the end of January 1925 and finished within ten days. This was called 'Upon the Mountains'. It deals, significantly, with yet another triangular relationship. Tino and Mateo are two brothers. An unusually close bond unites them until Tino falls in love with a volatile, capricious woman called Fiora. After Tino has married Fiora, Mateo becomes increasingly resentful of his exclusion from his brother's side and his relations with Fiora deteriorate into a deadly rivalry for Tino's affections. Tino is subsequently killed in an air crash, but his death only increases the enmity between Mateo and Fiora, who become obsessed with discovering the sign, that Tino had once promised to give them should he die first, indicating which of the two had loved him better. Each tries to outdo the other in the most trivial and ingratiating acts of service to the dead man's memory.

This state of affairs continues for two years as Mateo and Fiora travel through Europe together, bound by their strange pact to accompany each other everywhere. The story ends in the rugged Carpathian mountains. Mateo has become a changed man, full of an unearthly serenity. He no longer hates Fiora and does not care any more which of them receives the sign from Tino. But in fact Mateo has made his way to the mountains on the strength of a message which an English friend claims to have acquired through a spiritualist medium. The message directs Mateo to a small chapel in the mountains. It is here that he is found dead at the story's close, slumped in a position of prayer and clutching a piece of paper which contains the quotation from Isaiah: 'How beautiful upon the mountains are the feet of him that bringeth good tidings, that publisheth peace.'

There are echoes here of the John/Ladye/Una triangle, and once again, as in *A Saturday Life,* the story assumes the existence of a spiritual domain that transcends the earthly world and takes the form of a spiritual quest. Through bitterness and conflict Mateo learns Christian love and in so doing acquires a kind of sainthood, but only at the price of removal from the real world and of his death.

'Upon the Mountains' was John's last (direct) fictional word on the subject of Ladye. Guilt is a powerful stimulus and the question arises whether John would have turned her hand to fiction without it. Much of her prose writing represents a quest for atonement. Since she was driven by a strong sub-conscious desire to punish herself for her 'betrayal' of Ladye, her fictional counterparts can only acquire 'absolution' through a process of ordeal and loss. The ultimate self-sacrifice is death itself, for this is at one and the same time the only 'punishment' which fits the 'crime' against Ladye *and* the only true means of being reunited with her.

John's sense of isolation as a homosexual would have given her fiction, as it gave her poetry, a strong streak of fatalism in any case. Her guilt over Ladye, reinforced by a self-dramatizing Catholic conscience, steered her towards protagonists who were the victims not just of external forces but of their own inner self-destructive impulses. Mateo is the first major character in her work to give his life in the quest for self-fulfilment. Since John's religion did not allow her to condone suicide, his act of self-sacrifice is characterized as the last step in a mystical process towards spiritual perfection. It therefore represents not despair but triumph and renewal.

The first Una heard of *Adam's Breed* was when she and John were lunching at one of their favourite haunts, the Pall Mall Restaurant:

> John became abstracted and inattentive. Her eye was following our obsequious waiter and presently she said to me with quiet decision, 'I am going to write the life of a waiter who becomes so utterly sick of handling food that he practically lets himself die of starvation'.[2]

This rather unpromising idea for a story-line was not the beginning but the end of a long process of reflection about the theme that preoccupied John. It seems likely that all her novels went through this lengthy gestation period. Only a handful of the short stories she wrote have survived, but they seem to have served to varying degrees as 'try-outs' for the larger works. Una tells us in her memoir that John also wrote what they called her 'trolley books'. These were serious attempts to embark on a new novel which, like *Michael West*, proved unsatisfactory or which were superseded by a more viable idea. For example, in the autumn of 1924 she had started a story called 'The World'. Judging by the title, this possibly represented another shot at the theme of spiritual perfection. By January 1925 Audrey Heath was telling John that 'The World' ought to be a novel. However, some three weeks later John began 'Upon the Mountains' and no more was heard of 'The World'.

If the trolley books represented a stage in John's creative method, they also fulfilled a psychological need born of a persistent professional anxiety. Unlike most of her novelist friends, who had begun writing fiction in their twenties, John was a late starter, well over forty when her first book was published. Acutely conscious of this (to the point of falsifying her age in later years), she saw herself as a writer in a hurry, driven by the urge to make up for lost time. She was therefore inclined to push herself to the limit, fretting about starting a new novel even before the previous one had been finished or published. 'That faint anxiety of hers,' recalled Una,

> would grow like Jack's beanstalk until it overshadowed every other consideration. Why was she still without an idea in her head? Was she never going to be able to write another book? She was getting no younger and her output might be over . . . she had not begun to write till maturity. Never had she known so prolonged a period of stagnation! Was I sure that the last book had been really first-class! After all, there had been some adverse reviews. Come to think of it, she couldn't remember many good ones! Did I remember such and such a criticism? Was it really worth while her writing at all? And yet again and again and again: why was she without the ghost of an inspiration? Head by head I would tackle this Hydra; infinitely pitiful of what she endured but perfectly confident of the ultimate issue, and almost invariably her misery would seek relief in the gestation or resurrection of a trolley book.[3]

A still deeper cause lay at the root of this chronic anxiety. As her poetry had shown, John felt a sense of dislocation from the world around her, ever conscious that her homosexuality set her apart. She had sublimated this feeling in her writing, which was now the central activity of her life. Through her books she had begun to meet people outside the small lesbian circles she frequented, important writers and intellectuals who held some influence in society. Therefore her work offered proof that she was worthy of respect and could make her mark. But by measuring her personal esteem against her success as a writer, her confidence was easily eroded by small setbacks and she dreaded the loss of her talent.

Exactly a fortnight after the publication of *A Saturday Life*, John began writing *Food*, the working title of the novel which would emerge as *Adam's Breed*. That same evening Rebecca West and May Sinclair came to dinner and John told them all about the new book. The two guests were no doubt flattering for Una reported the occasion as 'v. successful'.[4]

Rather less successful were meetings with their respective mothers. The Visettis had taken to wintering on the south coast and this year were staying in Bournemouth. On April 3 Marie was suddenly taken ill and John and Una had to travel down to Westcliff to see her. With *A Saturday Life* just out and John on tenterhooks about its reception, Marie's timing could not have been more inconvenient. John dreaded the inevitable hysterics from her mother and they only stayed in Bournemouth one night, long enough to make the necessary arrangements for Marie's treatment (for which John footed the bill).

Minna was no less 'tiresome' when she lunched with them on April 9. She had never come to terms with her daughter living with John. During and after Una's separation from Troubridge, they suspected that Minna was in touch with the admiral and might be used as a go-between to patch up a reconciliation. The final straw had been her conspicuous lack of support for them during the Fox-Pitt case, the first time, as Una saw it, that John and she had had their backs to the wall. Viola, who also disapproved of John, had blotted her copybook too. In 1921 she had married another journalist, J. L. Garvin, the editor of the *Observer*, a paper whose coverage of the slander action Una construed as an insult to John's integrity. In fact, the *Observer* proved less damning than *The Times*, but Una always expected family and friends to show blind support. By marrying Garvin, Viola had let the side down.

1925 was a busy year for John. Her career had reached that tantalizing stage where, with a measure of success behind her, great things were expected in the future. She was in demand. Her portrait was sketched and women's magazines started to show an interest in her. The American Women's Club invited her to lunch. She was to be found occasionally at the fashionable Kit-Kat Club, one of the Prince of Wales' haunts, in the company of Lord Ned Lathom, the stage producer, or the Dolly Sisters, Hungarian-born twins whose cabaret act had taken Paris by storm the previous year. She continued to meet new writers – Alfred Noyes, Hanslip Fletcher, Clifford Bax, Ralph Straus, Berta Ruck – many of them invited back to Holland Street in a series of dinner parties which she and Una hosted during the spring and summer.

Leonard and Molly Rees remained among their closest literary friends. John felt a debt of gratitude for their unstinting support and the couple were frequent guests at Holland Street. When the Rees' daughter died unexpectedly in May, John and Una were among the first to visit and console them. Alec Waugh, whom they had met through Rees, was another whom they saw quite often. His father had run Chapman and Hall at the time the firm published John's poetry. Alec Waugh liked John and Una, though they struck him as 'an austere Edwardian couple who expected conventional behaviour from their guests and hosts'. Of the two, he felt more at ease with Una. John had a somewhat blimpish, humourless manner that he found both disconcerting and risible. He recalled: 'She said once of Francis Laking "If you want to have a properly run house, you can't have people like him around. The servants won't stand for it." She never in my presence referred to her own amatory relations – anymore than a Victorian couple would. It was assumed that intimacies took place in darkened rooms when the world was silent.'[5]

In the company of other writers, especially men, John often felt inhibited and on her mettle. Her tendency on such occasions was to project a tight-lipped, forthright manner, with the result that she appeared more of a caricature than she really was. Beverley Nichols recalled what he described as her 'British policeman act':

> hands clasped behind the back, chin thrust up, knees bent and jerked outward in a springy, aggressive motion. While indulging in these callisthenics she would discourse intelligently about the latest novel. It was her boast that she knew nothing about housekeeping. She must have regarded this as a sign of virility, because she so often referred to it. 'Couldn't boil an egg', she would proclaim gruffly, jerking out her knees with extra gusto. 'Couldn't light a fire, couldn't dust a chimneypiece.'[6]

The publisher Rupert Hart-Davis remembered her as looking like 'a retired admiral': 'It was always said that at a dinner-party, when the women left the table, Johnny Hall (as she was always called) found it hard to make up her mind whether to go with the women or remain with the men.'[7] By contrast, her close women friends, not all of them lesbians, recalled her panache and sense of style, *and* her humour. Many of those who knew her well would later remark on her capacity for laughter and for making others laugh too.

Two secretaries now worked at Holland Street. The faithful Miss McLean, who had been with them since the early psychical research days, was joined in April by another typist, Miss Clark. John's career now generated a considerable work load. In addition to the constant demands created by 'polishing' her various manuscripts, a sizeable correspondence had to be answered. To keep interruptions to John's writing to a minimum, Una bore the brunt of this latter task, spending hours dictating to the two typists or penning her own replies on John's behalf.

Una was still writing articles for the SPR. She had also embarked in a small way on her own literary activities. In the summer of 1924 she had begun an English translation of Charles Pettit's *Le Fils du Grand Eunuque*, a florid romantic novel set amid the perfumed mysteries of the exotic Orient. She finished the task by the end of the year and, through Audrey Heath, began to hawk the book from publisher to publisher. In the meantime Audrey asked Una to become a reader for the agency on a part-time basis, as did Cassell, for whom she was already designing a jacket for *Adam's Breed*. And in the summer Leonard Rees asked her to write an article for the *Sunday Times*.

Though Una took pride in her own literary efforts, there was never any question in her mind that John's work came first and that her primary role was to create the right conditions under which John's genius could flourish. In effect, this meant that Una served not only as John's amanuensis but her full-time housekeeper and social secretary. She even, when necessary, prepared John's tax accounts and bought her clothes. This was devotion of a high order.

Having completed the first four chapters of *Food*, John signed her contract with Cassell at the end of July. The terms, including the £50 advance, were identical to those for *The Unlit Lamp*. At the last moment Newman Flower had baulked at the title. In June, while they were on holiday at the Cottage Hotel in Lynton, Flower rang through to say that the novel was bound to be mistaken for a cookery book. This hitch threw John into a panic and once again Una (who had earlier bought a lamb as a mascot for the book) came to the rescue. Firmly rejecting John's frenzied suggestions, she ransacked the local W. H. Smith's and found what they were looking for in Kipling's poem 'Tomlinson', which describes a dead soul's rejection by both Heaven and Hell: 'I'm all o'er-sib to Adam's breed that I should mock your pain' ran the line.

Adam's Breed was the first novel which John researched. She based Teresa's pasta factory in Soho on a real establishment situated in Old Compton Street which Una discovered. They managed to gain entrance to the place by passing off John as an eccentric Italian woman fascinated by the manufacture of macaroni. The 'Doric' restaurant in the book was modelled on Ladye's old favourite, the Berkeley Grill, whose kitchens they were allowed to inspect. In October John visited a public mortuary with a pathologist, Dr Brontë, in order to verify the procedures there. Towards the end of October the couple went for a weekend to Brockenhurst in the New Forest to retrace Gian-Luca's steps for the last part of the book. John had planned that her hero should meet a poor charcoal burner in the forest, remembering such characters from her Bournemouth childhood. They were not easy to find. 'I am not likely to forget our hunt for that charcoal burner,' wrote Una years later, 'we trudged and waded in abominable weather and found him at last; almost, it seemed, by chance, and [John] listened for hours while he expounded his lore. I remember that I beguiled a part of the time by extracting a sheep-tick from his kitten's ear!'[8]

In September Audrey Heath had introduced John to the American publisher Russell Doubleday, who was passing through London on his way to a European holiday. He read what John had written of *Adam's Breed* and she told him how she intended to end it. He eventually wrote to Audrey, from Venice, to make an offer on behalf of Doubleday Page and Company to publish the novel in the States.[9] A contract was signed a month later, giving John less good terms than Cassell's but a $250 advance *and* that all-important entrée into the American market. So as soon as the Cassell draft was delivered, John and Una turned their attention to Doubleday's, changing spellings and checking for anglicisms that might be unintelligible to the American reader. The work was finished on November 20 and they carried it off in triumph to Audrey Heath. On their way home afterwards they bought a small cockatoo to celebrate.

'We are hugely enjoying our well earned holiday,' Una wrote in the diary five days later. Once again, after such taxing endeavours, they gravitated towards their lesbian friends: Toupie and Gabrielle and Teddie's lover Etheline – who was now to be seen in the company of the novelist Eileen Bliss, Teddie having departed for America to take up another engagement. Not that Teddie seemed too concerned about fidelity. They received a homesick letter from her in New York in which she wondered 'who is with who amongst our bright young friends – I suppose the cards have been shuffled & reshuffled by now'. Enquiring after the new parrot, she added: 'I hope John won't teach him any bad language!!!'[10] For the first time for several months John attended a PEN dinner, escorting Violet Hunt. On December 2 there was consternation at Holland Street when they learnt that Thor, whom they had recently sold to some people called the Cholmondeley's, had been given by them to a hairdresser. This would never do. 'Home & wrote to get hold of him,' the diary recorded purposefully.[11]

Christmas 1925 was spent with the Temples in Datchet. Andrea, now fifteen, joined them. Since April 1923 the girl had been at a new convent school, St George's, Harpenden. Una had gone down to attend her sports day during the first term, but thereafter, as John's writing career took off, visits were few and far between. In the holidays Holland Street was not the most welcoming of homes for a teenager. While she worked John did not easily tolerate noise or interruptions, so Andrea was rarely allowed to bring friends to the house. If the girl wanted privacy, the cramped cupboard of a bedroom that was hers proved a less than inviting refuge. The knowledge that her mother was the lover of the woman who lived with them cannot have eased the normal growing pains of an adolescent. The fact that John tried to persuade Andrea to address her as 'uncle' only compounded her embarrassment.[12]

Chapter Sixteen

The entry in the diary for January 28 read: 'Admiral Troubridge died at Biarritz.' The stark, formal statement had been written on the 29th, the day that Minna broke the news to them. Una's lack of emotion showed how far apart she and Zip had drifted since their separation. The admiral had retired in 1924 after a second term as president of the Danube Commission. He had been attending a tea-dance in Biarritz when he collapsed with a heart-attack. The funeral took place in Biarritz on February 1, attended by a distinguished gathering of military and naval colleagues of the dead man as well as by Chatty, Tom and Mary, his first three children. Una and Andrea did not go. While her husband was being laid to rest in France, Una was scribbling a furious letter to her mother. Now that Troubridge had gone, Minna renewed her pressure on Una to leave John and remarry. There were strong financial grounds for this course, argued Minna, for Una had learned to her astonishment that the annual widow's pension she would receive from the Admiralty amounted to only £225, with a mere £24 in maintenance for Andrea. This would hardly keep her in the style to which she was accustomed. But Una rounded on her mother impatiently, calling her interference 'intolerable' and 'damnable'. In her letter she made it clear once and for all that she would never leave John and had no interest in marrying again.

On February 13 a memorial service for Troubridge was held at Westminster Cathedral. This time Una attended with Andrea, who had come from school for the weekend. John stayed at home and took one of the dogs for a walk. Her feelings are not recorded, but there had never been much love lost between her and the admiral. To her friends she now jocularly declared that, with Una single again, she would have to keep on her toes to compete with the young 'bloods' who would be coming a-calling on her.[1]

Troubridge died a puzzled and bitter man. He had found it hard to comprehend how his pretty young wife could have forsaken him for another woman. What embittered him most was a story which Una circulated among her friends at the time of their break-up to the effect that her ill-health during her marriage had been due to her husband giving her syphilis. She claimed John had cured her of the disease. There is no evidence to suggest that this was anything other than a fantasy of Una's imagining designed to justify her behaviour to those people who would have been horrified by any hint of homosexuality. Crighton-Miller made it abundantly clear that Una's problems were psychological and psychosomatic. The gynaecological troubles for which Dr Sachs and others treated her stemmed from a damaged Fallopian tube: their prescriptions, meticulously noted by Una in the diaries, were certainly not for syphilis. But the damage was done and Troubridge never forgave Una for a cruel blow which he considered added insult to injury.[2]

On March 4 *Adam's Breed* was published. Two weeks earlier the writer Alfred Noyes, who had a review copy, had rung them to say it was 'unquestionably by far one of the finest novels he had read in the last ten years'.[3] John herself believed it 'far and away the best thing that I have ever written'.[4] Word quickly got about that it was a book to buy (Cassell's advertisements billed it as 'The book that has set the literary world talking'). The first edition of 3,500 copies sold out within a week. A reprint of 1,500 copies was followed two weeks later by two further reprints, also of 1,500 each. In April a fifth impression appeared, while in May Doubleday reported that subscriber sales in America (where the book was not due out until July) already totalled well over 2,000. Una, who kept a careful tally of the novel's progress in the back of her diary, recorded that sales to the end of June reached almost 9,500 in England. John was on a royalty of 20% after the first 3,000 copies and Una calculated that she had made £637 from the book so far – no small sum at that time.

Flushed with success, John posed for her by now familiar post-publication photograph, taken this time by fashionable Douglas's of St James's Place. She also bought Una a Standard motor car (which they nicknamed The Squig). In April she invited a number of literary people to dinner at Holland Street, among them Audrey Heath, James Agate, Violet Hunt, and the elderly Mrs Alice Perrin, a novelist of Anglo-Indian life who had known Ladye. Both Violet and Mrs Perrin sat on the British committee of the Prix Femina Vie Heureuse, an award for the best English novel of the year sponsored by a French women's magazine. Violet had nominated *Adam's Breed* for the prize.

The reviews of *Adam's Breed* were enthusiastic. All found it moving and remarked on its originality. The *Observer* thought it just missed greatness (through a lack of humour), while the *Sunday Times* declared it stood 'head and shoulders above the general run of contemporary fiction'.[5] The *Sunday Herald* described it as a book distinguished by 'a sympathy, strength and skill in craftsmanship rare in these hurried, novelty-seeking days'.[6]

What impressed serious critics about *Adam's Breed* was the symbolic aspect of the novel and its poetic intensity. Indeed, without this quality the book would have amounted to little more than a quaint story about a sensitive boy who grows up in Soho to become a distinguished headwaiter and then, in a prolonged nervous breakdown, develops such a revulsion to food that he starves himself to death. But it is evident that, as in all her work, John's story-line provided the vehicle for a much more personal theme.

The novel was her first to take a whole life, from birth to death, and was set in a period (about 1890 to the mid-1920s) that roughly spanned John's own lifetime. The childhood of the hero, Gian-Luca, draws heavily on John's own. The boy has 'ashen-fair' hair. He is a child rejected from birth by his grandmother Teresa, the woman who brings him up, because she holds against him the fact that her daughter died in labour. He grows up lonely, aloof, and with a sense of spiritual exile that is reinforced by his confusion of national identity as the illegitimate son of an unknown Italian father and a naturalized English mother. His feelings of isolation are further compounded when he is sent to a Board School instead of a Catholic establishment, an unusual step in the Italian community dictated by Teresa's anti-religious views. Even though he works his way up to become one of the finest waiters at the famous Doric restaurant, he remains curiously detached from its hurly-burly and colleagues find him inhuman and other-worldly.

Gian-Luca eventually marries a simple Italian girl called Maddalena. The name, with its Biblical overtones, is no accident and like all John's heroic women Maddalena is a humble, gentle, placid earth-mother figure full of quiet peasant wisdom. What attracts Gian-Luca to her are her maternal qualities (passion is almost entirely absent from their courtship): '"I think my mother must have been like you,"' he tells her, and the girl's beauty is likened to an arbour where a man might rest after toil. To his wife's dismay, Gian-Luca makes it clear that he does not want children, which Maddalena ascribes to the fact that he never knew his father.

When the war breaks out, Gian-Luca enlists. He dreams of performing heroic deeds at the battle front but to his deep disappointment he is assigned to the catering corps and never sees action. He returns to Soho at the war's end and becomes head waiter at the Doric, but a change has come over him in the meantime. Gone are all his ambitions to start his own restaurant and he now questions his existence as a waiter. He has drifted away from Maddalena in spirit and now treats her with a cold unkindness. His disillusion reaches its peak when his boyhood hero, the poet Ugo Doria, dines at the Doric. Gian-Luca takes enormous pains to give his distinguished guest the very best hospitality the restaurant can offer, only to discover that the great man is a debauched sensualist held in thrall by a vulgar, brainless courtesan. That night Gian-Luca destroys all his copies of Doria's poetry. The irony is that, unknown to either man, they are in fact father and son.

After this Gian-Luca develops a positive disgust for his job and the whole business of food and eating. The proprietor of the Doric instructs Gian-Luca to take a holiday. He and Maddalena spend four months in Italy with her peasant cousins. Despite their idyllic rural surroundings, Gian-Luca's behaviour grows even odder. He cannot stand the cruelty he sees everywhere displayed towards animals and his interference finally alienates his relatives, obliging him to return to England with Maddalena.

Up to this point Gian-Luca has always thought of himself as an Italian. He now begins to realize that the 'home' he seeks, and has always sought, is not a physical place but a state of mind, a spiritual peace. Accordingly, he throws up his job at the Doric, starts to give away his possessions, and finally leaves home and takes to the life of a tramp. From here on the religious undertones of the novel become increasingly conspicuous and the final steps in Gian-Luca's quest acquire a more or less conscious parallel to the Passion story itself. He ends up as a hermit in the New Forest, communing, like some latter-day St Francis, with the birds and beasts and sharing the simple poverty of other outcasts like gypsies and charcoal-burners. In an incident that recalls Judas's betrayal of Christ, Gian-Luca is prevailed upon to 'sell' for three shillings a forest pony he has befriended – knowing that the poor beast is destined for a life of darkness in the coal pits. However, heavenly forgiveness and self-revelation at last descend upon him as, dying from starvation and exposure, he suddenly understands the wider purpose underlying all creation. God, he realizes, is within himself and with this knowledge his restless soul finds peace. Significantly, when Maddalena gazes down at his dead body and remarks that he looks as if he was not here at all, the priest present observes: '"Why should Gian-Luca be here? Did Our Lord remain in his Tomb?"'

The language and imagery of *Adam's Breed* constantly evoke the symbolic, spiritual aspects of the story. Much play is made on the notion of service, which makes it apparent why John chose a waiter for her hero. In his first waiting job it is quickly discovered that he possesses 'that rarest of all gifts, the instinct for perfect service'. His first love, for the wife of his employer, is no grand passion but a form of selfless service and worship. In the forest he feeds the birds from the palms of his hands: 'So it happened that Gian-Luca, who had served all his life, continued to serve in the forest, waiting upon the simplicity of birds as he had upon Milady's caprices.'

'Seeing' and 'sight' are also terms that are used for their double meaning (John's poem 'The Blind Ploughman' employed the same device), as Gian-Luca stumbles towards a growing insight into the world around him and his final self-revelation. At crucial moments in his development he 'sees' visions (his 'pictures', he calls them) in the form of dreams or hallucinations. Nowhere is the symbolic significance of sight better described than in a scene where Gian-Luca comes across a beggar-woman selling matches. The woman is accompanied by a blind child, who makes such an impression on Gian-Luca that he 'sees' for the first time both the beauty and the ugliness of creation. A passing coster's barrow full of flowers is suddenly illumined by a blaze of light as the sun emerges from behind the clouds: 'and because of a child who could not see, Gian-Luca realised the flowers'. Equally, he now 'realizes' with new intensity the misery and rottenness of the world.

In no other novel was John so preoccupied with the way in which the experience of the child moulded the outlook of the adult. The lonely, unloved boy quickly realizes that, to survive in the world, he has only himself to rely upon. This makes him ambitious and highly professional at his job, ensuring his ultimate success as a waiter. Yet he remains so emotionally vulnerable that his symbolic quest for a 'home' has a convincing psychological basis to it. When Gian-Luca visits Italy with Maddalena, he thinks of it as a 'homecoming' and he feels like a child again. When he sets out on his final journey to the New Forest, he crosses Kew Bridge and his mind drifts back to happy picnics as a child in Kew Gardens. In the moment of dying, he closes his eyes with the sweet peacefulness of 'a child who is heavy with sleep'. And it is no accident that his body is found in a stable by an inn and when Maddalena weeps over him, she weeps 'for her unborn children and for the father of her unborn children, himself so much her child'. Life has come full circle for Gian-Luca, for in death he has been reborn and the slate wiped clean.

All John's novels betray to some degree her emotional loyalty to an unhappy childhood, but in *Adam's Breed* this impulse is central to the development of her protagonist. It fuels Gian-Luca's sense of spiritual exile, of being adrift in a world of modernity in which he feels out of place. It also provides the soil in which his pity and compassion grow, for pity is the ability to discern the vulnerable child in others. But such a sentiment is inimical to maturity, for it expresses a deep sympathy with childhood which others are expected to share. Invariably, others do not live up to this standard and misunderstand. Pity on these terms is irresistibly driven into bankruptcy, producing a painful and precarious adulthood for its possessor. Hence the strong thread of determinism pushing John's characters to their inevitable fate.

However, one feels that in *Adam's Breed* John successfully found the formula that had eluded her in previous novels, to express both the paradox of her own divided nature and her vision of the unity and divinity intrinsic to all creation. The book develops these themes with an impressive skill and patience, reaching a peak of mystic intensity that has rightly been compared to the far more famous *Siddartha* (1951) of Herman Hesse.[7] The catering business, with its obsession for food and drink, provided an apt metaphor for the values of sensual materialism on the one hand, while Gian-Luca's intuitive search for self-knowledge represented spiritual idealism on the other. The two opposites warred with each other in John herself. Once again, as a writer, she could not envisage a resolution to the conflict which embraced something of both philosophies. As before, her natural inclination was to settle for the self-sacrifice of her protagonist. This time, however, the moment of supreme self-denial is also a triumph, representing rediscovery and redemption.

At midnight on May 3, 1926, the country found itself in the grip of a General Strike. Transport and railway workers stopped work in support of the miners' campaign against reduced wages, and many other unions followed suit. In common with others of their class – who were reading in the *Daily Mail* such alarmist headlines as 'The Pistol at the Nation's Head' – John and Una started storing their furs and jewellery and volunteered for emergency transport duties. The Conservative press, and some members of the Baldwin government, saw the strike as Communist-inspired and spoke in terms of a class war. John and Una ended up driving patients to and from Charing Cross Hospital. 'We drove Mrs Rice to Sutton to see her dead child,' reported Una on May 11, '& enquired for a boy at Peckham with a crushed foot.' Middle- and upper-class life was not seriously affected by the strike and these small errands constituted the extent of the couple's contribution to 'doing their bit'. They had had their first wireless installed at Holland Street on May 5 (BBC radio broadcasts had begun in 1922) and the Sunday of the strike they listened to the service from St Martin-in-the-Fields. The General Strike ended on May 12 at 1 pm. As if to proclaim the resumption of normal life, Una commented: 'My tooth began to ache at lunch.'

On May 21 Cassell informed them that *Adam's Breed* was selling so well that no extra advertising would be needed. Indeed, even G. K. Chesterton's latest book had had to be postponed to accommodate the printing of a further 3,000 copies of John's novel. John felt elated but the prolonged excitement was taking its toll of her fragile nerves. The doctor ordered a complete rest. So on May 26 she and Una motored down to Burgh Island, off Bigbury-on-Sea near Weymouth, for a month's holiday – accompanied by three dogs, the maid Dickie, and Bradley the chauffeur.

'Miss Ogilvy Finds Herself', a short story, was completed in early July shortly after their return from holiday. Burgh Island inspired its setting. Miss Ogilvy is a lonely, middle-aged spinster of masculine manner and appearance who returns to England at the end of the Great War after performing heroically as the leader of an Allied ambulance unit serving at the French front. In short, Miss Ogilvy is an older version of Toupie Lowther, even down to her habit (so characteristic of Toupie) of rocking backwards and forwards on her feet and thrusting her hands into her jacket pockets. As a girl Miss Ogilvy had been tomboyish. She was strong and athletic and always insisted her name was William not Wilhelmina. When war broke out her first thought had been 'If only I were a man!' Her wish to see action is fulfilled after she forms her ambulance unit and persuades the French authorities to let it operate at the front.

The war represents Miss Ogilvy's finest hour, both in terms of the heroism she displays and for its liberating effect on her masculine temperament. With demobilization she is thrust back into the mundane world where, as before, her type of woman is out of place. Her disillusion and her latent homosexuality are brought home to her forcibly when one of the girls from her unit announces she is to marry. Miss Ogilvy leaves her petty, neurotic family and goes to stay on the small island off the Devon coast, searching like Gian-Luca before her for some answer to her unhappiness. It is here that the story takes on a fantastical, mystic quality. For, like Sidonia, Miss Ogilvy experiences the pull of a previous incarnation, in which she appears to have been a caveman on the island during the Bronze Age. In a dream or hallucination she relives this former life and her love for an adoring cave-woman. Though the primeval world in which they exist is dangerous

and threatening, the couple find momentary serenity as they con-
summate their love in the womb-like interior of a cave in the cliffs. It
is in the same cave that Miss Ogilvy is discovered sitting at the
story's end: 'She was dead, with her hands thrust deep into her
pockets.'

In its quest for the ineffable and its yearning for a state of purity, a
time before the Fall, 'Miss Ogilvy Finds Herself' is an archetypal
Radclyffe Hall story. Nostalgia for the war, for a time of simple,
clear-cut values in which the mundane world temporarily became
heroic, is another familiar theme. But 'Miss Ogilvy' is also implicitly
about the dilemma of the homosexual woman. Such a woman is a
misfit, the story proclaims, because 'the world has no wish to
understand those who cannot conform to its stereotyped pattern'. It
is suggested that 'the marring of her' began in her earliest childhood,
that her masculine tendencies are in-born. Miss Ogilvy is therefore a
trapped being, destined to 'blaze a lone trail through the difficulties
of her nature'. With her arrival on the island, the story changes gear.
By veering into the realm of fantasy, it avoids a realistic treatment of
Miss Ogilvy's problem and becomes another spiritual quest. But
twelve days after the story was written, Una recorded in the diary:
'John began notes for "Stephen"' – the working title for *The Well of
Loneliness*.[8] And when 'Miss Ogilvy' was eventually published (in
1934), John admitted in a preface that the early parts of the story
provided the nucleus for those sections of the novel dealing with
Stephen Gordon's childhood and her war experiences.

At some point between finishing 'Miss Ogilvy' and starting work
on *Stephen*, John broached the idea for her new novel with Una.

> John came to me one day with unusual gravity and asked for my decision
> in a serious matter: she had long wanted to write a book on sexual
> inversion, a novel that would be accessible to the general public who did
> not have access to technical treatises. At one time she had thought of
> making it a 'period' book, built round an actual personality of the early
> nineteenth century. But her instinct had told her that in any case she must
> postpone such a book until her name was made; until her unusual theme
> would get a hearing as being the work of an established writer.
>
> It was her absolute conviction that such a book could only be written
> by a sexual invert, who alone could be qualified by personal knowledge
> and experience to speak on behalf of a misunderstood and misjudged
> minority. It was with this conviction that she came to me, telling me that
> in her view the time was ripe, and that although the publication of such a
> book might mean the shipwreck of her whole career, she was fully
> prepared to make any sacrifice except – the sacrifice of my peace of mind.
> She pointed out that in view of our union and of all the years that we had
> shared a home, what affected her must also affect me and that I would be

included in any condemnation. Therefore she placed the decision in my hands and would write or refrain as I should decide.

I am glad to remember that my reply was made without so much as an instant's hesitation: I told her to write what was in her heart, that so far as any effect upon myself was concerned, I was sick to death of ambiguities, and only wished to be known for what I was and to dwell with her in the palace of truth.[9]

What is clear from Una's somewhat reverential account of this key moment in John's career (written, of course, long after *The Well of Loneliness* had established the Radclyffe Hall legend) is that John's preoccupation with the plight of the homosexual woman was no sudden inspiration. In a sense all her previous work, including her poetry, was a sublimation of the confusion and frustration she felt as a homosexual. The doomed, compassionate misfits of her novels and stories represented her own sense of dislocation as a social outcast. She had once thought of writing a period novel about George Sand, whom she and Ladye had so admired, and perhaps *Michael West* was an early attempt at such a book. But the time had not been ripe. Not only was she then inexperienced and unknown as a novelist, but she was also too close to her subject, too unsure of her own identity, to do justice to her concerns.

On both counts she had now matured. Creatively, she had established a personal system of values, a philosophical outlook into which her theme could be fitted. This would be important in determining the kind of book she would write. Despite her own protestations to the contrary, *The Well of Loneliness* would be heavily autobiographical, but her approach was to be self-consciously 'objective', involving prior research into the literature and sub-culture of homosexuality. Though she expressed her determination to write a book that was not a medical treatise, it was to medical and scientific texts that she first turned. Within a few days of John starting her preparatory notes for *Stephen*, Una was reading her Havelock Ellis. Ellis was the greatest living English sexologist. The first volume of his famous *Studies in the Psychology of Sex* (published in 1897) dealt with 'sexual inversion'. Not only did he advocate toleration for homosexuals, but it was his unswerving belief that all homosexuality was 'congenital' in origin. His attraction for John, and his subsequent influence upon the creation of Stephen Gordon, therefore proved potent.

On August 12 John and Una crossed to Paris on their way to another rest cure at Bagnoles. The following day they dined with the

American literary agent Carl Brandt. John had recently met Brandt in London at the instigation of Audrey Heath, whose London agency had a reciprocal relationship with Brandt's in New York. Brandt was a shrewd, sociable man, over-fond of alcohol and good with writers – '"if perhaps a little bit slick"', according to Maxwell Perkins, the legendary Scribners' editor.[10]

After dining with Brandt, John and Una joined Natalie Barney, Mimi Franchetti, and the poet Anna Wickham. The five of them went off on a spree round a number of fashionable Left Bank bars, including the Sélect, the Dingo and the Regina. This presented John with the opportunity to collect copy for *Stephen*, parts of which took place in Paris, but the conviviality proved too much for her fragile digestion and the party broke up at 2.30 am with John feeling 'badly poisoned' – Natalie, Una noted, stayed behind at Mimi's.

Their five weeks' holiday in Bagnoles passed peacefully. Natalie had promised to introduce them to Colette and Una began reading John *Chéri* and, later, *La Fin de Chéri*. Both were in spending mood. John bought Una a large pearl choker, a bracelet, a light overcoat, and a bouquet of flowers. Una presented John with pearl studs. They also refurbished their wardrobe with new suits, John buying herself four men's shirts as well while Una invested in four pairs of camiknickers. On September 19 they stopped over in Paris for another two days (to shop at Sulka's, dine at Prunier's and La Pérouse, and buy a griffon bitch which they named Tyke after May Massola's dog) before continuing on to Monte Carlo. In those days Monte Carlo served as a winter rather than summer resort and the whole place was deserted and shuttered. The hotel they had booked turned out to be 'awful' and 'noisy'. They transferred to another not much better. As soon as they could, they took the sleeper back to Paris, where they booked into the quiet, pleasant Hotel Pont Royal in the rue du Bac. A suite of three connecting rooms was put at their disposal and it was here, in a bedroom converted into a study, that John started writing *Stephen* on October 11.

Several familiar faces were in Paris. Eileen Bliss and Etheline dined with them and they saw Toupie in the company of a new lover called Fabienne. They made a number of excursions to Renée Vivien's grave at Passy, taking photographs and laying bouquets of plastic violets (in memory of Renée's great love Violette Shilleto). Renée's epitaph read: 'My ravished soul, from mortal breath/Appeased, forgets all former strife,/Having, from its great love of Death,/Pardoned the crime of crimes – called Life.'[11]

On October 19 Natalie at last took them to see Colette, at her ground-floor apartment in the rue de Beaujolais. The great writer was now fifty-three. As a young woman she had been neat and slender, but she now weighed over thirteen stone, was twice divorced, and had fallen in love with a young man of thirty-six, Maurice Goudeket, a pearl broker (Colette called him her 'pêcheur de perles'), with whom she was rapturously happy. The famous 'bronze' voice, with its rolling Burgundian Rs, remained very much in evidence, as did her peculiar charm, a mixture of provincial innocence and earthy wisdom. Earlier in the year *La Fin de Chéri* had been published and she had just returned from the south of France where she had been appearing in a revival of the stage adaptation of her novel *La Vagabonde*.

John and Una had been captivated by the 'Chéri' books and they eagerly requested that Colette autograph their copies. On October 22 they took her to lunch at Prunier's in the company of Natalie and Lily de Gramont. John's opinion of Colette at this time is not recorded, but some years later, in a letter, she made it clear that her admiration for the great French writer was not wholly unqualified. She thought she possessed 'a well-nigh perfect style, and a great knowledge of human and sub-human nature'. She added:

> Colette, who loves good food & too much of it; Colette who loves the sexual act and too much of it, Colette who has a peasant's outlook on money the while she over-indulges herself. Yes, but Colette who adores the wind & the rain, the sea and the earth and the fruits of the earth . . . Colette, as hard as the sun-baked soil yet so able to perceive and to immortalise the pathos of life in all its forms – a great woman in her way and a masterly writer.[12]

In other words, John liked the humanist in Colette but not the sensualist. The two aspects were of course inseparable in Colette's nature and John's verdict perhaps says more about herself than Colette.

John and Una returned to London in early November. The healthy sales of *Adam's Breed* in England placed John much in demand. She was the guest speaker at the Writers' Club dinner on November 24, talking about the novel and its Soho background ('a great success' shrilled Una). A few weeks later she read her poems to the Club's Poetry Circle. More lionizing took place at the PEN Club Ball and the Society of Authors' Dinner ('decorations worn' noted the diary).

John was also beginning to receive her first fan mail, some of it from women who recognized her as a fellow homosexual. Not all these correspondents were entirely happy with the self-denying fate of her protagonists. One writer asked if the message of *Adam's Breed* was that only by becoming insane could one reach God. If so, wasn't this rather cynical?[13] Another, delighting in the depth and vitality of John's books, nevertheless questioned the purpose of Joan Ogden's 'final self-immolation' and Sidonia's sudden acceptance of placid motherhood. With revealing candour, she confessed that Frances (in *A Saturday Life*) was her favourite character: 'Frances should be the patron saint of all us happily unmarried women! – wise, gallant, full of that detached & dry humour which can transform life & keep alive the spirit of adventure.'[14]

Before the end of November Violet Hunt confided to them the exciting news that *Adam's Breed* had been shortlisted for the Prix Femina. A few days later Una had cause to celebrate her own little triumph: a special tribunal had at last agreed to an increase in her naval pension ('hurrah' exclaimed the diary). The same day the new Daimler John had ordered arrived to replace the old model and The Squig, both of which were now sold. In less than a month they had run through two chauffeurs, sacking one for insolence, the other for crashing the car, and they had seriously considered hiring vehicles from Harrods. However, Una discovered that this would cost some £800 a year, whereas she calculated that running their own car (chauffeur included) would amount to only £700. For a saving of £100 even unreliable chauffeurs could be endured.

1927 opened with fresh tribulations for John. Her mother was again the cause. The Visettis had spent Christmas and New Year at a hotel in Brighton. On January 2 John received an urgent phone call to say that Marie had developed pneumonia. John instantly dropped her book (which she was working on intensively at this time, sometimes twelve hours a day) and rushed down to Brighton with Una. It turned out to be a false alarm. Marie had bronchial catarrh. However, she would need some looking after for a time. Because she could not stay on in Brighton or go home (she had recently fired all the servants), John was obliged to arrange, at great effort and expense, to have her taken to London in a specially heated ambulance and installed in a nursing home in Kensington for two weeks.

Worried by the prospect of continuing interruptions to her work – not to mention the drain on her pocket – caused by 'those ghastly old folk', as Una called them, John decided that a service flat would be the answer for the Visettis. However, on looking into her mother's financial affairs, she discovered to her horror a state of utter chaos. The lease on their house in Phillimore Gardens had expired, bills were unpaid, Marie was spending £60 to £70 at a time on clothes, there was no provision for life insurance, and – worst of all in John's eyes – they had almost run through the capital left to them by Grandma Diehl and Aunt Mary. When John tried to suggest practical steps to remedy this situation, her mother refused to listen or just screamed furiously at her. 'The whole business has shocked me beyond words,' John confided to Jane Caruth's daughter Winifred:

> Albert is just frankly dishonest and as far as I can see always has been, making no provision & never attempting to pay his debts – my mother has developed into a worse fury than she used to be, & that's saying a good deal I can assure you. Are they both mad? I don't know, I only know that their house has such a dreadful name that no decent servant will go near it, and that this greatly shames me, who am living in the same neighbourhood, and who am now very well known owing to my books. There are moments when I literally feel in despair.[15]

The crisis refused to go away, for no sooner had Marie got better than Albert came down with 'flu. Marie refused to nurse him on the grounds that she was convalescing and two nurses had to be hired (again at John's expense). But Marie proved so impossible that the nurses soon left – by which time, luckily, Albert was up and about again. John seriously wondered if her mother was going insane, but the doctor assured her that Marie simply had an uncontrollable temper. He also pointed out that she violently resented John's literary success and advised John to avoid seeing her if she could. The upshot was that John decided to pay her mother and Albert a monthly allowance on the condition that all communication between them ceased. 'No grown up woman,' John explained to Winifred, 'could allow herself to be abused & insulted as I have been lately – such a state of affairs is unseemly between a mother & daughter, and I'm done with it for good & all.'[16]

Had the problem been Una's, one suspects that she would have been far more ruthless in dealing with it. John's tendency, entirely in character, was to endure it as yet another cross to bear, conscious of that phrase in its every sense. Had Marie been less relentlessly hostile, John's inordinate capacity for compassion would never have allowed her to tolerate the complete break which she now contemplated. Her deep regret was evident, therefore, when to Winifred, who did not get on with her own mother, she wrote: 'I want her [Jane] to love you, because I have so often felt the bitterness of having no mother.'[17]

On February 17 a seventh impression of *Adam's Breed* appeared on the bookstalls at a price reduced from 7/6d to 3/6d. The book's continuing popularity brought John further invitations to speak at literary gatherings. In January she had addressed the Writers Circle of the Institute of Journalists. The meeting was chaired by the columnist Wilhelmina

Stitch, who afterwards hosted a dinner at Gatti's in John's honour at which the menu consisted of dishes described in *Adam's Breed*. In March John lectured at Sion College to the Bookman's Circle on the subject of 'True Realism in Fiction'. Her theme was that a writer could be imaginatively truthful even with a limited knowledge of the world, and she cited Jane Austen and the Brontës. Signalling her antipathy to the 'experimentalist' trend in modern literature, she suggested that realism (which she defined as an accumulation of finely observed detail) should be used for a purpose: too much contemporary writing was simply an aimless leaking of the subconscious mind.[18] With her usual unswerving loyalty, Una noted that John spoke 'extraordinarily well'.[19]

Una was very busy on her own account. As well as reading manuscripts for Cassell and Audrey Heath, and reviewing books for the *Sunday Times* (in March she reviewed 'Dogs: Their History and Development'), she was engaged on a translation of Colette's *La Maison de Claudine* – the first into English of any Colette work. For her fortieth birthday on March 8, John bought her a portable Remington typewriter. With characteristic fervour, both women were going through a 'Colette phase'. Una bought John a pied French bulldog bitch pup which they named Colette and John ordered headed blue notepaper and envelopes in imitation of the stationery that was Colette's hallmark.

On April 8 John learnt that *Adam's Breed* had been awarded the Prix Femina. Messages of congratulation poured into Holland Street. Violet Hunt, who had consistently supported the book on the English committee, urged John not to forget foreign language editions. English authors, she said, too often neglected this aspect by asking for too much money. With endearing tactlessness Violet added: 'I want to see your new one [i.e. *Stephen*]. I believe I shall like it better than A.B'.[20] For the next few days John was swamped by the press. Many newspapers in America and on the Continent captioned their photographs of her 'Man or Woman?' English papers were not quite so blunt, but her mannish appearance was a constant, thinly-disguised theme (in an allusion to her close-cropped hair, the *Birmingham Post* observed that she had 'what many people consider the best shingle in London').[21]

The *Daily Mail* interviewed her for its series 'How Other Women Run Their Homes'. John confessed to the *Mail*'s reporter, Evelyn Irons, that she was a fussy housekeeper with 'a perfect mania for cleanliness'. While Una supervised the catering side, she supervised décor and furnishings. After hours of writing, she liked nothing better than to unwind by waxing and polishing her oak antiques. However, she never let the house 'vamp' her, she told Miss Irons, or get in the way of her writing: if it did start to encroach, she simply upped and took off on her travels.[22] Neither John nor Miss Irons had any illusions: the article was a piece of journalistic 'hype'. Privately, John confided to her interviewer that Una looked after the house and that if any dusting or polishing was necessary, she simply rang for the maid.[23]

Evelyn Irons was to become one of their 'regular' friends. A Scots woman in her mid-twenties and an Oxford graduate with a half-blue at tennis, she was the sort of intelligent, sturdy and independent-minded woman that John admired. Evelyn lived with Olive Rinder, a neurotic, tubercular young woman with a 'leftish' background who served in a bookshop opposite Evelyn's flat in Royal Hospital Road. Olive got on with Una as well as Evelyn did with John, so that before long the two couples were seeing each other fairly regularly. To Evelyn's surprise, John always addressed her as 'Irons', as if man to man, and in the diary the two were invariably referred to as 'Irons and Rinder'.

John and Una now saw Vere and Budge infrequently – largely because of Vere's deteriorating condition. Budge had rung them in desperation one day to report that Vere had 'gone out of her mind' and there were periodic alarms of the same kind over the following months. In July John and Una visited Vere for tea and pronounced her 'a tragic and well nigh hopeless sight'.[24] She was still bravely managing to write (Hutchinson would publish two new novels by her in 1928), but she could no longer walk and suffered epileptic fits. Una's doctor, somewhat indiscreetly, gave it as his confidential opinion that Vere had inherited syphilis, for her father was similarly paralyzed. Budge refused to believe that her friend would ever get better, but she looked after her with a fierce, if morbid, devotion which did not fail to impress John.

In mid-August John and Una paid another visit to Bagnoles. The Hotel des Thermes was full of visitors, many of them British, whom they recognized from last time. There were also, John noted, large numbers of rich Jews – 'and no wonder, for the prices are in no way Christian.'[25] A new doctor devised a fresh regime for John's bad leg. She told Evelyn:

> I am to be violently sprayed all over with a thing like a fire hose – also I am to be 'brushed' in my bath until, as he describes it, I am scarlet, also I am to do deep breathing until I nearly explode *every hour*, also (but this at my own request as I am fat as always when I write for hours) I am to be slapped and pinched and rolled and kneaded and pummelled and stretched every morning at 7 a.m. prior to breakfast...Dear Irons, you won't know me when we meet, either I shall be a complete wreck or so

beautiful that you will have to put on smoked glasses, but I fear the former.[26]

If John was overweight, she needed little encouragement to eat less. During her most intensive periods of writing, she normally took very frugal meals, sometimes not eating at all for long stretches (much to Una's consternation). Though she and Una when abroad nearly always visited the best restaurants (they usually hated hotel food), John could be very fussy, harbouring a deep suspicion of foreign methods of preparation and sanitation. Since both women were prone to digestive disorders, this caution was well founded – though, as with many of their 'golden rules', they were apt to take them to extremes. From Bagnoles John sent Evelyn a list of culinary items to be avoided if 'dear abroad' was to be properly enjoyed:

> 1. Mussels. 2. Oysters. 3. Crabs. 4. Lobsters. 5. Langouste. 6. Cray-fish. 7. Eals (sic). 8. Mushrooms. 9. Prawns. 10. Shrimps. 11. Salad (unless you are sure that the water is not drawn from Tite Street) [a reference to the bad plumbing at her flat in Shelley Court]. 12. Sausages of *all kinds*! Una has helped me with this list – she knows all about it from bitter experience. No, but seriously when these days it is safest to live on prayer & fasting.[27]

Whenever they booked into a hotel, they would make arrangements to have 'café complet' instead of proper meals. After John's death, Una fondly recalled the countless rolls and croissants that the two of them had eaten in hotels across Europe: 'the bread of the communion of perfect companionship.'[28]

Back in England, Una wrote in her diary on November 13: 'I read (John) W. of L. all day – 14 chapters – and she talked out the latter part.' 'W. of L.' stood for *The Well of Loneliness*, the new title which had now replaced *Stephen*. Once again, the inspiration was Una's. By mid-December John had written a further one hundred pages of the novel. The seemingly unstoppable progress of *Adam's Breed* served to dispel any faint-heartedness she might have felt at the prospect of finishing *The Well*. *Adam's Breed* was being translated into German, Danish and Norwegian (remembering Violet Hunt's advice, John accepted relatively small sums for the foreign rights). Towards the end of November she was invited to turn the novel into a film, to be produced by the Hollywood mogul Sam Goldwyn and possibly starring Ronald Colman. The venture subsequently came to nothing, but it was soon eclipsed by more exciting news: *Adam's Breed* had won the James Tait Black Prize for the best literary novel of the year. Only

E. M. Forster's *A Passage to India* could boast of both the Prix Femina and the James Tait Black.

Somewhat to her amazement, at the age of forty-seven and less than four years after the publication of her first novel, John found herself at the very peak of her profession, a writer who had acquired that enviable 'double': commercial popularity *and* critical acclaim.

Part Four

JOHN
[2] THE MARTYR

1928–1934

Chapter Seventeen

John and Una had now been with Audrey Heath's agency for some six years. John's star had risen as the agency itself had grown and there existed a mutual respect on both sides. The office nicknamed the two women 'The Darlings', on account of their habit of addressing each other as 'darling' like a married couple. To Audrey's annoyance, they referred to her as 'little Audrey', which in time became simply 'Robin'. As clients they were glamorous, stylish and kindly, but could also be exacting and peremptory. Audrey normally dealt with them directly herself, which they expected as a matter of course, but an increasing workload (John's included) inevitably meant that others in the office were brought into contact with them. Chief among these was Patience Ross, then a young woman of twenty-two. Patience had joined the agency in 1926 as a typist on a temporary basis but had stayed on and assumed greater responsibilities. She lived with her parents in Kensington Church Street, adjacent to Holland Street, and found herself delivering messages and undertaking errands.

Patience recalled the visits of 'The Darlings' to the office as something of an event. They would be dropped in Piccadilly by an impressive chauffeur-driven Daimler, John looking pale and solemn in her jabot-fronted shirt and black satin lapels. Both women had deep voices and trailed a distinctive scent called 'Chypre'.

They inclined to a sardonic sense of humour and were both good mimics. John told stories in an entertaining, heavily facetious manner, often against herself. A favourite was her imitation of their long-suffering but punctilious typist, Miss Maclean, who had a way of retorting: 'You *said* a comma, Miss Hall,' which both irritated and amused.[1]

To Patience they were personally kind and generous, giving her small gifts and items of furniture, but they could be unnerving company. In restaurants John tended to fuss over Una's welfare, making endless small demands on the waiters ('Lady Troubridge would like this,' 'Lady Troubridge would like that,'), while at home in Holland Street Patience was often embarrassed by their outspoken discussion of sexual abnormalities. One of their favourite books was

L'Ersatz d'Amour, first published in 1923 and co-authored by Colette's first husband 'Willy' (Henri Gauthier-Villars). This told the story of a love-sick French artist who travels to Hamburg in search of other women to drown his sorrows but ends up, to his own surprise, finding consolation in the arms of a homosexual Prussian officer. It was one of several French novels with a homosexual theme that Una wanted to translate and the hero's bewildered exclamation: 'I did not ask you, O God, to send me "un petit officier boche",' became a catch-phrase with them which invariably invoked hilarity. Since Patience innocently assumed that John and Una were platonic friends who had a mission to help 'those poor people', her shock at such talk was understandable.[2]

On April 5, 1928, Una and Andrea came home from the first night of a play called *Thunder in the Air* to find that John had just completed the last chapter of *The Well of Loneliness*. Ten days of 'polishing' and retyping followed. John was highly keyed up. As the novel had entered its last stages, she had become more convinced than ever that she was engaged on a pioneering work. Never had writers felt they could be so candid and fearless, she told reporters who interviewed her after the Tait Black award, no subject was now out of bounds.[3]

On April 17 John delivered three bound copies of the typescript to Audrey, enclosing a covering letter for Newman Flower of Cassell (who contractually had first option on the new novel). The letter was friendly but firm. She had now put her pen at the service of some of the most persecuted and misunderstood people in the world, she wrote, and she would not allow one word to be changed or modified.

> So far as I know, nothing of the kind has ever been attempted before in fiction. Hitherto the subject has either been treated as pornography, or introduced as an episode as in [Rosamond Lehmann's] *Dusty Answer*, or veiled as in [Clemence Dane's] *A Regiment of Women*. I have treated it as a fact of nature – a simple, though at present tragic, fact. I have written the life of a woman who is a born invert, and have done so with what I believe to be sincerity and truth; and while I have refused to camouflage in any way, I think I have avoided all unnecessary coarseness.

John wanted a prompt answer from Flower for she intended that publication should take place not later than the autumn, to avoid the risk of interruption from the General Election scheduled for spring 1929. With all the uncompromising militancy of an author well aware of her star rating, John concluded:

I need not say how sorry I should be to sever my connection with Cassells, but unless you feel, upon reading the book, that you are prepared to go all out on it and to stand behind it to the last ditch, then for both our sakes, as also for the sakes of those for whom I have written, please don't take it.[4]

In the same letter John pointed out that she might be able to persuade Havelock Ellis to write a foreword to the novel. Her optimism was based upon a chance meeting she had had with Ellis in March. Roger Scaife of American publishers Houghton Mifflin had invited John to tea at Garland's Hotel in Suffolk Street. He introduced her to Ellis, who promised to read *The Well* when she had finished it – though he explained that he never wrote prefaces (being mindful of the traumatic Bedborough trial of 1898, in which a bookseller had been fined for selling copies of Ellis's *Sexual Inversion* and Ellis himself had had to give an undertaking never to publish his sex books in Britain again).

John and Una arrived at Ellis's address in Brixton on April 18 intending to hand him a copy of the typescript, only to find that he was away at his country cottage in Oxfordshire. That night John wrote to the man whom she regarded as the 'greatest living authority on the tragical problem of sexual inversion', reiterating her desire that he should read *The Well* and 'give it in a few words the support of your unassailable knowledge and reputation'. Only this, she believed, would prevent her worst fears being realized, namely that the book would be seized upon as a mere 'salacious diversion' by 'undesirable elements of the public'.[5]

Ellis returned to Brixton a few days later and replied to John's letter, emphasizing yet again that he could not write a preface to the novel but was still eager to read it. However, his professional curiosity had been aroused by the two formidable women – 'terribly modern & shingled & monocled & not at all Faun's style'[6] – and he did concede that if *The Well* appealed to him he would be happy to write an 'opinion' which could be quoted. 'I am deeply interested in the subject, having had many friends, both men and women, who were, as they sometimes say, "so",' he wrote.[7]

Newman Flower, meanwhile, had read *The Well* and come to the reluctant conclusion that he must decline it. He liked John. They had met socially on a number of occasions and he shared her interest in spiritualism, believing he was in contact with the spirit of Lord Northcliffe, the legendary newspaper baron.[8] Flower was determined to publish what he liked without interference. 'I own the whole box of tricks,' he told Compton Mackenzie, 'and what I say in my department will be law.'[9] Such resolution did not extend to *The*

Well of Loneliness, however, even though Flower acknowledged that it was 'one of the finest books that has gone through my hands'. The novel could harm Cassell's other titles, he explained to Audrey, and in any case his was the wrong house for it (true enough, since Cassell chiefly supplied circulating library fiction). But Flower was sorry to see John go. 'She is a great artist, and I take off my hat to her.'[10]

That principles were ultimately little match for expediency among publishers became clearer still over the next few days. Charles Evans of Heinemann was full of admiration for *The Well*, but admitted that its propagandist tone could bring damaging criticism down upon his firm.[11] Martin Secker, while praising John's 'gifts' (and declaring his willingness to publish any future novel by her), felt the book was too uncommercial.[12] He did not let on that he had another lesbian novel in preparation, namely Compton Mackenzie's *Extraordinary Women*, and was hoping to publish it in the autumn.

After Secker, Audrey sent the typescript to Jonathan Cape. Cape had been in business, with his partner George Wren Howard, since 1921 and had shown himself an astute modern publisher. In 1927 he had published an abridged version of T. E. Lawrence's *Seven Pillars of Wisdom* (under the title *Revolt in the Desert*), which sold over 30,000 copies in less than three months. Hemingway, Sinclair Lewis, Henry Williamson and Mary Webb (author of *Precious Bane*) were on the Cape list by 1928. The firm had a distinctive style that combined shrewd discrimination in its choice of authors with elegant production values and a flair for publicity.

Though Cape was prepared to take risks, he was cautious about what he called 'highly dangerous' books, that is, books with taboo subject matter. *The Well of Loneliness* came into this category. At the same time, his instinct told him that, given Radclyffe Hall's reputation as an author, the book could be a most commercial prospect – 'a good piece of publishing property,' as he put it to T. E. Lawrence.[13] Cape was at first so undecided about the book that he even asked Norah ('Jimmy') James, his publicity manager, to read the typescript and give him her verdict – the first time he had ever approached her with such a request.[14]

On May 8 John, Una and Audrey met Jonathan Cape for lunch at the Berkeley Grill. Cape set out his strategy for *The Well*. He agreed to John's insistence that it be published by the autumn but he proposed only to produce a limited edition of 1,250 copies priced at 25/- each, three times the cost of the average novel. If the book 'caught on', a cheaper, larger edition would follow. To John, straining at the leash to shout her message to the mass readership she believed she had acquired with *Adam's Breed*, such a scheme had the ring of pusillanimity. But by pointing out the financial risks he was taking and by emphasizing that the exceptional price would keep the book out of reach of the sensation-mongers, Cape was able to impress her with his sincerity. He offered her, moreover, an advance of £500, the largest by far she had ever received. After a minor hitch over liability – which, in John's pent-up state, created 'an agitated & worried evening & night' at Holland Street[15] – she finally signed a contract with Cape on May 11.

The same day Havelock Ellis sent word that he had read half the book and was confident that he would be able to write an 'opinion' in its support. This duly arrived on May 15 – except that Ellis now referred to it as a 'commentary'. John thought it 'perfect'.[16] In full Ellis's commentary read as follows:

> I have read *The Well of Loneliness* with great interest because – apart from its fine qualities as a novel by a writer of accomplished art – it possesses a notable psychological and sociological significance. So far as I know, it is the first English novel which presents, in a completely faithful and uncompromising form, various aspects of sexual inversion as it exists among us today. The relation of certain people – who, while different from their fellow human beings, are sometimes of the highest character and the finest aptitudes – to the often hostile society in which they move, presents difficult and still unsolved problems. The poignant situations which thus arise are here set forth so vividly, and yet with such complete absence of offence, that we must place Radclyffe Hall's book on a high level of distinction.

No wonder John was pleased, for Ellis had praised her on the two fronts which she cared about most: the novel's literary merits and its 'scientific' accuracy. One is reminded of her worshipping admiration for Sir Oliver Lodge in her early spiritualist days. As she embarked on a dramatic new phase of her career, she had to hand yet again, waiting in the wings, a special mentor and father-figure (with his long white beard the elderly Ellis admirably suited the part).

When John saw Cape on May 16 to discuss production details, she showed him the Ellis 'commentary'. Cape liked it but felt it advisable to change the phrase 'various aspects of sexual inversion' to 'an aspect of sexual inversion' – on the grounds that the former could be supposed to include male homosexuality, which was not only more ferociously deplored than lesbianism but was also a criminal offence. John duly passed on the suggestion to Ellis, who acquiesced. But then Cape had second thoughts. The word 'inversion' worried him. The phrase finally read: 'one particular aspect of sexual life . . . ' Whether or not these tinkerings with his text began to irritate Ellis, he proved less than happy with the final result in which his 'commentary' appeared at the front of the novel as if it were a preface. The misunderstanding seems to have been genuine on both sides and John apologised profusely to Ellis.[17] Cape, for his part, now decided to increase the numbers of the first edition to 1500, leaving the type set up for more copies if necessary, and to reduce the price by almost half to 15/-.

In America, meanwhile, *The Well* had still not found a publisher. Since meeting Roger Scaife, John was keen to send the book to Houghton Mifflin, but bowed to Carl Brandt's urgings that Doubleday (who had taken *Adam's Breed*) remained her best bet. However, by mid-May Doubleday had turned down the novel (on grounds of subject-matter) and Scaife was duly approached on John's insistence, despite the fact that Brandt had long before promised first refusal to Harper's should Doubleday decline. John felt indebted to Scaife for introducing her to Havelock Ellis. She had since corresponded with the American publisher, who had sent her a collection of Amy Lowell's poems which she had adored – 'Alas, that I should never have known this writer – I can only look forward to our meeting in the next world!'[18] However, as Carl Brandt had foreseen, Puritan Boston (where Houghton Mifflin was based) was not the place to launch a book advocating toleration for lesbians. Scaife admired *The Well* but understood only too well that to publish it would land him in the police courts. 'Such a novel as yours,' he wrote to John in June, 'is bound to arouse adverse comment and I imagine you not only expect it, but desire it, and so we would do you a poor service if we offered publication.'[19] Brandt could now pass the book to Harper's, but it took them less than three days to turn it down – poor Brandt insisting to John that they had 'almost' accepted it.[20]

While Roger Scaife was still considering John's typescript, she chanced to meet Blanche Knopf, the petite wife and partner of American publisher Alfred Knopf. According to the diary, Mrs Knopf 'insisted on immediately reading the W. of L.'[21] John sent a copy of the typescript to Mrs Knopf at the Carlton that evening. On June 4 Mrs Knopf asked for first refusal on the novel and a week in which to make a decision one way or the other. Though both Houghton Mifflin and Harper's were still officially in the running at this stage, John and Audrey did nothing to discourage Mrs Knopf. John had got on well with the American woman and she felt optimistic that this was the lucky break which they needed. A sitting with Mrs Leonard on June 6 appeared to confirm these feelings: 'v. interesting control anent B[lanche] K[nopf],' Una reported. Sure enough, on

June 8, with immaculate timing (for Scaife and Harper's had just retired from the field), Knopf's in New York told Carl Brandt that it would take *The Well*.

John and Una were jubilant and celebrated with Mrs Knopf at a party she hosted at Boulestin on June 11. But almost immediately problems arose. 'A thousand alarms & excursions anent Knopf & book,' the diary exclaimed on June 12. The hitch concerned the small print in John's contract. John had accepted a 15% royalty and no advance (lower terms than her usual), but she was not prepared to go along with a clause making her legally responsible for any action taken against the book by the American authorities. Such a provision was exceptional and ill-defined and could involve the author in endless legal costs. Accordingly John instructed Audrey and Carl to give Knopf until June 22 to withdraw the offending clause. If they failed to oblige, then the book was to be passed to Harcourt Brace.[22]

When by June 21 nothing further had been heard from Knopf, John's frustration boiled over in an extraordinary outburst to Brandt.

> My patience is completely at an end. It is not that I do not like Mrs Knopf personally, I do; but I am accustomed to dealing with men in business, to going perfectly straight for a point, and above all to sticking to essentials. I find it both difficult and tedious to deal with a woman, and this I have several times told her quite frankly, asking her to settle all business details with my agents. The trouble is that she has a great hankering for 'the personal touch', and this I consider a great mistake . . . I should hate to do her even the slightest injury in any way because, if her methods are somewhat unusual and tortuous, I put it down to the fact that she is a woman, and that in many cases it is better for women to keep out of business negotiations.[23]

This of course overlooked the fact that John's agent, Audrey Heath, was a woman. That night, in a self-dramatizing gesture expressing her martyred mood, John had Una read her the unpublished parts of Oscar Wilde's *De Profundis* (the eighty-page letter Wilde had written to Lord Alfred Douglas from Reading Gaol).

Knopf did comply by the deadline, however, agreeing to change the contract to John's satisfaction. To make doubly sure no last-minute complication arose which might get John more 'fussed up' than she already was, Audrey instructed the Brandt office to hand over John's signed copy of the contract *only* if the Knopf copy was an exact duplicate in every detail. John herself wrote to Carl's assistant, Bernice Baumgarten, explaining that she wanted the Brandt office to check all the Knopf proofs of the book extremely carefully to ensure that not a word was different or out of place. Her concern here stemmed partly from a sense of obligation to Havelock Ellis, who was anxious that his 'commentary' should be applied to the exact text he had read in typescript. But John also felt that the book was too important to be 'softened' or modified in any way, intentionally or otherwise. 'It is a pioneer work and I have risked much to write it, and therefore it feels to me very much like a child.' If the slightest word was altered or omitted, she told Bernice, she would consider it a breach of contract.[24]

For an agent, powerful clients can be a mixed blessing. John's intense concern for her 'pioneer work' did not make life easy for Audrey and Carl, especially as she tended to act on her own, only informing them later. It proved unfortunate for Brandt that after his own suggestions had failed to materialize, it was John herself who 'found' Knopf – which of course only strengthened her belief that she knew best. But John was not trying to be wilful for its own sake. She cared deeply about her book and wanted only the best for it. She had a sharp business sense and liked her affairs to be conducted in an orderly fashion. No detail of *The Well*'s production was too trivial for her attention. Hardly had the Knopf contract been settled than John wrote to Blanche Knopf about publicity for the book. She sent her the photographs of herself that she wanted used, and directed her attention to a silhouette picture displayed by Doubleday in their promotion for *Adam's Breed* which she did *not* want used. John had hated this picture which she said made her look like 'a middle-aged gent who is given to imbibing, or worse still a stout old lady masquerading'.[25]

Early in July Jonathan Cape switched his plans yet again. He decided to bring forward publication from the autumn to the summer, to July 27 in fact – less than a month away. This did not please Knopf, who had planned to bring out the American edition in tandem with the British one. Cape's reason for the change was his discovery in June that Secker (and the Vanguard Press in America) were proposing to publish Compton Mackenzie's *Extraordinary Women* in September. This set alarm bells ringing violently in Holland Street. Not knowing that Mackenzie's novel (a waspish satire on the lesbian colony he had once known on Capri) was very different from her own, John immediately saw it as a threat to *The Well*. Assuming (incorrectly) that Mackenzie had started his book the previous December, Una scribbled in the flyleaf of her diary that it 'must be either very bad or very short' to have such an early publication date. John was determined not to be pipped to the post. She cabled Carl to urge Knopf to rush through publication of *The Well* in America. Carl did not consider *Extraordinary Women* would affect *The Well* and advised that to advance matters too fast could harm a proper sales campaign, but he followed instructions and succeeded in extracting a reluctant agreement from Knopf that they would try to publish in October.

One further outcome of John's fears about *Extraordinary Women* was that she made a deal to share the preliminary advertising costs for *The Well*. She would add £150 to Cape's £300, making an unusually large promotional budget. Jonathan Cape had some qualms about this course and warned that the book should not be given an 'undue prominence' in case other publishers smelled a rat.[26] In normal circumstances John would have despised authors who subsidized their own publicity. It gave them an unfair advantage over 'their poorer brethren'. But these were not normal circumstances, she told Cape, and she trusted he would spend the money in 'the best and wisest way to defeat our rivals and steer *The Well of Loneliness* to success'.[27]

On July 10, with their usual flair for bad timing, John's family added to her anxieties: Albert Visetti died. Inevitably, the funeral arrangements were left to John to handle. Una reported that poor John was 'abominably received' by her mother at Phillimore Terrace. Marie apart, however, 'all going very well' read the diary entry on July 16. This referred to preparations for *The Well*'s publication at the end of the month. John had now received her advance copies of the novel. The book had been produced in large format style, with a sombre black binding and plain jacket. As Jonathan Cape made clear to the novelist Hugh Walpole (whom he sent a review copy), this muted presentation was deliberate: 'I don't want to strike an attitude – portrait of a publisher doing something daring and heroic – but I realise that the publication of *The Well of Loneliness* may be called into question unless it is soberly and carefully published.'[28] In accordance with this policy, review copies were sent only to the serious dailies and periodicals.

Behind the scenes John urged her friends in the press to show a 'proper spirit' towards her book. Writing to Una's brother-in-law, J. L. Garvin, editor of the *Observer* (she addressed him as 'Garvin'), she stated that it was high time her subject was tackled 'boldly', not simply for the sake of inverts but for society as a whole: 'Many writers have been nibbling at it just lately in fiction – but this I have felt to be wrong and only calculated to awaken in certain minds an unwholesome & salacious curiosity.' She praised Cape for producing a 'beautiful & dignified' volume.[29] Leonard Rees pleased her by asking Ida Wylie to review *The Well* for the *Sunday Times*.

On the eve of publication Una walked her bulldog, Mitsou, to W. H. Smith's and gazed admiringly at the rows of *The Well* neatly laid out in the window. Nothing could stop it now.

The Well of Loneliness is a long novel, over five hundred pages in the Cape edition. The action covers roughly the same time span as *Adam's Breed,* namely some thirty-five years from the late Victorian epoch to the early 1920s. It starts with the heroine's birth. Stephen Gordon is the only daughter of Sir Philip and Lady Anna Gordon, who reside at an ancestral country seat, Morton Hall, in Worcestershire. Stephen is so called because her father dearly wanted a son and saw no reason to change his chosen name when the baby turned out to be a girl. Much of what follows springs from this initial contrivance. For Sir Philip brings up Stephen as if she *were* a boy, encouraging her in such pursuits as fencing, riding astride, and exercising with dumb-bells – and later in formal scholastic studies. At the age of seven the child develops an infatuation for one of the house-maids, Collins, and experiences her first jealousy and sense of betrayal when she discovers this woman kissing the footman.

Stephen is very close to her father and as she grows older she looks more and more like him. She is a sensitive child and she divines his disappointment that she is not a boy. But he is loving and understanding and the two of them are more like bosom friends than father and daughter. Stephen's mother, on the other hand, is somewhat distant. She is a gentle, well-meaning woman but, despite her best intentions, she cannot overcome her growing distaste for her rather masculine daughter. As Stephen advances into her late teens, Lady Anna becomes openly critical of her, and there are quarrels over clothes and behaviour. By this date Stephen is acutely aware that she is not like other girls. She prefers the company of men, but they do not seem to take to her, finding her too clever and unfeminine. She does befriend one boy, a simple, unassuming youth called Martin Hallam who shares her love of nature. But when he eventually proposes marriage to her, she recoils in horror. The final seal is put on her sense of isolation by the tragic death of Sir Philip, killed by a falling tree. After this her only real confidante is her governess Miss Puddleton ('Puddle'), a benign, wise old soul who gives Stephen the emotional support she misses in Lady Anna.

Matters reach a head between mother and daughter when Stephen – who is now dressing in jackets and ties – falls in love with the wife of a local businessman, Angela Crossby. Angela is flighty, capricious, and bored by her marriage. She encourages Stephen's tremulous advances without any real intention of committing herself – only to find she has led the girl so far up the garden path that she is talking of their eloping together. Stephen's first lesson in disillusionment comes when Angela points out that women in love cannot marry each other; her second when she finds Angela in the embraces of a neighbour, Roger Antrim. Fearful that Stephen might now reveal their relationship to the world, Angela tells her husband that Stephen is a 'pervert' trying to foist her attentions on her. She shows him a passionate letter from Stephen. Ralph Crossby is horrified and indignant, and writes to Lady Anna, enclosing Stephen's letter. It is another betrayal for Stephen.

All Lady Anna's bewilderment turns now to a positive revulsion. In a terrible, bitter indictment, she calls Stephen 'a sin against creation' and refers to 'this unspeakable outrage that you call love': 'I would rather see you dead at my feet than standing before me with this thing upon you.' Stephen defends herself by stressing that her love for Angela was just as good and pure as Lady Anna's for Sir Philip, but her mother makes it clear that the two of them cannot go on living at Morton together. So Stephen leaves home with Puddle – having made another dramatic discovery: her father knew of her latent homo-sexuality but had not had the courage to tell her. This pains her more than her mother's contempt.

Stephen becomes a writer. Her first novel *The Furrow* is a great success, but the second falls far short and she is overwhelmed by feelings of failure and isolation. 'Why have I been afflicted with a body that must never be indulged,' she exclaims desperately, 'that must always be repressed until it grows much stronger than my spirit because of this unnatural repression? What have I done to be so cursed?' Soon after this she meets Jonathan Brockett, a successful playwright. He is witty, brittle, waspish, and homosexual, and Stephen is both attracted and repelled by him. He introduces her to Valérie Seymour, an American writer living in Paris. Valérie is 'a creature apart', a woman of extraordinary charm and culture who, though a lesbian, has friends equally among men and women. Unlike Stephen, she has come to terms with her nature.

When the war breaks out in 1914, Stephen is confused. She is not cut out for normal women's work, but as a woman neither can she fight at the front. However, the opportunity arises to join a women's ambu-lance unit in France and she volunteers. It is while serving with this group in the battle zone that Stephen meets her second great love, Mary Llewellyn. Mary is a simple, innocent orphan from the Welsh valleys and Stephen's love for her is born of a deep desire to protect and look after her. At the war's end (Stephen comes away with a scarred face and the Croix de Guerre) Stephen and Mary take a blissful holiday in Orotava. Up to this point Stephen has suppressed her love for the young woman, anxious not to push her into an attachment she might later regret. But Mary is so unhappy at Stephen's aloofness that she threatens to leave. At this Stephen's resolution fails her and they tearfully fall into each other's arms: 'and that night they were not divided'.

The two lovers set up home together in post-war Paris and Stephen resumes her writing. At first they are as happy as any newly married couple, Mary playing the attentive 'wife' to Stephen's protective, bread-winning 'husband'. But gradually insidious pressures emerge to sour the relationship. 'Normal' society does not accept them as a couple: Mary is not asked to Morton with Stephen by Lady Anna and an apparently sympathetic friend, Lady Massey, cancels her Christmas invitation to them when she learns the true nature of their friendship. At the same time Stephen's writing starts to come between them. Thrown back on their own company, Stephen buries herself in her work, closeted for long hours in her study day and night. Mary grows bored and lonely. In an effort to remedy this situation, Stephen introduces her lover to Valérie Seymour and her circle, and the two of them gravitate towards exclusively homosexual company.

But all their new friends are unhappy misfits. Wanda, the ungainly Polish painter, drowns her sorrows in drink. Jamie is 'a trifle unhinged' and a less than successful composer. Her lover Barbara is a consumptive. Margaret runs extravagantly from lover to lover, invariably ending up in tears and out of pocket. Even the learned Jewish designer Adolphe Blanc, though more resigned than most to his homosexuality, is a desolate, lonely figure. Far worse are the patrons of Alec's, a bar for male homosexuals of the most miserable kind, those who have lost all self-respect and resort to drink, drugs and despair.

In time, to Stephen's horror, the society they keep begins to affect a perceptible change in Mary. She who never used to drink now does so – and suffers hang-overs. Yet if the Lady Annas and Lady Masseys of this world will not accept them, where else can they go? Worse is to come. Barbara dies of consumption and Jamie, unable to face life without her, commits suicide. Stephen now feels that her love for Mary is 'shadowed by death'. Enter Martin Hallam again. Stephen resumes her friendship with him but gradually realizes that he has fallen in love with Mary. At first Stephen is determined to uphold her claims on her lover and resist Martin, but she then decides that to hang on to Mary is simply to drag her deeper into the degradation that she sees as the ultimate prospect for homosexual women. The book therefore ends with Stephen feigning an affair with Valérie Seymour in order to drive Mary into the arms of Martin. Stephen, abandoned and desolate, makes a final anguished plea: 'Acknowledge us, oh God, before the whole world. Give us also the right to our existence!'

So much attention has focused on *The Well* as '*the* lesbian novel' that its kinship to Radclyffe Hall's previous work tends to be overlooked.[30] Stephen Gordon is a heroine who, like her predecessors, is highly sensitive, deeply moral, abnormally protective, painfully lonely, and resolutely self-sacrificing. Even her sexual proclivity is not new, for the masculine lesbian has been strongly hinted at in both Joan Ogden and Miss Ogilvy. Lady Anna, like Teresa in *Adam's Breed*, is another aloof, unloving mother-figure. Equally, Mary is an English version of Maddalena.

Many of the themes and preoccupations of the novel are also familiar. Stephen's childhood and adolescence covers almost half the book and lost innocence is a major underlying motif. Stephen learns, about herself and the world around her, through a series of 'betrayals': even the adored Sir Philip has ultimately 'betrayed' her by failing to tell her what he knows. Mary is more a symbol of virginal innocence than a rounded character and it is no accident that Stephen finally abandons her to Martin when she sees the girl's purity becoming sullied by the company they keep. The careful, almost courtly language in which Stephen's hesitant wooing of Mary is described – culminating in the famous euphemism 'and that night they were not divided' – reflects the author's reverence for the notion of unspoilt purity.

This theme is reinforced in *The Well* by the idealized rural setting of Stephen's childhood. The Malvern countryside that John knew so well is lovingly described and Stephen is never to experience again such happiness as she feels when riding her horse Raftery or taking long country walks with the youthful Martin Hallam. Morton Hall (its description opens the book) is such an important influence in Stephen's early life that she treats it as almost a living friend. She talks to the house, confides in it, feels its 'moods', and misses it when she is away. Morton represents abiding values and comforting certainties in a changing, bewildering world. Once Raftery dies and Stephen is banished from Morton to the city (first London, then Paris), disillusion and tragedy unfolds, reaching a peak of degradation in the urban squalor of Alec's bar and Jamie's suicide in a garret.

Whereas the war has featured only perfunctorily in John's previous work, in *The Well* Stephen's service with the ambulance unit in France is related at some length. The reason is partly that the battle front provides a suitably dangerous setting in which Stephen can exercise her protective concern for the innocent Mary – and thus fall in love with her. But undoubtedly John's main aim here was to show that lesbians (it is strongly suggested that most of the women in the unit are 'inverts') could be just as gallant and patriotic as the next man. They too, John is saying, are capable of fulfilling that highest ideal called forth by war, the ideal of service to one's country and one's fellows. Stephen makes the grade by earning a medal and receiving a facial wound – both the emblem of her gallantry and the 'mark of Cain' (recalling John's poem 'The Scar'). John's attitude to the war proved more ambivalent than previously. She recognized that it was 'the most stupendous and heart-breaking folly of our times', and one moreover which had not created a land fit for heroes, still less for lesbian heroes. At the same time, the war had provided women like Stephen with a chance to play a worthier and more fulfilling role than either before or since. When that role ended, Stephen, like Miss Ogilvie, cannot help feeling a sense of regret.

The Well is not a novel of spiritual quest like *A Saturday Life* nor a story of religious redemption like *Adam's Breed*, but it is a book of high moral purpose and its undertones are, in the broadest sense, deeply religious. Stephen is not apparently a church-goer, but her empathy for the natural world, her search for the hidden meaning to her unhappy existence, and her final anguished plea to God, all suggest that she is a woman of religious instincts. Moreover, as a story that leads up to its protagonist's 'martyrdom', the novel contains submerged but pointed parallels to the example of Christ. It is no accident that Stephen is born on Christmas Eve and that her decision to sacrifice herself for Mary's happiness is finally affirmed in front of the supplicant Christ figure above the altar of a little church in Montmartre.

Contrary to popular theory, Stephen Gordon's story is not John's own, not in any literal sense at any rate. The romantic picture of Morton Hall and the Malvern countryside, the aristocratic forbears, the loving father, and the muscular daughter, none of this bears any resemblance to John's own unhappy upbringing in the more prosaic purlieus of Bournemouth and Kensington. Rather it is the childhood John would have liked, the companionship between Sir Philip and Stephen recalling Una's relations with Harry Taylor rather than anything John had ever experienced with Rat. Similarly, Mary is hardly a model of Una, whose 'marriage' to John was a far more sophisticated (and equal) partnership. Even the adult Stephen Gordon, though a writer, is no more a direct copy of John herself than Joan Ogden was. To state otherwise is to deny John's very considerable powers of characterization.

However, no one familiar with Radclyffe Hall's life can read *The Well of Loneliness* and fail to spot certain sentiments, circumstances, and even characters associated with its author. The major steps in Stephen's story parallel the principal stages in John's own life, but are deliberately condensed and jumbled in form. Thus John's hunting memories of Worcestershire are placed in Stephen's childhood. Ladye's intellectual influence is given to Puddle and brought forward to Stephen's adolescence. Similarly, John's early love affairs, with all their disappointments and frustrations, are condensed into the one youthful misalliance with Angela Crossby. The effect of this process is to enable Stephen to start her career as a writer, and be successful at it, almost as soon as she reaches her majority and leaves home – whereas of course John herself did not achieve this until her forties.

It would be surprising if Ladye did not figure somewhere in all this. Stephen's relationship with Lady Anna is curiously ambivalent. It is also central to the first half of the book. Stephen blames her mother for her lack of sympathy and warmth, but at the same time she cannot help admiring her beauty or feeling protective towards her. Until Stephen's homosexuality is fully revealed to Lady Anna in the letter from Ralph Crossby, relations between mother and daughter are less hostile than bashful and tentative ('it was almost grotesque, this shyness of theirs ... '). Stephen is capable of empathizing with her mother's moods and at times her need for consolation is so intense that she cannot resist grasping Lady Anna's 'cool hand'. Lady Anna finds such displays of physical affection faintly repulsive, but the sexual undertones to these scenes are strongly hinted at.

Stephen is a traditionalist at heart. Had she not been homosexual, she would have become much like her county neighbours, 'a breeder of children, an upholder of home, a careful and diligent steward of pastures'. When she does rebel, it is impossible for her not to because it is her in-born nature impelling her. This point is made several times in the novel and bears the unmistakable stamp of John's own character and feelings. Nineteenth-century women novelists and their early twentieth-century counterparts tended to choose heroines whose intellectual development thrust them into conflict with their backgrounds and upbringing. Stephen Gordon goes against this tradition. Her curious tragedy is that she *wants* to conform but can't. This was the paradox of Radclyffe Hall too.

In creating the homosexual milieu in which Stephen and Mary find themselves in Paris, John drew partly on her own personal experience. The squalid Alec's bar was based on those haunts that she and Una had visited in search of copy the previous summer in the company of Natalie, Mimi Franchetti and others. The lesbian set that Stephen and Mary befriend consists of composite characters modelled on women John and Una knew well on both sides of the Channel. The extraordinary Wanda seems to be a cross between Ida Rubinstein and Romaine Brooks. Hortense, Comtesse de Kerguelen, suggests the Duchesse de Clermont-Tonnerre. Barbara and Jamie recall the tragic Vere and Budge. According to Una, Adolphe Blanc was an idealized Adrien Mirtil, while Valérie Seymour represented Natalie Barney.[31] Even Stephen herself seems to have been a composite. Her singular prowess as a fencer and her war record irresistibly call Toupie Lowther to mind.

The Natalie Barney character is particularly interesting, for Valérie Seymour is the only homosexual woman in the novel who stands on equal terms with Stephen. The women with whom Stephen is associated are either less talented than her, or less wealthy which means less independent. Valérie is the exception. She is clever and rich, but above all she is at ease with herself – 'placid and self-assured' is how she is described. The tragic 'inverts' of her circle look to her for courage and comfort, so that she is 'a kind of lighthouse in a storm-swept ocean'. Thus even Stephen has something to learn from Valérie. Valérie understands the homosexual's problems and believes they should be faced up to with pride, but she retains an equanimity (and a sense of humour) towards the anguished posturing around her that is alien to Stephen. They are presented then as courteous friends who agree to disagree. But it is Valérie who puts her finger on Stephen's personal dilemma: the disharmony between the two aspects of her personality, her hypersensitivity on the one hand and her conservative, traditionalist values on the other ('all the respectable county instincts of the man who cultivates children and acres'). If Stephen could unite these two sides to her nature and put the result into her work, what could she not achieve? John must have asked herself the same question many times, and it suggests her genuine respect, even envy, for Natalie Barney's very different outlook on life that she puts these home-truths into the mouth of Valérie Seymour.

Acquaintance with fellow homosexuals was not John's only source of inspiration for *The Well*. She was also evidently well read in the relevant literature. She herself wrote that her novel aimed to be bolder than either *A Regiment of Women* or *Dusty Answer*. Some of her poetry bears witness to her knowledge of Sappho's works. She was fascinated by Oscar Wilde. She was certainly familiar with the 'spicier' French sapphic tradition. Ladye had introduced her to writers like Zola and

De Maupassant. Natalie Barney and Colette widened her horizons still further (Una's fluent French was a help here). John knew Natalie's *Pensées d'une Amazone* and Colette's *Claudine* novels. Her admiration for Renée Vivien stemmed directly from her connection with Natalie, just as her friendship with Colette led her to curiosities like Willy's *L'Ersatz d'Amour*. Natalie had also been a lover of Liane de Pougy and knew Proust, and it seems unlikely that John would have been unacquainted with, respectively, *Idylle Sapphique* and *Sodome et Gomorrhe*.

So far as one can tell, none of these works individually exerted an obvious influence upon *The Well of Loneliness*. But John's knowledge of the lesbian tradition in literature, especially the more outspoken Continental variety, gave her the necessary confidence to formulate her own vision, and one moreover which went beyond the pale discretions of English novelists. The tendency of most contemporary writers (outside pornography) was to focus on adolescent girls, with the implication that their homosexual impulses were a normal, passing phase which would be superseded in adulthood. The radical departure that John took in *The Well* was to create a heroine who, from birth, is irrevocably homosexual, a fact that colours her whole life and outlook.

The view that homosexuality was an in-born condition rather than acquired was one which John had long applied to her own case with growing certainty. By the time she came to write *The Well* she had elevated it to the level of a general theory. In this she was heavily influenced by the extensive reading she had undertaken among the works of contemporary sexologists during her preparations to write the novel. Here she had discovered the concept of the 'invert', a type of woman whose psyche was topsy-turvy: she rejected her femininity, was attracted to women not men, and engaged in masculine pursuits. According to the most influential theorists of 'inversion' – Richard von Krafft-Ebing and Havelock Ellis – the 'true invert' was almost always distinguishable by some congenital taint. In other words, somewhere in her family background invariably lurked a history of neurosis, instability, or worse. By logical extension, therefore, 'inversion' was inherited and in-born.

Despite the slender research on which these theories were based (Ellis cited only six lesbian case-histories in *Sexual Inversion*), John swallowed them wholesale. She *wanted* to believe them – just as she had wanted to believe that Ladye was speaking to her through Mrs Leonard. The 'invert' neatly defined her own case, providing a 'scientific' explanation both for her divided, tormented nature and the unhappy circumstances of her upbringing. Rat's restless, 'neuropathic' temperament and parental irresponsibility, Marie's violent, almost insane, hostility, these 'defects' in her parents more than bore out the sexologists' theories, as John saw it. Other investigators, notably Freud, did not subscribe to the hereditary theory. Some, like Magnus Hirschfeld, qualified their support by rejecting the element of morbidity and pathological taint. Significantly, John ignored Freud, and the only observations that Una noted from Hirschfeld's *A Manual of Sexual Science* (1926) stuck to the one theme: 'To the fact that homosexual desire is not induced but inborn its ineradicability bears witness.'[32]

Krafft-Ebing is actually mentioned in *The Well* – his is one of the books (presumably his *Psychopathia Sexualis*) which Stephen finds in her father's study after his death, indicating that he knew of her homosexuality all along. The air of degradation and vice that hangs over the lesbian fraternity in Stephen's story is a vision of homo-sexuality which smacks strongly of Krafft-Ebing's morbid case-histories. In most other respects, however, Havelock Ellis was John's chief model and it is hardly surprising that his 'commentary' to the novel proved so complimentary. For John took on board without qualification Ellis's distinctive definition of the invert's character and appearance. She was, according to Ellis, a nervy, artistic type, boyish in manner and looks, deep-voiced, capable of whistling, and prone to deeply felt, longstanding attachments. He was especially preoccupied with the invert's physical attributes, which invariably inclined to the masculine.[33] Thus John made Stephen a muscular baby, broad in the shoulders and narrow at the hip. She is good at masculine pursuits like hunting and fencing. As she grows older she begins to resemble a man, her father. Most of the other 'true inverts' in the book are also physically odd. Pat's ankles are thicker than they should be for a woman, Jamie is 'loose-limbed', Margaret's voice is like a boy's on the verge of breaking, and Wanda cannot dress as a woman without looking like a man or as a man without looking like a woman.

Ellis's view was that a lesbian relationship conformed to the tradi-tional male-female divide. Thus one invert would be inherently 'masculine', her partner invariably 'feminine'. Stephen and Mary clearly match this pattern. But the theory has problems, because if, as Ellis stated, true inverts are always 'masculine' women, how can their 'feminine' partners be true inverts? Why don't they gravitate to men? Ellis's less than ingenious solution was to distinguish a category of women who, though womanly, are not sufficiently attractive to appeal to most men, who have a low sex drive, and who are 'responsive' to true inverts. But this implied an element of seduction on the part of the true invert, suggesting that such liaisons might be vicious. Ellis's difficulty here is translated into *The Well*, for Mary seems on the one hand to 'respond' to Stephen quite happily and on the other to be capable of marrying Martin Hallam at the end (though, admittedly, with a broken heart).

Ultimately Ellis appears to be suggesting that lesbian relationships are inherently unstable and this impression certainly comes across in *The Well*. The fact that lesbian couples could not have children was, Ellis implied, a source of frustration to them that eventually led to a souring of relations. In Stephen's mind the knowledge that her union with Mary is ultimately sterile is one of the major causes of her growing unease about the girl's future. It is strongly suggested that if Mary had had the opportunity to be a properly fulfilled woman (i.e. by having children), she would not have grown bored and not begun to decline. By 'abandoning' Mary to Martin, Stephen hopes that her lover's womanhood (and thus her purity) will be redeemed. There is no indication that John and Una were acutely affected by their inability to have children – perhaps because Una had her own child. And certainly Una never grew bored with John. It is a good example of the way in which John's concern to be 'scientifically' accurate about her subject ran counter to the reality of her own personal experience.

The message of *The Well* is unequivocal: inverts have a raw deal out of all proportion to their 'crime'. They cannot help the way they are and society should therefore extend to them its fair share of Christian toleration and understanding. To drive home the injustice, John created a heroine of the highest moral character, superior in some ways to the 'normal' people around her. Here again she was in sympathy with Ellis's ideas. In his case-histories Ellis took pains to demonstrate the worthiness of the women concerned, their sterling intellectual qualities or their impressive achievements. As a rule, he felt, lesbians had to win social acceptance by being more remarkable that other people. This might be through brains or sheer force of personality, but it might also simply mean belonging to the ruling classes, a privilege which Ellis assumed conferred automatic moral superiority. In her correspondence with Ellis over his 'commentary' for *The Well*, John had suggested that inverts should 'work to make good'. Knowing his views, she cannot have been surprised by his reply: 'I heartily agree. I know only too many [inverts] who don't – and perhaps could. It is far from being a "craze" and applies equally to those who are not inverts.'[34]

One way that inverts could rise above their condition, hinted Ellis, was to cultivate a soulful spirituality, implicitly avoiding the physical side of lesbianism – the side, of course, that drew the fiercest social disapproval. Something of this notion creeps into *The Well*, for it is noticeable that Stephen herself never makes the sexual running in her two close relationships. Angela is the one who draws her on on the first occasion, while with Mary Stephen is at first so discouraging that she almost drives the adoring girl away. Equally, during the two affairs, physical intimacies are generally hinted at rather than described. Even where passions are allowed to run their course, the language employed is so gentlemanly and quasi-Biblical that it is difficult to believe that these are two people sexually involved with each other. So blameless is Stephen that she loses the two women she loves to men, thereby reinforcing the idea that she is more sinned against than sinning. In her own life John had wooed two women away from their husbands. The irony would be that, when *The Well* came to be prosecuted in the courts, it was the very excellence of its heroine that would count most against it.

Great as was Ellis's influence on John, *The Well of Loneliness* remains peculiarly the work and vision of Radclyffe Hall. It is arguable that had John stuck less to sexological definitions of inversion and drawn more on her own personal knowledge, a better novel would have resulted. For the early promise of the story, with its powerful depiction of a sensitive child's growing years, too quickly deteriorates into an assortment of stereotypes representing the Tragic Invert. On the other hand, as all her fiction had illustrated, John's personal vision of the world was essentially a tragic one and strongly determinist. Stephen's bleak progress towards the sacrificial altar is as irresistible as Joan Ogden's or Gian-Luca's. John *did* believe that homosexuality was an 'affliction' and that she therefore stood in some sense as an outcast. The fact that she had independent means did not lessen her sensitivity. Suffering lies in the heart of the beholder and no amount of money could shut out the knowledge of loneliness endured, of love unrequited, of trust broken, of embarrassment caused, of pretence and deception resorted to, all aspects of her own experience that John could lay at the door of her homosexuality. It took considerable courage and a strong conscience finally to declare her credentials and say: 'Enough is enough.'

On July 27, the day of *The Well*'s publication, telegrams and flowers poured into Holland Street. Both John and Una were out early to the bookshops to reconnoitre. John awaited the public verdict upon her 'pioneer work' in a state of high tension. Prudently perhaps, Una packed off Andrea to Guide Camp to keep her out of the way. John had embarked on no new work since finishing her book. This was unusual and signified her intense involvement with *The Well*. Instead, ironically, Una was the one busy writing throughout June and July, finishing off her second Pettit translation (of *La Chinoise Qui S'Emancipe*) for Boni and Liveright. John was far from idle, however. With crusading zeal, she set about getting her novel translated into as many European languages as possible, but especially into German. Germany had a progressive reputation for the toleration and discussion of homosexuality. Havelock Ellis recommended his own German translator, Eva Schumann. She was not an invert herself, but Ellis thought this would be for the better, warning John (not without a certain professional self-interest) against the sort of 'invert clique' associated with German experts such as Hirschfeld.[35]

The reviews of *The Well* were mixed. The first appeared in the *Saturday Review* and was by the novelist L. P. Hartley. He admired the novel's power and sincerity but felt it lost its way by turning into a polemic.[36] Many critics made the same point. As might be expected, Ida Wylie in the *Sunday Times* showered John with compliments, but even she had to admit that the controversial nature of the subject ran the risk of submerging the book's artistic qualities.[37] Leonard Woolf put it more bluntly: the novel was a failure, lacking form, too discursive, the whole lost in the parts. He liked the first 150 pages (up to the death of Sir Philip) but thereafter he considered that the novel's emotional impetus was sacrificed to the author's propagandist aims.[38]

If Woolf's criticisms could be dismissed (and were by John) as an example of male distaste for lesbians, Vera Brittain (in *Time and Tide*) showed that even the most sympathetic women had serious reservations about John's treatment of her theme. Miss Brittain thought *The Well* 'important, sincere and very moving', but she also questioned its simple reliance on male and female stereotypes and felt it unclear whether Stephen's inversion stemmed from psychological (i.e. environmental) or physiological (i.e. inborn) causes. The supposedly suspect tomboyishness of the heroine as a child, Miss Brittain observed, would seem to reflect the perfectly healthy preferences of any energetic young girl.[39] Implicitly, of course, this amounted to a criticism of the Ellis model that John had employed (though it is worth noting that Vera Brittain subsequently took care not to let her own daughter acquire a male nickname). In general, the critics (most of them, admittedly, male and heterosexual) considered *The Well* guilty of too much special pleading. At least, commented the *Tatler*, Stephen had money, whereas her squalid Parisian friends, whom the novel implicitly deplored, had none.[40]

However, *The Well* was certainly doing good business. Within a week of publication major outlets like *The Times* Book Club, W. H.

Smith's, and Truslove had sold out their stock. When the literary hostess Lady Ward came to tea at Holland Street in the second week of August, she arrived clutching her copy of the second edition. John and Una felt sufficiently confident of progress to leave London for a couple of days. An admirer of *The Well*, Anne Elsner, invited them down to her Tudor cottage in Rye. They were instantly taken with the house and the picturesque little town, which with its unspoilt medieval buildings and narrow cobbled lanes breathed history at every turn. 'We longed for a cottage there,' noted Una.[41]

In fact, not a cloud ruffled the horizon. John seemed set to achieve a steady if unspectacular success with *The Well*. On August 17 the *Daily Telegraph* gave the novel its best review yet: 'truly remarkable' and 'a work of art finely conceived and finely written'. This was what John, like any writer, wanted to hear – or was it? Was it all perhaps proceeding just a little too smoothly? After all, she had written the book to stir consciences and change public attitudes towards 'a misunderstood and misjudged minority'. Tasteful literary reviews, the good ones at any rate, would certainly help sales, but they hardly amounted to the dramatic impact John had had in mind when at the outset she had spoken to Una of being prepared for 'the shipwreck of her whole career'. She wanted to be seen as the bold 'pioneer' she believed she was, as the first person who had 'smashed the conspiracy of silence'.[42]

She did not have to wait long. On Sunday, August 19, the storm broke suddenly out of the blue.

Chapter Eighteen

The banner headline appeared on the features page of the *Sunday Express*: '*A Book That Must Be Suppressed*'. The article beneath, in large type and covering almost the whole page, was by the paper's editor James Douglas and represented a strongly worded attack on *The Well*. A large photograph of John accompanied the article, showing her in one of her more masculine poses – one hand in the specially-made pocket of her skirt, the other languidly holding a cigarette at waist height – and wearing a gentleman's silk smoking jacket, a high collar and black bow tie. The picture was cut off at the knee, thereby eliminating the stockinged ankles and low heeled shoes which would have softened the severe image.

'I say deliberately,' Douglas thundered, 'that this novel is not fit to be sold by any bookseller or to be borrowed from any library.' He was well aware, he went on, that sexual 'inversion' existed, but to flaunt it in the form of a novel which anyone could pick up and read was provocative and inadmissible. Perversion, he believed, had already gone too far.

> I have seen the plague stalking shamelessly through great social assemblies. I have heard it whispered about by young men and young women who do not and cannot grasp its unutterable putrefaction. Both aspects of it are thrust upon healthy and innocent minds. The contagion cannot be escaped. It pervades our social life.

Then, descending from the Biblical metaphor of Pharoah's Egypt to the more prosaic horrors of modern chemistry, the final *coup de grâce*:

> I would rather give a healthy boy or a healthy girl a phial of prussic acid than this novel. Poison kills the body, but moral poison kills the soul.

The article ended with a demand that the publishers withdraw the book, otherwise it should be suppressed by law. 'Literature as well as morality is in peril,' concluded Douglas.

This startling outburst had been carefully orchestrated. On the Friday before the *Sunday Express* denunciation, Douglas had sent

Jonathan Cape a copy of his forthcoming article. The next day the Beaverbrook stable-mate, the *Daily Express*, carefully aroused public expectations by printing a sharply edited resumé of Douglas's piece which omitted the name of the novel and its author. At the same time posters and bill-boards gave wide prominence to the impending thunderbolt. That Saturday night the *Evening Standard* obligingly kept the world on tenterhooks by reproducing the *Daily Express* 'teaser' word for word.

The result was that, come Sunday the 19th, other newspapers were leaping with gusto on the unstoppable *Express* bandwagon. *Amazing Story By A Woman*, gasped the *Sunday Chronicle*, which then proceeded, bathetically, to mumble mysteriously of 'one of the hidden cankers of modern life'. It coyly declined to name the novel.[1] The *People* proved equally shy on this score, but there its inhibitions ended. It invented the elaborate fiction that Scotland Yard was examining a 'secret' book that was so frank that even libraries and bookshops were trying to hush it up. The paper solemnly informed its readers that one of its staff had procured a copy: 'his verdict is *that nothing could justify its publication.*'[2]

On Monday, August 20, the 'story' was moving like a school measles epidemic through the national press. Most newspapers were content simply to repeat extracts from the *Sunday Express* article. Some sought out the book in a vain bid to reproduce its juicier passages. Beverley Nichols recalled being amazed when a Fleet Street colleague, whose editor had instructed him to skim the novel for 'dirt', confessed gloomily he could find nothing unprintable in it. The closest thing to an obscenity occurred at the end of a chapter where the heroine kisses her lover's hands. There followed: 'And that night they were not divided.'[3] Even this was a direct allusion to the Biblical story of Saul and Jonathan in the Second Book of Samuel where it says: '. . . and in their death they were not divided.'[4]

One daily newspaper, the Labour *Daily Herald*, challenged the *Express* position by widening the issue into a debate on censorship. The literary editor, Arnold Dawson, accused Douglas of 'stunt journalism' and hypocrisy. How could a paper which revelled in the confessions of murderers condemn such a profound work of literature? The standard of prurience held up by the *Express* would mean that writers of the calibre of Defoe, Swift, Smollett, Sterne and even Shakespeare himself would have to be suppressed.[5] Two days later Dawson would return to the attack with an article entitled *Should the Bible be banned?*[6] The *Evening Standard* leader on Monday night cautiously supported the *Herald*: readers themselves were ultimately the best judges of what they read, not some outside authority.[7]

The *Express*, however, remained unabashed. Its Monday leader reiterated Douglas's call to the Home Secretary to ban the book. It also announced a further scoop. Jonathan Cape had written to the paper staunchly defending the book and his decision to publish, and the letter was printed in that day's edition. However, he had also offered to send copies to both the Home Secretary and the Director of Public Prosecutions. If it could be shown that the best interests of the public would be served by withdrawing the novel, Cape gave notice that he would do so.[8]

In this same letter Cape pointed out that the *Express* campaign would simply alert the 'smut-hounds', thus nullifying all his efforts to ensure that the book reached the right class of reader. Indeed, the events of the week-end had made the book an instant sell-out. Bookshops and libraries up and down the country reported a run on stocks. One London library received 600 enquiries about the novel on Monday August 20 alone.[9] As early as the previous Saturday morning, when the *Express* posters publicizing the Douglas article were already on the streets, queues had started to form at Cape's trade counter in Bedford Square. Veteran collectors wanted copies, one firm alone ordering one hundred.[10]

By this time the author as well as the book was beginning to reap the full harvest of such unexpected publicity. Every paper displayed photographs of John and contained descriptions of her 'arresting' appearance and personality. The *Yorkshire Post* showed her in jacket and tie, a cigarette clamped raffishly between the teeth, looking every inch the smooth young man-about-town.[11] The *Manchester Despatch* dubbed her 'the most easily-recognised artistic celebrity in London' – which it put down to her straight-cut clothes and wide-brimmed blue Montmartre hat. The paper noted that both she and her secretary (a tactful reference to Una) smoked.[12] The *Newcastle Daily Journal* drew a reverential portrait of 'Titian hair in a close Eton crop' and characterized John as the epitome of the strong, silent type of woman: 'With her notably fine forehead and beautiful hands, her whole aura is high-brow modernism.' The report added (not without a certain tongue in cheek perhaps) that she probably never read Sunday newspapers.[13]

John was appalled by Douglas's attack. Its stark and unqualified condemnation of 'inversion' shocked her. To Toupie's friend Fabienne she wrote:

I know that those words have wounded many who cannot afford to be further wounded. If the result of that article is, as I honestly begin to fear that it may be, to cause certain weaker souls to feel despair, perhaps even to drive them out of existence, then I hope that his day of reckoning will come when he stands face to face with his and their Maker.[14]

John's anger drew strength from the enormous mailbag she had received daily since the publication of *The Well*. It reflected, as she saw it, the full suffering of 'my people'. Lesbians everywhere had written to thank her for breaking the silence. She told Gerard Manley Hopkins (who had complimented her on the book):

> One woman asked me if toleration of the third sex would ever come, and I replied that Havelock Ellis thought there was a faint light in the darkness, but that it would probably not come in our lifetime. She wrote back saying "I am just 23 – do you think it will be very long?" I could not help visualising the many stony miles that her feet must tread.[15]

At bottom, John regarded the *Express* attack as blatantly un-Christian. It was a theme she took up with vigour in her first public interview, in the *Daily Herald*. 'Does the *Sunday Express* editor's conception of Christianity,' she asked, 'lead him to think that because God permits certain types to be born into the world they should be thrust aside or ignored?'[16] This would always be the kernel of her defence: if sexual abnormality existed, then it must be a fact of nature. Consequently, 'inverts' should be given as much toleration as anybody else. By contrast, in talking of a contagion infecting innocent minds and souls, Douglas assumed that homosexuality resembled a transmittable disease. The moral difference between the two positions – the latter suggesting a corruptive influence – mattered crucially to John. Events, however, were fast overtaking such philosophical niceties.

Jonathan Cape had impressed John with his enthusiasm for *The Well* when other publishers had dared not take it. His ideas for producing and marketing the book matched her own desire to present it as a serious work without hint of titillation or sensationalism. She was wholly unprepared, therefore, for his sudden retreat, in his letter to the *Express* of August 20, offering to submit the novel to Home Office approval. Worse, he had taken this step (*and* sent copies to the Home Secretary) without consulting her. John was understandably furious. A flurry of phone calls between Holland Street and Bedford Square was followed by a heated meeting at Cape's offices. There is little doubt that Cape was engaged in hedging his bets, exploiting the fortuitous exposure given the book by the *Express* rumpus while carefully ensuring that he kept on the right side of the law. He tried to mollify John by pointing out that in himself the Home Secretary had no power – as the Lord Chamberlain had in the theatre – to ban a work. This of course overlooked the fact that in his letter Cape had agreed to withdraw the novel simply on the basis of the minister's adverse *opinion*. At bottom, as Cape later admitted, the publisher believed that the Home Secretary would vindicate his judgement.[17]

In this he revealed a considerable naivety. For the Home Secretary of the day was the unprepossessing Sir William Joynson-Hicks. Popularly known as 'Jix', he was a muscular Christian, treasurer to the fundamentalist Zenana Bible Mission and a fervent opponent of current attempts to revise the Anglican Prayer Book. A stern advocate of the Cold War, before that term had been coined, he scented Reds under many beds, especially trade union ones. He had had twelve leading British Communists arrested during the labour troubles of 1925. Jix had recently expressed his concern at the proliferation of immoral literature and, true to his kind, the mere mention of 'obscenity' called forth his most reactionary responses. Later in *The Well* case he would be dubbed 'The Policeman of the Lord' in a famous lampoon.

On the morning of Wednesday 22 August, an anxious John and Una attended a sitting with Mrs Leonard. Una simply wrote in her diary that the message was 'confused'. However, they did not have to wait long for news. On their return to Holland Street, a call came through from 'Jimmy' James to say that Jix had written a strongly worded reply to Cape instructing him to stop the book or face legal proceedings for obscenity. This unequivocal threat went beyond the Home Secretary's legal powers, but Cape now had no alternative but to honour his original offer. He therefore despatched a telegram to the printers to cancel the imminent third printing of *The Well*. He also wrote a letter to *The Times*, which appeared in the next day's editions,[18] announcing he was withdrawing the book and discontinuing publication. The *Daily Express* piously thanked the Home Secretary for his prompt action which, the paper declared, had earned the whole nation's gratitude.[19]

For the second time in forty-eight hours John cursed Cape, and shed her last illusions that publishers were anything but unreliable opportunists. That Wednesday afternoon another meeting took place at Bedford Square. This time Cape suggested an ingenious and practical plan of action. In his telegram to the printers he had expressly instructed that moulds of the type be made as quickly as possible and delivered to his offices. Given the continuing publicity surrounding the book – to which Cape's own letters to the press had added – he reasoned that there still existed a large and unsatisfied demand for the novel. No actual ban had been imposed but to continue publication in Britain would provoke official reaction. The publisher's plan, therefore, was to fly the type moulds to Paris, sub-lease the rights to an English-language publishing company there called the Pegasus Press, and solicit orders from English booksellers and other subscribers.

Determined not to let the book die, John suppressed her angry regrets and fell in with the plan. Any doubts she might have had as to the justice of her cause were removed by the hundreds of letters and telegrams which poured into Holland Street offering her support and sympathy. They marked a new phase in John's campaign. Perceptibly we can see her changing gear, almost revelling in her new role as champion of all threatened writers, of Literature itself. She and Una had planned to spend the end of August and September at their regular watering-hole of Bagnoles de l'Orne. They now cancelled the trip. On August 23 John gave another interview to the *Daily Herald*. The liberty of the pen was at stake, she declared. 'Is the reader to be treated like a kind of mental dyspeptic, whose literary food must be pre-digested by a Government office before consumption? Such action can only insult the public intelligence.' Then, in a clarion call to arms: 'On behalf of English literature, I must protest against such unwarrantable interference.'[20]

The withdrawal of *The Well* had prompted some of the great names of English letters to enter the lists on John's behalf. Arnold Bennett, who praised the novel when it first appeared as 'honest, convincing, and extremely courageous',[21] sent her a message of sympathy. He was angry that Cassell, his own publisher, had turned down *The Well*, and he openly voiced his opinion that he could cheerfully murder James Douglas. Bennett was already in touch over the case with E. M. Forster and Leonard and Virginia Woolf. Forster, reminded of his own 'unpublishable' homosexual novel *Maurice* (written in 1913), had taken a keen interest. On the day of *The Well*'s withdrawal he paid John a visit. He proposed, with the help of Leonard Woolf, to draft a public letter of protest which would be signed by Bennett, Lytton Strachey, and other of their influential literary friends. Always suscep-tible to the praise of those she regarded as her intellectual superiors, John felt flattered and agreed enthusiastically.

However, her mood changed when she received a copy of the draft letter. It dealt merely with the legal aspects of the suppression, offering 'no opinion on either the merits or the decency of the book'. Her quick sensitivity to criticism was instantly aroused. She hastily amended the Forster version to correct this omission and sent it back to him. John could not forget that it was Forster's co-drafter of the letter, Leonard Woolf, who had given her book one of its least favourable reviews. At the time she had called it 'a really dastardly attack, hitting below the belt with a vengeance'.[22]

On Friday 25 August Cyril Connolly's review of *The Well* appeared in the *New Statesman*. It did nothing to ease John's defensive state of mind. Connolly found the novel 'long, tedious, and absolutely humourless'. The idea that homosexuals were branded with the 'mark of Cain' and could therefore claim the right to martyrdom was preposterous, he wrote. The middle parts of the book constituted merely 'mechanical' writing, being 'a few pleas for kindness to animals, halos for inverts, and a special paradise for trees'. Connolly hoped it would pave the way for a better book on the subject. To make matters worse, an editorial in the same issue of the weekly compared *The Well* unfavourably with that rival lesbian novel about to be published, Compton Mackenzie's *Extraordinary Women*.

It was against this background that John had matters out with Forster when he finally returned to discuss with her the wording of the letter of protest. According to Virginia Woolf, who relayed Forster's account of the meeting to her friend Vita Sackville-West, the exchange was none too cordial. 'Radclyffe scolds him [Forster] like a fishwife, and says that she won't have any letter written about her book unless it mentions the fact that it is a work of artistic merit – even genius.'[23] The comment was more waspish than just, though it is conceivable that John's ready temper, easily fired, did overreact. What John could not accept was the unwillingness of the petitioners to back without reserve the moral integrity of *The Well*. She therefore appealed to Arnold Bennett, the one great writer, she felt, who had sincerely 'befriended' her novel. She was worried, she wrote to him, that the letter as it stood in the Forster version would compromise Bennett's published view of the book 'in the eyes of my public'. She made her own position absolutely clear:

> I do not *want* the support of anyone who will not vouch for the decency of my book ... I don't intend, if I can prevent it, to be made a peg for the possible future grievances of writers who express any doubts anent the purity of my intention in writing *The Well of Loneliness*.[24]

This plea put Bennett in a difficult position. Although his review had praised certain qualities in John's novel, he privately doubted its literary worth, and told Forster as much. In his reply to John, therefore, Bennett assured her that while he himself still stood by both the merits and the decency of *The Well*, he had been persuaded to agree to the Forster letter 'because it enable (sic) certain other, more timid, persons to sign'. He ended lamely: 'I do not think Forster's enterprise will result in anything. It is now rather late, and the difficulty of getting hold of signatories at this time of the year is extreme. Nor do I see how anything else can be done.'[25]

This held little comfort for John and by the end of August the protest petition looked still-born. She was bewildered by the fastidious conscience-juggling of the Bloomsbury writers. She saw only a principle at stake, that Truth was being suppressed. The episode vividly displayed the gulf which lay between herself and the intellectual clique that centred on the Woolfs. There was no mistaking, in Virginia's catty utterances, her tone at once amused, superior, and proprietary. John was simply too unambiguous to be taken seriously by her. At a week-end house-party held at the Woolfs' Sussex home in early September, Forster's equivocal personal feelings surfaced. In a slightly tipsy outburst, he confessed frankly that lesbianism disgusted him – partly out of a sense of conventionality but also because he disliked the idea of women being independent from men.[26] Virginia was not at all put out by such remarks. Though she herself was currently involved in a tentative love affair with the avowedly homosexual Vita Sackville-West, she found 'these people' strange and rather ridiculous.[27]

To Forster's credit, he did not let the matter drop entirely. In an article, albeit anonymous, in the September 1 issue of the *Nation and Athenaeum*, he deplored the suppression of *The Well* as 'an insidious blow at the liberties of the public' and called for further protest. In the following issue he and Virginia Woolf signed a joint statement saying the book had been victimized, not for indecency, but simply for its theme. Did that now mean, they asked, that such a subject could only be alluded to incidentally? What about other controversial issues such as birth-control, suicide, and pacifism? Could they be mentioned? 'We await our instructions!'[28]

If John felt disappointed with the organized protest on behalf of her book, she could take comfort from the knowledge that public support for her cause remained widespread. Letters and messages were still arriving at Holland Street in profusion. On September 1 alone her postbag contained almost 400 letters. Many came from 'normal' people who claimed that reading *The Well* had changed their views on 'inversion'. This more than anything confirmed John's belief in the struggle. To Fabienne she explained that she was prepared to risk all on behalf of 'these people': 'Nothing less than my all would have been enough to offer in view of the ceaseless persecution that has been meted out to abnormals for years.'[29] It suggests she hankered, like her heroine Stephen, for the wounds that the battle would inflict as a token of her faith and resolution. She assured Oliver Baldwin, the homosexual son of the Conservative Prime Minister Stanley Baldwin, that she was only too proud 'to stand the racket of having told the truth – I shall go on telling the truth and the truth and the truth whenever opportunity offers!'[30]

The Well, meanwhile, was far from dead. The Knopf edition in America remained scheduled for publication in October and plans proceeded for a number of foreign translations. Most exciting of all, Cape's Pegasus Press enterprise was now under way. On September 6 Cape's partner Wren Howard packed the papier maché type moulds into a suitcase and flew to Paris with them. The French printers of Pegasus at once cast a set of stereo plates and began printing a new edition. At the same time circulars were sent from Paris to a large number of selected individuals and booksellers in England (taken from Cape's mailing list) offering the novel for 25/- plus 11d postage. The circulars emphasized that each copy was 'a replica of the original London edition and appears without the alteration of so much as a comma'. By the 28th of the month the Pegasus edition was ready. Stocks of *The Well* moved into Paris bookshops and a steady flow of copies began crossing the Channel, some in the luggage of returning English travellers but by far the greater number in postal shipments.

There followed a brief lull, broken only by the flurry of activity which came on the heels of the news that Knopf had 'ratted' – as Una put it in the diary.[31] Knopf had appeared eager to publish up to the last moment. A postcard to John in mid-September from the *Aquitania*, on which Blanche Knopf was returning to America from a rest-cure in Europe, had read: 'Now I'm anxious for New York and full speed ahead.'[32] However, in Mrs Knopf's absence, her husband and partner Alfred Knopf had been getting cold feet. As a result, with only days to go before publication, the whole thing was suddenly off.

Blanche Knopf's explanation was that the withdrawal of the book in England had entirely altered its image in America. They could now only sell it as a 'dirty' book since demand would be for something salacious and sensational. Moreover, Knopf would be placed in the invidious position of having to defend a work which had not been defended in the author's own country. Resurrecting the vexed question of simultaneous publication, Mrs Knopf pointed out that had both the American and English editions appeared together, as originally intended, the present unfortunate situation could have been avoided: 'we feel we were definitely sacrificed to Cape's convenience,' she concluded.[33] What this piece of special pleading boiled down to was that the Knopfs were afraid that the heat would now be turned on them. Rather than face it out, they were prepared to cut their losses – though they wanted no one to take their place. Blanche Knopf advised John to keep the book out of the American market altogether on the grounds that no publisher there would now handle it except as pornography.

John had no intention of following this advice and considered the Knopf action outrageous. She had Audrey cable Carl that there should be absolutely no compromise with the Knopfs. Then Audrey was despatched to New York to help sort out the collapse of the contract while Jonathan Cape negotiated to take over the novel's American rights. On the morning of October 3 John and Una paid another visit to Mrs Leonard. Ladye cannot have 'got through' any unduly disturbing disclosure, for that evening they both took time off from the crisis to attend the first night of *Thunder On The Left* at the Kingsway Theatre. Fans mobbed John for her autograph.

But next day events took another dramatic turn. Customs officers at Dover, tipped off by the *Daily Express*, seized a consignment of 250 copies of the Paris edition of *The Well* on its way to the London bookseller Leopold Hill, Pegasus's English distributor. John and Una were about to set off for Rye. They cancelled the trip and called on Jonathan Cape. John was in defiant mood. Sensitive to Blanche Knopf's charge that the book had not been defended in Britain, she had no intention of letting Cape off the hook a second time. At her suggestion Cape telephoned John Holroyd-Reece, head of the Pegasus Press, who gave his assurance that he would fight the case all the way. For this unequivocal response, so different from Cape's devious manoeuvrings, Holroyd-Reece earned a lasting place in John's affections. John next rang Harold Rubinstein, a lawyer with a reputation as a writer as well, and asked him if he would take the case on behalf of Pegasus against the authorities. Rubinstein agreed to do so.

Now that the authorities had taken positive action, influential voices again spoke up on John's behalf. The *Daily Herald* took the lead, as before, using the issue as a stick with which to beat the Conservative government. On October 6 the paper contained interviews with H. G. Wells and Bernard Shaw. Both vigorously attacked the Home Office and deplored the Customs action. Shaw said he failed to understand why Cape had voluntarily withdrawn the novel in the first place, but such a step nevertheless gave the authorities no right of seizure. If their action was not contested, Shaw went on, there would soon be no books published in England at all. Wells also considered the seizure illegal and urged the publisher to fight it. The radical feminist Dora Russell described the move as 'monstrous' and advocated less timidity in the face of official brow-beating.

John too was quoted in the *Herald*. She called the Customs action 'an outrage against literature and an attack on personal freedom'. The newspaper challenged the Home Office to explain itself since no legal ban had been imposed on *The Well* – nor had any action been taken against Compton Mackenzie's *Extraordinary Women* when it appeared in September. The BBC, meanwhile, announced an hour long debate on the censorship of books between Mackenzie and James Douglas, to be chaired by Desmond MacCarthy. Mackenzie intended to defend his book personally should it be prosecuted and he viewed Douglas as nothing better than a 'literary scavenger'. In the event Douglas avoided the challenge. A few hours before the broadcast he claimed he was too ill to appear.

On October 18 the Customs suddenly released the seized consignment. John was jubilant. The next morning she and Una travelled down to Rye to renew their inspection of properties in the town. However, hardly had they arrived and installed themselves at the Mermaid Inn than a call came through from Rubinstein to say the police had raided the premises of Leopold Hill and reconfiscated all the copies of *The Well*. The two women rushed back to London. The Customs release proved only to have been a feint to allow the authorities time to prepare a more legally defensible move. They found what they needed in Lord Campbell's Obscene Publications Act of 1857, which empowered magistrates to seize and destroy material they deemed obscene. The Metropolitan Police had obtained search warrants under the Act and gone to Hill's shop in Great Russell Street where they seized 247 copies of the book.

A few days later Cape's offices at Bedford Square were also raided, during the lunch hour when Cape's secretary was alone in the front office. She directed the police down to the stockroom in the basement, then grabbed the only remaining Cape copy on display in the showcase and sat on it until the raid was over. The police left the premises with a meagre haul of six Pegasus copies and one Cape edition.[34] Hill and Cape, as the owners of the seized goods, were now summonsed to appear at Bow Street Magistrates Court on November 9 to show cause why the books should not be destroyed.

John cannot have been unduly surprised by this fresh action by the authorities. Nor overly disappointed, for it ended all the prolonged uncertainty. The fight now lay out in the open and even Cape would have to stand his ground. Never physically strong, John felt drained and exhausted after an unremitting two months in the limelight. Yet in the closing weeks before the court case she seemed to radiate a sense of intoxication. In an over-wrought letter to the biologist Julian Huxley, thanking him for consenting to be a witness for the defence, her vision of the forthcoming struggle had become heroic and apocalyptic: 'we dare not allow them to triumph otherwise it would mean an end to progress.'[35]

By the time *The Well* case came to court, John and Harold Rubinstein had approached over one hundred individuals in their search for defence witnesses. The response among writers proved disappointing. Faced with the prospect of supporting a homosexual novel in public, many authors suddenly become unaccountably shy or over-worked. John Galsworthy, president of PEN, insisted he was too busy and doubted that the question of literary freedom arose. PEN's general secretary, Hermon Ould, himself a homosexual, maintained he could not appear to speak on behalf of the membership as a whole. Everyone was of course against censorship, he explained, 'but that is not the question raised at the present moment'.[36] Evelyn Waugh proved characteristically curt: he had not read the book and he hated legal proceedings. Rebecca West disapproved of the Home Office action but thought the case a bad one on which to fight censorship. James Agate and G. B. Stern pleaded ill-health, Eden Phillpotts claimed he was a recluse, Harley Granville-Barker did not regard 'sexual perversion a fit subject for art', and Margaret Kennedy (author of *The Constant Nymph*) considered the law on obscenity so ill-defined that any testimony would be useless. Many other writers simply declared that they had not read John's book and therefore could not voice an opinion.[37] Such a negative response, especially from a body like PEN that was supposedly committed to authors' rights, throws John's own courage into even sharper relief.

A more predictable reaction came from those churchmen, scientists, academics and military men who were approached, showing the extreme caution of contemporary opinion towards the whole question of homosexuality. Some, while admiring *The Well* as literature, felt that to put the book into general circulation would only encourage an increase in 'abnormality' and therefore do more harm than good. A more substantial objection concerned the legal issues. The lawyer Stephen McKenna pointed out that by voluntarily withdrawing the novel at the Home Secretary's behest, Cape had undermined the defence in advance.[38] Hugh Walpole put the same point directly to Jonathan Cape himself:

I admire Miss Hall's courage in writing [the book] and would have admired yours in publishing it if you had stuck to it but you abandoned it to Jix and I don't see that a number of writers swearing that they don't think the book obscene has anything to do with it.

Walpole agreed to be a witness, but insisted that he disliked intensely all the publicity given to homosexuality, 'which ought I think to be "let lie" – on both sides'.[39]

A major disappointment was Havelock Ellis's refusal to testify:

I *never* have been in the witness box. There are two good reasons against it. The first is that I do not possess the personal qualities that make a good witness, and would probably make a bad impression, and certainly not a good impression. The second is that being the author of a book on this very subject that has been judicially condemned, I am 'tarred with the same brush'. The less said about me the better for you. In any case, for good or evil, my testimony is already contained in the book itself. It is people of the highly conventional and respectable kind, & occupying a high position . . . who will be really helpful.[40]

Amplifying on his decision a few days before the trial, Ellis pointed out that an adverse verdict against the book might be better publicity for it.

Whatever Ellis's reasons for excusing himself, his withdrawal from the battle at the crucial moment was characteristic. His own involvement in the Bedborough case thirty years before had shown him to be conspicuously irresolute in the face of authority. He was a scholar not a campaigner, preferring to stay in the background as a father-confessor figure while others (usually the strong-minded women to whom he seems to have been attracted) fought the good fight. While he stayed away from Bow Street, his mistress Françoise attended *The Well* hearing on his behalf. Remarkably, John's respect for Ellis was such that she accepted his withdrawal in good faith and continued to seek his advice. Lesser 'traitors' would not receive the same treatment.

A number of eminent people *had* let their names be put forward as potential defence witnesses. These included E. M. Forster, Virginia Woolf, Hugh Walpole, A. P. Herbert, Professor Julian Huxley, Oliver Baldwin, MP, Desmond McCarthy (editor of *Life and Letters*), Gerald Barry (editor of the *Saturday Review*), Dr Norman Haire (Harley Street sexologist), the playwright Clifford Bax, Laurence Housman (of the British Sexological Society), and the novelists Rose Macaulay, Storm Jameson, Sheila Kaye-Smith and Naomi Royde-Smith. By the time the case came to court, the list contained some forty names, twenty-five of them writers.

Some of the literary witnesses agreed to appear reluctantly and had qualms up to the last moment. Storm Jameson went to see Virginia Woolf, whom she had never met before, and anxiously enquired whether they were really expected to testify that *The Well of Loneliness* was a great piece of literature: 'Instead of snubbing or mocking me, as I deserved, she said gravely: No, there will be no need for that.'[41] In fact, Mrs Woolf herself was assailed by doubts on this point. She tried to convince herself that her stand was simply against censorship, but it pained her sensibility that the case rested on such a poor book.

> Leonard [Woolf] and Nessa [her sister Vanessa Bell] say I mustn't go into the box, because I should cast a shadow over Bloomsbury. Forgetting where I was I should speak the truth. All London, they say, is agog with this. Most of our friends are trying to evade the witness box; for reasons you may guess. But they generally put it down to the weak heart of a father, or a cousin who is about to have twins.[42]

In the event, Virginia did agree to give evidence, but asked that, because she might be nervous, 'for temperamental reasons', she be allowed to be one of the last to appear and then only if she was absolutely indispensable.[43]

Two literary giants who would not be at Bow Street on November 9 were Arnold Bennett and Bernard Shaw. Bennet claimed he was against a book being reintroduced which, however wrongly or unofficially, had been banned by 'properly constituted authority' – a strange excuse in view of his scathing attacks on Jix's conduct (one of which, written for the *Evening Standard*, was considered too libellous to print). He also felt that the legal definition of 'obscene' was so broad that it presented major difficulties for any defence. This did not stop him, however, from advising witnesses on the tactics they should employ:

> If prosecuting counsel, e.g. asks, 'Do you think this book is a proper one to put into the hands of young persons?' the witness should absolutely refuse to say either 'Yes' or 'No'. If he says 'No' he should add, 'And I say the same for the Bible and Shakespeare'.[44]

Shaw cheerfully declared that he was too immoral to stand as a credible witness for the defence. In his considered opinion, *The Well* could not be defended under the Obscene Publications Act of 1857, since it ruled that the judgement of the magistrate alone counted. In other words, any witnesses the defence put up could be ignored. Like Bennett, Shaw also hid behind the all-embracing legal definition of obscenity. The Act defined a book as obscene if it *tended* to corrupt those whose minds were 'open to immoral influence'. Such a definition applied to the entire British public, stated Shaw, 'not to say the human race', and necessarily included the whole of literature.[45]

John, meanwhile, remained busy soliciting support, not just among the distinguished but also from 'working people'. With the help of the Labour *Daily Herald*, she obtained signed protests from the National Union of Railwaymen and the South Wales Miners' Federation. In early November Una read her Virginia Woolf's latest novel *Orlando*, which would be published six days after *The Well* hearing. Perhaps John intended to meet Mrs Woolf before the case came to court but there is no record of this happening (equally possibly, Virginia took care to avoid her).

John's involvement in the lawyers' preparations proved no less intense. Since she and Cape were meeting the legal costs jointly, she assumed the right to take a full part in all their deliberations. She asked to be put in the witness box but counsel advised against this. Under the law, the publisher and the bookseller alone were prosecuted, not the author (this did not change until 1959). John felt bitterly disappointed. She saw *her* book on trial and found it difficult not to regard herself as the defendant in the case. She burned, moreover, to play a leading role in the battle ahead. She acquiesced in counsel's advice only on the assurance that the defence made it perfectly clear that she was not ashamed of her homosexuality nor was she afraid of giving evidence in front of her fellow writers. Her private life, she maintained, compared entirely favourably with that of ordinary respectable people. Further, she desired that counsel try to prevent any literary disparagement of her novel which might come from some of the defence witnesses, 'the literary world being what it is', as she put it. Evidently, John was quite aware of the reservations which some of the witnesses had about her book. She wished, finally, that the defence would throughout make a clear distinction between the terms 'inversion' and 'perversion'.[46]

If John had appeared in the witness box, it is likely that she would have expressed the sentiments contained in a long written statement she had prepared for Rubinstein. This reiterated her motives for writing *The Well*, her reasons for choosing fiction, and her conviction that the novel contained not 'one obscene word'. She referred to Havelock Ellis and Magnus Hirschfeld as her authorities on homosexuality – which, she declared (quoting Hirschfeld), now claimed fifteen persons out of every thousand. The statement concluded:

I claim emphatically that the true invert is born and not made. I have behind me in this claim the weight of most of the finest psychological opinion. This is precisely one of the things that I wished to bring home to the thinking public. Only when this fact is fully grasped can we hope for the exercise of that charitable help and compassion that will assist inverts to give of their best and thus contribute to the good of the whole. When I wrote The Well of Loneliness I had in mind the good of the whole quite as much as the good of congenital inverts. It is not too much to say that many lives are wrecked through the lack of proper understanding of inversion. For the sake of the future generation inverts should never be encouraged to marry.

I do not regret having written the book. All that has happened has only served to show me how badly my book was needed. I am proud to have written The Well of Loneliness, and I would not alter so much as a comma.[47]

Chapter Nineteen

Bow Street Magistrates Court was so crowded on November 9 that a notice had to be put up on the door reading 'Court Full' some time before the hearing began.[1] Most of the public seats were occupied by women, Una among them, looking (according to Storm Jameson) 'abominably over-dressed and over-made-up'.[2] In the well of the court sat the forty defence witnesses, which did not leave much room for counsel on either side. John was placed at the solicitors' table, a conspicuous figure in a dark blue Spanish riding hat and a leather motor-coat with astrakhan collar and cuffs. As the *Daily Herald* put it: 'Her features are refined and well-chiselled, the expression in the eyes being one of mingled pain and sadness.'[3]

The magistrate presiding over the case was the elderly, white-haired Sir Chartres Biron. Expectations varied of this key figure in the drama. Harold Rubinstein privately regarded him as 'pathologically boorish',[4] and it was rumoured that he had been overheard at his club saying he thoroughly agreed with James Douglas. There were those, on the other hand – and Shaw was among them – who placed some hope in the fact that Biron was something of a man of letters. Indeed, he had written two books, *Pious Opinions* and *To The Pure*, which appeared to support the view that the police should leave literature alone. In the latter work he had actually related the case of Lion Feuchtwanger's novel *Power*, which had been prosecuted for obscenity in Toronto. Biron expressed the opinion that the book was such that it would never have attracted those whom the law was designed to protect, and prosecuting it simply widened its sale. However, Sir Chartres was not known as one of the more progressive members of the Bench. One newspaper noted that he was using a quill pen to record the proceedings.[5]

The defence team was led by the eminent K. C. Norman Birkett, acting for Cape. A tall, bespectacled figure with a high forehead and vivid red hair, he had been brought into the case only three days before – which would perhaps account for his less than impressive handling of the matter in court. Appearing for the bookseller Leopold Hill was a younger barrister of considerable flair, James B. Melville, an eloquent

Irishman of left-wing persuasions (he had an African wife who was
popular in socialist circles). Opposing them for the prosecution was
Mr Eustace Fulton, accompanied by the Director of Public Prosecutions, Sir Archibald Bodkin (whose presence at the hearing, though
passive, indicated the gravity with which the authorities viewed the
case).

Fulton began the proceedings by calling the prosecution's only
witness, Chief Inspector John Prothero of Scotland Yard, the police
officer who had supervised the raids on Hill's bookshop and the Cape
offices in Bedford Square. Prothero gave evidence of the seizures,
after which he was cross-examined by Birkett's partner Herbert
Metcalf. Metcalf pointed out that *The Times Literary Supplement*'s
review of *The Well* had described the book as 'sincere, courageous,
high-minded, and often beautiful'. Prothero agreed that it was sincere
and courageous but not high-minded and beautiful. He said the theme
of the book was offensive: it dealt with physical passion, which should
remain the domain of doctors and scientists only. When Metcalf then
asked him if he would be impressed by the evidence of certain
distinguished people, Biron intervened to declare: 'I do not think that
the *opinion* of the witness would be of any great importance.' It was an
ominous pointer to the line the magistrate intended to take.

As it was incumbent on the prosecution to prove their case from the
text of the book as well as from its theme, Fulton re-examined
Prothero and singled out page 351 of the Pegasus edition – which
described a sad farewell at a railway station between Stephen and
Mary. This scene contained little evidence of physical affection, but it
was obvious from the context that the two women were lovers.
Fulton asked: 'Does that convey to your mind a normal or Lesbian
passion?' To which the police inspector replied: 'It conveys a Lesbian
and physical passion.'[6]

After the prosecution had closed their case, Birkett rose to address
the court. He contended that the action against *The Well* was a misuse
of the 1857 Act and, if successful, would have repercussions for the
whole of literature. The book dealt not with perversion, he continued,
but with what medical science termed inversion, which he defined as a
physical disability afflicting certain individuals who could not help
themselves. So far so good, but at this point Birkett began to get
himself into a tangle. To the amazement of those who had read the
novel, he proceeded to explain that the relationship between Stephen
and Mary was not physical but only romantic and sentimental, 'a
schoolgirl crush transferred to adult life and innocent of sexual
implications', as Sheila Kaye-Smith put it.[7] The magistrate interrupted to enquire incredulously: 'Do you say that [the book] does not deal

with unnatural offences at all?' Birkett replied: 'I say not.' Then added, hastily changing tack: 'Nowhere is there an obscene word, a lascivious passage. It is a sombre, sad, tragic, artistic revelation of that which is an undoubted fact in this world.'[8]

More trouble lay ahead. Birkett next turned his attention to the expert witnesses, though he had already clashed with Biron over the admissibility of such testimony. Professor Julian Huxley was first called. He failed to respond (though he was in court) and so Birkett requested Desmond McCarthy. McCarthy entered the canopied witness box and Birkett asked him: 'Having read "The Well of Loneliness", in your view is it obscene?', adding 'Don't answer until you have permission.' Biron refused to allow the question and went on to rule out any possibility of hearing the other thirty-nine witnesses – many of whom breathed an inward sigh of relief. Faced with the magistrate's intransigent view that no *opinion* could constitute evidence and that it was his duty alone to decide whether the book was obscene, Birkett shelved his plan to put Cape in the box and asked leave to consult his client.

Under the 1857 Act, Biron had acted within his rights – as Shaw had pointed out before the case. But Birkett had not handled the witnesses cleverly. He asked McCarthy the wrong question, given the law as it stood. Instead, he should have put other, less direct questions which would have elicited the answers he sought.

During the lunch recess John and Una adjourned to the Waldorf with John Holroyd-Reece (of the Pegasus Press), Rubinstein and Birkett. John was so angry with Birkett for the line he had taken that she was close to tears. 'Can you imagine my horror and despair,' she wrote later to Gerard Manley Hopkins,

> when Cape's counsel opened the case with a lie, with a blatant denial of the physical aspect that entered into my study of inversion! I can tell you that I sat there and sweated blood feeling that my work was both shamed and degraded. At lunch time I made it abundantly clear that unless Birkett got up and retracted his words I would get up before anyone could stop me and would tell the Magistrate the truth.[9]

Holroyd-Reece and Rubinstein supported John's stand and the contrite Birkett agreed to retract his statement – which he did during the afternoon session in court. It must have been a humiliating moment for a top barrister. In later years Birkett would recall his lunch with John as 'certainly the most miserable of my life'.[10]

After lunch it was Melville's turn to address the magistrate. He spoke in a quiet, confiding tone, asking Biron to judge the book as a whole and not on isolated passages. He quoted George Moore's distinction (in *Avowals*) between pornography and literature, stating that the latter dealt with descriptions of and thoughts about life rather than physical acts. He suggested that *The Well* neither praised nor apologized for sexual inversion, but rather accepted it as 'a fact of God's own creation'. Biron interjected that everyone was God's creature, even criminals, to which Melville retorted: 'I do not think one has got to consider, if I may respectfully say so, whether one agrees or disagrees.' *The Well* was written in a 'reverent spirit', Melville continued, Stephen's sacrifice at the end reflecting her 'inherent respect for the normal', her 'worship for the perfect thing which she had divined in the love that existed between her parents'. The book's moral, he concluded, was that inverts cannot accept charity but must try to exercise it themselves.[11]

'No actor,' reported the *Herald* of Melville's speech, 'ever held audience more tensely than this legal pleader with the quiet voice. When counsel sat down there was a silence that could be felt.'[12] It was 2.30 pm and Biron adjourned the hearing for a week to consider his decision. As the court rose, John rushed over to Melville and shook him warmly by the hand.

Una thought that Melville's speech had shaken Biron's 'rooted prejudice' and might possibly have swung the decision their way.[13] But the lawyers had little doubt that with the dismissal of the witnesses, the magistrate would pronounce for the prosecution. John was already decided on an appeal if necessary. 'This thing has got to be fought out to the end,' she told Hopkins, 'I for one would not tolerate any half measures . . . I will not desert the cause of these people or the cause of literary freedom.'[14]

The weather on November 16, the day the case resumed, turned appropriately dramatic. Severe gales swept across London and the south of England causing one death and injuring some twenty-five other people. This did not deter the crowds who flocked to Bow Street eager to hear the verdict, and scores of people had to be turned away. Conspicuous by their absence this time, however, were the forty witnesses, most of whom regarded the result as a foregone conclusion and were only too happy to make themselves scarce. John, of course, was very much in evidence, seated again in the centre of the court and sporting this time, for luck, a sprig of white heather in her Spanish hat.

Biron's judgement took almost an hour and was delivered in a subdued, conversational manner. From the start he made the most of Birkett's unfortunate retraction on the issue of physical relations in the

John's literary agent, Audrey Heath
(Robin)

Miss Radclyffe Hall
From a caricature by Matt

John as seen by *T.P.'s Weekly*, 1926

John by 'Pax' in *The Popular Pictorial*,
1927

Havelock Ellis

MISS RADCLIFFE HALL
(who has been awarded the Femina Prize for
her book "Adam's Breed").
"'At home on Pegasus, that valiant steed;
Yet finds romance in Soho—' Adam's Breed.'"

The Beresford Egan cartoon lampooning *The Well of Loneliness* that so shocked John

John in her Chinese silk smoking jacket

ohn photographed by Howard Coster
o mark the publication of *The Master*
f the House, 1932

John and Una at a First Night, 1933

Edy Craig (foreground) with 'the Boys',
Chris and Tony

Mickie Jacob with John and Una,
Sirmione 1934

Mickie and John

A photograph of herself that John sent to Souline. 'S.H.' stands for 'Same Heart'

Private View (1937), by Gladys Hynes. John and Una are unmistakable in the centre of the picture

John's study at The Forecastle, Rye. The photograph on the desk on the left is of Ladye, those on the right probably of Souline

John with Fido, one of her last dogs

John in her 50s

book. He also stuck carefully to the definition of obscenity under the 1857 Act, which meant that even a book containing no indecent words or phrases could still be accounted obscene on its theme or intent. If this was not the case, Biron argued, the best written books – and he acknowledged that *The Well* had some literary merit – could be as pornographic as they wished and always escape criticism. He conceded that a book describing immoral practices could be beneficial in its influence, but only provided it implicitly condemned or rejected such practices. However – and this was the nub of the magistrate's case – *The Well* put forth the view that 'unnatural vice' was wholly admirable and blameless of the ills which befell its practitioners.

To demonstrate his point, Biron opened his copy of the novel and systematically analysed those sections covering Stephen's love affairs with Angela and Mary. He singled out for special attention Stephen's defence of her love for Angela in the face of Lady Anna's horrified reproof, and commented: 'I am asked to say that this book is not a defence of these practices?' Biron's personal prejudice against homosexuality became obvious from his constant reference to 'these horrible practices', to 'these two people living in filthy sin', and to 'acts of the most horrible, unnatural and disgusting obscenity'. His tone sounded the ruder for being so matter-of-fact and John boiled with anger and humiliation. Turning to the case of Mary, the magistrate referred to her meeting with Stephen at the French front, 'where,' he went on, 'according to the writer of this book, a number of women of position and admirable character, who were engaged in driving ambulances in the course of the war, were addicted to this vice.' At this John could contain herself no longer and sprang to her feet. 'I protest! I am that writer!' she exclaimed. Without looking up, Biron said: 'I must ask people not to interrupt the court.' John stood her ground. 'I am the authoress of this book,' she repeated. Biron replied brusquely that if she could not behave herself in court he would have to have her removed, at which John sat down muttering: 'It is a shame!'[15] A police sergeant approached her and told her that she must keep quiet.[16]

John was itching to have her say in court. Biron had also been exceptionally provocative. But why did she choose to make her protest at this particular juncture? John was especially sensitive to the section of *The Well* dealing with the women at the front. There had already been some direct criticism of it, notably from the writer A. E. F. Horniman. In her reply to Rubinstein's questionnaire, Horniman had written: 'Personally I considered the remarks about the War calling on such women for help should not have been printed at all.'[17] John had obviously modelled Stephen's ambulance unit in France on the one run by Toupie Lowther (though she expressly denied this in an 'Author's Note' at the front of *The Well*). She knew several of Toupie's ex-colleagues. Therefore, any aspersions on the fictional unit could be construed as a slur on the real women. John's strong sense of loyalty was outraged by such a notion. But it went deeper than this. To John, there was something sacrosanct about those who had served at the battle front during the Great War. As her novels suggest, she saw their heroism as the supreme example of an ideal of self-sacrifice to which she herself aspired. She could not let pass unchallenged Biron's casual attribution of 'vice' to the ambulance-women in *The Well*.

Biron ended his address by saying he had no hesitation in declaring the book an obscene libel which would tend to corrupt those into whose hands it fell. He ordered the seized copies to be destroyed and imposed 20 guineas costs on both Cape and Hill.

Just before his verdict, Melville stood up and told the magistrate that, to avoid any misunderstanding, Miss Radclyffe Hall wished it to be pointed out that she would have gone into the witness box had it been allowed. And so, in a sense, John had the last word and honour, if not justice, was satisfied. As she left the court sympathisers, mostly women, swarmed round her, reaching out to shake her hand.

Notice of appeal was given on November 22. John, the Woolfs, and the sex reformer Dr Stella Churchill agreed to stand surety for Cape and Hill – though the Woolfs thought at first they were putting up bail for John in case the question of imprisonment arose. Dr Churchill started a defence fund and sent John £30, which she returned. Have-lock Ellis also suggested such a fund as a way of keeping the issue in the public eye (this had been done in the Bedborough case), but he advised that it should be organized by someone who was not himself an invert and should embrace the cause of 'Freedom and Progress' not merely homosexuality.[18]

In fact, the court decision had already spawned a number of independent initiatives on behalf of literary freedom. These focused on the need to change the law on obscenity. Shaw drafted a letter to this effect which appeared in the press on November 22: 'neither authors nor others should be subject to judicial defamation under cover, not of laws, but of ancient dicta which are too absurd to be discussed without a suspension of common sense,' the letter con-cluded. It was signed by forty-five writers among others.[19] An article by Arnold Bennett appeared in the *Evening Standard* on November 29 entitled '*Who Shall Select Books for Censorship?*' It did not mention *The Well* case by name, but Bennett pointedly backed up his attack on literary censorship with apt quotations from Sir Chartres Biron's *Pious Opinions*.

The appeal on December 14 proved largely a formality in which the same arguments were repeated on both sides. Birkett had withdrawn leaving Melville to handle the case for the defence, while the prosecution was led this time by the Attorney General, Sir Thomas Inskip. On the Bench sat twelve magistrates, two of them women, headed by Sir Robert Wallace – none of whom had read the book, according to Una.[20] Few of the original defence witnesses bothered to attend the hearing, though some new faces were present, notably Rudyard Kipling's and Marie Stopes's. Vita Sackville-West, who had waxed indignant at Biron's rudeness to John, looked in on the proceedings but soon grew bored and went shopping instead.[21]

The prosecution made the most out of Cape's duplicity in secreting the moulds of the book to Paris, making him look like a publisher more concerned with profit than principle. Inskip endeavoured to show up the heinousness of *The Well*'s offence by admitting he knew of only two other references in literature to lesbian women: one in the first chapter of St Paul's Epistle to the Romans, the other in the sixth Book of Juvenal. He characterized homosexuality as a 'well-known vice, unnatural, destructive of the moral and physical fibre of the passive persons who indulge in it'. Examining the novel in detail, Inskip singled out Stephen's conversation with Angela about marriage between women. He contended that 'a pure woman' or adolescent boy would not be able to keep their minds off 'libidinous thoughts' while reading the scene.[22]

The Bench retired for less than ten minutes to consider their verdict. Sir Robert Wallace announced the appeal dismissed with costs after a short address in which he declared *The Well* 'a disgusting book . . . prejudicial to the morals of the community'.[23]

John was not surprised by the decision. She wanted to fight on, she told the press, but was advised that further legal proceedings were impossible. She stoutly protested that both she and her book had been most unjustly treated. As she left the court, two women admirers stepped forward from the waiting crowd and kissed her hand.[24]

The view of most contemporary commentators after the banning of *The Well* was that the authorities had simply turned the book into an underground bestseller. Pegasus was still printing its edition in France and those who wanted a copy had merely to cross the Channel to obtain one. At the Gare du Nord in Paris, returning English travellers could buy the book for 125 francs from newsvendors' carts as they boarded the 'Golden Arrow'. Tucked into suitcases and handbags, the novel was smuggled into England with little difficulty. Dealers in the rue de Castiglione offered as much as six thousand francs (£40) for a copy of the banned Cape edition, knowing they could sell it on for far more. By Una's calculation, *The Well* had sold over 7,500 copies outside America by the end of 1928, 4,000 of these since James Douglas's attack on the book. By February 1929 Pegasus alone had sales totalling 9,000 and was reprinting more. As 'A Modern Mother' protested in a letter to *Time and Tide*, far from protecting those whose minds were 'open to immoral influences', the ban on *The Well* had created such a ballyhoo that no young girl or boy could now 'remain ignorant of certain facts which ordinarily would never have come to their notice'.[25]

John felt bitter and let down, as a loyal Englishwoman by her country, as an author by other writers. Even before the trial she had expressed disillusion at the government's action. She had confided to Fabienne:

> I have been a Conservative all my life and have always hotly defended that Party. When people told me that they stemmed progress, that they hated reforms and were enemies of Freedom, I, in my blindness, would not listen. I looked upon them as the educated class best calculated to serve the interests of the country. And yet, who was the first to spring to my defence, to cry out against the outrage done to my book? Labour, my dear, and they have not ceased to let off their guns since . . .[26]

John believed that Baldwin's government had been ruthlessly intent on making an example of her case. She claimed that 'secret orders' were issued to the appeal magistrates to make sure that they gave the book no chance of a reprieve.[27] As evidence, she circulated a confidential letter by the Director of Public Prosecutions, sending copies to Arnold Bennett and Lytton Strachey among others in the hope they might stir up the issue in the press. Bennett, wearying of the affair, proved less than encouraging. In a brusque reply, he wrote that he doubted 'whether any editor in London would now consider any item connected with the case as "news".'[28]

This sort of response typified the ambivalent stance which John had come to expect from many writers. She could not help seeing their hedging as cowardly and dishonourable. In particular, she felt deeply hurt by the unsupportive attitude of the official writers' bodies. After the case, she resigned from both PEN and the Writers' Club. PEN persuaded her to stay on as a member, but her departure from the Writers' Club was final. She had for a time sat on its executive committee and their lack of action was doubly wounding. 'I consider that the Committee *as a body*,' she wrote to the Club's president, Ranee Margaret Brooke, 'should have, at least, sent me a letter signed by all, expressing their indignation at the treatment I have received. By not doing so they implied an insult.'[29]

The *Well* case was not simply a watershed in John's life. It became a constant point of reference for her. As she saw it, she had laid her career on the line by publicly admitting her own sexual proclivity and by taking up the standard on behalf of all inverts. She expected her friends to show at least a measure of solidarity in return. Those, especially lesbians, who had displayed a conspicuous lack of support during the case or who favoured a traditional reticence in matters of homosexuality were now found wanting and given short shrift. Toupie Lowther became one of the first casualties. John and Una heard that she had resented *The Well* 'as challenging her claim to be the only invert in existence'[30] – though in later years she contended that she was the model for Stephen Gordon. Worse, she sought to conceal her homosexuality, according to Una, by shunning the company of 'her own ilk' and by wearing 'scarlet silk "confections" in the evenings with accordion pleated skirts and low necks'.[31] Toupie had often been tiresome and quirky and they dismissed her as 'essentially a crank'.

Relations with Evelyn Irons also noticeably cooled after 1928. John expected her to rally round the flag and use her position as deputy editor of the women's page of the *Daily Mail* to promote the cause. This was clearly not possible on a paper like the *Mail*, but John interpreted its failure to support her as backsliding on Evelyn's part. Minna and the Garvins, having been found wanting over the Fox-Pitt case, finally blotted their copy-book during *The Well* affair. Minna had never made any bones about her opposition to Una's liaison with John. It came therefore as no surprise to them when she deplored *The Well* and expressed horror at all the publicity of the case. Una, however, vowed never to see or speak to her mother again. Garvin was deemed guilty of a more positive 'betrayal' because, despite John's request to him to review her book in the 'proper spirit', the *Observer* was one of the few national papers not to review *The Well* at all. He and Viola had kept singularly silent during the court case, but then tried to get back in favour after realizing that most of their intellectual friends supported John. John and Una regarded this as all the more contemptible.

To some of John's friends *The Well* proved a revelation, if not something of a shock. May Sinclair was astonished to learn that the ménage at Holland Street was not platonic – and disapproved (having once had to rebuff another woman's amorous overtures).[32] Leonard Rees was very upset by the storm over *The Well* and assured Alec Waugh that John and Una were ' "nothing but deep friends" '. Waugh recalled: 'I made no very audible reply. A month or so later, however, Rees said, with trembling voice: "It's true, I'm afraid, it's true – my friends laugh at my innocence." '[33] It was a measure rather of the innocence of the times. *The Well* changed all that, bringing female homosexuality into the forefront of public consciousness – and reinforcing an image of the lesbian, as a masculine woman, which would prove remarkably durable.

Not all lesbians approved of *The Well*. Violet Trefusis thought the book a 'loathsome example' and longed to write her own novel on the same theme to correct the balance.[34] Vita Sackville-West felt more than ever that 'a really great novel remains to be written on that subject' and itched to try it herself: 'if one may write about [homosexuality], the field of fiction is immediately doubled.'[35] Romaine Brooks dismissed *The Well* as 'a ridiculous book, trite, superficial, as was to be expected' and labelled John 'a digger-up of worms with the pretention of a distinguished archaeologist'.[36]

What all these women disliked about John's novel was the stereotyping it projected, the notion that lesbian couples simply mirrored the male/female divide of heterosexual partnerships. John herself remained unrepentant. Having nailed her colours to Ellis's mast and been 'martyred' in the defence of the 'true invert', her pronouncements became increasingly sweeping and strident. In an interview with Evelyn Irons for the *Daily Mail* on the eve of *The Well*'s publication, she had declared: 'To be a good wife and mother is the finest work a woman can do.' She deplored the post-war trend encouraging women to go to work.[37] After the ban on the book she told an American woman reporter: 'In the heart of every woman is the desire for protection. In the heart of every man is the desire to give protection to the woman he loves. The invert knows she will never enjoy this and because of her affliction will face social ostracism.'[38]

The thousands of letters of support which John received during and after *The Well* case, many of them from fellow homosexuals who felt that her stand had given them new confidence, only strengthened her belief in herself as the leader of a 'defenceless minority'. This provided another outlet for her strong protective instincts: she could not let her 'people' down. Her conviction grew that she was a member of a third sex, neither man nor woman but uniting the best qualities of both (and, therefore, implicitly superior to either). She identified, in fact, with Stephen Gordon, reading back into her own life many of the attributes she had given to her heroine in order to back up her 'discovery' of the congenitalist theory. As we have seen, Una's memoir sought to do the same thing.

Just as she had self-consciously immersed herself in spiritualist theories, so John's self-appointed role as the inverts' spokesman led her to develop a pseudo-scientific expertise. She continued to read widely in sexological literature, corresponded with Havelock Ellis about his 'patients', and familiarized herself with the latest research work into glandular secretions and cell formations. Nobody minded, she told an American newspaper, when Professor F. A. E. Crew of Edinburgh University published an account of a chicken which, through an endocrine abnormality, both laid eggs and fathered chicks. Why then should inverts be treated so harshly?[39] But sometimes her zeal led her up strange paths. Taking Ellis's hereditary theory to its logical extreme, she privately came to believe that inversion could be detected in a baby's physical characteristics – in, say, the width of shoulders or the thickness of an arm.[40] It was the ultimate simplification: tape measures could predict lesbians.

Chapter Twenty

The legal fees of *The Well* case were heavy. The prosecution's costs at the Appeal alone amounted to some £300, all of which was borne by John and Cape. After some less than amicable exchanges between author and publisher over their respective share of the costs, Cape made what John considered a 'fair' offer: 'it makes me friends again with the loyalty to my Publisher that I always like to feel,' she wrote to Wren Howard.[1] Even so, John was obliged to sell 37 Holland Street to pay her way. Wealthy as she was, rising income tax in the post-war years combined with the impact of the Depression made the trial an extra financial burden she could ill afford. On January 11, 1929, John and Una moved back into temporary accommodation.

They intended to spend most of their time in Rye, at a rented cottage, 'Journey's End', making do with a small flat in London. John, however, was exhausted after the prolonged high drama of the court case and her doctor ordered a complete rest in the sun. They therefore changed their plans and decided to spend the rest of the winter and the spring in Paris and the south of France. With characteristic generosity, John paid Mabel Bourne, the amiable housekeeper at Journey's End, three months' wages to tide her over till she found another job.

There was plenty to do before they left England. John was still answering a heavy correspondence connected with *The Well*. Since the book's publication, she had received some 5,000 letters personally, only five of them abusive.[2] Many societies and magazines approached her for permission to quote from the book, but she remained adamant that any reproduction must be of the novel as a whole and without so much as a word altered – which ruled out serialization. When the Dutch publishers admitted they had abbreviated certain chapters, John was furious and had Audrey instruct them to make changes. Newspapers which suggested she was making large sums out of *The Well* were also taken to task and obliged to point out that she earned only a standard royalty and received nothing from the high black market prices.

On January 25 John gave a talk about *The Well* to the Southend branch of the National Council of Labour Colleges' Student Association as a gesture of gratitude to the Labour Party for their support. She repeated her defence of the book and declared herself a victim of gross injustice. She called Biron 'that old man' and strenuously denied that the novel was a plea for licensed debauchery. 'No government under heaven shall stop me writing,' she proclaimed, 'if I feel there is a great social problem which you have a right to know and which you can help solve.'[3]

Another debt of gratitude which John paid off at this time was to the miners, whose union had protested to the Home Secretary at the ban on *The Well*. The mines were again strike-bound and many mining communities were suffering great hardship. John sold one of her most treasured possessions, the Sargent portrait of Ladye. It was bought by the Glasgow Art Gallery for £1,000 and John presented the sum to the Lord Mayor of London's Fund for the Relief of Distress in the Coalfields.

In America, meanwhile, *The Well* had run into more trouble. After Knopf's withdrawal, the book had been picked up by a new, progressive publishing firm, Covici Friede. It appeared in December and instantly began selling in huge numbers, the news of the English ban having preceded it. John was eager to break into the American market. She noticed a review in one newspaper which referred to 'a woman writer named Radclyffe Hall'. 'Truth is,' she told Audrey ruefully, 'that I am completely unknown in America so far – *but completely unknown.*'[4]

Not for long, however. Several weeks after the publication of the Covici Friede edition, the New York police arrested Donald Friede and seized over 800 copies of the book on a charge of obscenity. The raid resulted from a complaint against the novel by John Sumner, secretary of the local Society for the Suppression of Vice and an active campaigner against 'risqué' literature. The publishers had expected Sumner's action and had already hired the services of Morris Ernst, an attorney with a reputation for fighting book censorship. By contrast with Cape in England, Covici Friede continued to sell the book while they awaited the official verdict of the authorities, exploiting to the full the attendant publicity of the case. Ernst, meanwhile, was soliciting the endorsements of well-known writers on behalf of *The Well* and collecting an impressive list of admiring reviews. Theodore Dreiser, Sherwood Anderson, Scott Fitzgerald, Ernest Hemingway, Sinclair Lewis, H. L. Mencken, Upton Sinclair, Carl Van Doren, Edna Ferber, Ellen Glasgow, and John's old friend Ida Wylie, were among the authors who came to the book's defence. John wrote to Covici Friede conveying her thanks and gratitude to 'my American brothers and sisters of the pen'.[5]

The Sumner case came to the Manhattan Magistrates Court in February. Friede was found guilty and *The Well* judged obscene: it 'idealised and extolled' perversion and would 'debauch public morals'. By contrast with the English trial, in the American court the defence played down the homosexual nature of the book, characterizing Stephen Gordon rather as 'thwarted in the development of her emotional life'. According to Ernst, the vital question at issue was, will the law condemn a book otherwise unobjectionable simply on its theme? 'To put it another way, if Stephen were a man and not a woman, the book would be merely a rather over-sentimental bit of Victorian romanticism.'[6] The court thought otherwise.

This decision was not unexpected and Ernst immediately appealed. He stepped up his search for distinguished supporters of the book. Hundreds of letters and telegrams were despatched to eminent public figures in all walks of life. This in turn boosted heavy newspaper coverage. To their delight, the publishers discovered they had a runaway best-seller on their hands. Friede, who believed that 'any publicity was good publicity if they spelled your name right', tried to get more of it by provoking the New York Watch and Ward Society into prosecuting him too, but without success. 'They assured me that they saw nothing wrong with the book,' he recalled with regret.[7] He need not have worried. By the end of February sales were moving towards 50,000 copies.

John was keeping abreast of developments from Paris. She and Una had arrived in the city on February 5. The weather was bitterly cold and they spent much of their time huddled in front of John Holroyd-Reece's fireplace in the rue Boulard, for the central heating in their hotel proved so poor that ice formed on the *inside* of the windows. John was tremendously grateful for Reece's staunch support during the court case and he and his wife Jeanne ('a wonder', Una called her) could do no wrong in her eyes. In her self-dramatizing way, John saw herself as an exile in Paris from an 'ungrateful England' and the Holroyd-Reeces as a safe haven from the storm. 'But for you and Mitsie [their dog Mitsou],' Una wrote on John's behalf to Audrey, 'I wouldn't care if I never saw England again.'[8]

Paris had its compensations, however. Copies of *The Well* were everywhere in the bookshops. Galignani's had a large display featuring a huge photo of John and at Brentano's she was accosted by autograph-hunters. The Pegasus edition was selling over one hundred copies a day and Gallimard showed interest in a French translation.

John and Una were soon seeing all their old friends – Colette, Natalie, Lily de Gramont, Romaine ('who is still Romaine!' exclaimed Una). 'Our John is a reluctant Lion!' Una reported effusively to Audrey.[9]

In early March Donald Friede arrived in Paris and met them for lunch at his hotel. 'As U.S. Publishers go he's quite decent and honest,' Una told Audrey. They were impressed by his assurances that Covici Friede were determined to fight the American prosecution to the end.[10] But Carl Brandt was not in their good books. He had done next to nothing to promote the Covici Friede deal, had not answered John's letters, and appeared to be ignorant of current developments concerning *The Well*. To cap it all, he arrived in Paris in late February and was not only 'v. tight' at lunch but had the effrontery to ask John to lend him money. 'He really is just a spineless drunken lout & worse than useless,' Una fumed.[11]

In March Gallimard agreed to publish the French version of *The Well*, a considerable coup since it made John the first female author on their list – thus risking, Una thought, the wrath of all French women writers. Other translations of the novel proceeded less smoothly. The Dutch publishers had again incurred John's anger by their sloppiness. In the hunting scene of the book, the Dutch translation had the fox being shot in the stomach: 'It is the sin against the Holy Ghost . . .!' John exclaimed in exasperation.[12] She was also concerned over the Danish translation. A reputable Danish author Karin Michaëlis had offered to do it but was worried that unless there were some small omissions the book might risk being suppressed in her country. John's instinct was to stand firm but she was impressed by Miss Michaëlis's admission that the book had revolutionized her views of homosexuality. She therefore instructed Audrey to 'let her rip': 'I must not lose our important friend for the inverts.'[13]

'What a life!' John wrote ruefully to Audrey, 'Do you remember the time when no publisher much wanted John Hall, and now they're all at each other's throats – oh, well, as long as we get the dollars!!!'[14] In an earlier letter she admitted that she was beginning to 'simply dread being Me' and longed for anonymity. She would rather be

Annie Jones of Putney who lives in a villa with father & mother and plays in the local lawn tennis tournaments! Or better still a retired ironmonger with a fat bank account, a wife and four children – I want to read the lessons on Sunday feeling placid, because all sinners are damned, and because unlike Lot I have never been tempted to rape my elderly daughters.[15]

John was also regaling Audrey with her increasingly entrenched views on homosexuality. She reported a depressing visit to a Paris bar for male 'inverts' where a youthful hermaphrodite called Charpini sang in 'an *enormous* soprano voice': 'everyone was trying to be light-hearted while looking deeply unhappy'. She went on: 'What does it all mean and what are we to do in order to help such people? [Charpini] is very good looking at the present moment, but that will not last & then drugs or drink or both and a slippery tobogan (sic) down hill . . .'[16] John now believed that 'true inverts' should be allowed to marry and had been intrigued to learn that in Berlin lesbian marriages were going to be legalized ('If so, *I'm* for Berlin!! Am Tag!!' gushed Una). She was therefore dismayed to hear of the extraordinary 'Colonel' Barker case in England, which she saw as giving the very worst publicity to her cause. Barker was in reality an Englishwoman called Lilian Smith who for years had masqueraded as a military hero. She had projected herself as the most blimpish of hunting, shooting, fishing men, had even taken up boxing and, incredibly, was married for three years to an unsuspecting woman whom she later abandoned. She was finally exposed in a case for bankruptcy. 'I would like to see her drawn & quartered,' John told Audrey.

> A mad pervert of the most undesirable type, with her mock war medals, wounds, etc.; and then after having married the woman if she doesn't go and desert her! Her exposure at the moment is unfortunate indeed and will give a handle to endless people – the more so as what I ultimately long for is some sort of marriage for the invert.[17]

What intrigues here is the distinction John evidently made between her own case – a woman with a masculine psyche – and a mere masquerader like Barker. The key difference for John was one of deception.

John was upset to learn that in England Compton Mackenzie's *Extraordinary Women* was to be published in a cheap popular edition and without interference by the Home Office. She saw it as a deliberate insult aimed at her by the government. 'Here and now,' she declared angrily to Audrey, 'I renounce my country for ever, nor will I ever lift a hand to help England in the future.'[18] Her attention had also been drawn to a 'disgraceful' advertisement which Macy's had placed in the *New York World* to promote the Vanguard edition of Mackenzie's novel. This deliberately linked *Extraordinary Women* to *The Well* by proclaiming that Radclyffe Hall – 'herself . . . an EXTRA-ORDINARY WOMAN' – was one of the principal figures in Mackenzie's 'brilliant satiric fictional divertissement'.[19] Mackenzie later wrote that each character in his novel (except one) was an exact portrait of a real person,[20] and presumably John was the model for Hermina de Randan, who possessed a 'finely-cut profile' and whose hobbies included spiritualism, gardening and collecting antique furniture (the list of John's 'recreations' as it appeared in *Who's Who* in 1928). John believed she had a strong case for sueing Mackenzie for defamation of character, but she wearily instructed Carl Brandt to do everything possible, short of legal action, to get the Macy's advertisement withdrawn.

Far better news arrived from America on April 19. A cable from Covici Friede informed her that the Appeal Court had overturned the obscenity verdict against *The Well*. John was jubilant. 'Here's to the Saints, God bless them! And to Hell and Damnation with Jix and Co.!' she wrote excitedly to Audrey.[21] She urged her agent to write to '*all* the nations of the earth who would be likely to translate the Well' and tell them of its triumph on the other side of the Atlantic.[22] Covici Friede had plans to bring out a Victory edition of the novel containing reports of the English and American trials in its preface. On May 3 John met Ezra Pound at one of Natalie's salons and he suggested that the full text of each country's obscenity laws be included as well since they made such 'humorous reading'. John passed on the advice to Donald Friede.[23]

In the midst of all these dramas John was still being bombarded with fan mail, dutifully relayed to Paris by Audrey. So many presents (including a vase from a German admirer) were being delivered at the agency that Una jokingly advised Audrey to open a special depository. Some of the letters greatly amused John. One ardent American admirer, who described herself as 'one of those unfortunates' and regarded *The Well* as 'so gorgeous it hurt', addressed her letter mistakenly to Audrey and gushed: 'What sort of a gorgeous creature are you, Miss Heath? How much of yourself is in your book? And why oh why is England so far away ...?'[24] Whether this letter was genuine or not, John responded playfully by penning a humorous pastiche and sending it off to Audrey:

> What sort of a gorgeous creature are you Miss Heath? What is the colour of your adorable eyes that have gazed upon your flaming words as you wrote The Well of Loneliness? What is the size of your snow white hand and the make of your particular fountain pen? As a hart panteth for the living water my spirit is panting to know these details! And why oh! why do you live in England? Were I there I could be so happy to wait for aeons outside your door in the Burlington Arcade, sniffing the exotically fragrant air of the perfumed shops of that romantic passage. Oh, but I know that you are *utterly* gorgeous! ... Miss Heath, I simply and entirely adore you ... (asterisks here for Sir Chartres Biron).

What a letter, dear Audrey, well this is what comes of your writing The Well of Loneliness – I always advised you not to do it![25]

On May 17 John and Una finally left Paris for their long overdue holiday in the south of France. Colette had recommended St Tropez, where she had recently bought a villa, and they decided to make the journey by hired car after discovering that the trains went no farther than St Raphael. Accompanied by their maid Barber and John's latest acquisition, a tiny griffon called Tulip, they proceeded at a leisurely pace (the French chauffeur Pierre had been given strict instructions not to drive fast). 'We stopped for the night as we felt inclined and allowed the ex-chefs of royalty to feed us,' Una recalled later, 'and as the weather grew warmer we expanded, our tired nerves relaxed and we were very happy.'[26]

With their money worries now behind them (John was to make £6,000 in royalties from the American edition of *The Well* alone by the end of June) they were able to enjoy that high style of living to which they were accustomed. The English-run pension in St Tropez which Colette had recommended was thus discarded for its inferior meals and they moved instead into the more palatial Golf Hotel in Beau-vallon, with light, airy rooms on the top floor overlooking the bay and a private beach. This was to be their base for the next two months and more. They were rarely to be so relaxed, 'a holiday of holidays', Una recalled. 'I am dark red brown all over except for an insignificant middle piece where my swimming suit can't quite come off', Una told Audrey, '& John looks fifteen years younger, a fine brown & all the lines smoothing out of her day by day.'[27] She added in another letter: 'Wherever we live eventually she *must* have sea part of the year . . . It is life to her.'[28]

But John was never content simply to laze for long. For the first time since finishing *The Well*, she set her mind to some serious work again. In Paris she had dabbled with *The World*, the trolley-book she took up and put down again several times in between writing her published novels. But with their arrival in the south of France a new project emerged. Called *The Carpenter's Son*, it was, as so often before, no sudden inspiration but an idea that John had been mulling over for months. As she explained it to Una, 'she was haunted by the desire to write a book about a boy of our own times, the son of a carpenter, who, as he grew up in the carpenter's shop, would have memories and impulses that he did not understand, that linked him with the Carpenter's Son of Nazareth'.[29] But John could not think where to set the story and so the book had remained dormant – which suggests the importance of *place* as an inspiration to her writing. Una had forgotten about the idea until John suddenly resurrected it on their journey down to St Tropez. As they drove through Fréjus, John grabbed Una's arm and ordered Pierre to stop the car. 'What had caught her eye was a low stone archway and under the archway, half in and half out of it, a carpenter's bench and a carpenter at work. "Look", she said, "there is my carpenter's shop. That's where Christophe Bénédit was born . . ."'³⁰

To John there were pressing reasons why *The Carpenter's Son* should be the successor to *The Well*, reasons which stemmed from a painful emotional reaction to the furore the novel had caused.

In the late summer of 1928 a lampoon on *The Well* case had appeared called *The Sink of Solitude*. Published anonymously by the Hermes Press, it took the form of a mock-heroic poem accompanied by elegant but biting cartoons drawn by the artist Beresford Egan. *The Sink* poked fun less at John than at the other main protagonists in the drama, notably James Douglas, Jix and Jonathan Cape. Each was wittily savaged for his hypocrisy, self-righteousness and (in Cape's case) moral cowardice. But what deeply shocked John was one particular Egan cartoon unmistakably directed at herself. This took its cue from Stephen Gordon's anguished 'martyrdom' in the closing pages of *The Well* and depicted Radclyffe Hall, Spanish hat and all, nailed to a cross in imitation of the Crucifixion. Cupid is shown cocking a snook at her while Jix, Pontius Pilate-like, turns his back on her with an expression of distaste. A naked woman dances round the cross and another, severe and close-cropped, gazes stonily at the scene.

Egan took the view that the anguished tone of *The Well* was totally unjustified given that lesbians, unlike male homosexuals, could not be charged with a criminal offence. But this seems to have been a rationalisation of a more personal reaction, for he had once pushed to the ground a woman who made amorous advances to his wife. When she protested she was a woman, Egan countered: 'Why do you try to be like a man then?'³¹ To John, however, Egan's cartoon seemed a terrible blasphemy. She was so pained by it that she could barely speak of it for years afterwards, blaming herself in some way for having been used to insult her God. Absolution could only come through her writing. And so *The Carpenter's Son* was born.

She did not actually start the book in the south of France. Instead, having decided on Provence as its setting, she used their stay to collect copy for the new novel. It turned out that Pierre, the chauffeur, was a native of the region. Exchanging his peaked cap for a beret, he proved an indispensable guide, acquainting them with the local dialect and customs which John would later make such a feature of the book. St Tropez would become the fictional St Loup-sur-Mer and most days would find them at the Café de l'Escale. On one occasion they climbed at midday to the top of the town's Citadel so that John could experience for herself the sensations Christophe and his friend Jan would enjoy on a similar ascent.

In England in May Labour had won a narrow victory at the polls and Ramsay Macdonald became prime minister for a second time. In the last months of the Conservative administration the censorship debate initiated by *The Well* case had continued to rage in a number of influential journals, with demands for a change in the law from Havelock Ellis, E. M. Forster and others.[32] Moreover, James Melville, who had so impressed John at the trial, had received a post in the new government. Cape therefore expressed hopes of republishing the novel and John looked forward to ending her self-imposed exile abroad (during the summer she felt increasingly home-sick). It soon became clear, however, that Labour, fearful of its slender majority, was in no mood to rock the boat by resurrecting the issue. Rubinstein's representations on behalf of Cape met with little response and Melville 'funked' his responsibilities (as Una saw it) by failing to answer John's letters. 'I am afraid that Labour is going to rat on me,' John told Audrey, 'how rotten a thing is power for the spirit!'[33]

One comforting repercussion of *The Well* affair was its beneficial effect on sales of John's other novels. Arrowsmith reprinted *The Forge* and *A Saturday Life* and both books were selling steadily throughout 1929. *The Unlit Lamp* and *Adam's Breed* fared even better, the former in particular selling with 'amazing strength', according to Una[34] – perhaps because people now understood its homosexual undertones. Cape had skilfully exploited the commercial potential created by *The Well*'s ban in England by setting up a sister company in the States (Cape & Harrison Smith Inc), a move he had completed before the Appeal hearing. He bought the American rights of *Adam's Breed* from Doubleday and produced an American edition of *The Unlit Lamp* under his new imprint. By October 1929 *The Lamp* had achieved US sales of over 15,000 copies.

In October Andrea joined John and Una for a week's holiday in Paris. They had not seen her since the previous Christmas (when she had disgraced herself by arriving late for dinner). Somewhat to their surprise, she had written in March to announce she had won a scholarship to Oxford, where she was due to start on October 12. Andrea was now almost nineteen but Una still found it difficult to consider her as a grown-up. She told Audrey: 'John and I are paralysed to realise that she will next week be wearing a cap and long (scholar's) gown! She looks about thirteen.'[35]

One cannot help feeling that there was more to Una's attitude than simply a parent's natural reluctance to let go the guide-reins. She positively disliked the softening curves and budding tumescences that signalled the onset of womanhood and awakening sexuality in a girl. Her preference was for the androgyne figure, as epitomized by the principal boy of her childhood dreams, an ideal glimpsed in Nijinsky's Faun and later transmuted into her love for John. Her relations with Andrea, not improved by the long periods apart, had become increasingly strained as the girl had grown older and more independent – and less willing to accept the priority which her mother extended to John in all things. Others had noticed that Una was unnecessarily strict with her daughter. Her brother-in-law, J. L. Garvin, urged her not to 'repress' Andrea too much: 'she's full of sap & must follow nature. She will follow it more or less reasonably if emancipation comes by rather liberal degrees.'[36]

Una showed Andrea round Paris while John worked. On her last evening they took her to a night-club and stayed till one in the morning. 'Andrea blissful!' exclaimed the diary with more than a hint of motherly pride.

On October 14 John started on the first chapter of *The Carpenter's Son*. In the following days she worked intensely on the new book, usually going on past midnight, one night stopping at 6 am. Within a fortnight the first chapter was being typed up. By this date they had made up their minds to return to England. The truth was they had wearied of playing exiles and longed to be home again, despite Labour's 'betrayal' over *The Well*. With the Gallimard translation of the novel now complete (Una vetted it and judged it 'careful & sensible'), there was little to keep them on in Paris. John had pressing practical reasons for going home: another legal storm threatened and the need to consult solicitors in London could not be put off much longer.

The trouble this time stemmed from an ill-judged attempt to cash in on *The Well*'s huge success. Earlier in the year an American actress working in Paris, Wilette Kershaw, had bought an option on the stage rights to the novel for £100. The first snag was that nobody suitable could be found to dramatize the book. John had no wish to and Clemence Dane declined on the grounds that it could not be made into a play. In August John and Una saw Miss Kershaw performing on the Paris stage: 'an awful shock!' reported the diary.[37] They felt she would be utterly inappropriate as Stephen Gordon, which was hardly surprising since the American specialized in ultra-feminine ingénue roles. John then discovered that Miss Kershaw had not signed her copy of the contract (which had proved difficult to negotiate) and in a fury she returned the option fee and demanded to cancel. This proved easier said than done, however. For John's letter of cancellation crossed with one from Miss Kershaw in which she finally agreed to the contract John had stipulated and declared she had signed it. A moot point at law therefore arose whether John could now cancel the arrangement, especially since she had previously accepted the option fee.

It was the sort of quandary which seemed peculiarly sent to plague John. Miss Kershaw does not come out of the episode in a very attractive light, but John's extreme sensitivity in any dealings concerning *The Well* made her liable to over-react in a way that was not always helpful. Audrey was obliged to come to Paris in September to discuss the matter and a meeting in Boulogne took place between John and her solicitor. John got so worked up that for a time she believed that Audrey was siding with the opposition against her. In October she took out an injunction against Wilette Kershaw, who eventually backed down. She quit-claimed her rights in the project and even tried to send back the £100. However, it was not the last they had heard of the American actress.

Chapter Twenty-one

In 1930 John and Una put down new roots. Before their departure to France they had been much taken by Rye. They now decided to make their home there and John bought an ancient house in the High Street called 'The Black Boy'. It had leaded windows and a crooked oak door and got its name from 'Black Charles', the nickname bestowed by his opponents on King Charles II, who was reputed to have stayed in the house. The Black Boy was John's present for Una and was purchased in her name. The house rekindled their enthusiasm for the Stuarts and they were soon applying to join the White Rose Club, a society for Stuart admirers.

Rye attracted them because of its old-world charm and in some measure their decision to live there represented a conscious retreat from a present which they felt had let them down. Rye, in this sense, was the exile they chose for themselves in England, the one place, according to Una, 'where you can get away from this hideous age of progress'.[1]

In fact, the town had a solid association with writers. Henry James had lived for many years in Lamb House, a large and attractive Georgian villa set in its own grounds. In 1930 the novelist E. F. Benson (known to his friends as 'Dodo' after the title of his first novel) resided there. He was one of the first to make the acquaintance of John and Una, being introduced to them by another Rye resident, the publisher Vincent Marrot, who quickly became a regular (and not always welcome) visitor to The Black Boy. J. D. Beresford and his wife had a house in West Street. In the surrounding area of Rye lived several well-known artistic and literary people. The painter Paul Nash resided in nearby Iden, Sheila Kaye-Smith farmed, between books, from a remote converted oast-house at Northiam called 'Little Doucegrove', and Noel Coward was to be found from time to time at his home near Aldington.

Like all their homes, The Black Boy had to be 'refurbished' before they moved in. Una wanted to strip the interior to uncover the original walls and beams and a local firm of builders, Breed's, was hired. The work would take some eight months. In the meantime they stayed first at the Mermaid Inn, then in March rented Number 8, Watchbell Street, a small terraced house which faced the Catholic church of St Anthony (they were impressed by the fact that they could see up the nave to the altar from their front door). Most days, while John worked at her book, Una would walk down to The Black Boy and don overalls to supervise the builders. The house was fourteenth-century in origin with sixteenth-century additions and in the course of the renovations they discovered a secret priest's hole, a fresco, several Jacobean shoes and clay pipes, and a Henry VIII gold coin. This made the place something of a showpiece and visitors were invariably given a guided tour.

At Watchbell Street Mabel Bourne once again became their house-keeper. Though she never lived in, she was responsible for most of their general needs. She was usually assisted by a trained house-maid – though, as in London, the turnover of staff was rapid, for sloppiness or impertinence was never tolerated for long. For formal entertaining John and Una preferred to hire a banqueting room at the Mermaid, where they were on good terms with the chatty Irish manageress, Miss Breen.

Since their return to England, the couple's visits to Mrs Leonard had resumed on a regular and frequent basis, sometimes as often as once a week. The medium now had a cottage in Tankerton, near Canterbury, and John and Una would drive over to see her in a chauffeured car hired from the Rye garage. No records exist of these sessions, but they tended to be briefer than in previous years. We can safely assume that Ladye was still the chief 'communicator', though it is clear that Una thought she was also in touch with Troubridge. If the sittings were no longer the object of intense concern they had once been, John made sure that in Rye as elsewhere she paid her respects to Ladye's hallowed memory. In June she presented a large red and gold Byzantine cross to St Anthony's. It was hung from the sanctuary beams above a brass plate in the floor engraved with the words: 'Of your charity pray for the soul of Mabel Veronica Batten/In memory of whom this rood was given. 1930.' In October John paid off the outstanding debt on the church's building costs, a sum of over £500, donating it anonymously in memory of Mabel Batten.

Relations with the local Catholic priest Father Bonaventure, a plump Franciscan of Maltese origins, were at first friendly. Una thought he had reservations about inverts but that their open example had impressed him enough to modify his views. It seems more likely, however, that the priest was willing to overlook such peccadilloes in parishioners who had proved themselves extremely generous bene-factors. He came to call John 'The Boss' and they referred to him as

Father Bony. He became a regular guest at their Mermaid gatherings and, since they lived so close to the church, he was always calling at Watchbell Street. As was their rule, however, John and Una did not confess to him, instead seeking out a priest in nearby Hastings.

Trips to London grew rarer. At the end of June they travelled up by chauffeur-driven Daimler to have John fitted for reading spectacles. They stayed for ten days and took the opportunity to renew old acquaintances. The novelist Ellen Glasgow and Gabrielle Enthoven dined, Axel Munthe came to tea, and they saw Harold Rubinstein and Ida Wylie. They also consulted with Audrey, who was able to report that sales of *The Well* showed no signs of flagging: over 100,000 copies had been sold in America alone, which amounted to royalties of $60,000 for John. Patience Ross was now in their bad books and they spoke to Audrey of her 'impudence'. They had been shown the manuscript of a young writer whom Patience knew and they got it into their heads that it was a 'steal' from *The Unlit Lamp*. John insisted that Patience should have no further hand in any of her dealings.[2] Plagiarism was becoming an obsession with them, for they had earlier expressed their belief that Galsworthy had 'pirated' an idea of John's. It was a sign of their growing isolation.

Back in 'our Rye' after their London visit, John and Una met for the first time some 'locals' who were to become among their closest friends in the early 1930s. They were invited in mid-July to a pageant being staged in a barn on the edge of Romney Marsh at Smallhythe. The show was mounted by the elderly daughter of Ellen Terry, Edy Craig, who since her mother's death in 1928 had converted the barn into a small theatre for the purpose of annual performances to Ellen's memory. Edy lived just up the road from the barn in a timbered cottage called The Priest's House, sharing a curious ménage à trois with two female companions, the writer Christopher St John (whose real name was Christabel Marshall) and a painter, Clare Atwood (known as Tony).

Edy and Christopher had lived together for over thirty years, having met as a result of Chris's passionate devotion to Ellen Terry (whose memoirs she later edited). The two young women were active suffragettes and set up house together in a flat in Covent Garden. Edy first acted at the Lyceum under Irving, then produced plays with her own company The Pioneer Players while Chris eked out a living as a music and drama critic. They were not an easy couple. Edy acquired a reputation for being difficult and autocratic, for she lacked her brother

Gordon Craig's endearing charm and her mother's infallible sense of humour. She had an undeniable streak of brilliance but she was too overbearing to reap the rewards her talent deserved.

Chris was a heavy, ugly woman, clever, fastidious, stubborn, and cripplingly sensitive to her looks and cleft palate. Una was later to dub her 'a sort of "Ugly Duchess"' (Virginia Woolf, less kindly, called her 'a mule-faced harridan'). She had converted to Catholicism and took the name St John as a mark of devotion to the Baptist. When Edy fell in love with a young musician, Martin Shaw, in the early years of their relationship, Chris put a stop to the romance by threatening suicide. However, Edy, a committed feminist, was always more at ease with women than men.

Tony Atwood arrived on the scene during the war, at Edy's behest. Accepted only grudgingly at first by Chris, she became in time an indispensable member of the household, her quiet, tactful manner and sweet nature serving to keep the peace between the other two. Like Chris, Tony adopted mannish attire, wearing jackets and trousers, and in old age never went without her Panama hat. She accepted the soubriquet 'The Brat' to Chris's 'Master Baby', both in turn deferring to Edy's natural leadership.

The Priest's House had been a present to Edy from Ellen Terry, who lived in her retirement in Smallhythe Place, a picturesque cottage beside the barn. Relations between mother and daughter had often proved stormy and were not helped by Chris and Tony's interfering ways, but on the actress's death the trio had no hesitation in turning Smallhythe Place into a memorial museum. By 1930 Edy, Chris and Tony, now in their sixties, were already something of a local phenomenon. Visitors to the ramshackle Priest's House with its wild but lovingly tended garden on the edge of the Marsh were invariably struck by a quality of enchantment and other-worldliness. The place was a hive of bustle and energy and chatter, some new scheme always afoot, Edy in her blue country smock supervising operations with a deep, commanding voice that had the faintest hint of a lisp.

John and Una took an instant liking to the redoubtable trio, and the feeling was reciprocated. In August they were invited to tea at Smallhythe. They returned the favour a week later, the 'Handsome Pair' (as Una ironically dubbed Edy and Chris) visiting Rye accompanied not by Tony but by Vera Home (known as Jack), a close friend from their suffragette days who now acted as a helper with the Barn theatricals. To Una's annoyance, Vincent Marrot 'pushed in too & outstayed them'.[3] Since he was often less than sober, Vincent was fast becoming what Una liked to call 'a bug-bear'.

At the end of August The Black Boy was at last ready for occupation. All their furniture had arrived from Taylor's Depository in London the week before and it took three days (during a heatwave) to get the house shipshape. On the 28th they slept their first night there.

Four days later they received the bad news from Paris: Wilette Kershaw was putting on a production of *The Well* in defiance of John's embargo. Trouble had been brewing since July. Miss Kershaw had suddenly submitted a new synopsis for a play in the hope that John would relent and agree to a fresh contract releasing the stage rights to her. Audrey was despatched to Paris to meet the American actress and came back confident that she would sign a proper deal this time. Treading cautiously, John wrote to Miss Kershaw telling her that she would only consider a scenario *after* she had signed the contract. It soon became clear that the American had been advised by her solicitors not to sign the contract. John wrote again to Paris, urging Miss Kershaw to put matters on a legal footing and emphasizing that until such time there could be no binding agreement between them. To this letter came no reply, since Miss Kershaw had now decided to go ahead with her production and was already in rehearsal with a script that John had never seen.

The play opened at the Théâtre de la Potinière on September 2. Entitled *The Well of Loneliness*, it was advertised as 'From the Novel by Radclyffe Hall'. The posters quoted from the book's reviews as well as from statements in its defence by Shaw, Wells, Bennett and Havelock Ellis. There was no indication who had adapted the novel for the stage and the clear intention was to leave the impression that the project had been set up with John's approval. As for the production itself, 'nauseating is no word for it' wrote John Holroyd-Reece in a letter to John and Una penned straight after he had seen the show. He went on: 'All that I can tell you is that when you consider the obvious vulgarity and an excess of the greatest extreme of American sloppy sentimentality, you will be able to form an idea of what the performance must have been like.'[4] At the end of the play Miss Kershaw came on stage, having changed out of clothes modelled on John's own into a very feminine white dress, to make an emotional appeal to the audience on behalf of inverts. 'Everyone thought the only thing lacking,' commented another friend of John's who had attended the first night, 'was to pass the plate round for the building of a "home of refuge". Really!! it made me boil for everyone left the theatre guffawing with laughter.'[5]

On Holroyd-Reece's prompting, John issued a press release to the French papers denying she knew anything about Miss Kershaw's production and threatening legal action. The actress countered with an interview in the *New York Times* in which she stated John *had* given her permission in return for a 'substantial' cheque[6] (it now became clear why Miss Kershaw had sent back the £100 fee that John had returned to her). However, the legal arguments soon grew academic for the Paris production was shortlived. It was poorly attended and received a roasting from the critics that ensured its permanent demise. The kindest comment Janet Flanner could pass on Miss Kershaw's performance was that 'she made up in costume what she lacked in psychology: dressing gown by Sulka, riding breeches by Hoare, boots by Bunting, crop by Briggs, briquet by Dunhill, and British accent – as the programme did not bother to state – by Broadway.'[7] Ironically, the whole affair, though personally upsetting for John, simply boosted sales of her novel yet again. Wisely, she dropped any idea of taking action against Miss Kershaw.

Hardly had one theatrical fiasco finished than another began. The Stage Society, whose aim was to promote new plays which had little chance of commercial sponsorship, had agreed to produce Una's stage adaptation of Colette's *Chéri*. Gabrielle Enthoven was a member of the Society's council and had helped push through the idea. Casting proved difficult. After Noel Coward, Una suggested Ivor Novello and then John Gielgud in the title role, and Mary Clare or Edith Evans as Léa. In the event, they secured Mary Clare but had to make do with Hubert Langley as Chéri.

Rehearsals began on October 21 at the Prince of Wales theatre under the supervision of a French producer, Alice Gachet. John and Una were not content to play a passive role, seeing it very much as *their* production. Tempers became frayed, culminating in a row with Gabrielle, an acknowledged costume expert, over the dress of the Baroness ('Gabrielle Enthoven behaved disgracefully,' fulminated the diary).[8] The first night took place on October 26. The 'Handsome Pair' came up from Smallhythe for the occasion, Edy bringing Una Ellen Terry's medal for luck. 'Not to my mind a warm reception,' Una reported after the performance, 'but four managers approached at once.'[9] The managers were not much in evidence next day when the production received terrible reviews. The critics generally regarded the play as weak and dull and the acting (with the exception of Mary Clare) as poor: 'Mr Langley made an honest shot at Chéri and missed,' declared the *Telegraph*.[10] On October 30 Gabrielle Enthoven chaired a meeting of the Stage Society to discuss the production. John and Una were conspicuous by their absence, having returned to Rye the previous day.

The failure of *Chéri* confirmed their mood of isolationism. More than ever, they now resolved to stay out of London and keep to their own small circle in Rye. Through the Smallhythe trio they were beginning to meet like-minded women. Sixty-year-old Lady Maud Warrender, a daughter of the Earl of Shaftesbury, lived at 'Leasam' in Rye in the company of the singer Marcia van Dresser. One of their close friends was a Miss Goldingham, whom they called Toto. Through the latter they were introduced to another curious pair, Commandant Mary Allen (known as Robert) and her companion Miss Taggart, who lived at a house in Lympne called 'Danehill' with two St Bernards. Robert Allen had been a militant suffragette (she was once force-fed while on hunger-strike in prison) and helped found the Women's Volunteer Police Force during the war, subsequently becoming its Commandant. After the war, however, despite her protestations, the Home Office disbanded the organization and it had since existed in an unofficial capacity only, kept alive largely by the efforts of Miss Allen who was never happier than when wearing her uniform and highly-polished boots. It seemed unlikely that the force would ever be resurrected and the dejected Commandant was reduced to hoping that coal or transport strikes might lead to a call upon her services. John and Una sympathized, agreeing that the authorities were against her because she was an invert (all they wanted, Una declared contemptuously, were 'fluffy policewomen'). The two couples were heartened to find that they shared common beliefs on the subject of homosexuality. 'To feel that they are in sympathy with John's aims & mine is good indeed for they are fine citizens,' Una confided to her diary.[11]

John and Una's first Christmas in Rye (their fifteenth together) was a quiet affair. They delivered a hamper to the nuns at the local convent and dispensed sweets and sixpences to the slum children in Hucksteps Row. On Christmas Eve they attended midnight mass at St Anthony's in the company of Sheila Kaye-Smith and her husband Penrose Fry. Sheila was a diminutive woman of impish features and Una affectionately dubbed the couple 'the small Fry'.

The year ended on a less muted note. On December 28 Noel Coward dropped in for tea accompanied by his friend Earl Amherst and his devoted secretary Lorn Loraine. The Black Boy (which Noel '*adored*', Una noted exultantly) rang to 'howls' of boisterous laughter. Coward was in top story-telling form. 'He is one of the only people I

know,' wrote Una, 'who succeeds in being chronically and excruciat-
ingly witty without victimising anyone.'[12]

From the end of 1930 Una started writing a second diary which she
called her 'Day Book'. This was a fuller version of the short records
she had kept for years and seems to have been an attempt to chronicle
her life with John in a form that might be publishable at some later
date. Given this aim, one might expect the Day Books, like the
eventual memoir that was published, to be little more than hagiogra-
phy and guardedly discreet. In fact, however, they constitute a highly
revealing record in which Una aired her private feelings with a
forthrightness both vivid and entertaining. They show her to be a
considerable stylist, with an ear for the pithy phrase and a merciless
eye for the shortcomings of others (John excepted, of course). We
should not always assume that the views Una expresses were John's
too (John was invariably more compassionate), but the general
outlook of the Books represented a shared attitude of mind.

Thus, in February 1931, Una made clear their position on the vexed
question of 'closet' inverts. She had nothing but contempt for the
cowardice of those who refused to declare themselves – *if*, that is, they
possessed independent means. The male homosexual had some excuse
because he risked prosecution under the law, and the impecunious
female invert stood to lose her livelihood through prejudice. In any
other circumstances, though, the invert had a duty, Una maintained,
to 'show' herself and by example give courage to her less fortunate
sisters.[13]

A visit to Paul Nash at Iden gave Una the opportunity to vent her
spleen on modern art. Nash was an 'ass', she thought, for champion-
ing surrealism – and the painter's wife, Bunty, took her side. In Una's
opinion, the surrealist movement was simply 'a compound of
hideousness, sadism and anal-erotism heavily and constantly coloured
by sacrilege against Christ in particular and all that he stands for'. She
felt that Natalie and Romaine, whose work was becoming less
figurative, had both been seduced by this insidious trend.[14] Modern
theatre had even less to recommend it. In a felicitous phrase, Una
condemned it as 'innuendo accompanied by the closest possible
imitation of copulation in the strongest possible limelight'.[15]

But it is Una's 'warts-and-all' appraisals of the Rye 'locals' that
provide the most diverting reading in her new diaries. In 1931 they got
to know a female couple, Wilma and Dickie, who lived in the
Hucksteps. True to the lesbian stereotype of Havelock Ellis, Dickie

was stout and beefy, with a ruddy alcoholic complexion, while Wilma wore heavy make-up and looked, Una wrote unflatteringly, as though 'she had been buried and dug up just as decomposition set in'. Wilma led Dickie a merry dance, for she was apparently 'supersexual' and chased anybody, man or woman, who took a fancy to her. In June she went off to Devon for two weeks' holiday in the company of a fresh lover, Pat Chambers, whom she then insisted on bringing back to the Hucksteps. For a time there existed a tempestuous ménage à trois, and Dickie brought all her troubles to John and Una, who were so scandalized that they refused to have Pat and Wilma to their house.

Another couple who had John and Una shaking their heads at the frailty of human nature were the writer Francis Yeats-Brown and his girlfriend Rosalind Constable. Until 1928 Yeats-Brown had been assistant editor of the *Spectator*. He had left the job to concentrate on his writing and in 1930 his autobiography *Bengal Lancer*, about his early years as a cavalry officer in the Indian Army, became a best-seller in America and won the James Tait Black Prize. He had taken a house in Rye and was soon on friendly terms with the occupants of The Black Boy. Early in 1931 he announced to them he had fallen in love with a young woman called Rosalind Constable. From what Una had heard, the match had little to recommend it. Both had been married once and, in Una's opinion, both had homosexual tendencies. On February 28 Yeats-Brown invited them to lunch to meet his 'inamorata'. The Day Book takes up the story:

> What a couple! Y. B. [Yeats-Brown] a bag of nerves, yellow grey in colour – might be anything from India to cancer, running from treatment to treatment & sexually a bisexual, moreover he is over forty & the girl looks a mere child. A charming, pathetic dissipated wrong-headed child with baby blue eyes and flaxen wisps of hair, boasting that she can drink limitless quantities of alcohol & feel no effects; boasting that she wishes to sample satanism and attend a Black Mass...Looking bloodless and washed out, asking for aspirins and finally lying down on the dining room floor because she felt sick! Y. B. entirely inadequate removed her at that stage in his rotten little Baby Austin to put her (alone) into the Hastings train & thence to Hadley Wood. She is obviously heading straight for a ruined constitution – his is already done for & he has no idea at all of looking after or controlling anyone else ... where will it end![16]

They concluded that Rosalind was not really in love with him, especially after he told them that she had refused him once already. He would make a hopeless husband but an excellent wife, Una later wrote, adding: 'he has now rather touchingly confessed to me that most of his teeth are false.'[17]

Father Bony found frequent mention in the Day Books. His

behaviour struck them as more and more eccentric. He would ramble through Mass in almost unintelligible English, looking wild and dishevelled. When, in May, he festooned the church in white, pink and mauve roses ('Maltese gaudiness gone mad'), they were horrified, feeling he had no right to take such liberties without consulting people like John (by now she had donated over £1,000 to St Anthony's). On another occasion, when Una had gone into the church to pray, Bony had his radio on so loud in the adjoining Friary that she could hardly hear herself think – the fact that he was listening to a football match only made it worse. The final straw came when they suspected him of starving a red setter called Rodney that had been entrusted to his care in the absence of the owner. It confirmed their belief that he was not just eccentric but off his head. On their instructions, Rodney was instantly transferred to kennels, where Una doused the dog with a bottle of Lourdes water while John distracted the kennelman's attention.

Life at The Black Boy, meanwhile, settled into a comfortable routine. John and Una adhered to the 'husband/wife' division in their roles. Except when it became necessary to hire or fire servants, Una protected John from any domestic encroachments that might disturb her writing. Fan mail for John or admirers seeking her autograph were strictly vetted by Una. A certain number of ardent female correspondents wrote regularly, sending photographs of themselves, enclosing lilies, swearing undying devotion, and from time to time hinting at suicide. Three American women were especially persistent and taxed Una's patience. Each claimed to be like Stephen Gordon. 'They write in a vein of inexcusable common familiarity,' complained Una, 'and they are all of a pachidermity that ignores silence or rebuff. Their letters arrive with clockwork regularity, are opened, glanced through, and as regularly burnt by me. John never reads a word of them.'[18]

Mabel Bourne had stayed on with them, but she was now part of a larger establishment which included a cook (Mrs Hobbs), a lady's maid (Mary Pitt), a parlour-maid (Finn) and a gardener (Hailes). In addition, they had a call on Mr Hughes, the local chauffeur, whenever they required him. The maids were the problem. In February they discovered Mary Pitt talking to imaginary companions in the kitchen. The doctor was called and tried unsuccessfully to sedate her. Because she lived in, 'we took dogs and bird & camped in my bedroom on the qui-vive all night,' Una reported.[19] The poor woman was dismissed the next day. In March they learnt that Finn, who was unmarried, was suffering from morning sickness, so she too was soon on her way. In her place they hired a parlour-man, Quilter – perhaps to prevent any recurrence of Finn's troubles.

In the spring of 1931 John decided to invest some of her money in property. Rye by this date was already a considerable tourist town (they hated the 'bungaloids' which were sprouting up on its outskirts) and houses were much sought after by the more affluent artistic set (of whom Yeats-Brown was a typical example). John first bid for a cottage in Watchbell Street, then offered £900 for another, Oak Cottage in Trader's Passage, owned by a homosexual couple, Jack Green and Captain Geoffrey Bendall – Una described them as 'the nice type of Jews'. The offer was accepted, but the deal fell through abruptly when Jack Green admitted that the house had bugs. Finally, in April, they bought an old house in West Street from J. D. Beresford for £1,000 – and named it 'Sancta Maria' after Columbus's flagship. It proved a bad buy. It had no view or garden and required constant repairs. When John came to sell it in 1937, it fetched only £900.

Edy Craig and 'the Boys' (Una's nickname) were by now regular visitors. John and Una had grown extremely fond of them, delighting in their honest quirkiness. Una wrote: 'There is great consolation and gratification to me in the company of these friends who like us & want to be with us because they know us for what we are and respect what John has done for her kind.'[20] In June, while Edy was away on holiday, they had the key to The Priest's House and spent a blissful afternoon lounging in hammocks in the garden by themselves. In July another gala took place at the Barn, in which John Gielgud, Edith Evans and Violet Vanbrugh performed scenes from Shakespeare. Edy was there looking vague, Chris appeared in a blue boiler suit and a moth-eaten beret, while Tony, colourfully attired in a canary yellow golf coat, beamed patiently from under her Panama. Clemence Dane delivered the address on Ellen Terry. Afterwards John and Una overheard one of Gielgud's famous gaffes. He spoke to Clemence Dane about her latest novel (*Broome's Stages*), referring less than tactfully to a bad review in the *Observer*. 'Blenching Clemence Dane replied unconvincingly that she had not seen it . . . to which Gielgud replied: "Oh, he said it was much too long and that he couldn't read it, and so he gave it to his mother to read for him!" John remarked to me: "There goes Clemence Dane's evening."'[21] Una made a point of reading *Broome's Stages* and pronounced it 'an uncontrollable attack of literary diarrhoea'.

Another highlight of the summer scene at Smallhythe were Edy's jumble sales. 'We gazed with rapture,' Una wrote, 'at the second hand clothing depot – very popular – where Christopher's shrunken vests jostled things of such unthinkable dilapidation that they seemed only ready for decent cremation.'[22] Only John and Una could lure the trio out of their lair in the evenings. When they came to dinner at The Black Boy in August, it was the first time they had dined out in all the years they had lived at the Priest's House. (Chris appeared in a black velvet smoking jacket with enormous bell-bottom trousers 'and bearing an offering of all the best zinneas from their garden'.) What all of them loved best was to lounge in the 'gun-room' at Smallhythe (this was really an out-house which served as Tony's studio) and swap gossip about mutual friends. In later years Una would look back on these moments as among her most relaxed and peaceful with John, the two of them holding hands in utter tranquillity as the idle chatter floated out over the garden to the mysterious expanse of the Marsh.

In the autumn of 1931 John was working intensively on the final chapters of *The Carpenter's Son*. Cape had agreed to publish it and the title had changed (in August) to *The Master of the House*, another inspiration of Una's who, 'doubling from book to book', had eventually found what she was looking for in St Mark's Gospel (ch. 13, v. 35: 'Watch ye therefore: for ye know not when the master of the house cometh . . .'). John completed the novel on November 25 at three in the morning. She was up again at 9.30 am to dictate what she had written to the secretary, Miss Tyler. They then sent a wire to Edy and the Boys, telephoned Audrey and Wren Howard, and walked over to St Anthony's 'to say thank you and light candles'.

It had been a long haul, taking John over two years in the writing. Una regarded it as her best book yet, but it had proved difficult and painful for John all the way through. After the trials and tribulations of *The Well*, she did not find it easy to get back into the rhythm of writing. There were frequent and disheartening periods of 'block', and to Una's concern she increasingly went on working into the night, often till the small hours. The days when they would breakfast together every morning were long over, for John would still be sleeping, exhausted from her labours.

But the book proved an ordeal for John in another way, too. Because it had been consciously planned as an act of penitence, she wrote it in a spirit of deliberate austerity. Driving herself to work for over twelve hours at a stretch was part of this, as was ignoring her own health and comfort. One night in January Una crept down to her study at half past twelve 'to find as I suspected – fire out – bitter cold & she had made no effort to light the electric stove'.[23] Both women succumbed again to recurring bouts of 'flu and indigestion. John's face, so tanned and relaxed after their French holiday of 1929, reverted to its more habitual pallor and strain. It seems also that she kept herself celibate, if not for the whole two years, at least for long periods. She and Una had separate bedrooms, but gossip among the servants had it that late-night altercations had been heard between the two women, with Una sometimes pleading at John's locked door to be let in.[24]

John also underwent a strange experience during the writing of *The Master*. The hero of her book meets his death, like Christ, by crucifixion, which is prefigured earlier by intuitive sensations which the boy does not understand. Early in 1930, when John had completed only four chapters or so, she began to complain of discomfort in the palm of her right hand. The pain had soon spread to her left hand as well and became so intense at times that she could not sleep or write properly. At first there were no marks at all and they thought it might be some form of invisible eczema. But gradually livid red stains like bruising appeared in the palms of both hands, in the right one extending in a line to the wrist. Radiological treatment by a London specialist followed but the pain merely increased. The specialist confessed himself at a loss and from then on John bore her curious affliction as best she could, writing with her hands in bandages. Very gradually the red marks faded and the pain disappeared of its own accord.

Una believed that this singular phenomenon stemmed from John's complete identification, albeit sub-conscious, with the religious theme of her book. John's temperament certainly contained that austere, self-dramatizing element that characterizes the hysterical stigmatic. The 'martyr' motif had been strong in all her novels and after *The Well* she saw herself as a martyr to her Cause. She had come to look upon the writing process itself as something that necessarily involved pain if quality was to be achieved. In *The Well of Loneliness* Stephen Gordon, reflecting on the writer's art, imagined that fictional characters drew life from their creators as infants grow strong at the mother's breast, except that blood not milk was the element of nourishment: 'surely thus only are fine books written, they must somehow partake of the miracle of blood – the strange and terrible miracle of blood, the giver of life, the purifier, the great final expiation.'[25] We are reminded yet again of Una's earliest impressions of John in 1915: 'I had met for the first time in my life a born fanatic . . .

one who, if the need arose, would go to the pillory or the stake for her convictions.'

Christmas 1931 was, again, a strictly local affair. Robert Allen and Miss Taggart came for lunch on December 23, the Commandant appearing in 'mufti' – pale fawn breeches, a scarlet golf coat and patent leather pumps. John and Una had earlier become associate members of the Women's Auxiliary Police Service, though no duties were involved, only support for the principle of women's employment in the public services.

The Smallhythe 'darlings' stayed at The Black Boy on Christmas Eve. In November John and Una had been deeply touched by a gesture of Tony's designed to mark the completion of *The Master of the House*. She entrusted to their care what she believed was a relic of the True Cross, reputedly given to an ancestor of hers by the Pope 150 years before. Una placed the gift reverently in the fourteenth-century chalice that formed part of the small shrine to St Anthony in her bedroom. Although doubt was later cast on the authenticity of the relic, it remained a token of the respect and friendship between the two households. Una would later write : 'Tony has that greatest of all qualities: a steady faithfulness ... As one grows older one realizes more and more how rare it is.'[26]

On Christmas Day 'John & I & Edy breakfasted downstairs,' Una noted in the diary, 'and the Boys joined us afterwards & we all opened presents.' The 'small Fry' made up the party for lunch. Conspicuous by her absence, for the third year running, was Andrea. In her first year at Oxford she had taken Pass Mods in French, Greek Literature and Logic, but her ambitions had turned increasingly to the theatre and she spent most of her time acting in college productions. This did not improve relations with Una, who complained that the girl was lazy and secretive. She had Harold Rubinstein check on Andrea's London address in the vacations (a rented flat in Westbourne Grove) and was surprised to find it both authentic and respectable – though it appalled her to hear that when Andrea answered the door at 9.40 am she was still not dressed. 'Lord, how I wish she would marry and some man assume responsibility for her,' Una sighed.[27]

Her fear was that Andrea would end up as a 'sponging loafer', for which she blamed the Troubridges whom she felt had never been keen on the girl going to university. On her daughter's twenty-first birthday Una simply noted in the diary: 'Andrea comes of Age'.[28] She and John did not see the young woman and there was no celebration.

Any prospect of a reconciliation was shattered when, on December 11, Andrea suddenly appeared at The Black Boy and announced she intended to leave Oxford without taking her degree to try her luck on the professional stage. 'She went at 3.30 leaving us appalled,' read the bald entry in the diary.

The Master of the House was due out in February 1932. Cape planned two editions, a de luxe two-guinea version limited to 150 copies (each signed by John) and an ordinary edition priced 7/6d. John secured good terms: a £1,500 advance and a 20% royalty on the first 30,000 copies, 25% thereafter (her royalty on all the de luxe copies was 25%). Such a favourable deal reflected John's strong position after *The Well* (which had now sold 150,000 copies world-wide) and, to some extent, a conscious attempt on Cape's part to make amends for his past conduct.

Nevertheless, John determined this time to assert her control over her publisher. She insisted that the de luxe edition should have a real vellum binding, with her name and the title in gilt lettering. To Cape & Harrison Smith, who were publishing the book in America, her instructions were even more definite. She wanted no cover 'blurb', claiming that the novel's theme was too subtle to summarize, and in any case she felt it would be better not to disclose whether the book was another story of inversion. It was to be stipulated that it was her first novel since *The Well*. She gave notice that she intended to enforce to the absolute limit the clause in her contract concerning omissions and alterations in the text, for she had been appalled by the number of typographical errors in the Cape & Harrison Smith edition of *The Unlit Lamp*.

The only concession she was prepared to make, with an eye to speeding up publication in America, was to relinquish her right, fiercely upheld with *The Well*, to read and check the galley-proofs herself – provided it was done personally by Robert Ballou (Cape's managing editor in New York) from a corrected English page-proof. She concluded: 'It is a great concession I am making in view of the nature of this book'[29] – by which she meant its widespread use of Provençal words and phrases (Una had written a preface and glossary to explain these). John would not, however, allow the novel to be serialized. This, she felt, would be disrespectful to the subject. Una contrasted such admirable scrupulousness to the more mercenary attitude of other writers: 'I would rather live with John and one servant in a cottage for the rest of our lives than ever see her prostitute her genius to material ends.'[30]

All the omens looked good for *The Master*. A week before publication the de luxe edition was already sold out and advance sales of the ordinary edition numbered over 7,000 copies. John and Una went up to London to be on hand for publication day on February 29. John had her usual photographic portrait taken (by Howard Coster) – in tweeds and chequered bow-tie – to mark the occasion. In the first week of business 500 copies of the book were sold and Harrods ran out of stock. In a flamboyant gesture, John announced that she was giving Una for her birthday (on March 8) one of her most treasured possessions, the diamond and platinum hair comb which had been a gift from Ladye. Una recorded her gratitude in the diary with all the appropriate exclamation marks. A fortnight after publication Cape was able to report total sales of almost 9,000 and *The Master* reached the top of the *Observer*'s best-seller list.

The reviews, however, told another story. The ones that really counted expressed disappointment, suggesting once again that the book failed as a novel. Ralph Straus in the *Sunday Times* admitted he was perplexed by the intention of the author and *The Times*, in what Una called a 'vicious' review, concluded that the novel's serious spiritual aims were not realized in the telling.[31] By April sales of *The Master* had slowed dramatically and the book disappeared from the best-seller lists.

In hindsight it is not difficult to see that, even in 1932, *The Master of the House* was unlikely to be a novel with wide appeal. It was almost as long as *The Well* without possessing either that book's controversial theme or its sense of melodrama. The main character, Christophe Bénédit, unlike all John's other fictional protagonists, has still not come of age by the time of his death and the story's end. And yet from the outset he appears to have all the attributes of a mature adult. This was obviously deliberate on the author's part, giving the boy a mysterious perfectability that echoes the real Carpenter's Son, but it means that the novel lacks that tension which comes from the gradual development of character. Unrelieved virtue, across almost 500 pages, makes for dull reading.

Early on in the novel we are made aware of Christophe's ultra-spiritual aura. He is unusually compassionate for his age and is subject to strange visions. He is human enough to experience the pangs of love, but on the one occasion when he is about to embrace a girl, he is forced to hold back by a sudden intense pain in the palms of his hands. When the war comes, Christophe enlists and is posted to Palestine to fight the Turks. He gets separated from his patrol and, in a visionary state of near madness, walks into the enemy lines to try to persuade the soldiers to end the war in the name of humanity. Instead, the Turks tie him and beat him and finally crucify him on the planks of a timbered door. The closing words of the book leave us in no doubt of the divine parallel: 'Presently he became very still and his dying eyes gazed out to the east — to the east where the flaming, majestic dawn rose over the world like a resurrection.'

This final tableau was intended, like the Passion itself, to leave the reader with a message of spiritual hope and triumph, but after a long story peopled with a throng of quaint and humble village characters, it seems merely banal and out of keeping. As Gerald Gould put it in his *Observer* review: 'we do *not* feel in the mood for a last wild protest of suffering humanity against untold agonies.'[32] Though Una believed that John wrote herself more completely into the part of Christophe than any other she created, one cannot help feeling that, in fact, had the boy been less perfect and more like his creator, the story might have been more compelling. John's awareness that Christophe *was* really Christ inhibited the personal vision that had once given freshness and individuality to characters like Joan Ogden and Gian-Luca.

The Master of the House represented, if not John's final word, certainly her most unequivocal on the theme of compassion. All her novels had been preoccupied with this motif. The seeds of this outlook had their roots deep in her own personal development, in her view of herself as a 'victim'. But she had also read widely in French literature and in the Catholic tradition, especially the lives of the saints. Two of her favourite English writers, both Catholics, were Ford Madox Ford and Marjorie Bowen. Ford's early novels, culminating in *The Good Soldier* of 1915, are concerned with the dilemma of the decent, honourable man who tries to live according to an ideal code of morality but invariably suffers and is misunderstood as a result. Marjorie Bowen pursued a similar theme in novels such as *The Viper of Milan* (1906) and *The Burning Glass* (1918). Significantly, another Catholic novelist of a later generation, Graham Greene, was a great admirer of both Ford and Bowen. Like Radclyffe Hall, Greene drew inspiration from an unhappy childhood, and the hero-victims of his novels are foiled not by external circumstances so much as by their own fatal flaws and limitations. As one critic has put it, 'the artist's lust for suffering can be called a leading theme of Mr Greene's'.[33]

The down-turn in *The Master's* fortunes depressed John, leading to arguments with Wren Howard over sales figures (in April the 10,000 mark was barely reached). They repeatedly offered up prayers to Una's St Anthony shrine that the book might do better. John felt dragged down by a sense of failure, her 'complex' as Una called it, a feeling that the world was against her and was trying to stop her writing.

In this atmosphere petty slights and jealousies were easily aroused. Una, always blindly loyal to John, was quick to leap to her defence with insinuations that the success of others had somehow been achieved disreputably. Sheila Kaye-Smith especially irritated her. The prolific 'Sussex novelist', about to publish another novel, shocked Una by admitting 'she had wangled herself and her book into the Foyle's luncheon which she had had fixed for the publication day of her own book!'[34]

The Foyles Lunch took place on March 17 at Grosvenor House. John was a guest speaker and addressed the large gathering of some 700 guests on 'The Great Adventure of Fiction' – 'amusing without being precious', commented Una. John ended her talk by wishing Sheila Kaye-Smith the best of luck with her new book on its birthday, at which point, Una noted with satisfaction, 'Sheila went a deep crimson as the coals of fire descended on her head'. After the speeches John was kept busy for an hour signing autographs, Una 'marshalling' the queue.

Ten days later Sheila and Penrose called at The Black Boy. They had just started reading *The Master* and, according to Una, uttered not a word as to what they thought of it. Sheila mentioned *The Times* review (the worst) and ventured only that John seemed to have collected a remarkable amount of data about Provence. Una felt Sheila was being deliberately catty because she still smarted from her 'eclipse' by John at the Foyles Lunch. John, 'who surpasses the normal human', remained unperturbed. She praised Sheila's book and presented her with a signed copy of *The Master* – 'which I would oh so gladly have torn out of her mean little hands,' exclaimed Una.[35]

Privately, Una had regarded the 'small Fry' with scorn for some time. Little Doucegrove was a joke in her opinion: damp, badly heated, in constant need of repair, and with no proper drinking water. Penrose was weak and timid and an abominable driver. Sheila wore the wrong clothes for the country. She had prostituted her talent by agreeing to write pot-boilers for American magazines (no doubt to feed the soaring costs of her 'Moloch abode'). She was incorrigibly accident-prone, on one occasion twice fusing the crimping machine at the local hairdresser while under it (with the result that 'she was tied to the ceiling for forty five minutes instead of seven, had to be revived with water and a fan and has a very badly waved head to show for it').[36]

The truth was Una relished gossip and, after over two years in Rye, there were few locals whose peccadilloes had not been eagerly written up in the Day Books. But because of her tendency to dramatize and because she saw her primary task as one of protecting John from an exploitative world, she tended all too readily to discern the worst in other people. Thus Dodo Benson had fallen in their estimation for being over-reticent about his own homosexuality. They also suspected he had anti-Catholic leanings (he was the son of a former Archbishop of Canterbury), that he tippled on the quiet, and was stingy (Lady Maud Warrender had told them he had 'one way pockets'). He had especially angered them the previous summer when they had dropped in to Lamb House on a very hot August afternoon and been offered tea only grudgingly. The novelist claimed he had already had tea twice, once for himself and a second time when Vincent Marrot called. Una noted dryly: 'Shrewdly suspecting that both the earlier teas had lived in a bottle and been drunk with the aid of soda water, we left.'[37]

This somewhat jaundiced outlook on the world was not improved by another Cape 'betrayal' at the end of April: the publisher suddenly announced that his American company (now called Cape, Ballou) was bankrupt. It meant calamity for *The Master* in the States. The book had just appeared. Sales were promising and the reviews good, better than in England. John was convinced it would make 'a big sweep'. Now its circulation was stopped and all copies were seized by Cape's creditors. John was furious, especially since rumours had previously reached her of the vulnerability of the Cape-Ballou operation and she had expressly begged Cape to relinquish the book if he felt there was the slightest risk of his company's going under.

There followed a stormy interview at Cape's offices in London, with Audrey in attendance, at which John finally lost her temper with her publisher's excuses and prevarications. To Una's private delight, she twice called Cape 'a dirty blackguard' and once 'a skunk'. She told him he had ruined *The Well* in England and was now doing the same to *The Master* in the United States. Unless he advertised the book and carried it through, she fulminated, she would make his name mud. Cape 'went the colour of weak lemonade & murmured "don't threaten me" & we made our grim departure'.[38]

However, that same afternoon Cape agreed to release the American rights of *The Master*. A couple of days later, in a further interview with Wren Howard (conducted by Una and Audrey while John waited outside in the taxi), the publisher gave assurances that John was still their top author and that four large advertisements (designed by Una) would be placed in the Sunday press on behalf of the English edition. If that helped sales, then more would be spent in the same manner. This went some way to mollify John, but she felt Cape's conduct was the last straw. Although she and Una discussed the possibility of transferring allegiance to a different English publisher, when it came to the point the alternatives looked unpromising. Secker was 'as big a ruffian', Gollancz too. Collins and Chatto had been asleep for years, Constable was 'a wash out', and Heinemann stumbled along under the rule of a sick man who could not delegate (Charles Evans). Cape would just have to be endured.

The outcome of the American crisis was that in May Houghton Mifflin bought the rights to *The Master*. Good reviews continued to appear, but it took time for the new edition to come out and the momentum was lost. By September the figures showed that only some 7,000 copies had been sold in the States – a bitter disappointment to an author whose previous book had achieved American sales six times that number within three months. As John would put it later, *The Master* simply died, 'murdered by its publisher'.[39]

In the summer of 1932 a more domestic drama overtook them. Una's gynaecological history had seldom been trouble-free and as she approached the menopause (she was now forty-five) she was experiencing recurring bouts of menorrhagia (heavy menstrual bleeding). In June she was examined by a specialist in Brighton who diagnosed fibroids and recommended an immediate hysterectomy. A second opinion was sought and the verdict confirmed. Accordingly, on July 4 John escorted Una to London, where she entered a clinic in Welbeck Street.

The operation took place the following morning at 9 am. John had been in at eight to see Una and waited anxiously outside the theatre. All went well and Una awoke to find John at her bedside. John remained with her all next day, pampering her with fruit and flowers. Una felt they had never been so close and loving, and the diary noted with a hint of trepidation: 'a good day, too good!' Her premonition was realized, for on the 7th complications set in and she became seriously ill. For a time her life hung in the balance and she later recalled an overwhelming sense of weakness and weariness 'that refused all nourishment'. But the crisis passed. She opened her eyes one day to see 'John sitting beside me with her head in her hands in an attitude of complete and utter despair'. This sign of her lover's devotion, that John *wanted* her, was a more powerful medicine than anything the doctors could prescribe: 'I could not leave her and dragged myself back to life.'[40]

It was August before Una was well enough to leave the clinic. With a nurse in attendance, John took her to Brighton where they encamped at the Royal Crescent Hotel. There followed days of walks and drives in the bracing sea air, John pushing Una about in a bath-chair. When the nurse left them after a few days, Una could not have been happier: 'we are at last alone together. Deo Gratias.'[41] This illness proved a nightmare for John, but Una remembered it as a period of unblemished contentment for her. After a difficult period in their relationship, when Una had felt hurt and bewildered by John's self-imposed abstinence during the writing of *The Master*, her operation had forged a new intimacy. For almost two months John had been at her side day and night, an administering angel attentive to her every need and comfort (the diary, listing with the usual precision the number of bouquets sent by friends and relatives, underlined John's generosity: 'so many times that I could not possibly count'). Una acknowledged that her attitude was selfish, but she could not help exulting that the worry she had caused John had also made her 'absolutely essential to the one being on earth who is all in all'.[42]

Chapter Twenty-two

As if Una's illness had brought sudden intimations of mortality, a new mood of restlessness seized them as 1932 drew to a close. They decided to spend Christmas in London and left Rye as early as November 29, John buying Una a bunch of yellow roses to commemorate the seventeenth anniversary of the day their love affair had been consummated in Malvern. Edy and the Boys were also in town and the five of them shared Christmas dinner at Edy's flat in Bedford Street.

Even Andrea was partially readmitted to the fold. They saw her for an hour on Christmas Day and she came for lunch and tea on Boxing Day – when they gave the 'poor child' a sympathetic hearing. Una had been touched by her daughter's evident concern at the time of her operation (Andrea had sent flowers on three separate occasions and, dining with them a few days before Una entered the clinic, had greeted her mother with a warm embrace and the enquiry: 'Oh, mother, is it dangerous?'). She was, noted Una, 'much improved and really a handsome well-bred looking girl . . . hope springs eternal that she is shaping into a good citizen and a nice daughter'.[1] Early in 1933 they bought her a fur coat at Harrods and attended her first night in a play in Wimbledon. She invited them to her flat for 'China tea & rolls filled with honey' and they were pleasantly surprised by its spaciousness and comfort.

John and Una returned to Rye in the New Year but throughout 1933 they made extended visits to London. In March John bought a furnished flat (17 Talbot House) in St Martin's Lane and for a time they even considered letting The Black Boy (Sancta Maria, their other house in Rye, had long had tenants). So once again they were on the move and tackling the familiar problems of repairs and renovations and the transfer of possessions. It was a cycle to which they seemed incorrigibly addicted. Some years earlier Una had reflected on this propensity of theirs in an essay entitled 'The Tyranny of Home'. The problem, she admitted, was that both of them dearly loved to put down roots but neither had the reposeful temperament needed for settling. A house in London *and* the country ended up as a home in neither. 'The book sought in the Country will always be in London and vice versa. A summer season spent in London will mean missing the fruit blossom, the cuckoo, the bluebells, the nightingale; a season in the Country will mean no Russian Ballet, no Opera, no Wimbledon.'[2]

The solution they attempted in 1933 was to divide their time between both worlds. In London they were soon back in the swing of the kind of life they had known in the late '20s – theatre-going, parties, restaurants. As before, the society they moved in was primarily artistic and theatrical, though this time publishers and literary people were markedly less in favour. So too were a number of old friends who had since blotted their copy-books. Relations with Gabrielle Enthoven, for example, had never recovered from the *Chéri* fiasco and they now felt she had 'ratted' on her breed by deliberately distancing herself from her homosexual friends.

The Arts Club became one of their favourite haunts (along with the Ivy restaurant) and there they met the leading theatrical lights of the day, notably Gladys Calthrop, Lilian Braithwaite, and John Gielgud. Gielgud was then starring in his first popular success in *Richard of Bordeaux*. John and Una adored his performance and saw it three times, weeping 'buckets'. For a time the actor showed interest in collaborating with John on a play based upon *Adam's Breed* and they visited him at the huge attic flat he shared with John Perry. The project never took off (Una thought John was too like him in temperament for their partnership to work) but they were intrigued by a certain unrestrained, forthright quality to him that over-awed them. Una wrote: 'He's so wild, like a stag that has just broken cover and stands erect and watchful & you wonder, if you move, will it be gone in an instant.'[3] One is reminded yet again of John's attraction to people with charisma, a quality that obviously fascinated her and that had earlier drawn her to actresses like Teddie Gerard and Tallulah Bankhead. Una shared her fascination and later wrote an essay, entitled 'It', in which she singled out Joan of Arc, Napoleon, Charles II, Mary, Queen of Scots – and Mussolini.

Though *The Master of the House* had not made the impact of its predecessor, John still ranked as a considerable literary figure and was much in demand on the lecture circuit. On February 27 she addressed the Oxford University English Club on the subject of the propaganda novel. The meeting was held in the august Taylorian building and attended by some 500 students. In preparing her talk John was more than usually nervous, a sign of the respect, almost reverence, with which she regarded ancient academic institutions. Her custom was to speak impromptu from a list of headings, but on this occasion she felt she had to write out a full-length script. She appeared before her audience resplendent in a severe-cut flowered silk jacket, a waistcoat with a faint floral design, and a Gladstonian stock and cravat. The gist of her lecture was that it was easy to write on behalf of *popular* lost causes, but it was the *unpopular* ones that needed support. Once an author had settled on an injustice he wished to remove, she advised, he must forget the consequences however unpleasant. Her own case proved 'to the hilt' that persecution could often be a blessing in disguise: 'the field must submit to being torn by the plough before it can hope to bear a rich harvest.'[4] John's talk came a few days after the famous 'King and Country' debate at the Oxford Union (which passed a pacifist resolution) and she and Una formed a less than favourable impression of the undergraduates – odd, rather unclean, and affecting a slithering, slurring diction which they thought was scarcely intelligible and meant even less.[5]

A week later John delivered a similar talk to London University Literary Society. The audience was appreciative but constant interruptions came from a noisy Socialist Club meeting next door which had been invaded by Tory opponents. John remarked dryly that it was a pity such a disturbance had to be made in the name of brotherhood.

At another literary gathering, John met Lord Alfred Douglas for the first time. After Oscar Wilde's death, Douglas had written a memoir (*Oscar Wilde and Myself*, 1914) running down the playwright and vindicating his own behaviour. This was followed in 1929 by a mellower autobiography in which he proclaimed himself proud to have known Oscar. Wilde had long been one of John's heroes, a martyr to the Cause like herself. In Paris in 1929 Natalie had introduced them to Dolly Wilde, the great man's niece, a lesbian who looked uncannily like him (Una thought her 'the better man' of the two).[6] Dolly had charmed them. She had the same indolent, urbane wit as her uncle and her shabby black suits and Schiaparelli scarves made it possible to imagine that Wilde himself had come back to life. Douglas therefore ranked in their eyes as a contemptuous coward. After *The Well* case he had proved pathetically eager for John's approbation but on the occasions when they had spotted him across crowded rooms they had coldly ignored him.

However, in November 1933 he was present at a meeting of the Catholic Poetry Society which John and Una also attended. At sixty-three he looked frail and lonely and John took pity and shook hands with him. With characteristic compassion, she was once again ready to forgive if not forget (on the day after the failure of *The Well* appeal, she had presented Norman Birkett with a copy of the novel inscribed 'To my friend . . . from his grateful client'). Una was invariably less tolerant. On this occasion she pronounced Douglas 'utterly hideous' with his wizened face and fluttering, piping voice: 'a weak, petty, mean spiteful nature and a coward who has missed every opportunity of nobility, but who has had enough intelligence and imagination to find himself intolerable to live with!'[7]

If in 1933 the political climate, both nationally and internationally, was becoming more unsettled (Hitler had become German chancellor in January), the cosy world of Rye was also experiencing its own upheavals. Father Bony's eccentricities had reached a point where John and Una seriously questioned his sanity. Rumours were circulating that collections and donations were being mis-used, to install, it was said, new panelling in the Friary. At mass in July the priest 'pounded down to the rails at Benediction & bawled "Why don't you sing" or "Sing up can't you" & a long rigmarole anent prima donnas'.[8] John and Una set about campaigning for his removal on the grounds of ill-health. Under Harold Rubinstein's auspices, they prepared statements which were sent to the diocesan authorities.

The matter remained unresolved in September when Father Bony was accorded place of honour at the ceremony to consecrate St Anthony's. When the Bishop of Southwark spoke of the church as being 'the crown to Father Bonaventure's labours', John and Una hoped this signalled the priest's retirement. However, shortly afterwards the diocese announced that Bony was to stay at Rye, adding pointedly that his congregation should search their consciences. On the next occasion, therefore, that a young priest at mass referred to the consecration of the church as a 'miracle' wrought by Bony's goodness, John got up, genuflected and marched out, followed by Una. They vowed never to go back until Bony departed. (He finally requested his own transfer early in 1934 when falling attendances at St Anthony's could no longer be ignored.)

Even at Smallhythe unusual tensions were shaking the tranquil routine. In the summer of 1932 Chris had quite suddenly fallen hopelessly in love with Vita Sackville-West, who lived at nearby Sissinghurst. Vita had at first responded then tried to withdraw, but Chris had clung to her with all the intensity of infatuation, penning countless long letters (addressed to 'My Lord Orlando') and imagining she was St Christopher to Vita's Christ.[9] The affair dragged on into 1933, causing terrible scenes at The Priest's House which taxed even Tony's remarkable peace-making skills.

John and Una first learned of the crisis at a Barn performance in September 1932, when they had sat next to Miss Sackville-West. It was the first time they had seen her since *The Well* trial. She was cordial to John and they thought her intelligent and unaffected (but 'no beauty' – noting her swarthy features and the heavy growth of hair on her upper lip). At another Barn gathering in April 1933 Chris seemed distracted, having eyes only for Vita and offending them by her nervous abruptness. Then in October it became clear that Vita had dropped Chris, leaving her suicidally depressed. Una had seen it all coming and labelled Vita a 'snoop', meaning someone who habitually broke up couples and then passed on to fresh pastures.

By this date relations with the trio were beginning to cool. In August John and Una were making plans to sell The Black Boy and began looking at other houses in the area. Encouraged by Edy, they toyed with the idea of having a house built in the vicinity of Smallhy-the Place. However, on a visit in September to inspect a parcel of land adjacent to the cottage, they were startled to find Tony of all people stumping angrily round the field and muttering in a loud voice 'We can't possibly have a house out here!'[10] The scheme was abandoned and they concluded with some relief that they had probably escaped many future entanglements with the unpredictable threesome.

On November 15 the diary read simply: 'Andrea's Wedding Day.' John and Una deliberately stayed away. Despite the rapprochement between mother and daughter earlier in the year, relations had once again deteriorated. Andrea's financial security was precarious. She received £36 a year from an Admiralty pension, topped up by an allowance from Una and some money from her step-brother Tom. As an actress in repertory she could expect an irregular wage at best. Una therefore saw her salvation through meeting the right man. When the girl had seen them at Christmas, she had admitted being in an 'almighty snarl' with two men, one of them a decent, honourable divorcee, the other a 'bounder' with a mistress and strictly dishonourable intentions. Andrea said she preferred the bounder. To make matters worse, she had given up her faith. About the only thing that did not shock Una was her daughter's announcement that she intended to use contraception in marriage, something that John and Una had long advocated.

They were therefore pleasantly surprised when in June Andrea introduced them to a new young man, Toby Warren, who seemed eminently suitable. He was tall and fair, with a winning smile, and they accounted him polite and handsome (despite a glass eye). He had joined Mosley's Fascists (which proved to Una he had good sound principles) and, so he told them, ran a chain of roadside cafés. More crucially, his father Sir Norcott Warren was a KCMG and the family was rich enough to own a villa in Cannes and live in hotels in London. With somewhat premature optimism, Una gaily pictured the young couple with babies.[11]

Lady Warren came for tea in July and she too proved charming – despite Una's description of her as 'a withered Anglo-Indian'. Shortly afterwards Andrea appeared wearing an engagement ring (and kept glancing surreptitiously at it like 'any maiden of the '90s'). Wedding plans were made. Andrea relented on the idea of a Catholic ceremony and Una accepted that Tom Troubridge should give away the bride. All appeared to be going smoothly.

In August, however, Una was shocked to learn that Andrea and Toby were staying in a caravan at Dorking together with her former bounder and his mistress. Toby was a louse, Una now felt, and Andrea had cheapened herself. Moreover, it transpired that Toby's 'chain' of cafés was grander in name than substance. Events moved inexorably towards disaster when Toby and his mother lunched at The Black Boy in early September. On their guard and expecting the worst, John and Una were annoyed when Lady Warren smoked *their* cigarettes incessantly despite having her own. She appeared to condone the caravan episode, was vague about dates for the wedding, and cheerfully encouraged the young couple's notion that, on top of a cottage in the country and a flat in town, they should each run a car and own several dogs. Toby put the final seal on his disgrace by saying he expected Andrea to continue working and talking blithely of her going into films now that she had 'pull'. When the Warrens left the house at four o'clock, the previously 'handsome' Toby had become 'pasty and dissipated'. 'John and I,' concluded Una's report. 'kept asking each other who will look after the unfortunate dogs.'[12]

When Andrea next came to the house, she was on her own and in belligerent mood. Bitter recriminations broke out on both sides, ending with the girl making an abrupt departure shouting: 'And if you like to go about saying I'm living with Toby I don't care!' John was angry but kept silent. For Una it was the last straw. She resolved to wash her hands of the wedding and instructed her bank to pay over the nest-egg of £267 that she had been saving for Andrea. 'She never was really flesh or spirit of mine and this affair has been the last illusion and the last disillusion I shall endure on her behalf,' recorded the Day Book with finality.[13]

A week before the wedding, which was to take place at St Mary's Church, Cadogan Place, a formal invitation arrived at The Black Boy. It made no mention of John and the reception was to be held at Tom

Troubridge's – putting it out of the question as far as Una was concerned. She believed that this final snub was a deliberate ploy by Andrea to keep her out of the way so that all the Troubridges could be invited. To her annoyance, Minna announced she would attend, out of duty. On the day itself, Una did admit to feeling a little sad.[14]

After the publication of *The Master of the House*, over six months elapsed before John felt inclined to start work on a new project. She was offered an American lecture tour and a stint in Hollywood writing screen-plays, but declined both.

At the end of 1932 she was writing again. This time she went back to the short stories that over the years she had taken up and put down. She rewrote some, polished others, experimented with new ones. She looked again at her poetry, digging out the material that had not been published and reworking it. She even had Una reread her some of her earliest fiction: thus *The Forge* had them in wistful mood in early January 1933 as they searched for a new home in London. It was as if John was taking stock of herself, retrenching, recuperating her creative powers after reaching a peak. For both she and Una believed that *The Master* was her finest achievement, despite the verdict of the critics. Religious motives accounted for their view, for to John it was inconceivable that a story inspired by the Passion itself could not be the thematic summation of all her work. Una's list of John's books, in order of merit, is revealing. At the top she placed *The Master*, next came *Adam's Breed*, then *The Well* and finally *The Unlit Lamp* (the other two novels she labelled as merely pleasant diversions). Posterity would judge otherwise.

By the autumn of 1933 John had settled on five short stories which she considered fit to be published. Three of these represented a reworking of old material – 'Miss Ogilvy Finds Herself' (first written in 1926), 'Upon The Mountains' (1925), and 'The Lover of Things' (1924). The other two, so far as one can tell, were fresh efforts – 'Fräulein Schwartz' and 'The Rest Cure – 1932'. Taken together, all five stories present an extremely bleak vision. Each of the main protagonists inhabits an introspective, isolated private world where love and friendship are almost entirely absent. Attempts to extend sympathy or seek understanding are invariably rebuffed but, as in Radclyffe Hall's novels, it is the fatal flaws *within* the personalities of her characters that bring about their ultimate disgrace or failure. Significantly, with the exception of 'The Lover of Things', each story starts with the First World War and uses it implicitly as a point of comparison to show that far more terrible things can be perpetrated in the ostensibly peaceable and mundane world.

The deeply pessimistic message the stories convey suggests that a dark and despondent mood had overtaken their author. The Day Books reveal that their writing caused quite as much anguish and frustration as John's novels, whereas in earlier years she had been able to polish off a short story in a matter of days. Una tells us of one occasion when only her tactful intervention saved John from giving way to despair (showing once again that her loyal support was an indispensable part of John's literary achievement):

> At dinner she was down & out, looked wretched, wouldn't eat, said she was a mass of skin irritation & rash & that anyway her day had gone for nothing as 'Fraulein Schwartz' could never be made into a short story, or at any rate she had lost her talent and was finished and would never write again. After about an hour of this I got some cold tongue and salad eaten and got her back to her room where I read her aloud Fraulein Schwartz just as she is and convinced her that she was trying to alter what did not require alteration & that just as it is now it is one of the best things she has ever done in her life. And so got her calm and quiet and happier & put her to bed.[15]

To Una's consternation, and despite her attempts to discourage it, John began working through the night again in the summer and autumn of 1933.

By November the collection of short stories (entitled *Miss Ogilvy Finds Herself*) was making the rounds of potential publishers. In June Jonathan Cape had had an amicable lunch with John and Una at the Eiffel Tower, but when he tried to bid for the new book John instructed Audrey to disregard him. Heinemann finally signed up the book (an ironic twist since it had been William Heinemann, now long dead, who had originally enthused over her short stories way back in 1915). In the States Harcourt Brace took *Miss Ogilvy* after Houghton Mifflin had turned it down on the grounds that the stories were too gloomy (John believed rather they were put off by her forenote to the collection which pointed up the connection between Miss Ogilvy and Stephen Gordon).

Miss Ogilvy was published simultaneously in Britain and America on March 5, 1934. Heinemann's advance sales numbered over 1,800 copies. But the reviews were a disappointment. Accustomed to prominent coverage of her work, John was depressed by the patchiness of it all, consoling herself that short stories would inevitably be overshadowed by novels. The *New Statesman* (on March 20) came out with a poor review, but this was in line with the hostile reception it had habitually accorded John's work since (and including) *The Well*. They automatically put it down to the journal's vindictiveness against

John, who had threatened to sue over an article in 1928 suggesting that she had connived at Jonathan Cape's move in sending *The Well* to the Home Office for approval. It proved less easy, however, to dismiss a review by H. E. Bates in the *Spectator* (March 11) which asserted that John was not at home in the short story form.

Something went out of John in the early '30s. With her rise to international fame after *The Well* and her move to Rye, the impression grows that not only the art but the vitality as well has begun to dry up. The sudden return in 1933 to the hectic merry-go-round of smart London society expressed less a genuine change of heart than the apprehension of two middle-aged performers that the best parts were starting to pass them by.

The truth was that John was retreating more and more into herself, a process reinforced by Una's unswerving determination to shield her from outside intrusions. The martyr of *The Well* had become the penitent of *The Master*. With the 'murder' of the latter and its relative failure, her temperamental antipathy to the modern world and its materialist values was fuelled afresh and assumed an alarmingly morbid character. The despairing tone of her new work, the exhaustingly long hours, the all-night vigils, each signalled her descent into a stubborn, self-lacerating mood of isolation. So too did the dropping of old friends and colleagues. She had finally resigned from PEN in the autumn of 1931: 'it is chiefly a Club now I think of nobodies who attend the dinners in the hopes of meeting somebody,' Una commented.[16]

The high standard of loyalty John expected from all those who had dealings with her had become a paranoia that ascribed hostile motives to the slightest setback. Though she continued to hire his services, her confidence in Harold Rubinstein was shaken when, in 1932, she learnt he was now working for Jonathan Cape as well. Even Audrey Heath was no longer regarded as the staunch ally she had once been. Her reputation in John's eyes never recovered from the Wilette Kershaw fiasco, and John began to imagine that she had not been as openly supportive as she might have been during *The Well* case. Whenever she came to see them in Rye, she was not invited to stay at The Black Boy, being farmed out instead to the monastery next door (though, partly, this was a protective health measure since they reckoned that half the colds they had suffered in the time they had known Audrey had been caught from her). Sadder still, they no longer trusted her professional judgement. While she was negotiating the Cape contract for *The Master*, they were running behind her back to Harold Rubin-stein to check she was not making a 'muddle' of things.

But Una, too, was a victim of John's escape into herself. It never crossed Una's mind that their union could be anything but the most sacred commitment on both sides. In 1931 they had read the journals of the Ladies of Llangollen (two upper-class Irishwomen who had eloped together in 1778 and shared a Welsh cottage for over fifty years) and compared this legendary couple's 'sweet rural seclusion' to their own in Rye. They determined one day to visit Llangollen and lay flowers on the Ladies' graves, 'a pilgrimage to the pioneers' as Una put it. In Una's mind she and John formed a special couple, bound by an insoluble bond, spiritual as well as physical. John, she believed, was a unique individual whose greatest quality was an immovable loyalty. 'Never in all the eighteen years we have lived together,' Una wrote in 1933, 'has any new excitement, any emotional stimulus made her less careful of my every need, less solicitous of my safety and comfort . . . it is a rare quality indeed and the one of all others that makes for the perfection of human relationships and foreshadows the future union of spirits in another state.'[17]

These words were about to reap a bitter harvest. For John's self-absorption entailed, however sub-consciously, a rejection of Una, or at the least a distancing of herself from her. John was not demonstrative of her deepest feelings. Even Una could be mystified as to her real thoughts, recalling that 'there were times when she was so silent that she would take the trouble to reassure me and would say: "If I'm silent, it isn't bad temper, darling, it's just that I'm 'broody' over my work . . ."'[18] In hindsight, it is clear that for some time, perhaps for years, John's broodings extended to other, more intimate, areas of her life and reflected a growing sense of dissatisfaction.

Una, like Ladye before her, had not weathered well. Though still in her forties, she often looked older (and older than John, whose face and figure retained a remarkable youthfulness), an impression enhanced by the monocled eye, a coiffeur which was now almost as severe as John's, and a manner altogether too managing to be entirely attractive. The hysterectomy had left her in precarious health, a prey to headaches, colic, heart flutters and a general state of hypochondria. John displayed devotion, sympathy and patience, but she could not ignore that stifling sense of entrapment so familiar to her once before in the company of the ailing Ladye.

Una took her partnership with John for granted. John took nothing for granted. She was too self-aware, stood too far outside herself, ever to be entirely at ease with conventional notions of domestic bliss. Both in public and in private she advocated the virtues of hearth and home, the importance of fidelity in relationships (especially among inverts), and the sanctity of marriage. And yet, as her fiction attested, she understood only too well how more sensitive souls could find no lasting happiness within such norms. Her father's example may have been important here. The image of the anguished loner, a veritable ancient mariner roaming the seas like some lost spirit, powerfully appealed to that streak of masochism and self–destructiveness in her nature.

Part Five

SOULINE

1934–1939

Chapter Twenty-three

The decision to sell The Black Boy was a financial one. In the course of the early 1930s John's income fell by almost half as a result of losses incurred in the American Depression (she had always invested heavily in US stocks). Since *The Well* had achieved world-wide sales of over 200,000 copies by the end of 1933, she cannot have been too badly off, but she had never been a reckless spender and evidently felt a measure of retrenchment was called for. As they were keen to maintain the London flat, a smaller establishment in Rye with fewer staff and less upkeep became necessary.

As luck would have it, in December 1933 Journey's End, the small cottage which had been their first Rye home in 1928, came on the market. They had always regarded the house with affection (Una thought it had a 'jovial and carefree' spirit) and John quickly bought it for the bargain price of £750, putting it again in Una's name. They rechristened it 'The Forecastle', for it hung on the edge of the cliff and had uninterrupted views of Romney Marsh, the river Rother, and the sea beyond. On clear nights as many as four different lighthouses could be seen from its windows.

The Forecastle was to be their last proper home in England. It lay at the end of Hucksteps Row, which at this date was still little more than a slum, a dark, narrow alleyway bounded by ramshackle Tudor cottages and populated by local fisherfolk (the Row was popularly known as Jolly Sailor Lane). The Forecastle was relatively grand, being detached and having its own small garden. But the drains were in a bad state of repair and the Tudor charms of its interior had been disguised over the years by ugly modern embellishments. So once again the builders were sent in to supply new oak beams and uncover old ones, to modernize the plumbing, and generally to restore the house to its original state while installing the proper comforts.

The cottage was ready in the spring of 1934. One of the treasured items which they brought with them from The Black Boy was a small square tombstone. It was a memorial to Tulip, the tiny mahogany-coloured griffon that had been one of John's favourite dogs. Tulip had died on May 25, 1931, the fifteenth anniversary of Ladye's death – a coincidence John and Una did not fail to notice. John wept inconsolably, for Tulip had shown extraordinary devotion to her, sitting for hours by her desk while she worked and refusing to go anywhere without her. According to Una, the behaviour of their other Brabançonne, Mitsou, proved exemplary throughout the crisis. 'She kept close to John all day, actually leaving me at times to stick to the bereaved parent. When I said to her: "Mitsou, where's father?" she turned her head and gazed adoringly at John.'[1]

John's extreme sentimentality over animals had involved her in many animal causes down the years. In the late '20s she was elected a Fellow of the Royal Zoological Society and in 1930 she had been awarded a medal by the Animal Protection Society. She wrote frequently to the newspapers, and advocated special lectures in schools designed to teach children 'to reverence the true ideal of strength which is, or should be, the protection of the helpless'.[2] She was more than just an animal crank. Her attitude was consistent with her wider, humanist outlook and the ethical message that so strongly stamps her fiction.

After Tulip, almost a year passed before John could bring herself to buy another dog. Finally, however, she procured a King Charles spaniel bitch which they named Jane – after the Jane Lane who had helped Charles II escape to the coast after his defeat at the battle of Worcester in 1651.

Hardly had they settled into The Forecastle than John and Una were on the move again. John's 'hunting' leg started to bother her and Una suggested another visit to Bagnoles. John was not enthusiastic. The Forecastle was just beginning to feel 'lived in' and she was anxious to get on with her new novel. Looking back Una was to write:

> I always remember how earnestly she opposed me and how I overbore her protests in my anxiety for the good of her health. She told me afterwards, many times, that she had an almost overwhelming instinct against leaving England on that occasion and had been unable to understand her own forebodings.[3]

They crossed to Paris on June 21, calling on Colette, Natalie, and their other friends before proceeding to Bagnoles and the Hotel des Thermes on June 26. Their old rooms awaited them, a suite on the fourth floor with french windows leading onto a balcony that overlooked the baths and the pine valley. For the first couple of days they luxuriated in the balmy, tranquil atmosphere. But then Una suffered a sudden and violent attack of enteritis and John found herself obliged to forego her rest cure and tend to the patient instead. Fearful of wrecking John's holiday, Una insisted they procure a nurse to look after her and rang through to the American Hospital in Paris. The die was cast. At the beginning of July Evguenia Souline arrived.

She was a plain woman, moon-faced, bespectacled, with slanting eyes and high cheek-bones. She was Russian and spoke little English, much to John's annoyance – though she was reassured when Evguenia told them she was a White Russian, the daughter of a Cossack general killed in the Civil War. She proved an efficient nurse and aroused their sympathy by her tales of her flight from Russia in 1922 and her present plight as a stateless citizen in France. Una was soon proclaiming her 'unmistakeably of our own class'.[4]

Within a week Una was well enough to get up. Bagnoles lay in a torrid heat, broken from time to time by thunderstorms and torrential rain. So that Una could rest undisturbed, John took to sleeping in Evguenia's room. It must have been during this time that John conceived her sudden passion for the Russian woman, what she called later a passion as intense as 'First Love'. It is clear that at this stage, while John made her intentions obvious, Evguenia reacted guardedly and with timidity. She can have had few doubts about the nature of John's relationship with Una and she was after all their employee. Una, who knew nothing of this startling development, noted that the nurse had sudden baffling moments of shyness and reserve and innocently ascribed it to the horrors she had witnessed during the Russian Revolution.

When Evguenia finally returned to Paris on July 14, the situation had not changed. Una was still none the wiser and John had not succeeded in breaking down the Russian woman's inhibitions. But John had sensed a response in Evguenia and her longing to bring matters to a head became intense and unquenchable. She later confided that when the time came to pay the nurse her fee and say goodbye, she had nearly lost control and taken her in her arms.[5] In the days following, letters and phone calls passed between John and Evguenia, John overriding all the nurse's apprehensions in her anxiety to see her again when she and Una passed through Paris at the end of the month. When Evguenia addressed her as 'Miss Hall' in her letters, John chided her: 'Never again can I be "Miss Hall" to you'. Plans were laid for a private meeting between them in Paris on July 26.

Una knew about this assignation but read nothing untoward into it. On July 26 she wrote of Evguenia in the Day Book: 'I am sorry for the poor child who is lonely and not happy.' Una, in fact, had already helped Evguenia. Freelance private nursing such as Evguenia undertook was precarious and poorly paid and Una strongly recommended to the American Hospital that they take her on. The result was that Evguenia soon joined the permanent staff.

After lunch in Paris John took the nurse back to the Hotel Pont Royal in the rue du Bac. There, in John's room, they kissed for the first time. Evguenia had suddenly asked: 'Do you want to kiss my mouth?' John had done so, but Evguenia's lips responded chastely like a child's ('so unwilling to give' was John's description) and as she drew back she said: 'This is the only way I know how to kiss'.[6]

In hindsight, one senses here the first signs of a tactic Evguenia was to use again and again with John, namely playing the innocent child in order both to lead her on and to restrain her. It is difficult to believe that the Russian was unaware of what she was doing. She was thirty-two years old at this date and had hardly led a sheltered existence. John, of course, proved easy prey to this ploy. Evguenia's innocence and apparent helplessness as a poor refugee aroused the usual powerful response in her. 'Never learn to speak English quite properly, will you?' John wrote to her in an early letter.[7] She also insisted that Evguenia let her pay for meals and taxis. She had begun to sign her letters to the nurse with that familiar, maternal catch-phrase of Ladye's: 'Bless you'.

On July 28 John and Una left Paris by train for Desenzano in northern Italy. The novelist Naomi ('Mickie') Jacob had invited them to spend a couple of months in Sirmione on Lake Garda, where she had a house. Before their departure, John wrote a passionate ten-page letter to Evguenia, whom she now preferred to call 'Souline'. It was the first of dozens that would pour from her pen in the coming weeks. She reassured the younger woman that this separation, though painful, was not the end, they would see each other again. In Biblical language, she continued intensely:

> Every mile of the road I am close beside you, and your hand is in mine, and your heart is in mine, and your pain is my pain, and your need is my need, and I cannot, no, I cannot see the light but just stumble along beside you in the darkness, and yet I know that this light exists, and this is Faith, to realise the light even only painfully and dimly, and I – poor unworthy sinner that I am, so hampered and tormented by my body that desires you, I have got to make you also realise this light is no less bright because I may fail to submerge the flesh entirely in the Spirit.[8]

This was guilt speaking. John admitted that she had wanted to take Souline's virginity in the hotel room – to 'bind you to me with the

Chains of the flesh' – but her spirit had triumphed over the body and saved her. 'Must I always save you?' she asked plaintively. She ended on a cautionary note, advising Souline to lock up her letters for she (John) was 'a marked woman'. Stephen Gordon had given similar warnings to Mary in *The Well*.

At Sirmione John and Una stayed at the Albergo Catullo, a small hotel overlooking the lake and close to 'Casa Mickie', as Miss Jacob's villa was known locally. The first couple of days were spent in 'pleasant idleness'. After amusing themselves in the morning, they would stroll up to Casa Mickie at about midday for cocktails. John then looked over the two-day old copy of *The Times*. Afternoons were for jaunts in the locality and then it was back to an evening with Mickie at her favourite café, Mario's, in the main piazza.

This tranquil routine was shattered, for Una at least, on July 30: John at last told her the truth about Souline. Next day's entry in the Day Book read simply: 'A very anxious day.' From John's letter to Souline of July 31, however, we learn that a violent row took place all night, culminating in Una throwing herself on the floor sobbing hysterically. She bitterly reminded John that she had always stood for fidelity in 'inverted unions' and that, as the inverts' champion, her own example imposed a 'terrific obligation'. Una insisted that John should not see Souline again: it would only shatter her (Una's) health. John admitted she could not blame Una, for they had been together for over eighteen years and Una had loyally stood 'shoulder to shoulder' in the great battle over *The Well*. The one concession Una would allow, John told Souline, was that they could continue writing to each other. By the next day, the nineteenth anniversary of John's meeting with Una at Lady Clarendon's, Una had relented and gave John permission to see Souline when they were next in Paris – provided she was not unfaithful 'in the fullest and ultimate meaning of the word'.[9]

Una was profoundly shocked by John's revelation. Nothing in their previous life together had prepared her for this moment. It never occurred to her that the Russian nurse with the 'curious face' would be anything but 'a bird of passage' in their lives. For a time the full implications did not sink in. On August 10 John dropped her new novel *The Unprodigal Son* and began another entitled *Emblem Hurlstone*, intended as 'a normal story about normal people'. Deceiving herself, Una believed that John's infatuation was simply a manifestation of her usual creative angst at the outset of a fresh project. On August 16 the two of them drove to Desenzano and then up to the lake at Salo. The beautiful warm weather and the magnificent scenery imparted a false sense of normality.

Our troubles seemed far away & John said 'I love to go off alone with
you on a jaunt' & we went slowly & saw all the beauty of lake &
mountains & olives, vines & cyprus – & she loved it and talked all the
time of her book & I felt happiness & peace for her looming in sight
again.[10]

On August 20 John started writing the first chapter of the new
book. Una breathed a sigh of relief: 'She is launched now & really it
seems that nothing else matters.'

This was far from the case. The daily letters to Souline, page after
page of them, continued with clockwork regularity, by turns
anxious, intense, reassuring. Una's reaction confirmed Souline's
worst fears and for a time she wanted John neither to write to her nor
to visit her again. John pleaded, remonstrated, threatened. She
wanted to send Souline £100 so that she could buy stationery and
stamps. When Souline refused this offer, she scolded her, telling her
that everything in love was equal and calling her 'you stiff-necked
little white-Russian'. If Souline was too tired to write her letters,
then postcards would do, because she had to know that Souline
loved her body and soul: 'Love is a kind of agony.'[11] When a day
passed without a letter from Souline, John sank into a fretful depression and sat down to pen a fresh plea. When two letters arrived in
one day she felt 'on top of the world'. When Souline finally agreed
she would see John again, John went into raptures. 'Darling, I think
you have bewitched me – there are times when I feel you so
intensely, as though you were dragging the heart out of me, as
though you were calling me.' She added a familiar note: 'For so
many years we two lived in the same world – were we always
waiting, we two, for our meeting?'[12]

Souline had qualms that their love was 'emotionally wrong'. John
took pains to put her right. She admitted that she herself was a
congenital invert: 'For me to sleep with a man would be "wrong"
because it would be an outrage against nature.' She asked Souline to
believe that inverts *existed*, that they were not evil or perverted. 'You
are being entirely childish and absurd, Souline, and I simply won't
have it, darling ... When we meet in Paris you shall tell me all about
it, and I will listen with infinite patience.' John said she thought
Souline was probably bisexual, many people were. But just because
she had once loved a man, so what? 'Nature, my darling, is not
limited by the views of ... a hospital Matron.' She explained that
inverts numbered some twenty to every thousand people, bisexuals
even more. 'I think we can hold our heads high, my Souline.'[13] Of
course, what is interesting here is the spectacle of John trying to
justify her seduction of Souline. In *The Well*, and all her public

pronouncements after it, strictures against true inverts 'influencing' the innocent or immature (even apparent bisexuals like Mary Llewellyn) were heavily implicit.

None of Souline's letters to John have survived (except one from a much later date), so it is difficult to tell how genuine was her response. From the tenor of John's letters, it seems clear that the Russian woman was volatile, blowing hot and cold by turns, deliberately or otherwise. At the end of August she suddenly announced that she might be going to America on October 3 as the nurse-cum-companion of a certain Mrs Baker. For days John's letters had been full of plans for her return to Paris on October 5 and this bolt from the blue sent her into fresh agonies. She immediately wired Souline that she and Una would now move forward their arrival to September 22. A protesting letter followed the same day, reminding Souline that she had fallen in love not just with anybody but with a famous author. She therefore had the power to affect the quality of John's work. For a week, John complained, she had fretted so much that work on the new book had been impossible. She begged Souline to stop 'wobbling': 'If loving's worth while it's worth while doing well, with every ounce of one's being.' An anguished postscript read: 'You are my despair – my utter despair.'[14]

Though John maintained that Sirmione was 'hell' without Souline, the little town was not without a certain curiosity value that summer. Mickie Jacob herself stood out as a larger-than-life personality. She was a big, heavy Yorkshire woman who had had to fend for herself from a young age. She had been successively a teacher, a vaudeville artist, a militant suffragette and a Labour Party campaigner. During the war she had joined the Women's Legion and became superintendant of a munitions factory. She went on the legitimate stage after the war and enjoyed some success in films. She had a history of tuberculosis and from the mid-twenties she gave up acting and turned her hand to novel-writing. Her first book *Jacob Usher* appeared in 1926 and sold well. She specialized in middlebrow romantic fiction and thereafter turned out a couple of books a year. In 1930, with her health deteriorating, she had moved permanently to Sirmione, returning to England at intervals to lecture and broadcast on the radio.

By 1934 Mickie had established herself as a well-known local figure in Sirmione, 'a kind of king,' John told Souline, 'loved and respected by the whole town, for Mickie has a most merciful heart and though poor herself gives much to the poor; her charity and understanding are great as is sometimes the way with the best type of invert.'[15] As a young woman Mickie had been married for a fortnight, a disaster never mentioned in later years. She was now unmistakably a 'ladies' man', sporting men's tailored suits and carrying a cane. She wore a skirt only to mass (like John, she was a Catholic convert), out of respect to the priest and God – 'the result is not good nor is it convincing,' John assured Souline, adding:

> She has short & very curly black hair, wears glasses, and is more than the average fat, but her face is good looking, intelligent & charming. She smokes all day & well into the night the rough & vicious little cigarettes that Mussolini imposes on his people, and sometimes she drinks a great deal of red wine, but never gets drunk though she says she feels it! She is funny – a really remarkable mimic, and, it must be admitted, can tell very coarse stories – and yet she is really a tragic soul, very immotional (sic) and very courageous.[16]

Mickie lived at her villa with an ageing Pekinese dog called Sammy and six stray cats. She had a lover in England, Sadie Robinson, who came out to Sirmione for seven months of the year, but John and Una gathered that the affair had its complications, not least because Sadie was married with a six-year-old child. During their visit, Sadie was absent, but Mickie had two young nieces staying as well as a Yorkshire admirer whom John characterized as 'a youthful and most bloody bore – wears trousers one day & a picture hat the next . . . In appearance she is like a white maggot in a nut.'[17]

Staying at their hotel was Gladys Faber, widow of the actor-producer Leslie Faber. She had a reputation as a beauty, but John thought her so English that she seemed out of place – adding pointedly to Souline: 'I don't seem able to find any face attractive that has not got high cheek bones and funny brown eyes and very white and adorable teeth that I so much want to kiss but am not allowed to.'[18] John quarrelled with Mrs Faber one night on the subject of religion, calling her a 'bloody liar' in the heat of the moment. It was an outburst she regretted having made to a woman, John confided to Souline, but the alternative would have been a glass of wine in her face.

In early September Romaine Brooks appeared briefly in Sirmione, looking incredibly dirty and dishevelled, according to John. The artist was in a strange, cynical mood, complaining of Natalie and all her old friends and swearing she would never paint again. When she left, John and Una breathed a sigh of relief.

Romaine's passionate friendship with Gabriele d'Annunzio was long since over, but the ageing poet-patriot, now in his seventies, lived just outside Sirmione in a palatial villa, Il Vittoriale. Una had always been a keen admirer of d'Annunzio's work, which she had read in the original Italian, and she was determined to meet the great man. He had a reputation, however, for being extremely reclusive and Romaine advised Una that literary eminence alone provided access to his presence. Una therefore persuaded a reluctant John to go along with her plan. They bought in Verona an Italian translation of *The Well of Loneliness* (*Il Pozzo della Solitudine*) and sent it with a covering letter from John to Il Vittoriale.

For ten days not a word. Then on the eleventh day a breathless hotel waitress came running up to report that a message had come through to the only public telephone in Sirmione: John would be receiving a letter from the Commandante brought by car the following day. Sure enough, on September 12 an Alfa Romeo sporting a pennant drew up at the Albergo Catullo. An elderly lady got out bearing an impressive envelope embossed with two blue seals and addressed to 'Radclyffe Hall' in letters an inch high. She had also brought a huge bouquet of pink carnations and a large porcelain bowl full of golden muscat grapes bedecked with yellow rose petals. Other envelopes contained fabulous bracelets made from rubies, sapphires and platinum. There were also rare copies of d'Annunzio's own works, each inscribed to John personally. Since John was resting in her room with a swollen ankle that had been stung by a horse-fly, the elderly lady marched upstairs followed by a retinue of hotel staff each clutching an item from the treasure trove of gifts sent down from the Vittoriale.

John was overwhelmed. The poet's long letter praised *The Well* lavishly and when she had finished reading it John felt close to tears. Una was delighted for her: 'I wonder will she ever be able to sink into diffidence and doubt of her own genius again?'[19] All Sirmione soon talked of this event, a rare example of the god descending from his cloud, and John was stared at in the street as a person of extraordinary importance. According to Una, Mickie was visibly jealous – and shocked too when Una told her that d'Annunzio was the only man in the world whom she could never refuse (to which John rejoined: 'Well, he is seventy-four now, darling').[20]

To Una's disappointment, the Commandante wished to see John alone, artist to artist, 'a tre occhi' as he put it in reference to his one good eye. However, the elderly lady suggested that Una accompany them as far as the Grand Hotel in Gardone just in case a summons for her too came from the Vittoriale at the last minute. On September 16 John and Una were driven at great speed to Gardone in the Alfa Romeo by a chauffeur wearing a pistol and ammunition belt. Una was deposited at the Grand and John taken up to the villa. At eight in the evening word came through to the hotel that John and the poet were dining alone and that Una should fend for herself. John finally reappeared at 11.30. She was distressed that Una had been left out and triumphantly announced that d'Annunzio had agreed to see them both the following day. As the car took them back to Sirmione, John related her adventure at the Vittoriale. The poet had given her a guided tour of his bizarre private apartments (in one a bronze statue of St Francis was adorned with a gun belt). He had confessed that he first believed *The Well* to have been written by a man and then suggested that John take a villa in the grounds of the Vittoriale to write a book dedicated to him. At dinner he had talked throughout of *The Well* and John had clearly struck a responsive chord in him.

As it happened, Una was fated never to meet her hero. For the following day d'Annunzio went back on his promise. The melancholia that afflicted him (he hated to be seen in the ugliness of old age) had once again descended and he would meet no one. Una was bitterly dismayed. But she consoled herself with the loyal thought that at least the two geniuses had met: 'My own personal gratification if I could meet him weighs as nothing in the balance of realities as compared with this wonderful event.'[21]

John thought d'Annunzio eccentric but not mad, 'except in so much as all genius skirts the borderline of madness', as she put it to Souline.[22] Her brief and curious interlude with the poet was an important influence, however, in both confirming her affection for Italy and pushing her further to the right in the polarizing political climate of the mid-1930s. Though d'Annunzio was anti-Catholic (and effectively a prisoner of the state at his villa), he was an extravagant nationalist with strong Fascist connections. John met him at a time when her association with Souline was hardening her antipathy to Russian Communism and his rare display of friendship secured her lasting loyalty and respect. Both shared a passionate morbidity, a rejection of modern values and nostalgia for a romantic past. They would correspond at intervals over the years and there would be further invitations to the Vittoriale. But always his reclusive mood would prevail at the last moment and John never saw him again. When he died in 1938, she wept bitterly and sent a huge laurel wreath to the funeral.

Una left Sirmione with few regrets. Apart from her disappointment at not seeing d'Annunzio, she had thought the place dull, the meals inedible, and the atmosphere lacking in the sort of bohemian conviviality she liked. But Una's judgement was no doubt clouded by her anxiety at John's continuing preoccupation with Souline. Mickie

Jacob's nieces were amused by Una's tendency to fuss over John's health 'like a mother hen',[23] but privately she was suffering agonies, waking at 5.30 every morning drenched in sweat.

There seemed little prospect that things would improve. For weeks John had been making plans to see Souline when they got to Paris and, despite her promise to Una not to be unfaithful in the fullest sense, her letters show that she had whipped herself into a state of intense sexual anticipation. She talked of making a woman of Souline, teaching her the meaning of passion, even of wanting to give her a child. She longed to hold the Russian girl in her arms, to feel her body and lips pressed against hers. In one letter she fantasized serving Souline breakfast in bed: 'I'll be the nurse and you'll be my patient!'[24]

As soon as they arrived at the Hotel Pont Royal on the morning of September 22, John telephoned Souline. Now that John was once more on her doorstep, the Russian woman expressed fears and uncertainties, which prompted John to despatch a quick note full of assurances that she would not force her to do anything she did not want. The record suddenly goes silent for the next ten days. Or almost silent. On September 30 a brief entry in Una's Day Book tells us she has prayed 'desperately for help' to Our Lady of Victories. There is also a cryptic note from John to Souline asking why she is so disheartened: 'Is it what I said last night about Una protecting the situation?'

By October 3 John and Una were back in London, staying at the flat in St Martin's Lane. The letters to Souline begin again and it is immediately clear what has happened.

> Nothing is real but those ten days in Paris when I held you in my arms and taught you to love, when your heart beat close against my heart, and your mouth was on mine, and our arms were round each other straining our bodies closer & more close, until there was an agony in our loving . . .[25]

They had gone to Souline's lodgings at Passy. The younger woman was so apprehensive that John had spoon-fed her at table like a baby, soothing and calming her like a parent with a frightened child – the fantasy which would always fuel their relationship because it satisfied John's need to protect and to dominate. But they had eventually made love, awkwardly, hesitantly, because Souline was nervous and tried to resist at first. John assured her that physical relations were not always harmonious straight off and promised one day to teach her the 'lesser things' of homosexual love-making.[26] But at last they had done it, John emphasized, and now belonged to each other. 'Soulina, my most dear, you have suddenly grown up – I found you a child and I have made you a woman.'[27]

Plans were made for Souline to visit London in November. The nurse's trip to America with Mrs Baker had mysteriously evaporated and she went instead to Menton to stay with a Russian friend, Lysa Nicolsky, whom John had met in Paris. John had learnt that Souline had a history of tubercular trouble and the letters were now full of small anxieties about the girl's health. Was she wrapping up properly? She must be careful not to drink too much spirits ('Am I less than a cocktail?'). When she took the ferry to England, she *must* travel first class otherwise it would be 'too stuffy and vile' for her.

Una, meanwhile, was trying her best to go along with a difficult and painful situation. Her self-control was such that John had begun to believe, whether genuinely or not, that she now accepted the affair. After Paris Una had written a friendly letter to Souline and was now using her title to procure an entry visa to England for her (as John explained it to Souline, so many writers were 'Red' these days that if *she* applied for the visa, 'they might think I was "Red" also – damn them!'[28]).

John's guilt and compassion drove her to make reassuring noises to Una – 'She said to me yesterday: "Remain with me for ever and ever throughout eternity, Amen!" She said: "*You* are permanent."'[29] – which only built up Una's hopes that the infatuation was merely temporary. In a touching effort to brighten up her appearance and regain John's interest, Una took to wearing a 'uniform' that John especially liked consisting of a plain grey suit, black silk crêpe shirt and stock, and a Fascist cap (a fez with a tassle which she had bought in Padua in August). But her bitterness lay brooding beneath the surface. When Ida Wylie lunched on October 19, bringing her elderly American girlfriend Dr 'Joe' Baker, the spectacle threw Una into a fresh depression. Ida's promiscuity was notorious and the misery that Una detected in Joe's face she judged 'a living indictment of Ida's thoughtless sexual selfishness'.[30] It was the nearest she could bring herself to blame John.

The full humiliation of Una's position became painfully apparent when Souline arrived in England on November 4. While Una stayed at the flat in London, John greeted her lover off the boat at Folkestone and the two of them spent three days alone at the Grand Hotel. They rejoined Una in London for the next three days. Thereafter Una took herself off to The Forecastle, moving back to the London flat when John and Souline decided to come down to Rye. To have to give up her own home in this way was a bitter pill. In her desperation she turned increasingly to Ladye for comfort: 'Ladye holds my hand day and night; I feel her presence and help as never before and generally she can alleviate my worst anxieties.'[31] And a few days later:

> But for [Ladye's] help and for what she has said to reassure me and give me security for the future I don't know how I could have faced up to life. All that I did to hurt her she has repaid by helping me in almost exactly similar circumstances. I was utterly selfish and cruel to her . . . May being hurt at least teach me never again carelessly or deliberately to hurt anyone else . . . But first and foremost I want the best, morally, spiritually and in all ways for my only beloved. And Ladye wants it too and for our Threeship, as she calls it. All other persons, whatever their part in our existence & however much interest and affection they may evoke, are outside, and my John knows it as well as I do . . . hence conflict which is making her unhappy.[32]

John was certainly not enjoying peace of mind despite her efforts to romanticize her affair (she had ended one letter to Souline with: 'they will write on my grave: "Radclyffe Hall who died of love for Soulina".'[33]) After Souline had left England and returned to Paris on November 20, John succumbed to a fresh bout of guilt and depression, but put it down to 'the melancholy of the inverted'. She felt she would never 'make good'. 'I am back where I was many years ago with only one difference – I know that I am kinder & more considerate & understanding.'[34] A curious statement under the circumstances.

The situation was beginning to affect her work. For a time she tried to convince herself that the new novel in progress had been invigorated by her new-found passion. The theme of *Emblem Hurlstone* had changed during their stay at Sirmione. It was now the story of a man who attempts to avoid all pain, both physical and mental, until in the end he is made to face it – reminiscent, in fact, of John's short story 'The Rest Cure – 1932'. John told Souline that the new idea had sprung from their love. 'You see we have had a mental child you and I – a kind of mental – imaculate (sic) – conception . . . while I was in torment during the summer I found the details flooding into my mind. I *felt* the awfulness of unfulfilled love – the awfulness of longing, the awfulness of living. Then it was that I knew what my people would do, and when they would end it, and how they would end it.'[35]

But the book proved difficult, more difficult than John made out to Souline. By the second week in December she could report to Paris: 'our child has at last cut its 3rd tooth'[36] [i.e. the third chapter]. Una, however, detected another trolley-book in the making. By mid-December, with some 50,000 words written, John accepted that *Emblem Hurlstone* would be no more than a stop-gap. The book was no longer mentioned to Souline. Instead, John's creative frustration expressed itself in renewed sexual yearnings:

If you were in my flat at this moment, I would not protect you at all – I'd kill you with love – I'd kiss you until you asked for mercy. I'd kiss you all over that dear body of yours – I'd make that body of yours desire me until your desire of me was as pain.[37]

John and Una spent Christmas together at The Forecastle. Una felt emotionally exhausted but her hopes that the 'turmoil' was only temporary had been lifted after a sitting with Mrs Leonard at which Ladye had proved reassuring – and had declared enigmatically that in a sense the situation had had to happen. Una was amused when, on December 17, Edy Craig's forty-eight year old niece Olive Chaplin – a bisexual woman who had been married and had grown-up sons – came for lunch and made eyes at her: 'She is a darling and very attractive but my focus is fixed and has been since Aug. 1st 1915.'[38] A few days later Una was called on to shield John from one of *her* admirers. A gently spoken American woman swathed in furs arrived on the doorstep clutching a parcel for John. She told Una she had come from Chicago, refused to give her name, and insisted on seeing John personally. Una finally managed to get the woman to leave on the pretext that John was away – though in fact she was skulking on the stairs ready to dash down if the American showed violence. The parcel proved to contain framed photographs of John, and Una contemptuously dismissed the woman as 'a raving nymphomaniac with delusions!'[39]

Such scenes imparted a false sense of normality to their lives. For John's gloomy longings for Souline made impossible the cosy sort of Rye Christmas they had enjoyed in past years. 'Be an extremist in love, my heart,' went a letter John wrote on Christmas Eve, 'love me and love me, and mourn our separations.' Quarrels and tensions prevailed at The Forecastle – which John sought to play down, unconvincingly, as merely Una's strained health since her hysterectomy. On New Year's Eve, while John was telling Souline how she kept waking at night and trying to touch her, Una wrote sadly in the Day Book: 'The last day of a very unhappy year . . . The road ahead of me looks steep and rough & at present I can seldom see any hopeful end to it.' Ladye's diary had expressed very similar sentiments twenty years before.

Chapter Twenty-four

Had Una known that Souline would be a part of their life for the next nine years, her despair would have known no bounds. By 1935, even had John and Souline stopped being lovers, John's financial and moral commitment to the girl had become such that disentanglement was difficult. Under John's encouragement, Souline had left the American Hospital (John felt the work was too strenuous for her) and turned to freelance nursing again. To safeguard against periods of unemployment, John paid a quarterly allowance of 3,500 francs towards her rent in addition to £10 a month for living expenses. In the course of the year these payments became an annual allowance of £250, paid in monthly instalments. Souline put up merely a nominal resistance to this patronage and, though initially John did not wish her to stop working altogether, the effect was increasingly to reduce her necessity to find jobs. At the same time John had taken on the responsibility, with Una's help and connections, of obtaining French naturalization papers for Souline. Inevitably, all these arrangements tightened John's control over the Russian woman, but they also increased her anxiety and concern, enabling Souline to exercise her considerable powers of emotional manipulation.

What kept Una going was not just John's evident need for her but the way in which John gave the impression that she still cared. Thus when they returned to Paris in January to see Souline again, John remained constantly solicitous of Una's welfare while spending most of her time with the other woman. On one day, after a lonely lunch on her own, Una arrived back at the hotel to find a large azalea plant in her room with a card saying 'From your John' – which reduced her to tears. Another time, after an evening with Souline, John came to Una's room at midnight. She woke her up and sat on the bed, asking how she had been and insisting that she was never really happy away from her side – 'and so for over an hour, wiping tears that would keep welling from my eyes with her handkerchief, feeling me as she held me in her arms to know was I less thin.'[1] At moments like these Una consoled herself with the thought that the infatuation could not last: it was purely a sexual adventure on John's part and when the novelty wore off, she would see that Souline had insufficient character to satisfy her.

Had Una known what John was telling Souline – that she had not loved Una for years – her feelings would have been less sanguine. Even so, on occasions when Souline stayed the night with John at their Paris hotel, Una could not help giving way to momentary despair and bitterness:

> I am actually fond of Soulina and I would give her anything I have and help her in every way; but seeing the devotion that for twenty years was all mine, overflowing for someone else, a woman years my junior and who has never been to John all that I have been, hurts and hurts and hurts and is never for one waking moment out of mind and heart . . . Oh poor poor us . . . why oh why couldn't the poor lamb remain faithful to our union?[2]

Worst of all to Una's mind was the disruption to John's work. Since dropping *Emblem Hurlstone* she had done nothing. Souline had ventured to suggest that John's forte lay in films. Una exploded contemptuously: 'She [Souline] has not the dawning of an understanding of her genius . . . !'[3] Yet John had found the girl's ingenuousness 'refreshing' and even talked of living in Paris though she had always sworn never to be an expatriate. Una bleakly envisaged even her aesthetic influence with John being undermined.

Back in Rye in April, however, John did start a new book. To Una's delight, her heart and mind seemed wholly concentrated on the job this time. Within ten days John had reached the fourth chapter. Some nights she was working till five in the morning. 'This new book appears to be galloping through me,' she told Souline.[4] And a few days later: '*I* think it's the best thing I've ever written. It's coming so truely (sic) – it's so real and true. Una read part of it & my Agent and she thinks its one of my tip top efforts. Oh, I'm so glad, and its all, all You.'[5] She wondered if Souline could stand being with her while she worked at such pressure: 'Una has had to endure it for years – and they say that one can get used to hanging! . . . but if it were you I think I'd want to get up and kiss you, that would be the danger.'[6]

But her new creative impetus did not stop John's thoughts from drifting constantly to her lover across the Channel. 'This longing I have to spend the night with you – it is a positive craving.'[7] New plans were laid to see Souline in Paris in May, to be followed by a holiday for the three of them in the south of France. Una regarded the prospect with dread. She was already in a state of nervous exhaustion, suffering attacks of breathlessness and heart palpitations. They decided to sell the flat in St Martin's Lane because she found the five flights of stairs too much for her. She noted with consternation that John no longer carried Ladye's photograph with her nor did she care for Una to read to her.

In the summer of 1935 John and Una spent five days in Paris, most of them visiting Souline at a clinic where she had a minor operation on her sinuses, before proceeding on to Beauvallon, accompanied by Boulinka, the bull-dog pup that John had earlier given to the Russian girl. The arrangement was that Souline would shortly follow them. In Paris they had found her frequently sulky and volatile, and impatient with John's constant fussings. Once they had left Paris it became clear that Souline was hesitating about joining them. She would make a date then change her mind shortly afterwards. An abrupt phone call from Una on a bad long-distance line did not improve matters.

Una privately held out hopes that this was the beginning of an eventual rupture, but the suspense drove John into an agony of pent-up frustration that prevented her working. 'When, oh, when will you spare me, my Soulina?' she asked.

> Sometimes I think that the answer is: Never ... I'm the first artistic brain-worker that you have known intimately I think – and so probably you don't understand the tension in which we creative people live during the time of creation.[8]

Souline, in reply, intimated that she might not come at all. John wrote back desperately:

> Darling, I am falling by the way – yes I am – the strain of intensive hard work and the strain of our parting is being too much. You must come here at once as you promised ... I must have you – I *must* – I *must* – I *must*.[9]

The emphatic repetition recalled Ladye's manner of speech. Una tried her best to be sympathetic, but she could not help reminding John that until Souline had come on the scene they had been united and content. John wept miserably, then said 'Darling, we shall weather through' – 'and we clasped each other close and clung together.'[10]

However, in the end Souline agreed to come, as she had probably intended all along. Relieved, John sent a list of appropriate clothes to bring (in the tone of a mother to her child) and tried to analyse why she had got herself into such a state, why love was so painful. 'I think because all great emotions are one. This is hard to explain but I know what I mean. The circle meets in all great emotions – it is part of that curious Oneness that I feel – that I tried to write in The Master of the House.'[11] She met Souline off the train at St Raphael and the two of them spent a night together at a local hotel before rejoining Una at Beauvallon.

At first a degree of harmony reigned. Sun and sea helped. Una and Souline bathed naked, frolicking with Boulinka in the water, while John watched from the beach in her swimsuit. But Una could not help marvelling at John's infatuation for this girl with the 'negroid face & eyes like currants'. She was such an inferior intellect that it was 'like sharing one's life with a rather under-developed type of child … whose deficiencies of sympathy and perception would distress one were she one's own.'[12]

In August the trio made their way to Sirmione. They each had a room at the Albergo Catullo and Una was upset when John began going regularly to Souline's at night. The Catullo was a small family hotel and she feared the scandal if John should be caught. Eventually John agreed to limit her visits to mornings and evenings only. Mickie Jacob arrived on August 6. Her affair with Sadie Robinson had clearly deteriorated. She quickly sized up the situation between John and Souline and made a play for Una, a move that had been in the offing the previous summer. Una made plain her lack of interest, but when Mickie tried to exploit her affections by calling Souline 'a complete bitch', Una leaped to the girl's defence and told Mickie in no uncertain terms that Sirmione was no longer big enough for the two of them. The following day John wrote Mickie a stiff letter. Mickie left town the same day.

They had in any case begun to find Mickie's sneerings at Fascism and the Italians (she had also been rude about d'Annunzio) tiresome and disloyal. Mussolini was on the point of invading Abyssinia and Britain first tried to buy him off. When this failed and Italy sent her troops into Abyssinia in October, Britain persuaded the League of Nations to apply economic sanctions. Una believed Mussolini had every right to occupy what she characterized as 'a barbarian slave owning country incapable of developing its own resources'.[13] John's feelings were even stronger. She scorned British politicians as 'a self-seeking, dishonest, hypocritical crew who ought to be strung up on the nearest lampposts'.[14] In Sirmione in August, meanwhile, the two women openly displayed their support for the Duce by wearing Italian ribbons on their lapels. They also participated in a sing-song with some local fishermen at a taverna in nearby San Virgilio, which went on until one in the morning. 'At the end,' Una reported, 'John gave them a toast: "Italia" & they replied "Erviva" & all gave and received the Fascist salute.'[15]

By mid-September the three women were back in Paris. John had worried for some time that Souline's lodgings in Passy were too cold and damp for her latent tubercular condition. A new and larger flat was found in the 17th arrondissement, furnished and paid for by John – a move which started Una worrying about the increased financial burden of Souline's ever more lavish tastes. They were delighted to see that a new French edition of *The Unlit Lamp* had come out, but when Una read it aloud Souline began to fidget and asked John if she had not made Joan Ogden too grown-up for a girl of thirteen. John made a tactful reply but muttered later to Una that she could never tolerate a mistress with brains.[16]

Leaving Souline in Paris, John and Una returned to Rye on October 17 to find that a mighty storm had flooded many of the older slums in Hucksteps Row, necessitating the demolition of some houses and the removal of their occupants to new council estates. John confessed she was sorry to lose 'my poor, funny people', adding: 'Change, always change – how I hate it!'[17]

One thing that never changed was Marie Visetti's habit of running to John only when she needed something. They had last heard from the old woman in 1933 when an almost illiterate letter had related how a wardrobe had fallen on top of her, breaking three ribs, and she had demanded £100. Now it appeared she was suffering from pernicious anaemia and, since she was in her eighties, the prognosis did not look hopeful. 'I cannot pretend that this seriously effects (sic) my heart,' John wrote to Souline, 'as she and I have been so wide apart for many years . . . I could have wished that she would go quickly & painfully in her sleep, the poor, angry, cruel old woman . . . anyhow I forgive her her faults towards me and I hope she forgives me my faults.'[18] However, Marie was not finished by a long way and she was soon upsetting the nursing home John had found for her with her outbursts of hysterical violence. John had long wanted to put her mother in a permanent nursing home, but she insisted on staying in a hotel. As she was technically not insane, 'we can do nothing except let her go her own crazy way'.[19]

On October 28 John told Souline: 'The finest book I have so far written was finished last night at 10.15 after an almost unbroken spell of 48 hours work.' Una had read the last section of the novel hot from the pen and pronounced it 'sheer genius'. The story was firmly rooted once again in a sense of place. Rye became the little town of Rother on the edge of Romney Marsh and Crofts Lane stood for Hucksteps

Row. The colourful characters who populated the Hucksteps slums
provided the real centre of the book's focus and, as in *Adam's Breed* and
The Master, the reader is presented with a lively, warts-and-all portrait
of a strong local community. As John saw it, she had written an
unvarnished celebration of the poor people who had become her
neighbours since buying The Forecastle. She explained to Souline:

> Of my poor I have tried to write faithfully and simply. Sometimes they are
> funny, sometimes they are tragic – and always they are very, very poor –
> belovèd. Sometimes they are tiresome, sometimes they are good, &
> always – except for outstanding exceptions – they are childish, they behave
> much like children. [20]

It was not long before Una had found an appropriately spiritual
title: *The Sixth Beatitude*.

The central character in *The Sixth Beatitude* is thirty-year-old
Hannah Bullen, who works as a cleaning woman to support a
colourful but difficult family. The book is short, spanning just one
year in Hannah's life, and unfolds less as a developing story than a
series of episodes designed to show the woman's warm, generous
spirit against a backdrop of poverty and minor calamity. As one might
expect from a Radclyffe Hall heroine, Hannah possesses a superiority
of vision that enables her not only to rise above the disorder which
surrounds her but to perceive in it something of the beauty and
permanence of all created life. This comprehension, of what John had
called 'that curious Oneness', springs from her acute affinity with
nature, and some of the descriptions of the Marsh and the changing
seasons are among the best the author ever wrote. As so often before,
the keynote of the heroine's character is a deep compassion and,
inevitably and inexorably, the story leads up to a final act of self-
sacrifice in which Hannah gives her life trying to save a neighbour's
children from a blazing house.

John believed that her love for Souline had given her the strength
and vitality to write the new book after the emptiness she had felt
following *The Master*. But the heavily fatalistic tone of the story, the
inescapable sense of loss and impermanence behind the surface beauty
and joy, suggests that the Souline affair had taught John a darker
lesson. It had made her acutely conscious of her age, of the relentless
passing of time. It had also shown her the hollowness of her own
cherished values, of fidelity in particular. It is significant that the
perspective of *The Sixth Beatitude* is one that transcends conventional
social morality. However feckless and dishonest the inhabitants of
Crofts Lane may be, they are all ultimately redeemed by being seen in
the light of eternity. At one stage Hannah agrees to sleep with a sickly

young man who begs her to initiate him sexually before he dies. Her action is depicted not as promiscuity but as a gesture of compassion and spirituality. John had once observed to Souline that the physical act of love was 'our most intense expression of a longing that is really of the Spirit'.[21] But just as Hannah's young man dies soon after their night of passion, underlining once again the unity of life and death, so John's intense emotion for Souline was inseparable from a chronic sense of desperation so impassioned that ecstasy became a form of suffering. Hence the violence with which her sexual longings were expressed: 'I could kiss you till you bled – I could tear you to pieces Evguenia . . .'[22]

If John was looking for suffering, she was to find it in full measure in 1936. After an uneasy Christmas spent with Souline at The Forecastle, she and Una accompanied the Russian girl to Paris in January. Almost immediately new frictions arose as John and Una resumed seeing Natalie and Colette – whom Una described as 'a marvellous figure, almost as broad as she's long', with 'bare legs and feet with scarlet toenails in open black sandals'.[23] Souline felt left out and sulked. She accused John of keeping her down and just using her for sex, a charge which so shocked John that she later wept in Una's arms. When in February Souline was admitted to the American Hospital with a slight bleeding on her lung, relations became so poor between the lovers that Una found herself in the invidious position of acting as John's go-between. After one particularly stormy scene with Souline, John rounded on Una and blamed her for all her misery. For the first time Una threatened to leave, bitterly telling John that she could hardly be blamed for *minding* after twenty years together.[24]

Although the X-rays showed no sign of a recurrence of Souline's TB, John was anxious to take her south as soon as possible. One suspects that Souline, like Ladye and Una before her, was adept at using her health as an emotional ploy against John. In March the three of them travelled to Grasse, this time with another new dog in tow, a dwarf pinscher christened Mary. Souline continued to be tearful and difficult and John was rarely sleeping with her now.

The routine at Grasse gave an impression of two embattled aunts trying to cope with an unruly niece. John and Una would breakfast in their rooms, as in their early days. Then John would accompany Souline on a walk or excursion. All three would lunch together (if on speaking terms) and Souline would take a siesta in the afternoon while John spent time with Una. John and Souline would rejoin each other in the late afternoon, then part again for dinner when Una saw John for a private meal in their rooms. Sometimes Una would accompany the other two on their walks, but Souline had by now built up such a resentment against Una that she invariably sulked and wandered off ahead of them on her own.

One must conclude that John was driven by a positive lust for suffering. By that *and* a sense of duty and compassion so extreme that it amounted to a chronic defect in her character. It is likely that, had Ladye survived John's infidelity with Una, exactly the same tortured threesome would have resulted, fuelled by John's emotional indecision. But it is equally clear that John was sexually enslaved by Souline, a bond that tightened rather than loosened the less the girl made herself available. Souline knew only too well she possessed this power and evidently used it to suit her purpose, although she also understood the limits to which she could push John, dissolving into tears and penitence when she saw she had gone too far.

In June the trio were back in Paris. To add to her misery, John had reluctantly to acknowledge the 'failure' of *The Sixth Beatitude*. Heinemann had published the book in April to mixed reviews and sales proved sluggish. By July just over 6,000 copies had been sold in Britain, only 2,000 in America. Audrey wrote to console John with the thought that any novel selling 5,000 could be counted a bestseller in the current depressed climate of the book trade, but it did little to cheer her. Souline, meanwhile, was provoking her jealousy by insinuating a romantic liaison with her Russian friend Lysa Nicolsky. All these pressures boiled over in John in a stormy scene at Souline's flat. In an uncontrollable rage she rushed from room to room smashing everything that she had ever given her lover – photos of herself, every book and picture, even a crocodile handbag. But, as always, reconciliation came with renewed tears from Souline and forgiveness from John.

In July they were off on their travels again. Though Souline's health was usually the pretext, this restlessness also served to distract them from the stifling tensions of the moment. They went first to Alsace, then, in September, to Merano in the Italian Tyrol. At first they wondered if they had made a mistake, for they found the modern part of Merano distinctly unattractive. But the old town delighted them. In later years Una could still remember its frescoed arches, the cobbled piazza, the ancient cathedral with its giant St Christopher painted on the outer wall, and the beautiful walkway above the town known as the Tappeinerweg. John was so struck by the place that she began to work on a new book, about a Merano shoemaker called Otfried Mahler, and once again she immersed herself in a search for local colour. As a result, they stayed in Merano for almost seven months.

Shortly after their arrival in Merano the Russian girl had caught her finger in a door. When the doctor tried to lance the blister, she moaned and wailed and kicked her legs. 'I have never seen an adult of our class exhibit such unashamed cowardice,' Una declared.[25] But of course it was the child in Souline that fuelled John's infatuation and she remained helplessly enthralled. Discussing Edward VIII's affair in England with the divorcee Mrs Simpson, John told Una that the King's action was 'wicked' and she drew pointed comparisons between his 'weakness' and her own. Yet she would not give up Souline. 'Oh, where will it all end?' lamented Una as she watched her beloved becoming sicker and older by the day while Souline grew plumper and appeared to 'flourish like a vampire on the wrecking of this great artist so immeasurably her superior'.[26]

Towards the end of April 1937 the three women left Merano and made their way to Florence. Because of poor rail connections, they decided to go by road. No one car could accommodate all three of them, the dog *and* their mountain of luggage, so they hired a turquoise-blue charabanc and removed its fifteen seats. It was a stylish exit and all along the route they were cheered and saluted by passers-by.

The plan was to make Florence their base for the following winter, since its moderate climate would be suitable for Souline. Moreover, Una loved the city, had many Italian friends there, and John remembered it with affection from their last visit in 1922. The prospect of such a lengthy sojourn abroad would normally have unsettled John, but she was passing through another of her 'exile' moods, inspired by the 'failure' of *The Sixth Beatitude* and her contempt for the British government's anti-Italian stance over Abyssinia. In any case, now that she was engaged on her Italian novel, she felt it would not come amiss to stay close to the sources of her inspiration.

The new book went badly, however. Souline's continuing petulance did not help matters. They were looking for separate flats in Florence, one for the Russian woman, another for the two of them, but Souline insisted she wished to stay in Paris. In early June John signed the lease on a second-floor apartment at Number 18, Lungarno Acciaiuoli, with a view over the Ponte Vecchio and the ancient houses of the Borgo San Jacopo. The lease would run from August, but the aim was to furnish it and move in in the autumn after returning to Rye for the summer months.

When they arrived back in Paris in early July, Souline announced she would definitely not accompany them to Florence in the winter and would leave John rather than do so. There ensued eight hours of tears, despair and fury from John, most of it vented upon Una who tried to calm her throughout the night: 'I feel as if a harrow had passed over me', lamented the Day Book.[27] On July 8 John told Una she could no longer go on. It was all over with Souline. Yet the next day the two lovers reached some kind of rapprochement, Evguenia softening her attitude now that she could see the prospect of John abandoning her. Una felt only numbed bewilderment: 'I am simply exhausted in spirit, mind and body.'[28]

John and Una arrived back in Rye on July 14. They had been away for eighteen months but it felt more like twenty years (John thought all their local friends looked about a hundred years old). Andrea came down for the day on July 18. In November 1935 she and Toby had had a son, Nicholas Vincenzo Warren, who was now nearly two. The first Una had learned of the birth was reading it in *The Times*. She had sent a telegram of congratulations and visited her grandchild several weeks later on her own (while Toby was away). Andrea now looked thin, almost beautiful, but with a poor, shabby air about her. John told Souline: 'As usual she is out of a job and I think her husband is a flop. But she insisted on marrying him against all advice and so there is nothing to be done or said.' She added pointedly: 'She is loyal to him which is as it should be.'[29] Una absent-mindedly kept calling Andrea 'Evguenia'. 'It was too funny, and of course it will all go back to Viola & co.,' John confided to Souline.[30]

Edy and the Boys greeted them joyfully, as if they had never been away. The annual Ellen Terry gala took place at the Barn on July 25. The performance was enlivened by a pungent smell of burning rubber from some electrical short-circuit and for a time there seemed every prospect that the timbered building would erupt in flames. 'We all began to think of our sins and a possible meeting with St. Peter at the Gate,' John reported.[31] Rumours that an adder had been found skulking under the seats at rehearsal did little to reassure the spectators.

Olive Chaplin was also at the gala. She now lived in a cottage opposite The Priest's House with a large woman over twenty years her junior who 'wears a man's lounge suit & looks like hell in it, she being fat. Her name was Lucy once upon a time, but of late she has become Lucian!'[32] The Smallhythe trio considered 'Lou' a good influence on Olive, keeping her sober and restraining her recklessness with money. John and Una privately disagreed. They suspected that Lou herself was a bit of a tippler and her effect on Olive was to encourage the older woman to try to look younger than she was, with disastrous results: Olive merely gave the impression of being 'a distressful old tart'.

While John and Una had been abroad, Minna had undergone a colostomy operation and was now convalescing in a clinic in Slough. More out of duty than inclination, they visited her on August 8. In her letter to Souline the same day, John painted a graphic picture of the old woman's condition:

> She looks more frightful than words can describe – as thin as a bone, of course, and her poor foolish old death's head of a face smeared over with pounds of paint. She is a bad and inconsiderate patient ... [and] is, if possible, vainer than ever and thinks continually of her appearance, so much so that she flatly refuses to allow the nurse to put pads on the incision in her side, saying that pads will spoil the look of her figure. The result of this is that her clothes are constantly in a disgusting condition.[33]

Una, who was suffering from her own intestinal troubles again, was shocked and upset. On the way back to Rye, she said to John: ' "Do you think I could grow like Minna? You must tell me if you see me growing like Minna." '[34]

Since John's reconciliation with Souline in July, both sides were attempting to be more flexible. Souline had more or less agreed to accompany them to Florence in the autumn in return for John's promise that she would never again have to live with her and Una. John also promised to allow Souline a greater measure of independence. This, however, did not come easily to John. In her first letter after returning to Rye, she wrote:

> I know that you are big and independent & all that, but I demand of our love that you sometimes become as the little child for whom I so much long – the little Chink child – our child, our most precious, spoiled and naughty little Chink.[35]

From early in their affair, John had nicknamed Souline her 'Royal Chinkie-Pig', or RCP for short. The girl's 'Chinkiness' seemed an essential part of her physical appeal for John and mention of it invariably stirred John's sexual longings. She now talked about their starting afresh, of making Florence a second honeymoon. When at the end of July Souline went to stay in Haute Savoie for a month, lists of maternal dos and don'ts followed her – she must wear a wrap in the evenings, she must not lie in draughts, no vodka or spirits, and damp shoes or socks should be changed immediately (and last but not least: 'Remember always to love John').[36]

On August 25 John fell and twisted her ankle badly. X-rays showed that she had sustained a triple fracture. The incident marred an otherwise joyful day, for news came through at the same time that Souline had been granted an annual 'come and go' visa to visit England for six week intervals. This meant she could come to Rye, as planned, in September. The visa was obtained through the writer Humbert Wolfe, whom John had met in 1933 and who had connections at the Home Office. In her gratitude to him, John wrote to Souline: 'never again will I speak against the Jews for Humbert is a Jew though a Catholic jew and pious.'[37] Personal considerations invariably coloured John's political opinions.

The ankle was to take far longer to heal than any of them imagined. When Souline arrived in England on September 21, John was still laid up in the London Clinic in Devonshire Place and it was Una who greeted the girl at Victoria Station bearing a note which read: 'Welcome to England, my darling Heart. John.' Earlier John had written: 'Darling, are you too horribly bored at the thought of having a cripple for a lover?'[38] Evguenia soon demonstrated that she was. She stayed at the Clifton Hotel in nearby Welbeck Street and would arrive at John's bedside at a late hour every morning, rushing out again on the slightest pretext – whereas Una was at the clinic first thing and stayed almost all day.

When John finally left the clinic on October 13, it was on crutches and with her leg still in a plaster cast. She moved into the Clifton Hotel to be near Souline, while Una made her way disconsolately down to Rye. Although John telephoned her every day, Una's distress revealed itself in almost constant headaches. On October 18, the two sides exchanged places, Una coming up to London and John and Souline removing to The Forecastle with a nurse in attendance. John felt guilty that the arrangement caused Una so much misery but she dared not go back on her promise to Souline to avoid the old ménage à trois. Her enslavement was complete.

Souline returned to Paris on October 24. John and Una followed on the 30th, Una arranging relays of wheelchairs to carry John from train to boat and, on the other side of the Channel, from boat to train. The intention was to collect Souline in Paris and proceed straight to Florence. But they were held up for a week in the French capital when John's Achilles tendon gave her such pain that she could not put her heel to the ground. 'A manipulator attached to the American Hospital asked for a month in which to put it right,' Una recalled, 'but John, with her eye on the calendar and her mind on Evguenia, told him coldly that the most she would give him was a week. So at the cost of what he had warned her would be agonising pain, the desired end was achieved and we resumed our journey.'[39]

The invalid party, with yet another nurse in tow (for there was no question of Souline using her once expert professional skills for her lover's benefit), finally reached Florence on November 10. A fresh storm from Souline, who threatened to leave if a separate flat was not found for her quickly, petered out when John took a lease for her on a first-floor apartment in an old palazzo in the Via dei Benci. A maid, Angelina, completed John's provision for her lover. The penniless Russian refugee of 1934 had come a long way. In the course of December, while all three stayed at the Gran Bretagna hotel, furniture was bought and moved into the two flats and decorators made last-minute changes. By Christmas all was ready. Una secured the services of two maids for the Lungarno Acciaiuoli flat, a young fair-haired Tuscan girl called Maria and an old woman, Emilia. Both proved devoted servants, John's only reservation (for she was a stickler for correct dress) being that Emilia would persist in answering the front door in her greasy kitchen apron.

Under any other circumstances, Florence in 1938 might have provided John and Una with as happy a home-from-home as their restless natures could allow. Una's old friends May and Cencio Massola were there, and through her relatives the Tealdis, she and John gained access to many of the city's most aristocratic families. In addition, they got to know the Bernard Berensons and British expatriates such as Harold Acton and Isabel Graham-Smith. Social life was simple and leisurely, free from the alcoholic conviviality that John had increasingly despised in London (when they entertained orangeade or iced tea was now the order of the day). Florence's rich historical associations provided ample opportunity for the kind of exploring (and bargain-hunting for antiques) that both women relished, while equally inspiring ancient cities such as Siena and Lucca lay within easy reach.

Yet Souline soon grew bored and resumed her appeals to return to Paris. Notes from John sent over to the flat in the Via dei Benci pleaded pathetically for forgiveness or urged a more reasonable course. More ominously, John's health showed signs of a steady deterioration. By the spring of 1938 her ankle still gave pain and she walked with sticks and a pronounced limp. Her eyes were also causing her trouble. Since Merano she had been afflicted by a nervous spasm in the lower eyelids which had the effect of turning the lashes inwards against her eyeballs. A London specialist had diagnosed a form of chronic conjunctivitis and recommended a new pair of spectacles and a regular course of eyedrops. For a time this appeared to alleviate the condition. John was

suffering from physical and mental exhaustion. Once installed in
Florence, she had begun working through the night again on her
book. Always prone to insomnia, she now permanently lacked sleep.
In February a bout of flu and Souline's decision to return to Paris for
the summer precipitated what amounted almost to a nervous break-
down. A scribbled note to Evguenia full of anguish ended with a
despairing 'it's all useless, hopeless'.[40]

One of the casualties of this crisis was her book. For some time she
had felt that it lacked inspiration but she so desperately wanted to
believe in it, to feel that at the age of fifty-seven she had not lost her
talent, that she persisted doggedly, working sometimes for as much as
sixteen hours at a stretch. Now, in despair, she finally put it aside.
Without the will to resist any more, she also caved in to Souline. She
agreed to her returning to Paris for the summer and consented to her
taking certain exams necessary to qualify for the Sorbonne. She also
offered to raise her allowance to £300 a year, perhaps in the hope that
this might deter Evguenia from abandoning her completely. It was
not an offer the Russian woman was likely to refuse – and she did not.

Souline went back to Paris on June 4 – despite a last-minute appeal
from John to stay and work as her secretary for £300 a year. On June 13
the Russian girl sat her exams for the Sorbonne and failed. Though she
had talked of starting work again in Paris and used this as a further
pretext for leaving Florence, she now announced plans for taking a
holiday in St. Malo with her friend Lysa Nicolsky. The news sent John
into a fresh depression.

> I still love you, but if you go on tormenting me I may suddenly not love
> you any more . . . You have not been a good woman to me, my Evguenia,
> not as good as you might have been. You were not a kind woman to me
> during my recent breakdown – you could have taken care of me but you
> did not.[41]

But this only drew further suggestions from Souline that she would
never return to Florence – at any rate not until John got rid of Una, she
implied. John knew she could never do this, so she tried to minimise
Una's importance, denying that she hated Souline. 'What does it
matter so long as we two love each other?' Even were she a man and
married to Una, John protested somewhat illogically, the situation
would have been no better since, being Catholics, divorce was out of
the question. If Souline were to leave her now, John hinted she might
not have the will to go on living.

I don't want to do myself in, it's against my every religious belief, a great sin and a terrible sign of cowardice, but I feel that I am nearing the end, and a God who Christ told us was a God of Love must also, I think, be a God of Understanding . . . Wherever I look I see only darkness – You are going to fail me when I need you most, and because of this my work has gone from me, so what is there left to live for, Evguenia?[42]

Whether John really believed she would commit suicide or whether it was a threat designed to bring Souline to heel is difficult to tell. Their relationship had become such a ritualised contest that fact and fantasy were inextricably entwined. John's trump card lay in her financial patronage and she was not above exploiting Souline's fear that she would withdraw it. And yet, if anything, John made her infatuation so apparent that she became an easy prey for Evguenia's manipulation. John was not a person who played games with people. At the same time, faced over four years with Souline's transparently selfish manoeuvres, John's insistence on prolonging the drama and taking further punishment can only be explained, once again, by some inner compulsion for suffering.

In July John and Una were back in Rye. The Hucksteps looked like a bomb site, with rubble, timber and bricks everywhere, for the slum houses were being converted now that the old residents had been moved out. Only The Forecastle remained intact, but it seemed dead and bleak, with not a flower in the garden. 'Oh dear, something seems all wrong with the world,' John sighed.[43]

Relations with Souline had been patched up on their way through Paris. She was to come to Rye in August. Having secured her lover a 'come and go' visa to England, John had hopes of obtaining an unconditional visa, a Nansen, which would allow Evguenia to stay in the country indefinitely should this become necessary because of the international situation. In March Hitler had occupied Austria. Czechoslovakia looked to be next on his list. John had little respect for the German dictator. After hearing him make a speech on the radio, she labelled him 'an hysteric, I think an epileptic'.[44] But Italy was Germany's partner in the Axis and she remained implacably opposed to the Soviet Union. In May John, Una and Souline had watched Mussolini parade through Florence with Hitler at his side. 'I hardly looked at Hitler,' wrote Una at the time, ' . . . but kept my eyes fixed upon the Duce every second he was in sight, & yelled Du-ce, Duce until I could yell no more – with John doing likewise beside me.'[45] A rumoured Franco-Soviet alliance could jeopardise all their plans to obtain French naturalization for Souline (no progress had been made on her papers), since they felt that White Russians in France might be rounded up as part of the pact between the two countries. Despite her previous gratitude to Humbert Wolfe, John took out her anxiety over Evguenia's Nansen on a familiar scapegoat:

> The long delay anent visa is driving me quite mad, but if you knew how distracted our Foreign Office is! Jews! Jews! Jews! millions of them trying to push their way into England, and dozens & dozens of them managing to slip in without papers or passports via Ireland, or by arriving at small villages on our coast in fishing boats.[46]

On August 11 John and Una stayed a night at Canterbury in order to attend two consecutive sittings with Mrs Leonard at her house in Tankerton. Ladye 'came through' with her harshest criticism yet of Souline. She described her as 'only half human' and warned that she hated John's work. She intimated that they might soon be free of the girl. This sounds suspiciously as if the medium was telepathically inspired by Una, whom Mrs Leonard had always found a most congenial sitter. But in her last letter before Evguenia's arrival in England on August 15, John remained as passionate as ever: 'I have fallen in love with you all over again . . . Love me – love me *please*.'[47]

There followed another four weeks of misery for Una, made worse this time by the fact that John took Souline off to Malvern with her for the week of the Music Festival. As the place where Una and John had consummated their love, Malvern represented sacred territory. John's infidelity had, literally, come full circle. Ironically, had she known it, Una was witnessing not a new chapter in John's relations with the Russian woman but the beginning of the end. For Malvern marked the last occasion that the two lovers would sleep together.

On September 15, the day Chamberlain flew to Munich to see Hitler at Berchtesgaden, John heard that Souline's British Nansen had been granted. Amazingly, a French Nansen was also obtained at the same time, allowing Evguenia to re-enter France over a limited six-month period. John had cause to thank Humbert Wolfe yet again. They still hoped, however, that the Nansens would not be needed and the plan remained to go back to Florence for the winter. But rumours of imminent war abounded. They bought black-out curtains for The Forecastle and, with other Rye residents, practised air raid drill. John noticed that the faces of her friends had grown old and resigned. Olive feared for her two sons, who were of conscriptable age, while Lucian talked tipsily of joining the Air Corps. Only Edy seemed unperturbed and calmly got on with organizing her next jumble sale. 'As for me, John Radclyffe Hall, what do I feel?' John wrote to Souline.

I scarcely know beyond amazement and spiritual horror. I cannot seem to envisage the horror and yet I am haunted by it. No mere words can express this madness that has suddenly stricken Europe. Darling, I don't want to depress you, God knows, but these are terrible and dangerous days indeed.[48]

They managed nevertheless to extract some humour from the grim situation. 'Olive and Loo came over last evening and we laughed a great deal over a demonstration I gave them of how to carry an incendiary bomb away on a long-handled shovel after having thrown 30 pounds of sand on it.'[49]

Then came Chamberlain's Munich agreement with Hitler and the famous 'Peace for our time' announcement. John and Una resolved their doubts and crossed to Paris. Souline finally agreed to come to Florence at Christmas. By October 21 John and Una were back in Italy.

Just before leaving Florence the previous summer they had taken a new apartment. The Lungarno flat had proved hot and noisy, with unwelcome smells drifting in from the kitchens of the neighbouring Berchielli Hotel. Within days, chiefly through Una's persistence, they had discovered an infinitely superior replacement, a large, airy apartment on the second-floor of an old palazzo in the Via dei Bardi. It contained an enormous study for John, an impressive black marbled bathroom, two bedrooms linked by a connecting door and, the showpiece, a loggia on the floor above which gave an all-round view of Florence and the mountains beyond. To Una's delight her bedroom was connected to John's study by an arched doorway, which meant that at night she could lie in bed and keep an eye on her beloved. Appropriately enough, John was to do most of her work in a curious annexe in the corner of the large study, 'an austere little cell,' Una called it, 'which we furnished with an oak table and chair, a big carved crucifix on the wall, and little else.' The penitent had come home.

Christmas with Souline proved another nightmare of sulks and scenes. John had agreed to the girl's condition that there should be no further sexual relations between them. In her letters she insisted this did not matter, claiming a spiritual dimension to their love, but the new restriction clearly imposed added pressures on the relationship. John had once admitted to Una that her sexual infatuation for Souline was the revenge of a physical temperament too long subjugated to a purely intellectual life.[50] That temperament still demanded satisfaction and could not suddenly be switched off. When Souline went back to Paris at the end of January 1939, she refused to say goodbye to Una and slammed the door in their faces. The long love affair was over, at least on Souline's side.

Later, trying to analyse what had gone wrong, John thought she detected a familiar pattern:

> I very well know that the day I was really pretty bad with that broken [ankle] bone you fell out of love – my long illness did it; and that when you ceased to be in love much tenderness in your feeling went too. You see, my belovèd, I know these things for I myself have been a great lover – I have loved and then grown weary and bored and put an abrupt and brutal end to the thing just as you have done. Did I stop to consider the other person's feelings? No, I did not. Well, now perhaps I am paying for my past and the price is high you may believe me. And yet – and yet – would I have it otherwise? God help me, I am constantly torn in two. I am not going to write any more about all this. You no longer desire me, you have made that quite plain & you had a perfect right to do so. Am I jealous and suspicious? Of course I am. I tell myself that there *must* be someone else, knowing your temperament as I do, and then I suffer, doubting your word, I suffer like Hell, Evguenia. But I have what is left of it all – your friendship. Not yet, & perhaps never can I say a real goodbye and go on living – I don't understand it, I ought to hate you, but instead I must love you.[51]

Souline was now thirty-seven and John accepted that her thoughts had turned to marriage. 'Perhaps this is why I came into your life, to give you the freedom & time to look about you. A strange mission for Radclyffe Hall, a very strange mission, but it is not for me to question heaven.'[52] Stephen Gordon, of course, had made the same kind of sacrifice for Mary Llewellyn.

John admitted her big mistake had been to push what had begun as a friendship into a love affair. But then the memory of that solemn young nurse arriving in Bagnoles flooded back into her mind and she acknowledged she had been powerless to resist the familiar but potent impulse that rose up within her:

> You were thinner in those days and very pale, you looked delicate and tired and you were very silent, and one day you found the courage to come all the way upstairs to find out if I were ill because I was rather a long time coming down. 'I have come on my own initiative' you said. I loved you for it, Evguenia, though I laughed because the words sounded so pompous. And one day in the motor you suddenly said: 'May I take off my cap please?' And all that you were then, or that I thought you were, seemed to me so intensely appealing, and I felt the whole of me reaching out to you, crying out that I *must* and *would* protect you.[53]

Part Six

A SINGLE SOUL

1939–1943

Chapter Twenty-five

As Europe drifted inexorably towards war in the spring and summer of 1939, John and Una consolidated their plans for settling permanently in Florence. Like many people, they wished so fervently for peace that they could not believe war was a real possibility. John did wonder where Hitler would stop, but she viewed the partition of Czechoslovakia as an inevitable and necessary expedient: 'really the little nations have always been a most awful menace and as such cannot be allowed our assistance.'[1] She felt sure that Mussolini did not want war and blamed the Jews and the Treaty of Versailles for Europe's current ills. Swallowing wholesale Fascist anti-semitic propaganda (and pandering to Souline's evident anti-Jewish sentiments), she could write: 'Jews. Yes, I am beginning to be really afraid of them; not of the one or two really dear Jewish friends that I have in England, no, but of Jews as a whole. I believe they hate us and want to bring about a European War and then a World Revolution in order to destroy us utterly.'[2] Her identification with the Fascist order had become as forthright as all her initial allegiances tended to be. When an Italian shop sold her a new typewriter that turned out to be a refurbished old model, she got her money back by threatening to report the owner to the local Fascists: 'in such cases the Party is really a rock of comfort.'[3]

Another reason why they felt they should stay put in Italy was John's health. Though her ankle had now completely recovered, she could not throw off a continual leaden weariness. In June Una persuaded her to undergo a thorough medical examination. This revealed signs of scarring on her lungs (proving that a mystery illness during her adolescence had been a mild form of tuberculosis), an over-active thyroid, and an enlarged aorta in the heart. Una sought a second opinion from a specialist in Rome, who confirmed the diagnosis. He advised John to give up smoking immediately and warned that if she returned to a damp climate such as England's she ran the risk of pneumonia. To Una's surprise and admiration, John followed doctor's orders and stopped smoking at once. As she was a habitual chain-smoker, especially while she worked, the added strain of this abstinence must have been considerable – causing Una to wonder at times 'whether the remedy was not worse than any risks involved'.[4]

At Easter Souline came to Florence for several weeks, accompanied by her friend Lysa (John paid both their travel expenses). This suggests that Evguenia was determined to enforce the new 'friends only' agreement with John, but it did not stop John continuing to perform her anxious role as guardian and mentor. Her letters had remained full of cautions and admonitions. Street demonstrations in Paris drew the plea that Souline should stay indoors ('the French are so fond of kicking!') and when the Russian proposed that John should employ her Italian maid Maria as the nurse–cum–travelling companion she had wanted Evguenia to be, John riposted with horror: 'no servant can ever be a "companion". God save us, what an awful idea!'[5] John could not view Souline's resolve to stay in Paris over the winter with anything but apprehension and at one stage threatened to stop her allowance if she did not go somewhere warmer. However, the girl simple called her bluff and refused to budge. John relented, continued to pay up, and even invested £300 for Souline in British War Loan – 'there is nothing safer in the world than British government stocks . . . and if England falls, well, the world falls with it!'[6] Such patriotic sentiments sat oddly with her contempt for British foreign policy.

In July John and Una left Florence for England. The intention was to sell up The Forecastle and tie up their affairs before returning to Italy for the following winter. They stopped briefly in Paris, to see Souline and put their new dog, Fido, a large white poodle John had bought in Florence, into kennels to await their return. Evguenia greeted them in red hennaed hair, which made Una wonder whether she had begun another affair.

In August the three women were once again living in close disharmony in the cottage at Rye. Souline continued to torment John with her insistence that she could live only in Paris, while Una exerted her own pressure by relaying messages from Ladye (gleaned at solo sittings with Mrs Leonard in Tankerton) to the effect that if John continued to put up with Souline the strain would kill her. Matters reached a head on August 27 when, in the midst of arrangements to sell The Forecastle, a bitter row broke out between Una and Souline. The Russian woman tried to prevent Una leaving her room. She grabbed her shoulders and pushed her backwards and would only let go when Una called the maid-servant. John insisted Evguenia apologize to Una but she refused.[7]

While the occupants of The Forecastle came to blows, the world outside entered the conflict that had been so long coming. On September 1 Hitler invaded Poland. The following day John, Una and Souline listened to Chamberlain's announcement on the radio that Britain was now at war with Germany. Almost immediately the air-raid sirens went off and they rushed into the garden with their gas-masks. It proved to be a false alarm and moments later Dodo Benson's valet appeared breathlessly at their door in a tin hat to enquire if they were all right. Rye's first morning of the war ended with their taking sherry at a neighbouring cottage and raising their glasses to 'Victory'.

For the time being, they decided to remain in England – though Una doggedly kept up her enquiries into ways and means of returning to Florence. With the sale of The Forecastle complete, they were homeless, but then they remembered Lynton with its temperate West Country climate and made up their minds to take up temporary quarters at the Cottage Hotel. On September 19 they left Rye just as streams of London evacuee children began pouring into the town. They travelled by hired car, the three of them wedged in the back, Souline sucking sweets 'interminably' and wishing aloud she were back in France. Since their fight in August Una and Evguenia (whom Una secretly and contemptuously nicknamed 'Florrie') had maintained a cold aloofness towards one another. The Russian woman made a show of pointedly ignoring Una by turning her back on her when speaking to John.

Under such circumstances, it was hardly surprising that before the end of the year Souline had taken herself off to Exeter where she found a nursing job. Even Una, not without a certain satisfaction, had to admit that Lynton held few attractions for a 'town bird' like Evguenia. Souline's departure, however, meant another wrench for John. Sick at heart, she sent letters after the girl begging her to steer clear of political 'undesirables' (Souline sometimes taunted John by pretending to 'Red' opinions) and listing the areas she was not permitted to enter as a resident alien. John had earlier set about 'polishing' the book she had been writing in Florence and pronounced it 'fine work', but her health remained precarious. Her eyelids were again causing her trouble and for most of the winter of 1940 (one of the worst in living memory in the West Country) a prolonged bout of flu kept her in bed or semi-convalescent.

Her only relief from this misery was her rediscovery of the delights of riding. Shortly after their arrival in Lynton, she and Una hired ponies from the local livery stables. However, when they came across one of the grooms beating a horse, they quit the stables in disgust and bought their own mounts, an Exmoor pony called Tommy and a farmer's nag, Star. On these, and other horses that later replaced them, the two women would set out each morning across the moors, come rain or shine. The bracing air and the exhilaration of moving across beautiful countryside soon revived John's flagging spirits and rebuilt her strength. In later years Una would look back on these last happy times together as one of her fondest memories of John.

In March they learned to their dismay that new foreign exchange controls meant they would be unable to draw money from England if they went abroad. Una cried at the prospect of losing their cherished Florence home and confided to her Day Book: 'I am beat this time and no mistake.'[8] Their escape was soon irrevocably cut off by Italy's declaration of war against the Allies on June 11. Rumours of Mussolini's move had been circulating for months, but Una had refused to believe it possible right up to the last minute (chiefly because Hitler was allied to the arch-enemy Russia under the Nazi-Soviet Pact). When the blow came, just days before the Germans entered Paris, Una pronounced it 'the foulest action of its kind in centuries'.[9]

The fall of France finally confined Souline to England. Amid rumours of an imminent German invasion across the Channel, John persuaded her to turn in her nursing badge and rejoin them at Lynton. Lodgings were found for her at a Mrs Widdon's house (called 'Spraytonia'). Sick of hotel living, John and Una took the opportunity to rent rooms as well, at a cottage named 'The Wayside' which stood conveniently near the local Catholic church and the convent of the Poor Clares. The house was owned by a couple called Jack and Marjorie Hancock, who not only agreed to let them the whole of the first floor plus the sitting- and dining-room but became their housekeepers as well. They must have been tolerant folk for before long a whole menagerie of pets had followed the new tenants into the cramped cottage: a pekinese called Me (after Mickie Jacob's 'Me' books), another spaniel named Jane, a grey parrot, Charlotte, and a canary, Pippin. In October they were also reunited with Fido, who had been retrieved from Paris by a friend in the spring and had since languished in quarantine kennels at Taunton.

John's experience of the Second World War would be as detached as that of the First. Though they could hear bombing from time to time,

Lynton was never the target of a raid. When the sirens went off, they would gather in the hallway of The Wayside with the animals, for there were no shelters to go to.

John talked of doing war work but her health was not up to it. Occasionally she helped Una man the local Air Raid Patrol telephone. When her eyes made it impossible to write, she took up knitting woollens (though this, like the gum she chewed 'like a vulgar American', served also as an antidote to smoking). In the autumn she began suffering severe attacks of colitis, which the local GP, Dr Anderman, ascribed to an inflamed gall bladder. Without Una, John's plight would have been much worse. Una's energy during these dark days was remarkable for a woman whose own health remained fragile. Not only was she nursing John but she coped singlehandedly with all her correspondence, her business affairs, and the endless frustrations thrown up by her work. In addition, she found time to exercise the dogs, write up her diaries each day, and make shopping expeditions to search for extra meat or butter to supplement their rations.

Souline, of course, had to be considered too. Cooped up in a remote rural community which she hated, the Russian woman went out of her way to be difficult. Dr Anderman confided to Una that Evguenia ranked as the worst hysteric he had ever come across. He blamed her for much of John's ill-health and suggested that if only John would agree to her taking a job elsewhere she would be spared considerable stress. Una hardly needed telling. But Souline turned up her nose at every suggestion. She took up some French coaching locally, but the job was only part-time and she obviously regarded it as a chore. They heard that she showed more interest in chasing a young grammar-school master who was a cousin of Mrs Widdon. She had also become friendly with a family in Lynton called Benn. The Benns had a reputation for left-wing, pro-Soviet leanings and it seems that Souline deliberately used them as a means of baiting John.

By the end of 1940 relations had reached rock bottom again. Souline held a party at Spraytonia on New Year's Eve without inviting John and Una. When she did see them she made such provocative and outrageous statements that John refrained from replying simply to preserve her strength and peace of mind. But her nerves were so shattered that she cried practically every day. Una took care to keep her temper for fear of inflaming the situation. Privately, however, she had come to regard Souline as a monster. At a drinks party hosted by John at the Valley of the Rocks Hotel in Lynton, Una described Evguenia looking fat and almost forty, 'tightly poured into a flowered georgette'. As soon as she arrived, the Russian woman made a bee-line for the 'liquor trolley' where she became increasingly 'crimson and shiny with potations of inferior sherry'.[10]

In the summer of 1941 John's eyes began to give serious cause for concern. The nervous spasm in the lower lids occurred almost continuously and a dry, gritty mucus clogged her upper lids. Una took her to Bath to see an eye specialist, Dr Tizzard. Tizzard recommended an immediate operation on both eyes to save John's sight. The surgery on the left eye was not wholly successful, giving rise to haemorrhaging. John experienced considerable pain and feared disfigurement, but she bore it all with stoicism. In the letters which she insisted Una write to Souline for her, Una reported that Tizzard had pronounced John 'the bravest woman he had ever known'.[11] By October John was still convalescing in the Bath clinic, but she could see well enough to write to Evguenia herself: 'The eyes do not match in size but Tizzard thinks they will do so eventually, in any case there is now no gaping corner or other horror to shock the expectant mothers into miscarriages.'[12] The next letter expressed her exasperation: 'I was supposed to give at most ten days to fourteen days for each eye & I have been here nine weeks!!! I am bloody well fed up.'[13]

On October 25 the doctors finally released her. She returned to Lynton with Una, to be greeted by Souline with a 'chilly peck' on the cheek and few words. Within a month complications set in. The spasms reappeared and her eye-lashes showed signs of growing too far back. Further visits to Tizzard followed. Having apparently botched the operation, the Bath specialist could offer no obvious solution. In exasperation, Una hastened John up to London to see the royal physician, Lord Dawson, and two eminent eye-surgeons, Sir Duke Elder and Dr Williamson Noble. Dawson told John she must give up any idea of further intensive work and John wondered bleakly if she would ever write well again. Then, quite suddenly, her whole system seemed to break down. Abscesses on her gums required the extraction of several teeth. Double pneumonia followed, accompanied by an attack of pleurisy, causing constant retching and coughing. As if this were not enough, her old complaint, haemorrhoids, returned and her digestion fell into turmoil.

The eye operation had to be postponed. Una had taken rooms for them at the Rembrandt Hotel in South Kensington and John lay for weeks in a state of semi-consciousness. Despite John's protests, Souline had applied for a typing course in Oxford and was now established in lodgings there. Once again Una began writing to her on

John's behalf, urging her to send John a daily letter and scolding her when she mentioned her own ailments. On the rare occasions that John could muster the strength to write herself, she tried to be brave and cheerful: 'how I do long for a breath of fresh country air with R.C.P. (Royal Chinkie-Pig) very pompus (sic) & self-important taking me for a walk! Can't you see it with its crown over one ear & its hoofs (sic) polished?'[14]

March 24, 1942, marked the first day that John felt well enough to get up and go for a short drive. London lay blanketed in a thick yellow smog and she was touched by the blitzed Georgian terraces in Regent's Park. 'The poor, helpless old scarred and wounded houses, the dead houses and such an army of ghosts' is how she would describe them on another occasion.[15] In the first week of April Souline appeared at the Rembrandt on one of her rare visits from Oxford. She delivered a bombshell. She stood at the end of John's bed, 'fat & pasty & bloated, her eyes glinting like boot buttons' (as Una put it), and announced that she intended to take a typing job at Basingstoke with the Red Cross. John had always understood that, at the end of her course in Oxford, Evguenia would return to Devon. The Russian insisted she would henceforth do as she liked without reference to John. John grew angry and said she would cut off her allowance. Souline retorted that she didn't care and intimated that she had already sold off some of the British War Loan John had invested for her. 'It is *my* money, anyway!' she insisted. She went on to tell John that she had given her all the best years of her life and received nothing in return. At this point Una tried to intervene but Souline shouted her down. John threatened never to see her again if she did not agree to return to Lynton as arranged. Souline sneered at her, claiming her illness was no more than a ploy, and flounced out openly defiant and abusive. John, Una tells us, looked 'grey & shrunk and trembling'.[16]

The same day Una wrote Souline a letter which began simply 'Evguenia' and was signed 'Una V. Troubridge':

> I think it only right to repeat what I have already told you: that Lord Dawson warned me that [John] had been in a very low state when she fell ill, that she had been 'very *very* ill', that her convalescence could only be a very lengthy one. He is sending her to Lynton to recuperate for the further operation [on her eyes] & if, in such circumstances you decide to go away without keeping her informed of your address (& this at a time when air raids are frequent) and if the strain breaks her down & she dies it will be your doing & on yr. conscience all yr. life.[17]

Two days later an ambulance ferried John back to Lynton. She hoped that Souline might have relented and would be there to greet her. But there was no sign of her.

The next time they saw Evguenia was in July, when she stayed at The Wayside for a week-end. By this time she had been working for a couple of months in Basingstoke, despite the fact that John had cut her allowance to £100 as a mark of disapproval. She now announced she had been offered a job with the BBC foreign monitoring service at Wood Norton in Evesham, Worcestershire. She would be working on French and Russian broadcasts, at a salary of £300, she emphasised pointedly. John did not try to fight her decision. Instead, she fretted anew, over air raids in the Midlands, and implored Souline to write. She also warned against 'plum fever': the Vale of Evesham was a major plum-growing area and if Evguenia should eat too many she would suffer from awful tummy upsets.

By the end of 1942 Souline had changed jobs yet again, this time to a department of the Foreign Office near London. Presumably it entailed using her languages, but the work was apparently of a secret nature and the only address she chose to send John proved to be a box number at the central post office in New Oxford Street. John agreed to supplement her salary (of £156) by continuing the allowance of £100 and adding £24 for heating expenses. The arrangement was intended to be in perpetuity, whatever Souline's salary in the future, provided only she kept John informed of her movements. Evguenia claimed that the peculiar demands of the new job would make it difficult for her to get to see John. Whether this was true or just another excuse (probably a bit of both), John resigned herself to the fact that Souline would now go her own way. 'It is as though', she wrote sadly, 'a dark, thick curtain had been dropped between us, so strange after all these years. But I am glad that you should be doing serious government work for my country . . .'[18]

Una inwardly breathed a huge sigh of relief at this turn of events, but it was not in John to let go completely. 'Remember', John wrote on Christmas Eve 1942, 'that your John, once so active and all over the place, is in the Lynton Prison Camp asking you to feed it once in a while through the prison bars.' The imagery of 'dumb animals', so much a part of her relationship with Souline, always came easily to her when she felt sad and sentimental.

One subject they no longer fought over was Russia. When Churchill announced Britain's alliance with Stalin in the summer of 1941, John was staggered. Una called it 'the final and utmost shame of our country'[19] and they resolved to emigrate as soon as the war ended. But John could not help admiring the Russians' heroic resistance at the siege of Stalingrad in the autumn of 1942: 'Courage they most certainly have to an enormous & glorious extent', she conceded to Evguenia.[20] The impact of events obliged her to review other atti-

tudes too. Reports of the Nazi concentration camps and mass depor-
tations of Jews from Vichy France to the gas-chambers horrified her:

> Bad Jews there certainly are and always have been, but *this*, Ah, no! I love
> France, but I cannot excuse her, she has sunk too low . . . Control the bad
> Jews, yes, by all means, *and* punish good & strong, but a woman is a
> woman and a child is a child, and both should be protected.[21]

Thus, in her own curious way, John's old streak of compassion for the
weak and defenceless, the dominating impulse perhaps in her troubled
life, helped her finally to make her peace with England.

Chapter Twenty-six

At the early sittings with Mrs Leonard, Ladye had repeatedly predicted that John would die before Una. At the time Una had believed it and been much distressed. On occasions since, the thought had crossed her mind, but now, over twenty-five years later when John was in worse health than she had ever been, Una remained curiously resistant to the true gravity of the situation. Perhaps in her relief at the almost complete break with Souline, she suppressed her worst fears and looked forward resolutely to a resumption of her former life with John. She would later write:

> I sometimes wonder that I missed the writing on the wall; that, although from as far back as our later days in Italy John's health had in so many ways been failing, I, who knew her so well and should have been wiser, concentrated upon lesser ailments and remote possibilities, and was misled into attributing much to overwork and to that convenient formula: 'nervous exhaustion'. In common, it must be admitted, with all the doctors who examined her, I never faced up to the fact that there must be some fundamental and sinister cause for the steady decline of her general condition.[1]

At the end of March 1943 John's health collapsed again. Severe attacks of colitis were accompanied by extremely painful haemorrhoids. A local doctor, Nightingale, examined her and declared she had caught a chill, probably from going fasting to mass on cold early mornings (an explanation that Una dismissed as mere antipathy to Catholicism). When John's pains refused to go away, Una quickly lost patience with Nightingale and decided on a proper examination in London. But beds in hospitals and clinics were full and no place would take Una as well, a prerequisite for both of them: whatever lay ahead, separation was out of the question.

In the end they had to settle for adjoining rooms at the Ritz, at five guineas a day. John required attention day and night, so a nurse, Miss Baldwin, whom they remembered from the London Clinic in Devonshire Place, was hired and came down to Lynton to help with their departure. She was a diminutive woman (John quickly nicknamed her 'little B') and proved good-humoured, resourceful and devoted – 'all that a nurse should be,' Una remarked, mindful perhaps of Souline's bad example.[2] On Sunday, April 11, the little party set out from The Wayside in a Daimler ambulance, accompanied by the dogs which were to be deposited at the kennels in Taunton en route. It was an exit accomplished with their customary sense of style. John, however, would not see Lynton again. Her long 'pilgrimage of grace' (as Una later called it) had entered its most severe stage yet.

Una's Day Books remained silent for almost five months. 'And what months!' she sighed when the record began once more on September 1, retracing the painful events of the intervening period. Installed in bed at the Ritz in her silk pyjamas, John had been examined by Dr Armando Child. He delivered a chilling verdict: an immediate colostomy was a matter of urgency. Horror-struck, Una protested strongly. Child insisted it was John's only hope. True to form, Una brought in a second opinion, Dr Cecil Joll, a leading cancer specialist. Joll confirmed Child's diagnosis, adding that even a colostomy might be only a temporary solution. Una trembled at the prospect, but John asked in a firm voice: 'Do I set my affairs in order?' – to which Joll replied gently: 'It is always wise to do that.' When the doctors had retired, leaving them to reflect on this shattering news, John took Una's hand and spoke almost matter-of-factly: 'Darling, you know, don't you, it may be cancer, and if so, it is God's will and we must not only accept it but welcome it.'[3]

The operation was planned for the following day. Souline, alerted by Una, put in a brief appearance and seemed genuinely shocked and chastened. John heard that Mickie Jacob had called and asked Una to invite her up. They had not seen her since the quarrel in Sirmione in 1935 but John remembered the big Yorkshire woman with genuine affection. 'Hello, Mike – this is a nice business, isn't it?' John exclaimed cheerfully when Mickie shook hands with her. Mickie told her that everything would turn out fine, that they would again visit each other in Italy, but when John asked her to promise to look after Una if she did not survive the operation, Mickie's eyes welled with tears. After she had left them, John smiled and said to Una: 'Poor darling old Mike, she cried so much that she washed her eyeglass out of her eye!'[4]

That same afternoon, after Father Geddes from the Jesuit mission at Farm Street had anointed her, John was taken to Lady Carnarvon's nursing home in Hadley Wood. The home was on the point of closure and a skeleton staff remained behind, John being its last patient. To

Una this counted as an advantage, for it meant less red tape and a relaxation of rules that might have kept John and her apart. At nine that night Dr Joll performed the operation. Afterwards he told Una they had found inoperable cancer of the rectum, but he assured her that the tumour had been isolated by the colostomy and should not cause much pain. This proved less than the truth. During the night the morphia John had been given wore off and she awoke in agony, calling for Una to come to her. A fresh injection was administered and Una sat beside the bed holding her hand throughout the night. 'Every time she opened her eyes she saw my face, knew that I was there and drifted back to sleep. In the morning they told me that she would live.'[5]

After a second operation, Dr Child spoke to John and proved reluctant to tell her the worst. John smiled: 'It isn't fair that you should have been left to hold the baby. Stop trying to think how to tell me I've got inoperable cancer, I know it quite as well as you do . . . '[6] Those around her found this cheerful courage remarkable, as indeed it was. But, as always in a major crisis, John seemed able to project an heroic front. Minor ailments and inconveniences, like a threatening sky which never breaks, left her nervous and irritable. But now that the deluge poured down upon her, she appeared almost to rejoice in its finality and completeness. She had probably known for a long time that she was dying without ever telling Una. She saw it as her war, the war that would make up for the two conflicts she had lived through but not served in, and she intended to die with gallantry. 'I've never seen her show a sign of fear,' marvelled Dr Child.[7] She drew strength from her religious faith, in particular from the conviction which shone through her books that only through suffering could true spirituality be achieved. As Una would put it, 'she wished to be worthy of the fellowship of death'.[8]

During these days Una evidently experienced terrible anguish and trepidation. Yet, curiously, she too felt a kind of elation. 'I wonder whether I, who am unskilled in writing, can ever find words to describe, even dimly, that strange and fulfilling happiness that blossomed for us as we knelt together in the Garden of Gethsemane,' she wrote later.[9] As the inevitable drew closer, never in all their twenty-eight years together had she been so confident of John's complete love and devotion. It represented the perfect ending after all the heartbreak of the Souline years, the final vindication of Una's unwavering fidelity. Holding hands in the shaded stillness of the clinic room or taking communion together at John's bedside, there were moments during these long weeks of pain and sorrow when they were utterly content and at peace. One day John turned to Una and suddenly exclaimed fiercely: 'I want you, you, *you*; I want only you in all the world.'[10]

The repetitive emphasis, again so reminiscent of Ladye, only made Una's triumph the sweeter. For years she had shared John with others. In the beginning there had been the ever-present, sometimes oppressive shadow of Ladye. Then had come the only too physical reality of Souline, a worthless 'chit' of a girl whose hold on John Una found frankly inexplicable. Over and above all this burned that other flame which John tended so lovingly, her writing, a silent passion that consumed her for days and nights at a time and rendered her oblivious to anything else. Now each of these rivals was forgotten and John turned only to Una: 'you, you, *you*'. John emphasised that it was entirely for Una, not Souline, that she clung to a life she considered hideous and hopeless. She showed kindness and concern whenever Evguenia called, and continued to write short notes to her signed 'Your John'. But to Una she explained she did it merely for form's sake. The Russian woman had been relegated to being no more than 'the object of a mild benevolent and tolerant affection'.[11] John scarcely ever asked to see her now, Una noted with quiet satisfaction.

John spent seven weeks at Lady Carnarvon's home. She had her own day and night nurses round the clock. A bed in a connecting room was made available for Una, but she never once used it, preferring to sleep by John's bedside stretched out across two arm-chairs. She would leave the clinic for a brief twenty minutes each day, to take a walk in the gardens or along the golf links where they had once exercised the dogs together in the Chip Chase days.

When the nursing home in Hadley Wood finally closed, Una moved John to another in Primrose Hill. They hated the place. It was dingy and oppressive, but the only one available which could take them both. After a 'nightmare' week, a vacancy suddenly came up at the London Clinic. They were given a single room divided in two by sliding doors, with a divan for Una when she did not sleep on the chair by John's bed. Mickie Jacob visited every Sunday afternoon, Una coming downstairs to see her and relate John's progress.

Finally, at the beginning of August, Una rented a flat in Dolphin Square, a huge residential block of luxury apartments on the embankment in Pimlico. It surrounded a quadrangle of trim gardens, contained its own arcade of shops, and was divided into 'houses', each named after a famous British admiral. John and Una moved into 502, Hood House, a spacious furnished flat in which a bed was made up for John in the drawing-room. The devoted 'little B' had to leave them, to be replaced by two special nurses, Reid and Sailes, who attended the patient in shifts day and night.

Adept at self-deception where John was concerned, Una still believed she could make a partial recovery. The tactful Dr Joll, though privately sceptical, had hinted at the possibility. She envisaged wheeling John about the gardens before the warm weather gave way to autumn. Dr Child could not bring himself to disillusion her. John exclaimed incredulously: 'Is no one going to tell Lady Troubridge that I'm dying?'[12]

However, by mid-September the truth could no longer be disguised even from Una. A devastating pain crept over John, kept at bay only by increasingly heavy doses of morphine. The doctors expressed surprise – or perhaps they just pretended to – that the cancer had not affected her earlier, for it lay up against her sacrum, close to the major spinal nerve. John experienced constant nausea, retching every two hours or so, the effort leaving her weak and exhausted. As the pain became more intrusive, spreading to her back, her bladder and her right leg, Dr Child switched her to heroin injections. The morphia had made her delirious and for the first time Una realized from John's ramblings the full extent of her pent-up disgust at the indignity of her pitiful condition. Una knew now that the end could not, must not, be prolonged. 'What a life!' John murmured one day to the nurse. Then, seeing Una, added quickly: 'I wouldn't do it except for you; I wouldn't fight. It's only for your sake . . . '[13]

Both women were acutely conscious of the symbolism of the moment. This was John's Calvary. In describing the unearthly beauty of John's face in the hour of her suffering, Una compared it to a medieval ivory carving of the crucifixion:

> Her head droops in the pillow with closed eyes and resigned mouth, with the lovely clean planes of her wasted oval face as it were His after death on the Cross. Her hands too are of a beauty that makes my heart ache, so white and thin and spiritual, and so utterly heartbreaking in their weak confidence of touch; hands that were so muscular and strong and decided in their grasp and in all their movements.[14]

Throughout it all John preserved a Christ-like stoicism. 'She is patient, courteous and courageous; thanking the nurses; apologising to them for what they must do for her; telling me how good I am; that I shall be rewarded; that this is no life for me; that I look tired . . . Several times she has cried at the thought of my loneliness when she is gone.' Una could hardly bear it when, in an effort to be cheerful, John's smile broke through. 'On her pale, emaciated face, it has the gallant sweetness, the touch of rakeishness (sic) it has always had, but it is a faint ghost, an essence of its former self.'[15]

From time to time Evguenia called and looked grieved by John's pitiful state. But Una could not help feeling that the Russian woman's emotion was a shallow display, her visits timed to fit conveniently between hair appointments or invitations to lunch or dinner with friends. Andrea came, as did Viola. Both tried to persuade Una, with the best of intentions, that she had a future after John. There was, for example, her young grandchild Nicholas. Una inwardly flared with anger. 'Why should I live for them?' she asked herself.[16]

By the end of September the doctors predicted it could only be a matter of days. 'My whole soul shrinks from what must come,' Una wrote. 'But I have a secret hope that however honestly and earnestly I may try to resume life, I shall metaphorically bleed to death before very long and so be allowed to depart in peace from an earth that holds nothing for me.'[17] This plea became a calm conviction that she would rapidly follow John to her death. Yet, strikingly, at the height of her ordeal, Una's health had never been better. She was eating and sleeping well and her chronic headaches had disappeared – and this despite attending to John three or four times a night. In all their years together Una's well-being had been bound up with her love affair with John. Now that John was giving her the exclusive attention she craved, perhaps for the first time in their long relationship, her ailments fell away.

The two of them discussed whether, after John's death, they should try to re-establish contact through Mrs Leonard's mediumship. Both firmly agreed it was unnecessary. 'I don't think,' Una observed, 'I shall want a hypothetical John diluted by the worthy and honest but alien Mrs Leonard.'[18] In 1931 they had read the medium's auto-biography *My Life in Two Worlds* and judged it over-sensational, 'blatant spiritualism of the silliest brand'. They were glad the book did not mention them by name. Now, after years of flirting with the supra-normal, they preferred to put their trust in traditional religious faith, in the 'communion of saints', in the hope that John's 'pure spirit' would find its way to Una 'somehow through my obstructing flesh'.[19]

Father Geddes again anointed John and served private mass to the two women, Una sharing John's wafer. On September 28 Harold Rubinstein called and drafted a last Will. If Souline felt she still had any vestige of influence over John, she was to be disappointed. Una's hold proved, in death, to be all-embracing. John left her everything, entrusting her only 'to make such provision for our friend Eugenie (sic) Souline as in her absolute discretion she may consider right knowing my wishes for the welfare of the said Eugenie Souline'. What this meant, as Una understood it, was that Evguenia should not be allowed to starve but neither should she be so mollycoddled as to avoid working. When Rubinstein had left and they were alone, John cried tears of happiness at the thought that Una's future was now fully safeguarded.

The final days, in the first week of October, passed with a numbing, dull clarity. Physically and emotionally exhausted, Una fretted that the record she was keeping would seem lifeless, that it would not fulfil its purpose 'of seizing and preserving some fragments of this precious and terrible time'.[20] One can see that she was already planning for the future in her organized way, already constructing the legend of which she alone would be the keeper.

On Saturday, October 2, John woke quite coherent. Una kissed her and John kissed her back. When Una left the room to answer the telephone, John exclaimed pathetically: 'Don't leave me!' That evening they could hear the boom of guns. John asked: 'There's a raid, isn't there?' Una nodded and said: 'I'll put on my slacks and sit beside you.' John lay quietly listening, then remarked, as if to herself: 'Well, I can't do anything about it anyhow.' With that she drifted off to sleep – 'and so did I in the armchair beside her.'[21]

As Dr Child increased her doses of heroin, John slipped into an unreal world somewhere between waking and unconsciousness. She wept frequently at the thought that Una would be alone after her death. At other times she showed a curious telepathy, or perhaps she was simply confused, accepting matter-of-factly whatever Una told her and saying she knew already. One day, à propos of nothing, she remembered her faithful old collie of Ladye's time and remarked quite suddenly in a quiet tone: 'Rufus is standing beside me with his head on my arm.'[22] When John was conscious, Una read aloud from the works of Robert and Elizabeth Barrett Browning. In Florence a marble tablet on the Casa Guidi bore testimony to the poets' stay in the city and John and Una had eagerly sought out every book about the couple that they could lay their hands on. 'As we read of the peace and beauty of their life together John evolved the idea that after the war, if and when we returned to Italy, we would try to obtain a lease of their apartment. She would say thoughtfully: "I think I should like to work in the rooms where Robert and Ba were so happy together . . ."'[23] It was no more than a fond dream now.

On October 5 Una reminded John that their old friend Dom Thomas Symons of Downside, with whom John had recently corresponded, had spoken of her ordeal as her 'purgatory'. 'She looked upwards and said quite collectedly: "I offer it to God." '[24] It was her last coherent statement. In the early hours of October 6 her pulse beat so feebly that Una thought she must be dying and fervently murmured prayers over her. John rallied slightly, then sank back into a coma. At 6.30 that evening Souline appeared but went out again within half an hour, leaving, Una noted, no phone number where she could be contacted. 'But what does it matter?' she confided to the Day Book with calm resignation, 'John does not want her or anyone but me.'[25]

The end came the following night, at seven minutes past eight: 'my belovèd went straight to God and saw the Beatific Vision'. The 'final severing of the silver cord', as Una put it, occurred peacefully, marked only by a slight spasm as of something passing through a difficult narrow opening. For the last two hours John had silently gazed up at Una 'in a perfect communion of heart and spirit'. Her final gesture was to squeeze Una's hand gently. The two nurses in attendance declared it the most extraordinary thing they had ever witnessed.[26]

Looking down on John's lifeless body, Una felt it had been transformed:

> At one moment it was my belovèd – wasted, drawn, lividly pale and at times distorted – the next a stranger lay there on the bed. Very handsome, very peaceful, very calm, but with scarcely a traceable resemblance to my John. After she had been laid out and later when the bandage was removed from her head, Sailes and I stood looking down at her and I said: 'Poor boy, he must have suffered a lot before he died . . . ' It seemed a young airman or soldier who perhaps had died of wounds after much suffering. Ivory clear and pale, the exquisite line of the jaw, the pure aquiline of the nose with its delicate wing nostrils, the beautiful modelling of eyelids and brow. Not a trace of femininity; no one in their senses could have suspected that anything but a young man had died.[27]

Una had kept her vigil at the bedside for over sixty hours without proper sleep, sustained only by cups of tea and coffee. After it was all over she lay down on the bed made up next to John's and slept soundly beside the corpse, confident that for John at least release from her suffering had come: 'now the agony is only mine.' The next day Mickie Jacob called and asked if she could have a glimpse of John, for old times' sake. Una politely but firmly refused. 'You have no right, Una!' Mickie suddenly flared. 'I have every right,' Una replied quietly, 'Now, Mike, please go.'[28] The Guardian of the Lamp already stood at her post. Henceforth she alone controlled the gateway to the inner sanctum.

Chapter Twenty-seven

Una had John's body embalmed and laid in a mahogany coffin lined with lead. The brass name plate read:

Radclyffe Hall
Author
1943
". . . And if God Choose I Shall
But Love Thee Better After Death"

The quotation came from one of Elizabeth Browning's *Sonnets from the Portuguese*. The coffin lay for a time in Westminster Cathedral and was then transferred to the vault in Highgate Cemetary. Behind the tomb's iron grille Ladye's coffin reposed longitudinally on the stone bench to the right. Una had John's laid in pride of place horizontally facing the entrance. When her own time came, she intended to take up her rightful position on the left flank, forming once and for all the appropriate memorial to '*Our Three Selves*'. Later, on the left of the doorway, Una arranged for a marble plaque to be erected which bore the name '*Radclyffe Hall*' and the same quotation from Mrs Browning. Underneath that one name was inscribed: '*Una*'.

On October 28 a requiem mass for John took place at the Jesuit chapel in Farm Street. Una had invited Agnes Nichols to sing a solo at the service but on the day the famous soprano was too ill to attend. In her place a tenor from the resident choir sang 'Panis Angelicus' by César Franck, which pleased Una because it struck a note of hope not sorrow. Over one hundred guests came, including the Holroyd-Reeces, Andrea, Viola, Souline, Audrey Heath, Patience Ross, and Harold Rubinstein – in other words, 'family' and business associates rather than old friends, a measure of their isolation in the last years. Una donated a huge floral wreath and at the end stood at the chapel door calmly receiving the condolences of the congregation as they filed out.

A few days later she carefully redrafted her Will. Her chief concern was to safeguard the future of John's literary property, the copyright of her novels in particular and of *The Well of Loneliness* above all others. Since the ban of 1928 several pornographic imitations of the novel had appeared, purporting to be the unexpurgated edition, and Una was determined this should never happen again. Accordingly she entrusted all John's literary rights to the publisher John Holroyd-Reece. Of all their supporters in *The Well* affair, he had appeared to them the most consistently loyal and helpful.

Just before her death John had asked Una to destroy her last book, the one about the Merano shoemaker. Though both believed it was up to her highest standards, it remained only half finished. John had also felt that too much of her suffering at the hands of Souline had gone into the novel. By the end she forgave Evguenia and had no wish to open old wounds with an account of their affair that might be identifiable. Nor, it must be said, did Una, despite her reluctance to obliterate anything that belonged to John. 'I gave her my promise,' Una recalled, 'and after her death I lost no time in carrying out that promise.'[1] Some people subsequently believed the book had been destroyed because it dealt openly with homosexuality again. When Una came to write her memoir of John, she took pains to deny this.[2]

In the first few weeks after John's death, Una experienced a strange calm. Her gruelling vigil appeared to leave no ill effects. She slept tolerably well and wept hardly at all. 'Where is the use of weeping as though it could bring relief?' she observed dully. After a week's silence, the Day Book began again 'in the quiet knowledge that, physically speaking, utter desolation must be my daily and hourly portion'. Up to John's death, the Day Book had run to some sixty volumes. After her death, scores of further volumes would be written but Una decided to call them 'Letters To John', addressing each entry personally to her beloved.

Her faith was now Una's only consolation – that and the cherished memory of the perfect love they had affirmed at John's death-bed. 'I can never now feel,' she wrote in one of the first 'Letters', 'as unhappy or as restless as I have felt during your earthly lifetime when for any reason there was a shadow of misunderstanding between us – this sorrow has *not* got that insupportable bitter quality – since now we are one for evermore.'[3] This confidence in their ultimate and eternal union was confirmed when, shortly after John's death, Una found a letter that John had secretly written and set aside for her. The letter has not survived but Una tells us that it ended 'God keep you until we meet again . . . and believe in my love, which is much, much stronger than mere death . . .'[4] The echo of Christ's parting sentiments to his disciples is unmistakable.

For a time Una stayed on at the flat in Dolphin Square. She felt in no hurry to leave the place where, as she put it, 'certain sacred and unforgettable things happened'. She slept in John's bed, wore the old French beret John had taken to in her later years, and even had John's blue and grey tweed suits altered to fit her. At first, the two nurses, Sailes and Reid, remained to keep Una company in her grief, but with characteristic impatience she quickly found them tiresome and over-familiar. Before long they were sent packing. Alone in the apartment, she talked to John aloud as if she were still present.

She had few English friends of her own. Occasionally she visited Andrea, who had divorced Toby Warren in 1941 and now worked for the BBC as its first woman news-reader. She also got back in touch with Jaqueline Hope (now Mrs Hope-Nicholson), who still lived at More House in Tite Street and who gave her a key so she could come and go as she wished. It was ironic that Una, by temperament so much more gregarious than John, should end up so isolated, but in the later years almost all their friends, Italians excepted, had been primarily John's admirers and associates. Yet Una had few regrets. In the future her single most important criterion of friendship would remain unqualified loyalty to or admiration for Radclyffe Hall. No widow could have served her husband's memory more faithfully.

The intense emotion generated by her experience of John's lingering death allowed Una to keep the full shock of her bereavement at bay for some time. She had only to recall John's heroic example to hanker for a similar martyrdom, willing herself to believe she wanted no lessening of her suffering: 'Rather do I want to bear the anguish of my love and pain as I would a stigmatisation, as an honour and spiritual gift to be endured and cherished.'[5] But by the end of 1943, having tied up John's affairs and with time on her hands, a growing sense of desolation swept over her. Wandering mournfully among the bomb craters and scarred buildings of Pimlico or riding back in the cab from one of her frequent visits to the tomb at Highgate, she would suddenly find herself in tears. In shops and restaurants she had to exercise an iron self-control to prevent herself breaking down. 'Darling,' she agonized in the 'Letters', 'this isn't just pain, it is torture . . . my God, if it weren't for a stubborn instructive holding to a faith that is in me . . . that we shall, we *must* meet again, I wouldn't endure this thing another hour . . .'[6]

In the New Year she finally moved out of Dolphin Square to a flat in Lincoln's Inn. It belonged to John Holroyd-Reece, who lived underneath. He and Jeanne had repeatedly urged her to take it, if only to be close to people who could look after her during air raids. Una eventually acquiesced, for the company rather than her personal safety. V-bombs meant nothing to her beyond the hope that she would end up dead without having to kill herself. Though sometimes frightened, she never once resorted to an air-raid shelter. She always slept in her flat and went about her life as if the Blitz scarcely existed. One night a flying bomb fell in nearby Chancery Lane, shattering a glass partition all over her bed. A large shard buried itself in her pillow. Though it happened in the small hours, Una had just got up to make herself a cup of tea in the kitchen. She suffered merely shock and minor cuts. 'No life is so immune as that which seems intolerable,' she commented drily.[7]

What kept her going was the abiding conviction that she would soon rejoin John. In January 1944 she issued precise instructions to Harold Rubinstein for her burial. Her body was to be embalmed, as John's had been, by Garstin's of Baker Street. She should be attired in her blue silk pyjamas and be wearing, among other jewellery, her two gold medallion neckchains with attached crucifix. In her clasped hands she wanted to hold her large cornchain and silver rosary, on her breast to be laid the wooden cross that normally hung over her bed. The coffin-plate would bear the inscription:

> Una Vincenzo Troubridge,
> The Friend of Radclyffe Hall:
> Arrive at last the blessèd goal
> When He that died in Holy Land
> Would reach us out the shining hand,
> And take us as a single soul.

Opposite the dedicatory plaque to John in the entrance to the Highgate tomb was to be erected another, bearing the same lines as on Una's coffin lid but with the addition (after the name 'Radclyffe Hall') of the words: *'with whom she shared a home for nearly twenty-nine years'*.

Una was to survive John by almost exactly twenty years, and die and be buried several thousand miles away from the sacred shrine to *'Our Three Selves'*.

Even before John's death, the question of Radclyffe Hall's reputation had begun to exercise Una. She worried about the potentially harmful effect of the Souline affair. After John's death, word reached her that

Evguenia was spreading fictions about this period of John's life –
fictions which, however absurd, could only reflect badly on John's
character and judgement. John's conduct during the Souline years
had indeed frequently been embarrassing and culpable. Una asked
herself whether this record of John's 'weakness' should be destroyed. Her inclination, after rereading the Day Books, was that it
should at any rate never be made public. She left an instruction to
this effect in the front of volume 22 of the Day Books, emphasizing
that nothing was for publication after June 28, 1934 – the day she
fell ill in Bagnoles and telephoned the American Hospital in Paris
for a nurse.

At the same time her conviction grew that she must leave behind
her an unequivocal record of her life with John, as the Ladies of
Llangollen had done, 'to cheer and encourage those who come after
us'.[8] Somehow the Souline episode had to be accommodated within
this record but in such a way as to underline John's exemplary qualities and the mutual devotion of John and Una. 'It is my duty,' Una
told John in the 'Letters', 'as "guardian of the lamp" of your genius
and our enduring love.'[9]

The result was *The Life and Death of Radclyffe Hall*, which Una
wrote in one intensive burst over four weeks in early 1945. It is a
strange book, in the form of a letter to her readers, almost two
hundred pages long, with no chapter headings, few dates, and little
chronology. In the preface Una declares that she aims to tell 'the
truth, the whole truth and nothing but the truth', for John herself
'always dwelt of choice in the palace of truth'. In fact, apart from
some waspish aspersions against friends who later dropped out of
favour, the account is resoundingly discreet and, as we have seen,
must be used cautiously as a reliable source. In many ways it tells us
far more about Una than John. The memoir rarely rises above hag-
iography. What is less to be expected is its artlessness. In her letters
and diaries Una showed she was quite capable of an elegant and
vivid style, with a sharp, often humorous, eye for character and
detail. Little of this is evident in her biography. One can only
wonder yet again at the remarkable way in which Una sacrificed her
own considerable talents and judgement to her obsession with John.

Una's account of the Souline affair merits barely three pages in
her book. It gives no impression that the relationship was physical,
still less that John was sexually enslaved to the Russian girl. Evguenia is portrayed as selfish, volatile, and supremely uninterested in
John's literary endeavours. She and John – 'a sensitive, highly-
evolved European' – are as incompatible as 'oil and water'. Una
implies that, once the novelty wore off, the liaison became for John

largely a matter of doing her best for an unprotected refugee girl with TB:

> in John all that was finest came at once to the surface; all her genius for compassion and protection was concentrated upon a determination to restore this afflicted friend to health. I can look back upon her patience, her endurance, her complete selflessness with immense pride and I am thankful to remember that in spite of my inevitable jealousy, and my distress at such a disastrous interruption to her work I rallied whole-heartedly to her determination that we should devote our combined energies to that end.[10]

Una's own diaries and John's passionate letters tell a different story.

Una withheld publication of the *Life* until 1961, when almost all the people mentioned in it were dead. Perhaps she recalled John's own reason for wanting her last novel destroyed: '"It isn't forgiveness if one leaves a record that might be recognised and give pain ..."'[11] Certainly Souline had died by this date – by an ironic coincidence, of cancer of the bowel. Up to the last she preyed upon Una for money. By making Una her executrix, John had effectively created a parallel situation to that which had prevailed between John and Cara after Ladye's death. Evguenia claimed she had been cheated of her due and resorted to angry tantrums and abusive letters. Una, to her credit, scrupulously abided by the letter (if not always the spirit) of John's injunction. She continued Souline's existing allowance of £125. While she lived, the Russian woman was to have priority over the Order of the Poor Clares, whom John intended should be the ultimate recipients of most of her wealth after Una's death. In case, as seemed likely, Una predeceased Souline, the Russian woman would receive a tax-free annuity of £350 for the remainder of her life.

As Evguenia came to terms with the fact that Una held the purse-strings, her mood grew more conciliatory. After the war, when well into her forties, she married a Russian emigré, Vladimir Maka-roff, who worked in a London bookshop. For a time she had a job with the BBC Foreign Service but by 1950 was pressing for more money. She reminded Una of a scene that had taken place at John's bedside during her last days. She related how John had joined their hands and said: '"I want you to be friends. There will be enough for both of you if not to live in luxury – in comfort. But you, Evguenia, shall ask Una's advice ..."'[12] Una furiously denied any such scene had occurred and rebuked Souline for inventing fantasies. However, she did send her small sums to supplement the allowance, and later helped the Makaroffs repay a loan they had borrowed to set up a boarding-house. The wheedling tone of Evguenia's letters to Una speaks for itself. She sugared her entreaties for money with staunchly anti-communist opinions (this during the Korean War) that sat oddly with her previous pro-Soviet views, and repeatedly insisted she was paying regular visits to 'dear Johnnie's' tomb and saying prayers for her. None of it deceived Una.

After Souline's death, Una made an effective job of expunging her from the official record. She released to her literary executor only the pre-1934 diaries. Had not Makaroff sold his wife's letters, which eventually surfaced at the University of Texas, the full story might never have come to light. Of the almost 700 items of correspondence in the Texas collection, covering the period 1934-42, only one is from Souline to John – a whining letter, appropriately enough, justifying her plans to set up a shop in Paris. Others have never been found and one must assume that Una destroyed them.

Marie Visetti was eighty-nine when John died, a chronic invalid crippled with arthritis and firmly ensconced in a Brighton hotel. Age had never mellowed her and she nursed her resentment of her daughter to the bitter end. 'You will see by the enclosed that Margarite (sic) is dead,' she wrote to Jane Caruth in October 1943.

> The shock was rather terrible one of the guests came into my room at lunch and asked me if I had seen the Telegraph – I said no I was in a hurry to get out, she showed me the deaths and wondered if that was a relation of mine, of course when I saw 'author' I knew I told the woman I did not think so. [13]

Her chief concern after John's death was that her annuity of £200 should be safe, for the Will did not mention her. She believed that Una had exerted some sinister control over John – a view confirmed when Una told her she *might* receive 'a hundred or two' if she co-operated with photographs and other 'unmalicious' material for the memoir on John.

Marie died in 1945. Though sorely provoked by her mother, John had never been able totally to ignore her or forget her filial responsibility. Marie, in fact, must have powerfully reinforced John's long-standing belief that compassion was invariably destined to be misconstrued and exploited.

Postscript

After the war Una returned to her beloved Florence, where she and John had intended to put down permanent roots. At first she was afraid to go back. The thought of walking alone those familiar streets and bridges, sitting without John in Doney's tea rooms or in Giacosa's, seemed intolerable.[1] But as time passed, her reasons for staying in England began to look increasingly threadbare. Minna died in 1947 (the same year as Edy Craig) and in 1948 Andrea remarried, to a forty-six year old brigadier, Douglas Turnbull, who took her off to Abyssinia where he was the British military attaché. Thereafter Una's loneliness, her loathing for England's damp grey climate, and her nostalgia for the consolations provided by a Catholic country, all combined to make the move to Italy an obvious one.

Before she left, she achieved one last ambition. At John's death, *The Well of Loneliness* was still selling a remarkable 100,000 copies a year world-wide. But it remained excluded from Britain. In 1934 she and John had tried unsuccessfully to get Cape to republish the novel through their medical list. After the war, Una persisted in her efforts to reinstate the book in England. After all, *The Times* obituary of John had spoken of 'her sterling literary qualities, her well-controlled emotional pitch, her admirable prose style'.[2] In 1946 Una lobbied the Labour Home Secretary, J. Chuter Ede, submitting him a first edition of the book. He proved unhelpful. In fact, what was required was not a change in the law so much as a publisher resolute enough to test whether the law would still be applied. Such a publisher materialized a couple of years later in the Falcon Press (subsequently Hammond & Hammond), which finally brought out the novel in 1949 without official reaction.

The Well of Loneliness continues to sell steadily today in many languages and has passed through numerous imprints. The latest edition (1983) was brought out by the feminist publishing house Virago and, the final irony, it has even been broadcast to the nation on the BBC's 'Book at Bedtime'.[3]

Una arrived in Florence in early 1949 and settled into a spacious garden-flat in the Palazzo Guicciardini, near the Ponte Vecchio. She put up a name-plate on the front door which bore the names 'Radclyffe Hall' and 'Troubridge', one above the other. In the hallway stood shelves of books containing the first editions of all John's work. Every volume in her library (some 4,000 in all) carried a small printed name-plate on the fly-leaf inscribed 'Radclyffe Hall/Una Troubridge'. In the vaulted living-room, dominated by a huge radiogram, pictures of John hung on the walls or were ranged about the room. In front of one, a framed photograph in the living-room, Una would place fresh flowers each morning – a ritual that John too had once carried out after Ladye's death.

Una was a wealthy woman, for John had left her over £118,000 (and this excluded royalties on her books). She lived comfortably but with a certain frugality. She attended early mass every morning, ate only two meals a day, rarely drank, and never slept more than six hours a night. A single maid, Prinetta, looked after her cleaning and cooking. To those unused to her, Una could project a severe, almost intimidating image. Small and slight (she weighed only seven stone, as on her wedding day), with greying, close-cropped hair, no make-up, a collar and tie, and a deep, blunt tone of voice, she now commonly wore John's clothes and jewellery – giving rise to the catch-phrase 'Una's weeds are John's tweeds' among amused observers. Her loyalty to John's memory remained unswerving and unqualified. Other women, and notably other lesbians, were expected to support to the hilt the objectives for which John had stood in her lifetime. Not surprisingly, Una had few close women friends, preferring instead the company of the homosexual or aesthetic type of man who could talk easily about art, books and music.

James Lees-Milne met her at a dinner party in Florence. She wore John's dinner jacket and black bow tie, and Lees-Milne was surprised to discover when they were introduced that she was not a man. She dwelled entirely in the past, he recalled, talking constantly about John. She spoke intelligently about d'Annunzio but then caused some embarrassment by bluntly asking her fellow-guest Julian Amery: 'Are you the brother of the boy they hanged?' – which he was, his brother having been executed after the war for acting as a sort of Lord Haw-Haw figure (the affair shattered the Amery family).[4]

Una could be equally disconcerting to those who knew her well. When young Felix Hope-Nicholson, Jaqueline's son, reached Rome in 1949 on a return journey from Greece, he found that he had run out of money (British travellers abroad were only permitted to take £25 out of the country). He wrote to Una asking her for a loan. She replied that she never, on principle, lent money and she advised him to get back into the 'sterling area' as fast as possible.[5] It was a harsh rejoinder after all the support and hospitality Jaqueline's family had shown Una after John died.

As it became obvious that her expectations of an early death were not to be fulfilled, Una began to pick up old interests again, art and music in particular, the twin enthusiasms of her youth. She and John had collected a number of medieval 'Old Masters', or so they believed, and Una now scoured Florence for further 'finds'. She became very excited when she thought she had discovered a Botticelli, which was proudly displayed to visitors to her apartment. Harold Acton regarded it as bogus.[6] She took up translating again, notably Guareschi's *Don Camillo* books, one of which *The Little World of Don Camillo* was turned into an Italian film that Una translated for English dubbing purposes. Above all, she revived her early interest in opera, an art form that John never really liked. Her record collection in Florence was enormous. She spent many hours listening to opera on the radio and regularly attended performances at La Scala, Milan, and all over Italy. She adored Wagner and a new production of *Parsifal*, her favourite opera, would always draw her.

One such, conducted by Fürtwangler at La Scala in 1951, provided the occasion for a meeting that marks the postscript to Una's long and remarkable life. Staying at her hotel in Milan was a young Italian bass, Nicola Rossi-Lemeni, who stood on the threshold of a distinguished operatic career. He was rehearsing for another production in the La Scala repertoire, Grunsberg's setting of Eugene O'Neill's *The Emperor Jones*. Within days he and Una became friends and she subsequently assisted with the opera's libretto. Thereafter she immersed herself in the singer's career, acting as a combination of patron, admirer and confidante. She was convinced of his greatness and he admired her impressive knowledge and understanding of music.

In the mid-fifties Una moved to Rome, to a flat in the Piazza Novella just across the square from Rossi-Lemeni and his family. The total absorption in another's life which had marked her relationship with John was now repeated. Rossi-Lemeni became for her 'the son I never had'.[7] Every morning she would sit at the window of her apartment and watch for 'Nika' to make his appearance. She followed him all over the world wherever he was singing, even, despite her fear of flying, as far afield as Brazil and San Francisco. By her death she had attended some 500 of his performances. 'Thanks to my John,' she told

Mickie Jacob, 'I can do most of the journeys in sleepers in which I sleep like a dormouse, an inheritance I sometimes think from my father, the King's Messenger.'[8]

As well as Mickie Jacob, Una kept in touch with Colette, Natalie and Romaine. Apart from Colette (who died in 1954, the same year as Lily Clermont-Tonnerre), they would be among the few old friends to outlive her. Andrea too remained a regular and affectionate correspondent. Una had been touched by her daughter's ready sympathy and support at the time of John's death and revised her previously harsh opinion of her. In 1944 she re-read the sections of the Day Book for 1931 in which she had lambasted Andrea as a liar and a sponger. She wrote in the fly-leaf of the volume that, should it ever be published, all unkind references to Andrea should be erased since she had become 'an admirable, unselfish, generous woman'. It did not prevent her, however, from labelling her grandson Nicholas 'an altogether odious brat' and a 'hooligan',[9] and she later refused to help towards paying the boy's school fees.

Despite this rapprochement, Una preserved a certain detachment from Andrea. Her characteristic self-absorption (which meant her absorption with John) reasserted itself once she had established her life in Italy. But perhaps, also, there lingered a residue of resentment that rankled, a suspicion (not unfounded) that Andrea had never reconciled herself to John's place in her life. There could be no real forgiveness, in Una's eyes, under such circumstances.

Andrea was to die, tragically, in 1966, the victim of a car accident in Gloucestershire. Despite her unorthodox upbringing, she appears to have grown into a stable, cheerful woman with a capacity for loyalty and affection. More settled backgrounds have produced less.

Una died in Rome at the age of seventy-six on September 24, 1963, of cancer of the liver. She never lost her conviction that she would rejoin John, and she wrote the 'Letters' till within days of her death. On August 12 she had remembered, as always, John's birthday: 'I sent Nada [her maid] to get flowers.' She had rarely felt entirely at home in the post-war world. Her wealth allowed her to go her own aloof way, but she admitted she felt 'older than God' in her last years.[10] Sending her condolences to the widow of her step-son, Tom Troubridge, who died in 1949, she had written: 'I can truthfully say I wouldn't if I could bring one I loved back to the world as it is today: no place for people who can think and suffer. They are *so* much better off where they are.'[11]

Just before she died Una redrafted her Will. To the last her chief concern remained John's work and reputation. Relations with John Holroyd-Reece had long since deteriorated, for she suspected that his loyalty owed more to mercenary motives than literary considerations. In his place she appointed as her literary executor a friend of Harold Rubinstein, the publisher Lovat Dickson, with whom she had already discussed an authorized biography of John.[13] She left £2,000 to Andrea, and £2,000 to Cancer Relief (not Cancer Research as this involved vivisection, which she and John had always deplored). The rest of the estate, well over £100,000, was to be given to the Order of the Poor Clares in Lynton – as John wished. The document reflects Una's priorities: God and John before family. Dickson was charged with ensuring that nothing 'detrimental to the dignity and nobility' of John's works would ever be permitted, and none of her books was to be expurgated or abbreviated. As for Una's own diaries and Day Books (including the 'Letters'), some 200 volumes in all, these were left to Nicola Rossi-Lemeni. They remain in his possession today, an indispensable source for the life behind the legend of Radclyffe Hall.

Una was buried before the instructions she had given to Rubinstein in 1944 were discovered (they lay unopened in her bank at Minehead). Moreover, in the intervening years she had never insisted to the Rossi-Lemenis that her body should be interred in England. Perhaps, after all, she had come to believe that physical separation mattered little to her reunion with John as 'a single soul'. Her grave rests in a small plot in the section of Rome's Verano cemetary reserved for 'Foreign Catholics'. It is marked by a flat marble slab engraved in bold letters. Her Christian names are given, wrongly, as '*Una Vicenzo*' and, beneath a line from St Francis's 'Song of the Beasts' ('Laudato Si', Mi Signora, Per Sora Nostra Morte Corporale'), stands the ringing phrase '*There is no death!*', attributed to '*John Radcliffe* (sic) *Hall*' (the quotation, inscribed in the fly-leaf of John's Bible, is in fact from Longfellow). Despite such inaccuracies, the sentiments were appropriate and Una would have approved.

Shortly before Una's death, the author Ethel Mannin, long an admirer of Radclyffe Hall, wrote and asked her how she and John had squared their relationship with their religion. What did they do about confession? Una replied simply: 'There was nothing to confess.'[13]

Notes and Sources

Most of the material for this book was drawn from three sources: the Lovat Dickson Collection at the National Archive in Ottawa; the Radclyffe Hall Collection at the Humanities Research Centre, University of Texas (mainly Radclyffe Hall's correspondence with Evguenia Souline); and a private collection (containing chiefly Una Troubridge's Day Books and 'Letters to John') in the hands of Nicola Rossi-Lemeni in Fregene, Italy. In the notes I allude to these three collections as, respectively, Ottawa, Texas, and Fregene.

I have used additional material from Radclyffe Hall's literary agent A. M. Heath and Co, from Cara Lancaster (Mabel Batten's diaries and letters), and from the archives of the Society for Psychical Research (SPR) in London (notably John and Una's records of their sittings with Mrs Leonard). References to these sources should be obvious, as should others, which in every case will appear as the last name in each note.

In referring in the notes to John, Una and Ladye, I have used only their initials – RH, UVT, and MVB respectively – a practice much employed by the trio themselves.

Unless otherwise stated, all publications are published in Britain.

M. B.

Prologue

1. 'The Modus Vivendi in so-called Mediumistic Trance', *Proceedings of the Society for Psychical Research*, vol. XXXII, p. 365
2. Leonard Sitting, 7.2.17. SPR.
3. Ibid.
4. *The Life and Death of Radclyffe Hall*, Hammond & Hammond, 1961, p. 80.
5. The scene occurs in Chapter 2 of *The Well of Loneliness*.
6. It is the opening line of L. P. Hartley's novel *The Go-Between*.

PART ONE: MARGUERITE

Chapter One

1. Unfinished essay by RH entitled 'Forbears and Infancy'. Fregene.
2. Ibid.
3. RH to Evguenia Souline, 16.6.42. Texas.
4. *Confessions of an English Opium-Eater*, Collins Clear-Type Press, 1908, p. 48.
5. *The Life and Death of Radclyffe Hall*, p. 7.
6. 'Forbears and Infancy'.
7. Ibid.
8. Ibid.
9. Ibid.
10. *The Times* report of the case, 27.2.1882.

Chapter Two

1. Marie Visetti to Jane Caruth, 3.3.44. Texas.
2. *The Well of Loneliness*, Barrie & Jenkins Ltd, 1976, pp.64–65.
3. 'Forbears and Infancy'.
4. *The Life and Death of Radclyffe Hall*, p.15.
5. See the unpublished history of the Royal College of Music by Guy Warrack, vol.1, p.110. RCM Library, Kensington.
6. *The Life and Death of Radclyffe Hall*, p.16.
7. Ibid., p.17.
8. 'Forbears and Infancy'.
9. This volume is in the possession of the Humanities Research Centre in Austin, Texas.
10. 'Forbears and Infancy'.
11. *The Life and Death of Radclyffe Hall*, p.19.
12. Ibid., p.20.
13. Nigel Nicolson, ed., *The Letters of Virginia Woolf, 1923–28*, Hogarth Press, 1977, p.520.
14. The picture is in the possession of Nicola Rossi-Lemeni. He acquired it from Una Troubridge, who told him this story.
15. *Adam's Breed*, Jonathan Cape (Florin Books), 1933, p.122.
16. Evelyn Irons to author, 13.4.83.
17. *The Well of Loneliness*, p.59.
18. *The Life and Death of Radclyffe Hall*, p.21.

Chapter Three

1. *The Unlit Lamp*, Jonathan Cape (Florin Books), 1933, p.206.
2. *Musical Times*, 1.4.1895 & 1.1.1897.
3. *The Life and Death of Radclyffe Hall*, p.25.
4. For an appreciation of Agnes Nicholls' career, see *Opera*, November 1959, vol.10/11.
5. *The Life and Death of Radclyffe Hall*, p.26.
6. Ibid., p.25.
7. UVT's 'Letters to John', 6.11.43. Fregene.
8. *The Unlit Lamp*, p.206.
9. *The Life and Death of Radclyffe Hall*, p.23.
10. Ibid., pp.22–23.
11. Ibid., p.27.
12. Ibid.
13. Ibid., p.32
14. In fact, it was not quite John's first publication. In 1902 Novello & Co published 'Two Miniatures', a couple of songs with words by John and music by her step-father Albert Visetti.
15. 4.7.06.
16. 5.7.06.
17. 28.7.06.

PART TWO: LADYE

Chapter Four

1. *The Life and Death of Radclyffe Hall*, p.30.
2. Quoted in Elizabeth Longford's *A Pilgrimage of Passion*, Weidenfeld & Nicolson, 1979, p.162.
3. Ibid., p.152.
4. *The Poetical Works of Wilfrid Scawen Blunt*, Macmillan, 1914, vol.1, p.142.
5. *Modern Society*, 15.3.02.
6. *The Life and Death of Radclyffe Hall*, p.30.
7. Ibid.
8. Ibid.
9. Ibid.
10. MVB to Cara Harris, 21.2.10.
11. Ibid., 25.1.11.
12. Ibid., 8.4.11.
13. Ibid., 29.4.11.
14. *The Life and Death of Radclyffe Hall*, p.34.
15. MVB's Diary, 6.12.11.

Chapter Five

1. MVB to Cara Harris, 1.9.12.
2. Ibid., 22.11.12.
3. *The Life and Death of Radclyffe Hall*, p.36.
4. 14.3.13.
5. 13.3.13.
6. *The Life and Death of Radclyffe Hall*, p.37.
7. II, *Samuel*, chapter 1, verse 23.
8. MVB to Cara Harris, 7.2.11.
9. 16.6.12.
10. *Pall Mall Gazette*, 5.3.12.
11. *The Life and Death of Radclyffe Hall*, p.38.
12. MVB's Diary, 30.8.13.
13. RH to Cara Harris, 19.4.14. Cara Lancaster.
14. MVB to Cara Harris, 24.3.14.
15. Ibid., 7.8.14.
16. MVB's Diary, 2.8.14.
17. MVB to Cara Harris, 7.8.14.
18. MVB's Diary, 13.3.13.
19. See Frederick Covins, *Malvern Between The Wars*, Book Production Services, 1981, pp.1–9; and the *Malvern Gazette*, August–September 1914.
20. MVB to Cara Harris, 30.8.14.
21. Ibid., 13.9.14.
22. *Malvern Gazette*, 11.9.14.
23. MVB's Diary, 15.9.14.
24. Leonard Sitting, 30.12.16.
25. MVB to Cara Harris, 12.6.15.
26. RH to Sladen, undated. Sladen Collection (vol.66, p.32), Richmond Library.
27. Sladen to RH, 30.12.13. Sladen Collection.
28. *Twenty Years Of My Life*, Constable, 1915, pp.114–115.

29 'In the Days of My Youth', *T.P.'s Weekly*. 20.2.26.
30. *The Life and Death of Radclyffe Hall*, p.41.

PART THREE: UNA

Chapter Six

1. *The Life and Death of Radclyffe Hall*, pp.45–46.
2. UVT's unpublished essay, 'Hero-Worship'. Ottawa.
3. Ibid., 'On Being Ill'.
4. Ibid., 'Bores'.
5. Ibid., 'Holidays'.
6. Ibid., 'Clothes'.
7. Ibid., 'Religion'.
8. Leonard Sitting, 2.4.19.
9. Troubridge's first wife was a Canadian, Edith Duffus. They married in 1891 and she died in 1900.
10. UVT's unpublished essay, 'Clothes'.
11. UVT to Jaqueline Hope, 25.8.08. Felix Hope-Nicholson.
12. Crighton-Miller to UVT, 4.3.13. Ottawa.
13. UVT's unpublished essay, 'The Play'. Ottawa.
14. For a fuller account of the 'Goeben' incident, see Barbara Tuchman's *August 1914*, Constable, 1962, and Redmond McLaughlin's *The Escape of the 'Goeben'*, Seeley Service & Co, 1974.
15. May Massola to UVT, 17.10.14. Ottawa.

Chapter Seven

1. *The Life and Death of Radclyffe Hall*, p.46.
2. Ibid., pp.46–47.
3. MVB's Diary, 24.8.15.
4. *The Life and Death of Radclyffe Hall*, pp.48–49.
5. MVB's Diary, 15.10.15.
6. UVT's Day Book, 23.8.38. Fregene.
7. MVB's Diary, 28.1.16.
8. MVB to Peter Harris, undated.
9. MVB's Diary, 26.2.16.
10. Ibid., 28.4.16.
11. UVT's Day Book, 8.9.31.
12. MVB's Diary, 13.5.16.
13. *The Life and Death of Radclyffe Hall*, pp.53–54.
14. Ibid., p.55.
15. See MVB's Diary, 19/20.2.15.
16. RH to Cara Harris, undated. Cara Lancaster.
17. *The Life and Death of Radclyffe Hall*, pp.54–55.
18. Ibid., p.55.

Chapter Eight

1. Introductory statement to RH's records of the Leonard Sittings. SPR.
2. RH to Cara Harris, 19.8.16. Cara Lancaster.

3. Leonard Sitting, 20.10.16.
4. Ibid., 15.11.16.
5. UVT's Diary, 9.1.17. Ottawa.
6. Ibid., 11.1.17.
7. Ibid., 12.1.17.
8. Ibid., 28.2.17
9. Leonard Sitting, 19.1.17.
10. Leonard Sitting, 17.1.17.
11. Ibid.
12. UVT's Diary, 15.2.17.
13. Ibid., 25.3.17.
14. Felix Hope-Nicholson to author, 7.11.81.
15. UVT's Diary, 25.7.17.
16. Ibid., 19.8.17.

Chapter Nine

1. Leonard Sitting, 3.1.17.
2. UVT's Diary, 15.8.17.
3. Ibid., 29.8.17.
4. Ibid., 16.9.17.
5. Ibid.
6. Leonard Sitting, 3.10.17.
7. UVT's Diary, 6.10.17.
8. Ibid., 21.10.17.
9. Leonard Sitting, 10.10.17.
10. UVT's Diary, 24.10.17.
11. Ibid., 29.12.17.
12. Ibid., 6.1.18.
13. Ladye's remarks were made in Leonard Sitting, 18.10.16.
14. UVT's Diary, 22.3.18.
15. Mrs Salter's notes to the interview. SPR.
16. UVT to Mrs Sidgwick, 11.6.18. SPR.
17. Mrs Sidgwick to Mrs Salter, 27.6.18. and 30.6.18. SPR.
18. Mrs Sidgwick to UVT, 12.6.18. SPR.
19. UVT to Mrs Sidgwick, 14.6.18. SPR.
20. RH to Sir Oliver Lodge, 2.7.18. SPR.

Chapter Ten

1. UVT's Diary, 26.2.18.
2. Ibid., 11.11.18.
3. Leonard Sitting, 1.1.19.
4. *The Life and Death of Radclyffe Hall*, p.62.
5. Leonard Sitting, 8.1.19.
6. UVT's unpublished essay, 'Beds'. Ottawa.
7. UVT's Diary, 17.2.17.
8. Ibid., 6.6.19.
9. UVT's unpublished essay, 'Pleacher'. Ottawa.
10. UVT's Diary, 17.7.19.
11. UVT's Diary, 7.11.19.

Chapter Eleven

1. *The Life and Death of Radclyffe Hall*, p.69.
2. Ibid., p.70.
3. Ibid.
4. Ibid., pp.72–73.
5. Fox-Pitt's views on the 'spirit hypothesis' are best represented by a letter he wrote to the SPR *Journal* in 1898. See vol.8, pp.184–6.
6. UVT's Diary, 26.1.20.
7. *The Life and Death of Radclyffe Hall*, p.64.
8. UVT's Diary, 9.4.20.
9. UVT's unpublished essay, 'A Dog's Life'. Ottawa.
10. See Hackett-Lowther Papers. Imperial War Museum.
11. *The Times*, 5.8.19.
12. UVT's Diary, 22.8.20.
13. Ibid., 29.9.20.
14. Ibid., 15.10.20.
15. Ibid., 30.10.20.
16. Ibid., 6.11.20.
17. From *The Times* report of the case, 19.11.20.
18. Ibid.
19. Ibid.
20. *The Times*, 20.11.20.
21. UVT's Diary, 19.11.20.
22. SPR Council minutes, 9.12.20. SPR.
23. I am indebted to Mr J. Fraser Nicol of Lexington, Mass., for this biographical information on Fox-Pitt.
24. UVT's Diary, 14.3.21.
25. Leonard Sitting, 3.11.20.

Chapter Twelve

1. *The Life and Death of Radclyffe Hall*, p.65.
2. *Life for Life's Sake*, Cassell, 1968, p.142.
3. MVB's Diary, 5.9.15.
4. Ida Wylie to RH and UVT, undated. Ottawa.
5. Ida Wylie to UVT, 28.9.21. Ottawa.
6. Ibid.
7. Quoted in Meryle Secrest's *Between Me and Life*, Macdonald and Jane's, 1976, p.49.
8. The description is Faith Compton Mackenzie's from *More Than I Should*, Collins, 1940, p.16.
9. Mackenzie, *My Life and Times*, Chatto & Windus, 1965, Octave V, p.176.
10. *More Than I Should*, p.24.
11. UVT's Diary, 25.7.21.
12. Ibid., 10.9.21.
13. Ibid.
14. Romaine Brooks to RH, 11.9.21. Ottawa.
15. Romaine Brooks to UVT, 25.10.21. Ottawa.
16. *The Life and Death of Radclyffe Hall*, p.68.
17. UVT's Diary, 14.11.21.

18. *The Life and Death of Radclyffe Hall*, p.51.
19. Romaine Brooks to UVT, 23.12.21. Ottawa.
20. Ibid.
21. *The Life and Death of Radclyffe Hall*, p.82.
22. UVT's Diary, 15.1.22.
23. Marjorie Watts, *PEN.: The Early Years, 1921–26*, Archive Press, 1971, p.14.
24. *The Life and Death of Radclyffe Hall* p.74.
25. Ibid., p.149.

PART FOUR: JOHN – [1] THE NOVELIST

Chapter Thirteen

1. The description is Sir Francis Rose's in *Saying Life*, Cassell, 1961, p.190.
2. Quoted in Natalie Barney's *Souvenirs Indiscrets*, Flammarion, Paris, 1960, p.130.
3. UVT's Diary, 21.11.22.
4. *The Unlit Lamp*, pp.5–6.
5. Ibid., pp.63–64.
6. Ibid., pp.66–67.
7. Ibid., p.250.
8. UVT's Diary, 12.6.23.
9. Romaine Brooks to UVT, undated. Ottawa.
10. UVT's Diary, 2.6.23.
11. *The Sweet and Twenties*, Weidenfeld & Nicolson, 1958, p.21.
12. UVT's Diary, 30.10.23.

Chapter Fourteen

1. UVT's Diary, 31.11. 23.
2. A. M. Heath to Arrowsmith, 17.1.24; Arrowsmith to A. M. Heath, 28.1.24. A. M. Heath.
3. *The Forge*, Arrowsmith, 2nd ed., 1925, p.318.
4. *Sunday Times*, 10.2.24.
5. *The People*, 2.3.24.
6. Violet Hunt to RH, undated. A. M. Heath.
7. Vere Hutchinson to RH, undated. Ottawa.
8. Quoted in Meryle Secrest, op. cit., p.291.
9. Romaine Brooks to RH, undated. Ottawa.
10. According to Brendan Gill's *Tallulah*, Holt Rinehart & Winston, NY, 1972, p.37.
11. John's letter is printed in the SPR *Journal*, June 1924, vol.XXI, p.285.
12. SPR Council minutes, 7.4.24. SPR.
13. Secrest, op. cit., p.292.
14. Ibid., p.291.
15. Romaine Brooks to UVT, undated. Ottawa.
16. *The Life and Death of Radclyffe Hall*, p.83.
17. UVT's Diary, 25.6.24.
18. Natalie Barney to RH, 20.10.24. Ottawa.
19. *Sunday Times*, 28.9.24.
20. UVT's Diary, 9.2.25.

Chapter Fifteen

1. *The Queen*, 29.4.25.
2. *The Life and Death of Radclyffe Hall*, p.79.
3. Ibid., p.75.
4. UVT's Diary, 14.4.25.
5. Alec Waugh to Lovat Dickson, 20.5.70. Ottawa.
6. *The Sweet and Twenties*, p.105.
7. Rupert Hart-Davis to the author, 22.4.81.
8. *The Life and Death of Radclyffe Hall*, p.80.
9. Russell Doubleday to Audrey Heath, 15.10.25. A. M. Heath.
10. Teddie Gerard to RH and UVT, undated. Ottawa.
11. UVT's Diary, 2.12.25.
12. Beresford Egan to author, 22.12.81.

Chapter Sixteen

1. Patience Ross to author, 2.7.82.
2. Ted Troubridge to author, 11.11.84.
3. UVT's Diary, 20.2.26.
4. RH to Jane Caruth, 22.1.26. Texas.
5. *Observer*, 14.3.26; *Sunday Times*, 7.3.26.
6. *Sunday Herald*, 21.3.26.
7. See Claudia Stillman Franks, *Beyond the Well of Loneliness*, Avebury Publishing Co, 1982, p.3.
8. UVT's Diary, 20.7.26.
9. *The Life and Death of Radclyffe Hall*, pp.81–82.
10. A. Scott Berg, *Max Perkins, Editor of Genius*, Pocket Books, NY, 1978, p.465.
11. Quoted in Lilian Faderman, *Surpassing the Love of Men*, Junction Books, 1981, p.363.
12. RH to Evguenia Souline, 12.4.35. Texas.
13. Anon. to RH, 9.1.27. Ottawa.
14. Grace Spencer to RH, 23.1.27. Ottawa.
15. RH to Winifred Macy, 23.1.27. Texas.
16. RH to Winifred Macy, 15.2.27. Texas.
17. Ibid.
18. John's talk is summarized in *The Bookman*, April 1927.
19. UVT's Diary, 16.3.27.
20. Violet Hunt to RH, undated. Ottawa.
21. 11.4.27.
22. *Daily Mail*, 11.5.27.
23. Evelyn Irons to author, 13.4.83.
24. UVT's Diary, 21.7.27.
25. RH to Evelyn Irons, 15.8.27. Evelyn Irons.
26. Ibid.
27. Ibid.
28. *The Life and Death of Radclyffe Hall*, p.87.

PART FOUR: JOHN – [2] THE MARTYR

Chapter Seventeen

1. Patience Ross to author, 18.8.82.
2. Ibid., 2.7.82.

3. *Glasgow Daily Record*, 4.1.28.
4. RH to Newman Flower, 16.4.28. Ottawa.
5. RH to Ellis, 18.4.28. Ottawa.
6. Quoted in Phyllis Grosskurth, *Havelock Ellis, A Biography*, Allen Lane, 1980, p.398.
7. Ellis to RH, 21.4.28. Ottawa.
8. Flower to RH, undated. Ottawa.
9. Quoted in Mackenzie's *My Life and Times*, Chatto & Windus, 1967, Octave 6, p.107.
10. Flower to Audrey Heath, 23.4.28. Ottawa.
11. Evans to Audrey Heath, 27.4.28. Ottawa.
12. Secker to Audrey Heath, 3.5.28. Ottawa.
13. Quoted in Michael S. Howard, *Jonathan Cape, Publisher*, Jonathan Cape, 1971, p.109.
14. Norah James, *I Lived in a Democracy*, Longmans, Green & Co, 1939, p.211.
15. UVT's Diary, 10.5.28.
16. Ibid., 15.5.28.
17. Grosskurth, op. cit., pp.398–399.
18. RH to Roger Scaife, 17.5.28. Houghton Library, Boston, Mass.
19. Scaife to RH, 5.6.28. Houghton Library.
20. Brandt to RH, 8.6.28. Ottawa.
21. UVT's Diary, 23.5.28.
22. RH to Audrey Heath, 12.6.28. Ottawa.
23. RH to Brandt, 21.6.28. Ottawa.
24. RH to Bernice Baumgarten, 29.6.28. Ottawa.
25. RH to Blanche Knopf, 8.7.28. Ottawa.
26. Cape to Audrey Heath, 27.6.28. Ottawa.
27. RH to Cape, 29.6.28. Ottawa.
28. Quoted in Michael S. Howard, op. cit., p.103.
29. RH to Garvin, 15.7.28. Texas.
30. For an excellent corrective view, see Claudia Franks, op. cit.
31. *The Life and Death of Radclyffe Hall*, pp.83–84.
32. UVT's Diary, 1928, end fly-leaf.
33. Ellis's theories on female homosexuality can be found in his chapter 'Sexual Inversion in Women', *Studies in the Psychology of Sex*, F. A. Davis Co., Philadelphia 1897, vol.I, Part IV pp.77–102.
34. Ellis to RH, undated. Ottawa.
35. Ellis to RH, 28.7.28. Ottawa.
36. *Saturday Review*, 28.7.28.
37. *Sunday Times*, 5.8.28.
38. *The Nation*, 4.8.28.
39. *Time and Tide*, 10.8.28.
40. *Tatler*, 15.8.28.
41. UVT's Diary, 9.8.28.
42. RH to Gerard Manley Hopkins, 15.8.28. Berg Collection, New York Public Library.

Chapter Eighteen

1. *Sunday Chronicle*, 19.8.28.
2. *The People*, 19.8.28.

3. Beverley Nichols, op. cit., pp.106–107. The line '... and that night they were not divided' comes at the end of Chapter 38 of *The Well of Loneliness*.
4. II, Samuel, I, v.23.
5. *Daily Herald*, 20.8.28.
6. Ibid., 22.8.28.
7. *Evening Standard*, 20.8.28.
8. *Daily Express*, 20.8.28.
9. Reported in the *Scots Pictorial*, 22.8.28.
10. According to Michael S. Howard, op. cit., pp.103–104.
11. *Yorkshire Post*, 24.8.28.
12. *Manchester Daily Despatch*, 22.8.28.
13. *Newcastle Daily Journal*, 22.8.28.
14. RH to Fabienne, 27.8.28. I am indebted to David Chesanow for permission to quote from this letter.
15. RH to Hopkins, op. cit.
16. *Daily Herald*, 21.8.28.
17. See Cape's sworn statement to his defence counsel. Morris Ernst Collection. Humanities Research Centre, University of Texas.
18. *The Times*, 23.8.28.
19. *Daily Express*, 24.8.28.
20. *Daily Herald*, 24.8.28.
21. *Evening Standard*, 9.8.28.
22. RH to Hopkins, op. cit.
23. Quoted in Nigel Nicolson, op. cit., p.520.
24. RH to Bennett, 27.8.28. Bennett Collection, London University.
25. Bennett to RH, 28.8.28. Bennett Collection.
26. See P.N. Furbank, *E. M. Forster: A Life*, OUP, 1979, vol.II, p.155.
27. Nigel Nicolson, op. cit., p.45.
28. Furbank, op. cit., p.154.
29. RH to Fabienne, op. cit.
30. RH to Baldwin, 2.9.28. I am indebted to Richard Payne for permission to quote from this letter.
31. UVT's Diary, 27.9.28.
32. Blanche Knopf to RH, undated. A. M. Heath.
33. Blanche Knopf to RH, 20.9.28. A. M. Heath.
34. Michael S. Howard, op. cit., p.107, note 1.
35. RH to Huxley, 7.11.28. Huxley Collection, Woodson Research Centre, Rice University, Texas.
36. Ould to Rubinstein, 26.10.28. Michael Rubinstein.
37. All letters in the possession of Michael Rubinstein.
38. McKenna to Rubinstein, 31.10.28. Michael Rubinstein.
39. Walpole to Cape, date indecipherable. Michael Rubinstein.
40. Ellis to RH, 20.10.28. Ottawa.
41. Storm Jameson to author, 27.3.81.
42. Virginia Woolf to Quentin Bell, 1.11.28. Nigel Nicolson, ed. op. cit., vol.3, p.555.
43. Defence Counsel documents. Ernst Collection.
44. Bennett to Mrs Amabel Williams-Ellis, 29.10.28. Michael Rubinstein.
45. Defence Counsel documents. Ernst Collection.
46. Ibid.
47. Ibid.

Chapter Nineteen

1. *Daily Express*, 10.11.28.
2. Storm Jameson to author, op. cit.
3. 10.11.28.
4. Quoted in Vera Brittain, *Radclyffe Hall: A Case of Obscenity?*, Femina Books, 1968, p.87.
5. *Daily Herald*, 10.11.28.
6. Ibid.
7. *All The Books Of My Life*, Cassell, 1956, p.137.
8. *The Times*, 10.11.28.
9. RH to Hopkins, 14.11.28. Berg Collection.
10. Quoted in Vera Brittain, op. cit., p.92.
11. Papers on *The Well* trial. Ottawa.
12. op. cit.
13. UVT to Ranee Margaret Brooke of Sarawak, 11.11.28. David Chesanow.
14. RH to Hopkins, op. cit.
15. Transcript of Biron's judgement. Ottawa.
16. *The People*, 17.11.28.
17. Horniman to Rubinstein, 30.10.28. Michael Rubinstein.
18. Ellis to RH, 30.11.28. Ottawa.
19. See the *Daily Herald*, 22.11.28.
20. UVT's Diary, 14.12.28.
21. Vita Sackville-West to Harold Nicolson, 15.12.28. I am indebted to Nigel Nicolson for permission to quote from this letter.
22. Transcript of the Appeal. Ottawa.
23. *The Times*, 15.12.28.
24. *Daily Express*, 15.12.28.
25. *Time and Tide*, 23.11.28.
26. op. cit.
27. RH to Vita Sackville-West, 16.12.28. Nigel Nicolson.
28. Bennett to RH 17.12.28. Bennett Collection.
29. RH to Ranee Brooke, 18.12.28. David Chesanow.
30. *The Life and Death of Radclyffe Hall*, p.113.
31. UVT's Day Book, 21.11.32.
32. According to Marjorie Watts, op. cit., p.31.
33. Alec Waugh to Lovat Dickson, op. cit.
34. Quoted in Philippe Jullian and John Phillips, *The Other Woman: A Life of Violet Trefusis*, Houghton Mifflin, Boston, 1976, p.228.
35. Vita Sackville-West to Harold Nicolson, 4.8.28 and 8.8.28. Nigel Nicolson.
36. Quoted by Secrest, op. cit., p.291.
37. *Daily Mail*, 26.7.28.
38. *New York Telegram Magazine*, 15.12.28.
39. *New York World*, 21.10.28.
40. Sybille Bedford to author, 5.7.81.

Chapter Twenty

1. RH to Wren Howard, 19.11.28. Ottawa.
2. So she told Laurence Housman. Housman to George Ives, 16.1.29. Housman-Ives Papers, HRC, University of Texas.

3. *Southend Observer*, 30.1.29.
4. RH to Audrey Heath, 17.1.29. A. M. Heath.
5. RH to Covici Friede, 11.2.29. A. M. Heath.
6. Defence brief submitted by Greenham, Wolff and Ernst. Ottawa.
7. Quoted in Paul S. Boyer, *Purity in Print: The Vice-Society Movement and Book Censorship in America*, Saunders, NY, 1968, p.133.
8. UVT to Audrey Heath, undated. Ottawa.
9. Ibid.
10. UVT to Audrey Heath, undated. Ottawa.
11. Ibid.
12. RH to Audrey Heath, 27.2.29. Ottawa.
13. Ibid., 4.3.29. A. M. Heath.
14. Ibid., 28.3.29. A. M. Heath.
15. Ibid., 19.3.29. Ottawa.
16. Ibid.
17. Ibid.
18. RH to Audrey Heath, 7.4.29. Ottawa.
19. *New York World*, 25.4.29.
20. Mackenzie, op. cit., Octave 5, 1966, p.138.
21. RH to Audrey Heath, 20.4.29.
22. Ibid., 24.4.29. Ottawa.
23. RH to Donald Friede, 4.5.29. Ottawa.
24. Anon. to Audrey Heath, undated. A. M. Heath.
25. RH to Audrey Heath, 28.4.29. A. M. Heath.
26. *The Life and Death of Radclyffe Hall*, p.97.
27. UVT to Audrey Heath, 3.6.29. A. M. Heath.
28. Ibid., 19.6.29. A. M. Heath.
29. *The Life and Death of Radclyffe Hall*, p.100.
30. Ibid., p.101.
31. Egan to author, 22.12.81.
32. See *Nineteenth Century*, April 1929, and *New Adelphi*, January 1929.
33. RH to Audrey Heath, 23.8.29. A. M. Heath.
34. UVT's Diary, 8.8.29.
35. UVT to Audrey Heath, 3.10.29. A. M. Heath.
36. Garvin to UVT, 22.12.26. Ottawa.
37. UVT's Diary, 8.8.29.

Chapter Twenty-one

1. UVT to Jaqueline Hope-Nicholson, 22.4.30. Felix Hope-Nicholson.
2. Patience Ross to author, 2.7.82.
3. UVT's Diary, 23.8.30.
4. Holroyd-Reece to RH & UVT, 2.9.30. Texas.
5. 'Bignor' to RH, 4.9.30. Texas.
6. *New York Times*, 17.9.30.
7. *Paris Was Yesterday 1925–39*, Viking Press, NY, 1972, p.71.
8. UVT's Diary, 25.10.30.
9. Ibid., 26.10.30.
10. *Daily Telegraph*, 27.10.30.
11. UVT's Diary, 9.1.31.
12. UVT's Day Book, 28.12.30. Fregene.
13. Ibid., 16.2.31,

14. Ibid., 11.2.31.
15. Ibid., 14.9.31.
16. Ibid., 28.2.31.
17. Ibid., 7.3.31.
18. Ibid., 24.1.31.
19. UVT's Diary, 22.2.31.
20. UVT's Day Book, 5.4.31.
21. Ibid., 20.7.31.
22. Ibid., 26.8.31.
23. UVT's Diary, 7.1.31.
24. According to Richard Ormrod, *Una Troubridge: The Friend of Radclyffe Hall*, Cape, 1984, p.203.
25. *The Well of Loneliness*, p.214.
26. UVT's Day Book, 21.5.33.
27. Ibid., 13.10.31.
28. UVT's Diary, 5.11.31.
29. RH to Jonathan Cape, 5.2.32. A. M. Heath.
30. UVT's Day Book, 31.12.31.
31. *Sunday Times*, 28.2.32; *The Times*, 4.3.32.
32. *Observer*, 28.2.32.
33. Frank Kermode, *Puzzles and Epiphanies*, Routledge & Kegan Paul, 1962, p.132.
34. UVT's Diary, 18.2.32.
35. UVT's Day Book, 27.3.32.
36. Ibid., 9.8.31.
37. Ibid., 28.8.31.
38. Ibid., 30.4.32.
39. RH to Mr Lloyd, 29.12.36. A. M. Heath.
40. *The Life and Death of Radclyffe Hall*, pp. 111–112.
41. UVT's Diary, 6.8.32.
42. *The Life and Death of Radclyffe Hall*, p.111.

Chapter Twenty-two

1. UVT's Day Book, 30.6.32.
2. Unpublished essay. 1927.
3. UVT's Day Book, 15.7.33.
4. *Oxford Mail*, 28.2.33.
5. UVT's Day Book, 28.2.33.
6. UVT to Audrey Heath, 14.3.29. Ottawa.
7. UVT's Day Book, 8.11.33.
8. UVT's Diary, 25.7.33.
9. Victoria Glendinning, *Vita: The Life of V. Sackville-West*, Weidenfeld & Nicolson, 1983, p.263.
10. UVT's Day Book, 21.9.33.
11. Ibid., 29.6.33.
12. Ibid., 2.9.33.
13. Ibid., 3.10.33.
14. Ibid., 15.11.33.
15. Ibid., 13.6.33.
16. Ibid., 29.9.31.
17. Ibid., 21.5.33.
18. *The Life and Death of Radclyffe Hall*, pp.100–101.

PART FIVE: SOULINE

Chapter Twenty-three

1. UVT's Day Book, 26.5.31.
2. *Daily Mirror*, 11.3.32.
3. *The Life and Death of Radclyffe Hall*, p.114.
4. UVT's Day Book, 6.7.34.
5. RH to Evguenia Souline, 19.8.34. Texas.
6. Ibid., 1.9.34 and 6.9.34.
7. Ibid., 24.7.34.
8. Ibid., 27.7.34.
9. Ibid., 1.8.34.
10. UVT's Day Book, 16.8.34.
11. RH to Souline, 11.8.34.
12. Ibid., 14.8.34.
13. Ibid., 19.8.34.
14. Ibid., 29.8.34.
15. Ibid., 12.8.34.
16. Ibid.
17. Ibid.
18. Ibid.
19. UVT's Day Book, 12.9.34.
20. Ibid.
21. Ibid., 17.9.34.
22. RH to Souline, 18.9.34.
23. Audrie Atcheson, *Mickie and Me*, unpublished MS. I am indebted to Mrs Atcheson for letting me read this book.
24. RH to Souline, 15.9.34.
25. Ibid., 3.10.34.
26. Ibid., 12.10.34.
27. Ibid., 5.10.34.
28. Ibid., 26.10.34.
29. UVT's Day Book, 2.10.34.
30. Ibid., 19.10.34.
31. Ibid., 9.11.34.
32. Ibid., 13.11.34.
33. RH to Souline, 28.10.34.
34. Ibid., 26.11.34.
35. Ibid., 1.12.34.
36. Ibid., 10.12.34.
37. Ibid., 13.12.34.
38. UVT's Day Book, 17.12.34.
39. Ibid., 22.12.34.

Chapter Twenty-four

1. UVT's Day Book, 18.1.35.
2. Ibid., 4.3.35.
3. Ibid.
4. RH to Souline, 23.4.35.
5. Ibid., 26.4.35.

6. Ibid., 21.4.35.
7. Ibid., 27.4.35.
8. Ibid., 19.5.35.
9. Ibid., 22.5.35.
10. UVT's Day Book, 23.5.35.
11. RH to Souline, 10.6.35.
12. UVT's Day Book, 30.6.35.
13. Ibid., 16.8.35.
14. RH to Souline, 6.11.35.
15. UVT's Day Book, 16.8.35.
16. Ibid., 16.9.35.
17. RH to Souline, 17.10.35.
18. Ibid., 18.10.35.
19. Ibid., 26.10.35.
20. Ibid., 2.11.35.
21. Ibid., 27.3.35.
22. Ibid., 3.11.35.
23. UVT's Day Book, 14.1.36.
24. Ibid., 7.2.36.
25. Ibid., 12.10.36.
26. Ibid., 9.12.36.
27. Ibid., 3.7.37.
28. Ibid., 9.7.37.
29. RH to Souline, 19.7.37.
30. Ibid.
31. Ibid., 26.7.37.
32. Ibid., 23.8.37.
33. Ibid., 8.8.37.
34. Ibid.
35. Ibid., 18.7.37.
36. Ibid., 1.8.37.
37. Ibid., 25.8.37.
38. Ibid., 7.9.37.
39. *The Life and Death of Radclyffe Hall*, p.131.
40. RH to Souline, 3.3.38.
41. Ibid., 23.6.38.
42. Ibid., 29.6.38.
43. Ibid., 21.7.38.
44. Ibid., 13.9.38.
45. UVT's Day Book, 9.5.38.
46. RH to Souline, 2.8.38.
47. Ibid., 12.8.38.
48. Ibid., 14.9.38.
49. Ibid., 18.9.38.
50. UVT's Day Book, 5.3.35.
51. RH to Souline, 5.2.39.
52. Ibid., 3.3.39.
53. Ibid.

PART SIX: A SINGLE SOUL

Chapter Twenty-five

1. RH to Souline, 15.3.39.
2. Ibid., 22.3.39.
3. Ibid., 15.3.39.
4. *The Life and Death of Radclyffe Hall*, p.169.
5. RH to Souline, 8.2.39.
6. Ibid., 29.1.39.
7. UVT's Day Book, 27.8.39.
8. UVT's Day Book, 20.3.40.
9. Ibid., 11.6.40.
10. Ibid., 27.6.41.
11. UVT to Souline, 2.9.41.
12. RH to Souline, 21.10.41.
13. Ibid., 22.10.41.
14. Ibid., 21.2.42.
15. Ibid., 10.8.42.
16. UVT's Day Book, 6.4.42.
17. UVT to Souline, 6.4.42.
18. RH to Souline, 17.12.42.
19. UVT's Day Book, 22.6.41.
20. RH to Souline, 25.11.42.
21. Ibid., 20.12.42.

Chapter Twenty-six

1. *The Life and Death of Radclyffe Hall*, p.168.
2. Ibid., p.183.
3. UVT's Day Book, 1.9.43.
4. Naomi Jacob, *Me and the Mediterranean*, Hutchinson, 1945, p.118.
5. *The Life and Death of Radclyffe Hall*, p.186.
6. UVT's Day Book, 1.9.43.
7. *The Life and Death of Radclyffe Hall*, p.181.
8. Ibid.
9. Ibid., p.182.
10. UVT's Day Book, 1.9.43.
11. Ibid., 29.9.43.
12. *The Life and Death of Radclyffe Hall*, p.190.
13. UVT's Day Book, 29.9.43.
14. Ibid.
15. Ibid.
16. Ibid.
17. Ibid.
18. Ibid.
19. Ibid.
20. Ibid., 1.10.43.
21. Ibid., 2.10.43.
22. *The Life and Death of Radclyffe Hall*, p.49.
23. Ibid., p.177.
24. UVT's Day Book, 5.10.43.

25. Ibid., 6.10.43.
26. Ibid., 7.10.43.
27. Ibid.
28. Naomi Jacob, *Me and the Swans*, Kimber, 1963, p.128.

Chapter Twenty-seven

1. *The Life and Death of Radclyffe Hall*, p.172.
2. Ibid., p.171.
3. 'Letters to John', 1.11.43. Fregene.
4. *The Life and Death of Radclyffe Hall*, p.190.
5. 'Letters to John', 1.11.43.
6. Ibid., 4.1.44.
7. UVT's unpublished essay 'War in the City of London, 1943–44'. Ottawa.
8. 'Letters to John', 27.1.44.
9. Ibid., 16.1.44.
10. *The Life and Death of Radclyffe Hall*, pp.116–117.
11. Ibid., p.171.
12. Souline to UVT, 6.10.50. Fregene.
13. Marie Visetti to Jane Caruth, 13.10.43. Texas.

Postscript

1. UVT to Jaqueline Hope-Nicholson, 16.5.46. Felix Hope-Nicholson.
2. *The Times*, 11.10.43.
3. In 17 episodes between 21 February and 18 March, 1974.
4. James Lees-Milne, *Caves of Ice*, Chatto, 1983, p.231.
5. Felix Hope-Nicholson to author, 7.11.81.
6. Acton to author, 2.7.83.
7. UVT to Naomi Jacob, 25.11.61. I am indebted to Mrs Sarah Turner for permission to quote from this letter.
8. Ibid.
9. 'Letters to John', 26.12.43.
10. UVT to Naomi Jacob, op. cit.
11. UVT to Mrs Lilly Troubridge, 5.10.49. E. St. V. Troubridge.
12. This eventually materialized in 1975 as *Radclyffe Hall at the Well of Loneliness: A Sapphic Chronicle*, published by Collins.
13. Ethel Mannin, *Young in the Twenties*, Hutchinson, 1971, p.54.

Published Works of Radclyffe Hall

Poetry

1906	*'Twixt Earth and Stars*, Bumpus
1908	*A Sheaf of Verses*, Bumpus
1910	*Poems of the Past and Present*, Chapman and Hall
1913	*Songs of Three Counties and Other Poems*, Chapman and Hall
1915	*The Forgotten Island*, Chapman and Hall

Novels

1924	*The Forge*, Arrowsmith
	The Unlit Lamp, Cassell
1925	*A Saturday Life*, Arrowsmith
1926	*Adam's Breed*, Cassell
1928	*The Well of Loneliness*, Cape
1932	*The Master of the House*, Cape
1934	*Miss Ogilvy Finds Herself*, Heinemann
1936	*The Sixth Beatitude*, Heinemann

Index

Throughout the index Marguerite Radclyffe Hall is often referred to as John or RH, Mabel Veronica Batten as Ladye, and Una Troubridge as Una.

Adam's Breed, RH's 3, 13, 20, 178, 191, 204, 206, 213, 214, 258, 283, 288, 314
    first title of *Food* 176
    language and imagery 184–5
    material and literary success 182, 184, 187, 191, 196
    projected film of 196
    publication, 1926 182
    research on 179
    reviews 182–3
    seventh impression appears, 1927 193
    shortlisted for Prix Femina 192
    story of 183–4
    storyline 174
    US rights sold 179
    wins James Tait Black prize 196, 197
    wins Prix Femina, 1927 194, 197
Adcock, St John 170
After Many Days (published as *The Unlit Lamp*), RH's
    autobiographical influences in 153, 155
    difficulty of finding publisher for 156–7, 160
    early title of *Octopi* 154
    story of 152–5
    See also *Unlit Lamp, The*
Agate, James 182, 234
Aldington, Richard 135
Allen, Commandant Mary (Robert) 267, 274
American Women's Club 176
Amery, Julian 354
Amherst, Earl 267
Anderman, Dr 333
Animal Protection Society 296
Arlen, Michael 159, 168
    The Green Hat 159
Arnim, Elizabeth von
    Elizabeth and her German Garden 145, 164
Arrowsmith's (publishers) 167
    publish *A Saturday Life*, 1925 171
    publish first and cheap editions of *The Forge*, 1924 and 1925 161, 171
    reprint *A Saturday Life* and *The Forge*, 1929 258
Austin, Peggy 116, 117
Atwood, Clare (Tony) 263, 264, 271, 272, 285, 286
    entrusts relic of True Cross to John and Una 274

Baker, Dr 'Joe' 306
Baldwin, Oliver 230–1, 235
Balfour, Arthur 94

Balfour, Gerald 106
Ballou, Robert 275
Bankhead, Tallulah 165, 283
Barker, 'Colonel' 254
Barney, Natalie Clifford 137, 141, 149, 164, 167, 168, 190, 191, 215, 217, 253, 296, 355
    appearance 142
    depicted in *The Well* 216
    independent spirit 141–2
    love affairs 162
        with Romaine Brooks 137
    Pensées d'une Amazone 217
    salons 142, 255
Barrett, Rachel 136, 145
Barry, Gerald 235
Bates, H. E.
    reviews *Miss Ogilvy Finds Herself* 290
Bath, Hubert 29
Batten, Cara, *see* Harris, Cara
Batten, George 34: marriage to Ladye 34; retires, 1882 34; accepts relation between wife and John 37–8; death, 1910 39
Batten, Mabel Veronica (Ladye) 2, 28, 123, 130, 215, 216
    appearance 33, 35
    belief in reincarnation 34
    burial chamber 78–9
    character 46–7
    early life and marriage 34
    her song 'Mother England' 78
    illness and death, 1916 77, 78, 79
    invalided by car crash, 1914 55–6
    love affairs 33, 34
    mentions war threats, 1914 52
    musical ability 34–5
    nicknamed Ladye 35
    paintings of 35, 251
    relations with daughter 38
    relations with John: first meeting 33; development of friendship 35–6; becomes John's lover 36; holidays together, 1908 and 1909 36, 37; complaisance of husband 37–8; visit to Teneriffe, 1910 39; visit to Mediterranean and Corsica 40; sets up house with John, 1911 41; introduces John to Catholicism 42–3; move to White Cottage, Malvern 44; holiday in Rome, 1912 44–5; summer of 1913 at Malvern with John 50–1; rift over John's affair with Phoebe Hoare 50, 51–2; continental holiday, 1914 52; visit to Harrises, 1914 52–3; effect of outbreak of

war, 1914 53; move to Malvern, August 1914 53; John tires of Ladye as lover 53–4; war-time life at Malvern 55–6; Ladye sends John's short stories to William Heinemann 58; visit to Ladye's sister Emmie, 1915 61; beginnings of John's affair with Una and 61, 72, 73, 75, 78; disposal of White Cottage 76–7; settles with John in London 74–5, 76–7; deathbed scene 78–9
  use of pet names 47
  will and funeral arrangements 79–80
Baumgarten, Bernice 207
Bax, Clifford 235
Bell, Vanessa 236
Bennett, Arnold 167, 246
  attacks censorship 244–5
  efforts in support of *The Well* 228, 229–30
  refuses to give evidence in *The Well* case 236
Benson, E. F. 261, 279
  Lovers and Friends 144
Beresford, J. D. 143, 152, 156, 261, 271
Berkeley Milne, Sir Archibald 67, 69
Birkett, Norman 284
  conduct of defence in *The Well* case 239, 240–1
Birmingham Post
  on John's shingle 194
Biron, Sir Chartres 251, 255
  Pious Opinions 239, 245
  presides in the obscenity case over *The Well* 239, 241–2
  pronounces judgement in *The Well* case 242–4
  To the Pure 239
Bliss, Eileen 179, 190
Blunt, Wilfrid Scawen 39
  love affair with Ladye 34
Bodkin, Sir Archibald 240
Bonaventure, Father, of Rye 262–3, 269
  eccentricities 270, 285
Bookman's Circle 194
Borgatti, Renata 138
Bowden, Father Sebastien 44
Bowen, Marjorie
  Burning Glass, The 145, 277
  God and the King 44
  Unfortunate, The 145
  Viper of Milan, The 277
Braithwaite, Lilian 283
Brandt, Carl 190, 206, 207, 208, 232, 253, 255
  literary agency 156
Breslau (German cruiser) 69
Brittain, Vera
  reviews *The Well* 221
Brontë, Dr 179
Brooks, John Ellington 137
Brooks, Romaine 136–7, 138, 139, 141, 149, 158, 159, 168, 216, 253, 302, 303, 355
  dislike of *The Well* 248
  John envies artist in 137
  love affair with Natalie Barney 137
  paints Una's portrait 166
  portrayed in *The Forge* 163, 164
Browning, Elizabeth Barrett 42, 52, 344
  Sonnets from the Portuguese 346
Browning, Robert 42, 52, 344
Burne-Jones, Sir Edward 62
Burroughes-Burroughes, Dorothy (Budge) 160, 164, 168, 169, 195, 216

Butt, Clara 77

Calthrop, Gladys 283
Cape and Harrison Smith Inc. (later Cape Ballou) 275
  bankrupt, 1932 279
  take over *Adam's Breed* and *The Unlit Lamp* in USA 258
Cape, Jonathan 204, 226, 232, 234, 239, 250, 257, 272, 280, 289, 290; accepts *The Well* for publication 204–5; publishing plans for *The Well* 208–9, 226; forewarned of *Sunday Express* attack on *The Well* 223–4; defends *The Well* 225; offers to withdraw novel 225, 226–7; arranges Paris publication for *The Well* 227–8, 245; raided by police 233; plans for *The Master of the House* berated by John, 1932 279
Carpenter's Son, The, see *Master of the House, The*, RH's
Casati, Marchesa 138
Cassell's (publishers) 168, 178, 179, 187, 194, 202, 228: accepts *The Unlit Lamp* 167; publishes *The Unlit Lamp* 168; publishes *Adam's Breed*, 1926 182; refuses *The Well*, 1928 202
Cecil, Lord William 63
Chains 157, 160
  published as *The Forge* (q.v.)
Chamberlain, Neville 324, 325, 331
Chaplin, Olive 308, 318–19, 324, 325
Child, Dr Armando 339, 340, 342, 344
Churchill, Dr Stella 244
Churchill, Winston
  orders *Goeben* and *Breslau* shadowed 68–9
Clare, Mary 266
Clarendon, Emmie, Lady 35, 61, 70, 99
Clarke, Dorothy (Dolly) 26–7, 38, 44, 50, 51, 55, 98, 100, 101, 106, 109
  estranged from John 108
  jealousy of Una 108
  marriage 28, 38
  note-taker at seances 88, 89
Clarke, Robert Coningsby 36, 38, 44, 50, 93, 100
  marriage to Dolly Diehl 27
  musical collaboration with John 27, 38, 46
  war service 55
Clermont Tonnerre, Lily de Gramont, Duchess of 149, 191, 216, 253
Cocteau, Jean 137
Colette 142, 190, 217, 253, 256, 296
  'Chéri' books 190, 191
  'Claudine' novels 194, 217
  death, 1954 355
  lunches with John and Una 191
  stage production of *Chéri*, 1930 266
  Vagabonde, La 191
Colman, Ronald 196
Connolly, Cyril
  reviews *The Well* 229
Constable, Rosalind 269
Covici Friede (publishers): publishes *The Well* in USA 251; secures large sales 252; loses court case over *The Well* 253, 254; wins verdict in Appeal Court 255

Coward, Noel 164, 260, 266, 267–8
  London Calling! 164
Craig, Edy 263, 264, 266, 271, 274, 282, 286, 308,
  318
  death, 1947 253
  jumble sales 272, 324
Crighton-Miller, Dr Hugh 69, 106, 113, 114,
  117, 182
  treats Una Troubridge 66, 67, 68, 112, 116
Crookes, Sir William 94
Cunard, Nancy 157

Daily Express 227, 232
  supports *Sunday Express* attack on *The Well*
  224, 225
Daily Herald 226, 237, 239, 242
  condemns attacks on *The Well* 224, 232,
  233
Daily Mail 115, 247, 248
  interviews John, 1927 194
  on General Strike, 1926 186
Daily Telegraph 15, 266
  reviews of RH's works 46, 222
Danby, Frank
  idea for feudal revival 50
  Pigs in Clover 50
Dane, Clemence 260
  Broome's Stages 271
  Regiment of Women, A 118, 202, 216
D'Annunzio, Gabriele 137, 139, 302–4, 312, 354
  Honeysuckle, The 134
  meeting with John, 1934 303–4
Dawson, Arnold 224
Dawson, Lord 334
De Maupassant, Guy 217
De Quincy, Thomas 7
Dickson, Lovat
  becomes Una's literary executor 356, 357
Diehl, Dorothy, see Clarke, Dorothy
Diehl, Sarah (grandmother) 12, 17, 18, 19, 25, 42
  death, 1910 39
  devotion to grand-daughter 14–15
Dolly Sisters 176–7
Doubleday Page and Co. 179, 258
  publishes *Adam's Breed* in USA 182
  turns down *The Well* 206
Doubleday, Russell
  acquires US rights in *Adam's Breed* 179
Douglas, James 226, 228, 233, 239, 257
  leads attack on *The Well* 223
Douglas, Lord Alfred 207, 284–5
  Oscar Wilde and Myself 284
  reconciled with John 284
Dresser, Marcia van 267
Drury, Sir Charles 65

Ede, J. Chuter 353
Edward VII, King 33, 64
  death, 1910 39
Edward VIII, King
  affair with Mrs Simpson 317
Egan, Beresford
  belief lesbians' anguish is unjustified 257
  cartoons for *The Sink of Solitude* 257
Elgar, Sir Edward 41
  'Dream of Gerontius' 77
Elliott, Enid 134

Ellis, Havelock 203, 217, 221, 226, 237, 244, 248,
  249, 258, 268
  Bedborough trial, 1898, and 203, 235
  'commentary' on *The Well* 205, 207–8, 218
  influence on John 217–20 *passim*
  on worthiness of lesbians 219
  question of writing preface for *The Well* 203
  refuses to testify in *The Well* case 235
  Sexual Inversion 203, 217
  Studies in the Psychology of Sex 189
  view of male-female divide in lesbianism
  218–19
  views homosexuality as congenital 189, 218
Elman, Mischa 35
Elsner, Anne 222
Emblem Hurlstone (uncompleted), RH's 299, 300,
  307, 310
English Review 135
Enthoven, Gabrielle 134, 150, 179, 263, 266, 283
  Ellen Young (play) 134
Ernst, Morris 251, 252
Evans, Charles 280
  turns down *The Well* for Heinemann's 204
Evening Standard 236, 244
  attacks *The Well* 224
  review of *The Forge* 164

Faber, Gladys 302
Falcon Press
  republishes *The Well* in England, 1949 353
Fargo, Gwen 158, 167
Farra, Gwen 158
Fauré, Gabriel 35, 51
Field, St John 130
Field, The
  reviews *The Forge* 164
First Sheaf of Little Songs, A, RH's 38
First World War
  Battle of Loos, 1915 83
  Battle of Mons, 1914 83
  'angels' of 83
  Battle of the Somme, 1916 83
  beginning 53, 68
  escape of *Goeben* and *Breslau* to Black Sea 68–9
  in Malvern 54, 55
  signing of Armistice, 1918 111
  Zeppelin raids on London 74, 75
Flanner, Janet 266
Flower, Newman 168, 202
  recommends *The Unlit Lamp* to Cassell's 166–7
  refuses *The Well* 203–4
Food, see *Adam's Breed*
Forbears and Infancy (unfinished), RH's 19
Ford, Ford Madox 135, 277
  Good Soldier, The 135, 277
  Ladies Whose Bright Eyes 135, 145
Forge, The, RH's 160, 166, 168, 172, 258, 288
  autobiographical details in 162, 163
  published, 1924 161
  reviews 163–4
  sells well 161, 164
  story of 161–3
Forgotten Island, The, RH's 57
Forster, E. M. 258
  agrees to give evidence in *The Well* case 235
  efforts on behalf of *The Well* 228, 229,
  230

Maurice 228
A Passage to India 197
Fox-Pitt, St George Lane 123
  litigious nature 131
  loses slander action brought by John 128–31
  opposes John's co-option on SPR council 123, 124
  resigns from SPR 130, 133
Franchetti, Mimi 138, 190, 215
Franz Ferdinand, Archduke
  assassination, 1914 52
'Fräulein Schwartz', RH's 288, 289
Freud, Sigmund 218
Friede, Donald 252, 255
  arrested for publishing *The Well* in USA 251
  meets John and Una 253
Fry, Penrose 267, 274, 278
Fulton, Eustace
  as prosecution counsel in *The Well* case 240

Galsworthy, John 144, 234
Garvin, J. L. 176, 209, 247, 259
Gauthier-Villars, Henri
  L'Ersatz d'Amour 202, 217
Gay, John
  The Beggar's Opera 127
Geddes, Father 339, 343
Genée, Adeline 64, 72
General Strike, 1926 186
George V, King 76
Gerard, Teddie 158–9, 164, 165, 179, 283
Gide, André 142
Gielgud, John 266, 283
  gaffe from 271
Goeben (German cruiser) 69
Goldingham, Toto 267
Goldwyn, Sam 196
Goossens, Eugene 157
Goossens, Ida 157
Gosse, Edmund 170
Goudeket, Maurice 191
Gould, Gerald
  reviews *The Master of the House* 277
Gourmand, Rémy de 141
Grainger, Percy 35
Granville-Barker, Harley 234
Greene, Graham 277
Guareschi
  Don Camillo books 355
Gurney, Violet 114

Hackett, Miss 'Desmond' 125
Hahn, Reynaldo 35
Haire, Dr Norman 235
Hall, Rev. Samuel 7
Hancock, Jack and Marjorie 332
Harcourt Brace (publisher)
  brings out *Miss Ogilvy Finds Herself* 289
Harris, Austin 38, 51, 52
Harris, Cara 34, 38, 44, 47, 48, 51, 55, 75, 78, 80, 87, 106, 109: gives birth to Karen 52; executrix of Ladye's will 79; resents John's spiritual communication with Ladye 101–2; visits Mrs Leonard with Una 102; objects to publication of paper on sittings with Mrs Leonard 106–7; permanently estranged from John 108

Harris, Karen 52
Harris, Pamela ('Honey') 38, 52
Harris, Peter 38, 75, 76
Hart-Davis, Rupert 177
Hartley, L. P.
  reviews *The Well* 221
Harty, Hamilton 24
Hastie, Mr (solicitor) 12, 25, 113
Hatch, Arthur 44
Heath, Audrey 157, 166, 167, 169, 178, 179, 182, 194, 201, 202, 204, 207, 208, 232, 250, 260, 272, 279, 289, 346
  agency 156
  becomes John's literary agent 156
  John's pastiche for 255–6
  loses John's confidence 290
Heinemann, William 156, 289
  recommends John turn to novel-writing 58
Heinemann, Wm & Co. (publishers)
  publishes *Miss Ogilvy Finds Herself* 289
  publishes *The Sixth Beatitude* 316
Herbert, A. P.
  agrees to give evidence in *The Well* case 235
Hermes Press 257
Hesse, Herman
  Siddhartha 186
Highgate Cemetery, London
  burial chamber for Ladye, John and Una 79–80
  John's burial at 347
Hill, Leonard (booksellers) 232, 239
  copies of *The Well* confiscated from 233
Hirschfeld, Magnus 218, 221, 237
  A Manual of Sexual Science 218
Hitler, Adolf 285, 323, 324, 329
  invades Poland, 1939 331
Hoare, Oliver 50, 52, 77
Hoare, Phoebe
  affair with John 50–3 *passim* 73, 77
Holroyd-Reece, Jeanne 252, 347, 349
Holroyd-Reece, John 232, 241, 252, 347, 349, 356
  literary rights of *The Well* entrusted to 347
  on stage production of *The Well* 265
Homburg, Germany 33
  first meeting between John and Ladye at, 1907 33
Hope, Jaqueline 74, 348, 354
Hope, Laura 74, 114
Hope-Nicholson, Felix 354
Hopkins, Gerard Manley 226, 241, 242
Horniman, A. E. F. 243
Houghton Mifflin Co. (publishers) 203, 206, 289
  takes *The Master of the House* 280
  turns down *The Well* 206
Housman, Laurence 235
Hueffer, Ford Madox, *see* Ford, Ford Madox
Hunt, Violet 135, 143, 164, 168, 180, 194
  nominates *Adam's Breed* for Prix Femina 182
  Tales of the Uneasy 135
Hutchinson, A. S. M. 160
  If Winter Comes 136, 145
Hutchinson, Vere 160, 164, 168, 216
  Great Waters 160, 169
  illness 169, 195
  Sea Wrack 160
Huxley, Julian 234, 235, 241

Inskip, Sir Thomas 245

Institute of Journalists
  Writers Circle 193
Irons, Evelyn 194, 195, 196, 247, 248
Irwin, Margaret 168
  Still She Wished for Company 145
Italy
  enters Second World War 332
  invades Abyssinia, 1935 312
  political disorder, 1921 140–1

Jacob, Naomi ('Mickie') 298, 301, 303, 312, 332,
    345, 355
  appearance 302
  'Casa Mickie' at Sirmione 299
  Jacob Usher 301
  life in Sirmione 301–2
  quarrels with John and Una, 1935 312
  visits John during last illness 339, 341
James, Henry 261
James, Norah (Jimmy) 204, 227
Jameson, Storm 144, 235
  worried about giving evidence in *The Well* case
    236
John, Augustus 165
John O'London's Weekly 164
Joll, Dr Cecil 339, 340, 342
Joyce, James 145
Joynson-Hicks, Sir William 227, 237, 257
  orders Cape to withdraw *The Well* 227

Kaye-Smith, Sheila 167, 235, 240, 261, 267, 274,
    278
  Joanna Godden 136, 144
  Sussex Gorse 150
Kennedy, Margaret 234
  The Constant Nymph 234
Kershaw, Wilette
  stage production of *The Well* 259–60, 265–6
Kipling, Rudyard 62, 245
  'Tomlinson' poem 178
Knopf, Alfred, 208
  accepts *The Well* for publication 207
  decides not to publish *The Well* 231–2, 251
Knopf, Blanche 206, 207, 208, 231, 232
Krafft-Ebing, Richard von 217
  Psychopathia Sexualis 218

Labour Party
  leaves obscenity laws alone 258, 353
  support for John in *The Well* case repaid 251–2
  victory in 1929 election 258
Ladies of Llangollen 291
Lady
  reviews of RH's works 29, 46
Laking, Sir Francis 165, 168, 177
Lanchester, Elsa 158
Langley, Hubert 266
Lathom, Lord Ned 176
Lawrence, D. H. 145
Lawrence, Gertrude 164
Lawrence, T. E. 204
  Revolt in the Desert 204
Lees-Milne, James 354
Lehmann, Liza 41
Lehmann, Rosamund 143, 216
  Dusty Answer 202
Leonard, Mrs Osborne 1, 2, 58, 84, 102, 103, 106,
    165, 343

communication with Raymond Lodge 84, 85
development into medium 85
early seances with John 85–7, 88–9, 90–3, 96–7,
    98
moves concerted with John and Una's 104, 112
My Life in Two Worlds 343
powers of telepathy 88
regular sessions with John and Una 116, 123,
    139, 151, 206, 227, 232, 262, 308, 324
relays Ladye's prediction that John would die
    before Una 338
Leonard, Osborne 85
Lewis, Sinclair 251
  Main Street 136
Lewis, Sir George 114, 123, 124, 125, 128
Life and Letters 235
Lodge, Lady 83, 88
Lodge, Raymond 83
  death in First World War 84
Lodge, Sir Oliver 93, 94, 99, 106, 107, 108, 128
  death of son in First World War 84
  exposes Mrs Scales, medium 84, 88
  falls from grace with John and Una 117
  investigates Mrs Leonard 85
  receives John and Una at home 94–6
  turns to spiritualism 83–4
  writes *Raymond, or Life after Death* 84, 95
London
  Arts Club 283
  Cave of Harmony 158
  Eiffel Tower restaurant 157, 165
  Ham Bone Club 158
  Kit-Kat Club 176
  Orange Tree Club 134
Lonsdale, Fifth Earl of 125
Loraine, Lorn 267
'Lover of Things, The', RH's 288
Lowell, Amy 206
Lowther, Barbara ('Toupie') 125, 134, 143, 151,
    179, 190, 244, 247
  infatuation with Romaine Brooks 138, 139
  love affairs 127
  makes friends with John and Una 126–7
  marriage and divorce 125
  passion for cars 127
  wartime ambulance work 125–6
Lowther, Claude 127
Lucas, E. V. 170
Lytton, Robert, Earl of 34

Macaulay, Rose 235
McCarthy, Desmond 233, 235
  witness in *The Well* case 241
MacDonald, Ramsay 161
McKenna, Stephen 234
Mackenzie, Compton 138, 167, 203, 233, 255
  Extraordinary Women 204, 208, 209, 229, 233,
    254
  portrayal of John in 254–5
  publicity in Macy's for 254, 255
Mackenzie, Faith Compton
  on life on Capri, 1919 138
Maddison, Adela 50–1
Makaroff, Vladimir
  marriage to Souline 351
  sells wife's letters from John 352
Manchester Despatch 225

Manners, Lady Diana 157
Mannin, Ethel 357
Marrot, Vincent 261, 264
Martin, Eathorpe 29
Massola, Baron Cencio 65, 321
Massola, May 65, 70, 139, 140, 190, 321
Master of the House, The, RH's 272–3, 281, 283,
  288, 291, 314
  beginning of work (on *The Carpenter's Son*)
  256, 257, 259
  completed 272
  early sales 276
  failure of 276, 277–8
  John's views on compassion in 277
  publication plans 275
  reviews 276
  story of 276–7
  US edition 279–80
Melville, James B. 258
  as defence counsel in *The Well* case 239–40,
  241–2
Metcalf, Herbert 240
Michael West (unfinished), RH's 58, 120, 153,
  175, 189
Michaëlis, Karin 253
Mirtil, Adrien 216
Miss Ogilvy Finds Herself (book of short stories),
  RH's 289
  published, 1934 289
  reviews 289–90
'Miss Ogilvy Finds Herself' (short story), RH's
  187–8, 288
  portrait of Toupie Lowther in 187
Moore, George 242
  Avowals 242
Morriss, Margaret 158
Munich crisis, 1938 324, 325
Murat, Princess Violette 164, 167
Murray, John 170
Murray, Prof. Gilbert 94
Mussolini, Benito 141, 312, 323, 329
  Abyssinian invasion, 1935 312
  brings Italy into Second World War 332

Nash, Bunty 268
Nash, Paul 261, 268
Nation and Athenaeum 230
National Union of Railwaymen
  supports RH in *The Well* case 237
New Statesman 229
  reviews *Miss Ogilvy Finds Herself* 289
New York Times 266
New York Watch and Ward Society 252
Newcastle Daily Journal 225
Newton, Isobel 103, 106, 123, 124, 128, 130
Nicholls, Agnes 22–3, 27, 77, 346
  marries Hamilton Harty 24
Nichols, Beverley 159, 224
  on John's 'British policeman act' 177
Nicolsky, Lysa 322, 330
Nijinsky, Vaslav 68
Nikisch, Arthur 17
Northcliffe, Lord 203
Noyes, Alfred 177, 182

Observer 176, 209
  reviews of RH's works 182, 277

Order of the Poor Clares, Lynton
  benefit under Una's will 357
Ould, Herman 234
Oxford Union
  'King and Country' debate, 1933 284

Pall Mall Gazette 49
Pegasus Press
  becomes Paris publisher of *The Well* 228, 231
  resolves to fight confiscation of *The Well*
  332
  sells *The Well* in France 245–6
PEN Club 144, 234, 246, 290
  Ball, 1926 191
  dinners 151, 160, 170, 180
People
  attacks *The Well* 224
  reviews *The Forge* and John's appearance 164
Perkins, Maxwell 190
Perrin, Alice 182
Perry, John 283
Phillpotts, Eden 234
Piddington, J. G. 123
Pius X, Pope 45
Plunkett, Eileen 134
Poems of the Past and Present, RH's 42, 54
Pougy, Liane de 217
  Idylle Sapphique 217
Pound, Ezra 255
Poynter, Sir Edward 35, 62
Prothero, Chief Inspector John 240
Proust, Marcel
  Sodome et Gomorrhe 217
Publisher and Bookseller
  reviews *'Twixt Earth and Stars* 29
Punch 50

Queen
  reviews of RH's works 29, 171
Queensbury, Marquess of 131
Quiller-Couch, Prof. 56

Radclffe family 8
Radcliffe Hall, John (great-grandfather) 8, 47
Radclyffe-Hall, Dr Charles (grandfather) 9, 10,
  12
  founder of family fortunes 8
Radclyffe-Hall, Esther (grandmother) 9
Radclyffe Hall, Marguerite (John)
  ambiguity over feminism 49
  anti-Semitism, 1939 329
  appearance 1, 61, 131, 201
  belief she was 'congenital invert' 18, 27, 217–18
  care for Una's welfare 201
  childhood nicknames 19
  concern with plight of homosexual women
  189
  desire to be a man 170
  early aptitude for music 17
  effect of childhood rejection on writing 18
  effect of guilt over Ladye on writing 174
  fanaticism 82
  fussiness about food 196
  jaundiced view of publishers 280
  life and career: birth and ancestry 7–8; last
  meeting with father 12–13; childhood
  attachments 14–15; relations with Granny

Radclyffe Hall, Marguerite *cont.*
    Diehl 15; acquires step-father 15–16;
    rudimentary schooling 16–17; childhood
    illnesses 17; childhood poems 17–18;
    develops into 'society girl' 19; conflicts with
    mother 21; heiress to grandfather's fortune
    21, 25; devotion to Agnes Nicholls 23–5; sets
    up house on her own 25; travels in USA
    25–6; relations with Jane Randolph 25–6;
    relations with Dolly Diehl 26–7; leases
    'Highfield' in Malvern Wells 28; publishes
    first book of poems 28–9; poems set to music
    27–9; visits Homburg, 1907 33; publishes
    second book of poems, 1908 36; hunting
    accident 36, 37; songs published, 1908 and
    1909 38; leases apartment in Cadogan
    Square, London 40, 41; abandons hunting
    40; sells house in Malvern 41; takes White
    Cottage, Malvern 41; publishes third book
    of poems, 1910 42; converted to Catholicism
    43–4; publishes fourth poetry book, 1912 45;
    affair with Phoebe Hoare, 1913 50–3 *passim*;
    activities in First World War 54–5; publishes
    final book of poems, 1915 57; first attempts
    at short stories 57–8; first attempt at novel
    58; sells London flat and White Cottage 74;
    moves into Vernon Court Hotel with Ladye
    75; moves to Cadogan Court flat with Ladye
    77, 78; remorse on Ladye's death 79, 80–1,
    82; keeps flat as memorial to Ladye 80; stays
    with Dolly Clarke 80, 81; converted to
    spiritualism 84; desire to communicate with
    Ladye through medium 84–5; meetings with
    Mrs Leonard, the medium, *see* Leonard, Mrs
    Osborne; checks on Mrs Leonard's honesty
    93; continued depression over Ladye's death
    96; worried about Catholic Church's
    condemnation of spiritualism 97; replies to
    Cara's criticisms of SPR paper 107; begins
    serious novel-writing, 1919 120; envies
    Toupie Lowther's war service 126; adopts
    more masculine appearance, 1920 131; cuts
    hair short 131–2; joins literary clubs, 1920s
    144; gets back to novel-writing 144, 150,
    151; prepares herself for prose-writing 145;
    ending of periods 150, 151; completes novel
    After Many Days 152; publishes *The Forge*,
    1924 160–1; runs down after heavy work
    165; resigns from Council of SPR, 1924 165;
    publishes *After Many Days* as *The Unlit Lamp*
    168; becomes literary lion 168; becomes
    theatre 'first-nighter' 170; literary standing,
    1925 176–8; begins work on *Food* (later
    Adam's Breed) 176; contracts with Cassell's to
    publish *Adam's Breed* 178; sells US rights in
    Adam's Breed 179; begins writing *Stephen*
    (later *The Well of Loneliness*) 190; in demand
    as speaker 191, 194; receives first fan mail
    191–2; support for mother and step-father,
    1927 192–3; newspaper interest in 194–5;
    completes *The Well* 202; makes
    arrangements for publishing *The Well*, see
    The Well of Loneliness; shares *The Well*'s
    advertising costs 209; arranges translations
    of *The Well* 221; reactions to newspaper
    attacks on *The Well* 225–6; agrees on transfer
    of publication to Paris 227–8; outraged at

    Customs seizure of *The Well* 233; prepares
    for *The Well* court case 237; lists motives for
    writing *The Well* 237–8; passive role in *The
    Well* trial 239, 242–5 *passim*; bitterness after
    The Well case 246–7; resigns from Writers'
    Club 246, 247; discards unsupportive friends
    247; sells house to meet expenses of *The Well*
    case, 1929 250; pays debts to supporters in
    The Well case 250–1; sells Ladye's portrait
    for miners' distress fund 251; begins work
    on *The Carpenter's Son* (later *The Master of the
    House*) 256, 257, 259; gifts to St Anthony's,
    Rye, in memory of Ladye 262; completes
    The Master of the House 272–3; acquires
    stigmata while writing 273; addresses Foyles
    Lunch, 1932 278; buys flat in St Martin's
    Lane, London, 1933 283; addresses
    University Clubs 283–4; prepares short
    stories for publication 288–9; retreats into
    herself 290–2; resigns from PEN Club 290;
    financial position, 1933 295; begins work on
    Emblem Hurlstone 299, 300; meets
    d'Annunzio, 1934 303–4; drops *Emblem
    Hurlstone* 310; begins new book (*The Sixth
    Beatitude*) 310; finds nursing home for
    mother, 1935 313; finishes *The Sixth
    Beatitude* 313; suffers broken ankle, 1937
    319–20, 321; suffers from conjunctivitis 321;
    medical condition, 1939 329; gives up
    smoking 329–30; pro-Fascist at start of
    Second World War 329; illnesses, 1940 331;
    attempts at war work 332–3; suffers from
    colitis 333; eye problems and operation,
    London, 1941–2 334–5; returns to Lynton,
    1942 335; changes views about Fascism
    336–7; breakdown in health, 1943 338;
    cancer diagnosed 339; moved to nursing
    home 339; operations 339–40; moved to
    London Clinic 341; moved to flat in Dolphin
    Square, London 341; stoicism in pain 342;
    final days 343, 344; given last rites 343;
    death, 1943 345; inscription on coffin 346;
    burial 346; requiem mass for 346
  love of animals 141, 196
  animals kept by 28, 40, 44, 51, 55, 89, 96,
    110–11, 115–16, 124–5, 127, 151–2, 179–80,
    190, 209, 252, 256, 295–6, 330, 332, 344
  love of riding and hunting 28
  love of the Brownings' poetry 42, 52, 344
  masculine taste in clothing 48
  method of writing poetry 28
  portrait at age of five 19–20
  portrayals of men in fiction 20
  preoccupation with spirituality 173
  professional anxiety as writer 175
  reading tastes 145
  relations with Havelock Ellis 203, 205
  relations with Ladye, *see* Batten Mabel
    Veronica
  relations with Souline, *see* Souline, Evguenia
  relations with Una, *see* Troubridge, Una
  ritual of seance with Una and Ladye 1–4
  romantic picture of father 20–1
  search for martyrdom 4
  theories on homosexuality 217, 248–9
  'trolley books' 174, 175
  writing methods 120–2

Radclyffe-Hall, Marie (mother) 14, 15, 17, 18, 20, 44, 106, 161, 209, 217
  hysterical outbursts 15, 21, 25, 176, 313
  life: unhappy marriage 10–11; divorce 12; rejection of daughter 14; marries Alberto Visetti 15, 16; ill health and financial difficulties, 1927 192–3; given allowance by daughter 193; supported in nursing home by daughter, 1935 313; reaction to John's death 352; death, 1945 352
Radclyffe-Hall, Radclyffe (father) 9–10, 64, 214, 217
  interests 9–10
  life: education 9; acting career 9; unhappy marriage 10–11; divorce 12; death 13
  relations with daughter 12–13
  scandal with fisherman's daughter 10–11
Randolph, Jane 25–6, 27
Reed. E. T.
  Tails With A Twist 64
Rees, Leonard 168, 177, 178, 209, 248
Rees, Molly 177
Reinhardt, Max
  The Miracle 43, 44
'Rest Cure – 1932, The', RH's 288, 307
Rinder, Olive 195
Robinson, Sadie 302, 312
Ross, Patience 263, 347
  recollections of John and Una 201–2
Rossi-Lemeni, Nicola
  sponsored by Una Troubridge 355
  Una's diaries and Day Books willed to 357
Rowe, Nellie 126–7
Royde-Smith, Naomi 235
Rubinstein, Harold 232, 233, 234, 239, 241, 243, 258, 263, 274, 291, 347, 349, 356, 357
  drafts John's will 343, 344
  loses John's confidence 290
Rubinstein, Ida 137, 216
  'The Weeping Venus' study of 149
Russell, Dora 233
Russell, Elizabeth 8

Sachs, Dr Alfred 151, 182
Sackville-West, Vita 229, 230, 245, 248, 285–6
St John, Christopher 263, 264, 271, 272, 285, 286
Salter, Mrs Helen 103, 106, 107, 108, 123, 124, 128, 130
Sand, George 48, 189
Sappho 216
Sargent, John Singer
  portrait of Mabel Batten 35, 251
Saturday Life, A, RH's 160, 165, 166, 167, 174, 176, 214, 258
  published, 1925 171
  reviews 171
  story of 171–3
Saturday Review 235
  reviews *The Well* 221
Scaife, Roger 203, 206, 207
Scales, Mrs (medium) 84, 88
Schiff, Mrs Sidney 158
Schumann, Eva 221
Scott, Harold 158
Scott, Mr (solicitor) 123
Secker, Martin 280
  turns down *The Well* 204

Second Sheaf of Little Songs, A, RH's 38
Shaw, George Bernard 241
  condemns Home Office action on *The Well* 232
  letter to press re law on obscenity 244
  Mrs Warren's Profession 49
  refuses to give evidence in *The Well* case 236–7
Sheaf of Verses, A, RH's 36, 43
Sidgwick, Eleanor 94, 107, 108, 117
Sidgwick, Henry 94
Simpson, Mrs Wallis 317
Sinclair, May 135, 143, 145, 160, 248
  Mary Olivier 143
Singer, Winnaretta 48, 50
Sink of Solitude, The
  lampoons *The Well* case 257
Sitwells, the 158
Sixth Beatitude, The, RH's
  publishing failure 316, 317
  story of 313–15
  writing started 310
  writing completed, 1935 313
Sladen, Douglas 57
Smythe, Ethel 48
Society for Psychical Research 84, 93, 94
  aims 94
  relations with John and Una: hears paper on Mrs Leonard 105–6; publishes paper 108; wish to co-opt John and Una on council 117; Fox-Pitt allegations against John and 123, 124, 128–31, 132; co-opts John onto council 134
Songs of Three Counties and Other Poems, RH's 45, 56
  'The Blind Ploughman' 46, 185
  'Willow Wand' 53
Souline, Evguenia
  anti-Semitism 329
  appearance 297
  background 297
  engaged to nurse Una, 1934 297
  Nansen passport 323, 324
  relations with John: John develops passion for, 1934 297; first assignation 297–8; Souline's tactics 298; John's letters 298–9, 300; John's justification of attempts at seduction 300–1; John's fantasies about 305; becomes John's lover 305; meeting in London 306–7; financial arrangements 308; together in Paris, 1935 309–10, 311; together in S. of France and Italy, 1935 311–13; together in 1936 315–18; together in 1937 320–1; in Florence together, 1938 321–2, 325; John's nickname for Souline 319; John threatens suicide 322–3; further financial arrangements 322, 330; end of love affair 325–6; John's analysis of affair 326; Souline's 'friends only' visit to Florence, 1939 330; turbulent stay at Rye 330–1; rejoins John and Una at Lynton, 1940 332, 333–4; visits sick John, 1942 335; visits Lynton, 1942 336; salary supplemented by John, 1942 336; visits John during last illness 343; provisions in John's will for 343–4; attends John's funeral 346
  sojourn in England: takes up nursing, 1939 331; moves to Oxford, 1941 331, 334–5; wartime work 336; preys on Una for money

Souline, Evguenia *cont.*
    351; marries after Second World War 351;
    death 351, 352
  suspicion of TB, 1936 315
South Wales Miners' Federation
  supports RH in *The Well* case 237
Spectator
  reviews *Miss Ogilvy Finds Herself* 290
Spiritualism
  cult during First World War 83
Stage Society
  production of Una's translation of *Chéri* 266–7
Stern, G. B. 234
Stewart, Prof. Balfour 94
Stitch, Wilhelmina
  hosts dinner for John, 1927 194
Stopes, Marie 245
Strachey, Lytton 228, 246
Straus, Ralph
  reviews *The Master of the House* 276
Sullivan, Sir Arthur 18, 19
Sumner, John
  brings case against *The Well* in New York 252,
    255
Sunday Chronicle
  attacks *The Well* 224
Sunday Express
  attacks *The Well* 222, 226
Sunday Herald
  reviews *Adam's Breed* 183
Sunday Times 178, 194, 209
  reviews of RH's works 164, 168, 182–3, 221,
    276
Symons, Dom Thomas 344
Syrett, Netta 170

Taggart, Miss 267, 274
Tatler
  reviews *The Well* 221
Taylor, Harry 62, 65, 214
  death, 1907 64
  devotion to daughter Una 64
  job as Queen's Messenger 62
Taylor, Minna 62, 64, 84, 106, 116, 176, 247
  colostomy operation, 1937 319
  death, 1947 353
  presses Una to leave John 181
Taylor, Sir Henry 62
Taylor, Viola, *see* Woods, Viola
Temple, Bill and Ida 110, 115, 180
Terry, Ellen 263, 264
Thesiger, Ernest 157
Time and Tide 246
  reviews *The Well* 221
Times Literary Supplement, The
  reviews *The Well* 240
Times, The 49, 176, 227, 318
  interviews Toupie Lowther 126
  reviews *The Master of the House* 276, 278
  obituary of RH 253
Tizzard, Dr 334
Tree, Iris 111, 157
Tree, Sir Herbert Beerbohm 63, 110
Trefusis, Violet 267, 274
Troubridge, Andrea (the Cub) 72, 74, 95, 98, 99,
    104, 111, 113–16 *passim*, 128, 133, 180, 282,
    346, 357: birth 66; sent to boarding school

    115, 118; intellectual ability at school 133;
    received Admiralty maintenance allowance
    on father's death 181; holidays in Paris with
    Una and John, 1929 259; life at Oxford 275;
    determination to go on stage 275;
    hullaballoo over wedding 286–8; gives birth
    to son, 1935 318; divorce, 1941 348;
    reconciliation with mother 355–6; death in
    car crash, 1966 356
Troubridge, Ernest 140: naval background 64–5;
    pays court to Una 65; marriage to Una 65–6;
    becomes Flag-Captain, Mediterranean
    Fleet, 1907 65; becomes Commodore of
    Naval Barracks, Chatham 66; moves to
    Admiralty, 1909 66; daughter born to 66;
    promoted Rear-Admiral 66; stationed in
    Malta 67, 68; fails to prevent German
    cruisers escaping 69; acquitted by court-
    martial 69, 70; posted to Belgrade 70; escapes
    from occupied Belgrade 75, 76; promoted
    Vice-Admiral 76; unhappy relations with
    Una on return to England 76; posted to
    Greece 89; returns to England, 1917 98;
    marriage breaks down 99; returns to Greece
    100; final attempt to get wife back 111, 112;
    promoted full admiral, 1919 112; arranges
    deed of separation from Una 112–13; final
    flurry over separation 114; receives KCMG
    116; part in Fox-Pitt case against John 122–3,
    124, 128, 130; death and burial, 1926 181;
    memorial service 181
Troubridge, Mary 74, 181
Troubridge, Tom 181, 286, 287–8
Troubridge, Una 28
  appearance 1
  condemns modern theatre 268
  condemns surrealism 268
  contempt for 'closet' inverts 268, 279
  deals with John's fans and fan mail 270, 308
  delight in dressing up as child 63
  describes childhood portrait of John 18–19
  devotion to father 64
  exhibitionist streak 63
  family 62
  fantasy of catching syphilis from Troubridge
    181–2
  life, excluding relations with John (q.v.
    below): wins scholarship to Royal College
    of Art 63; development as sculptor 63–4;
    conversion to Catholicism 64; becomes
    engaged to Ernest Troubridge 65; marriage
    65–6; gives birth to daughter Andrea, 1910
    66; develops nervous disorder 66; consults
    nerve specialist 66–7, 68; practises hypnosis
    as therapy 67, 68; joins husband in Malta,
    1911 67; works on bust of Nijinsky 68; in
    Mediterranean at outbreak of war, 1914 68;
    strain of Troubridge's court-martial on 69;
    accompanies husband to Belgrade, 1915 70;
    returns to England to raise funds for hospital
    in Serbia 70; moves house, 1917 97–8;
    unhappy relations with husband 99; learns to
    ride, 1917 103; gynaecological operation,
    1917 104; begins training dogs for exhibition
    110; illness brought about by final dealings
    with husband 111; separation from husband
    agreed 112–13; takes abbreviated rest cure

116–17; becomes Lady Troubridge on husband's elevation 116; menstrual and gynaecological troubles, 1920–1 150–1, 182; portrait painted by Romaine Brooks 166; designs jacket for *Adam's Breed* 178; receives Admiralty widow's pension on Troubridge's death 180; attends memorial service for husband, 1926 181; relations with daughter, 1929 259; failure of stage translation of *Chéri* 266–7; begins keeping Day Book, 1930 268; has hysterectomy operation 280; convalescence 281; aftermath of operation 291; procures entry visa to England for Souline 306; sees grandson Nicholas, 1937 318; redrafts will 346–7; moves to Lincoln's Inn flat after John's death 349; issues burial instructions, 1944 349; produces *The Life and Death of Radclyffe Hall*, 1945 350, 351; supports Souline financially 351; expunges Souline from record 350, 352; settles in Florence, 1949 353; life in Florence 354–5; translates *Don Camillo* books 355; reconciliation with daughter 356; redrafted will, 1963 356–7; death, 1963 356; burial in Florence 357

own literary career 178, 194, 221

pleasure in play-going 62–3

relations with John: first meeting 61, 70, 71; development of friendship 72; takes holiday with John and Ladye, 1915 72–3; make love for the first time 75; moves into same hotel as John and Ladye 75–6; stays with John at Maidenhead 78; aftermath of Ladye's death and 82, 89; holidays in Wales with John 89; appearance and dress influenced by John's style 89; attends seances with John 90–3; they join SPR 94; reports of seances passed to SPR 94; visit to Sir Oliver Lodge 94–6; John's sexual abstinence 96; nurses John through German measles 98; holidays at Southbourne, 1917 99–100; receives promise of burial at Highgate with John and Ladye 102; life together in Cadogan Court 102–3; preparation of joint paper on Mrs Leonard for SPR 103; holiday in Lynton, 1917, suggested by Ladye 103; first home together in Datchet 103–4; strains of living together 104–5; signs of telepathy between them 104; joint paper to SPR read by John, 1918 105–6; holiday in Lynton 106; upset at Cara Harris's objections to publication of their paper 106–7; begin to entertain 110; friends at Datchet 110; take up cycling 110; welcome Armistice, 1918 111; upset at reappearance of Troubridge 111, 112–13; meeting with Troubridge 112; happy at Una's deed of separation from Troubridge 112–13; move to Chip Chase, Hadley Wood 113–14, 115–16; entertain Sir Oliver Lodge at Chip Chase 117; honeymoon period, 1919 118–19; house burgled 118; permission received for Una to be buried with John and Ladye 118; beginnings of Fox-Pitt slander case 1919 122–4; breeding and exhibiting dogs 124–5; makes friends with Toupie Lowther 125–7; success in Fox-Pitt slander case 128–31; adopt clothes from theatrical

costumiers, 1920 132; move to Trevor Square, London 132; socialize with homosexual circle, 1920s 134–9; travel to Italy, 1921 139; holiday in Florence, 1921 139–41; enthusiasm for Fascism 140; experience Italian political turmoil 141; journey to Paris, 1922 141; return to England 142; move into house in Sterling St, London 142–3; reading lists, 1921 144–5; holiday in France, Summer 1922 149–50; 'marriage date', 18 August 1922 150; social life 157–9; holiday in W. Country 165; planned move to Holland St, Kensington 169–70; 'doing their bit' during General Strike, 1926 186; holiday at Burgh Island 187; first discussion on idea for *The Well of Loneliness* 188–9; holiday in France, 1926 189–91; admiration for Colette 191, 194; car problems 192; French holiday, 1927 195–6; visit Paris, 1929 252–4; holiday in S. of France 256–7, 258; return to Paris 259; return to England 259; move to Rye, 1930 261–2; social life in Rye 263–4, 267–72, 274–5; operation on Una and convalescence in Brighton, 1932 280–1; moves between Rye and London, 1932–3 282–3; avoid Andrea's wedding, 1933 286–8; strains in relations 291–2; move to new cottage in Rye, 1933 295, 296; holiday in France, 1934 296–8; Souline appears on scene 297; holiday in Italy 298–301; Una learns about Souline 299; return to Paris 304–5; Una's humiliation over Souline 306; Christmas at Rye, 1934 308; coping with the Souline affair 309, 310, 311, 315, 320; support for Mussolini 312, 323; ménage à trois, 1935–8 311–13, 315–18, 320–1; return to Rye, 1937, 318; ménage à trois continued 322, 325; plans to settle in Florence, 1939 329; hear that war has been declared 331; move to Lynton 331; take up riding again 331–2; confined to England by the war, 1940 332; settle in cottage at Lynton 332; Una tends John during wartime illnesses 333, 334–5; together during John's last illness 338–45; Una arranges John's funeral and requiem mass, 1943 346; destroys John's last book as requested 347; calm after John's death 347–8; Una feels eventual shock of bereavement 348

ritual of seance with John and Ladye 1–4

talent for drawing 62

unorthodoxy as parent 74

'Twixt Earth and Stars, RH's 28–9, 35–6

Unlit Lamp, The, RH's 17, 24, 160, 162, 164, 168, 170, 172, 178

accepted by Cassell's 166–7
advertised at St Pancras' Station 169
French edition 313
portrait of Agnes Nicholls in 22, 25
published, 1924 168
reviews 168
US edition 258, 275
See also *After Many Days*

Unprodigal Son, The (unfinished), RH's 299

'Upon the Mountains', RH's 173–4, 288

Virago (publishers)
  edition of *The Well*, 1983 353
Visetti, Alberto 17, 25, 44, 161, 192, 193
  death, 1928 209
  marries Marie Radclyffe-Hall 15–16
  work as music professor 15–16
Visetti, Marie, *see* Radclyffe-Hall, Marie
Vivien, Renée 150, 190, 217

Wallace, Sir Robert 245
Walpole, Hugh
  agrees to give evidence in *The Well* case 235
  reproves Cape over withdrawal of *The Well*
    234–5
Ward, Lady 222
Warren, Lady 287
Warren, Nicholas Vincenzo 318, 356
Warren, Sir Norcott 287
Warren, Toby 286, 287, 318, 348
Warrender, Lady Maud 267, 279
Waugh, Alec 170, 177, 248
  reviews *The Unlit Lamp* 168
Waugh, Evelyn 168, 234
Webb, Mary 144
  Precious Bane 204
Well of Loneliness, The 4, 17, 19, 21, 28, 288, 300,
    304, 346–7
  autobiographical portions in 214–15
  characters taken from life in 215–16
  court case over 239–44
    defence team 238–9
    dismissal of appeal 245
    heavy costs 250
    magistrate presiding 238
    magistrate's judgement 242–4
    prosecution case 240
    search for defence witnesses 234–7
    verdict given to Crown 244
  Dutch edition 250, 253
  expresses women's gallantry and patriotism
    213–14
  French edition 252, 253, 259
  idea for first launched 188–9
  influence of contemporary sexologists in
    217–20
  Italian edition 303
  kinship with RH's previous books 213
  literary influences on 216–17
  publishing history: finding publisher for
    203–4, 206–7; publishing arrangements
    204–5, 206, 207–8, 209; early publishing
    success 220–2; reviews 221, 228–9;
    newspaper attacks on 223–5; sales increased
    by attacks 225; publication transferred to
    Paris 227–8, 231; mail engendered 226, 230,
    250, 255; seized by Customs 232, 233;

    support of literary world for 228–31, 232–3;
    seized by police 233; republished in England,
    1949 353; latest edition, 1983 353
  reaches BBC 'Book at Bedtime' 353
  religious undertones 214
  sales
    by 1928–9 246
    by 1933
    on John's death 353
  stage production 259–60, 265–6
  story of 210–13
  success promotes sales of other RH books 258
  under working title of *Stephen* 188, 190, 196
  US edition: called off by Knopf 231–2;
    published by Covici Friede 251; declared
    obscene by court 252; cleared by Appeal
    Court 255; success of 252, 256
  use of Teneriffe location in 37
  writing of 190, 196, 203
Wells, H. G. 152, 167
  condemns Home Office action on *The Well* 232
West, Rebecca 143, 170, 234
Wickham, Anna 190
Wilde, Dolly 284
Wilde, Oscar 44, 131, 216, 284
  De Profundis 207
Wilhelm II, Kaiser
  abdication 111
Williams, Sir Ellis Hume 128, 129
Wolfe, Humbert 320, 324
Women Writers' Club 144
Woods, Maurice 67, 116
Woods, Viola 62, 65, 66, 116, 247
  marriage to Maurice Woods 67
  divorce 116
  marries J. L. Garvin 176
Woolf, Leonard 228, 236, 244
  reviews *The Well* 221
Woolf, Virginia 145, 228, 229, 230, 244, 264
  agrees to give evidence in *The Well* case 235,
    236
Wren Howard, George 204, 231, 250, 272, 277,
    279
Writers' Club 144, 191
  Poetry Circle 191
Wylie, Ida 135–6, 143, 151, 156, 163, 171, 209,
    251, 263, 306
  reviews *The Well* 221
  Towards Morning 136
Wyllie, Father Norbert 97

Yeats-Brown, Francis 269
  Bengal Lancer 269
Yorkshire Post 225

Zola, Emile 216